THE ABINGDON
PREACHING
ANNUAL
2005

THE ABINGDON PREACHING ANNUAL 2005

COMPILED AND EDITED BY

David N. Mosser

ASSISTANT EDITORS

Karen Dies
Ronda Wellman

ABINGDON PRESS
Nashville

THE ABINGDON PREACHING ANNUAL 2005

Copyright © 2004 by Abingdon Press

This book is printed on acid-free paper.

ISBN 0-687-00171-4
ISSN 1075-2250

All scripture quotations unless noted otherwise are taken from the *New Revised
Standard Version of the Bible,* copyright 1989, Division of Christian Education of
the National Council of the Churches of Christ in the United States of America.
Used by permission. All rights reserved.

Scripture quotations marked (RSV) are taken from the *Revised Standard Version
of the Bible,* copyright 1946, 1952, 1971 by the Division of Christian Education of
the National Council of the Churches of Christ in the United States of America.
Used by permission. All rights reserved.

Scripture quotations marked (KJV) are from the King James or Authorized Version of the Bible.

Scripture quotations marked (NIV) are taken from the HOLY BIBLE, NEW
INTERNATIONAL VERSION®. NIV®. Copyright © 1973, 1978, 1984 by International Bible Society. Used by permission of Zondervan Publishing House. All
rights reserved.

Scripture quotations marked (NASB) are taken from the NEW AMERICAN
STANDARD BIBLE®, © Copyright The Lockman Foundation 1960, 1962, 1963,
1968, 1971, 1972, 1973, 1975, 1977. Used by permission.

Scripture quotations marked (NLT) are from the *Holy Bible,* New Living Translation, copyright © 1996. Used by permission of Tyndale House Publishers, Inc.,
Wheaton, Illinois 60189. All rights reserved.

Scripture quotations marked (GNT) are from the Good News Translation in
Today's English Version-Second Edition © 1992 by American Bible Society. Used
by permission.

Scripture from *THE MESSAGE.* Copyright © Eugene H. Peterson, 1993, 1994,
1995. Used by permission of NavPress Publishing Group.

04 05 06 07 08 09 10 11 12 13—10 9 8 7 6 5 4 3 2 1
MANUFACTURED IN THE UNITED STATES OF AMERICA

CONTENTS

FEBRUARY

MARCH

APRIL

MAY

OCTOBER

NOVEMBER

INTRODUCTION

One of the difficulties about preaching week in and week out is that most preachers who practice the art of sharing the good news too infrequently hear other preachers practice the art. Certainly preachers assemble from time to time to confer about the particulars of persuasive preaching. However, we rarely allow ourselves the luxury of hearing others preach on any regular basis. As a result, this book of 156 sermon briefs is one attempt to allow preachers to examine the work of others with whom we share the Lord's vineyard.

The Abingdon Preaching Annual employs The Revised Common Lectionary to chart its (and possibly our) preaching course. Offset by about one month from the liturgical year, which runs from Advent through Pentecost, *The Abingdon Preaching Annual* begins and ends with the calendar year. If not liturgically correct in every respect, *The Abingdon Preaching Annual* at least aims at the neatness that the calendar year provides. The purpose of *The Abingdon Preaching Annual* is to help preachers plan a full yearly schedule for preaching the biblical good news. Each preacher has his or her own method for planning a preaching program for individual congregations, and this book allows preachers to sketch their preaching agenda from January through December, or any segment of the year. Many preachers, even those who do not regularly use the lectionary, find that lectionary texts can frequently augment their own range of preaching texts. Consequently, *The Abingdon Preaching Annual* attempts to be one helpful instrument in the preacher's "toolbox" to enhance a fuller and more faithful reading of the Bible.

Some pastors may rightly ask, "What kinds of preachers are we for whom Abingdon Press has prepared this book?" The answer would be those preachers who want to be in conversation with other preachers who take the preaching task with the kind of seriousness that you do. Therefore, the kinds of preachers who may profit from

13

this book may be young or old, experienced or novices, urban or rural. The sermon briefs are simply essays on lectionary texts for each Sunday in the church year. *The Abingdon Preaching Annual's* intention is to stimulate the discourse about the Bible that all faithful preachers need and want. Some of the sermon briefs provide excellent exegesis, while others offer an illustration or application that may help bring biblical texts to life for congregations. We point *The Abingdon Preaching Annual* toward those who desire to see how others use and understand the texts in their pursuit of delivering the biblical message to the people of God. However you choose to make use of this book, we trust it to be of assistance to those who want to preach more effective sermons for believers in 2005.

Some detractors charge that books in the genre of *The Abingdon Preaching Annual* often entrap preachers into plagiarism. Clearly, with the advent of the Internet and the overabundance of sermon helps now available, this concern is a valid one. However, *The Abingdon Preaching Annual's* goal remains to be one voice among many others speaking to preachers. These complementary voices also include biblical commentaries and the pastor's own unique experience. Only the pastor as preacher can preach well to his or her individual congregation. In the church of Jesus Christ there is never "one size that fits all." Rather, it is in the particularity of God's Word that the church grasps and lives out the Word. Each pastor and congregation has a particular and blessed relationship that no one else can replicate. Most pastors, in any event, do all the other ministerial tasks they do in order that they may preach the Word. Therefore, we trust that no one will be so dull or unmotivated by way of plagiarizing so as to let the temptation for shortcuts weaken effective preaching. At the same time, preaching is a task that is so difficult we can never do it by ourselves. *The Abingdon Preaching Annual* merely attempts to be one of the voices that the preacher listens to with discernment in preparing a unique word for distinctive congregations.

Reading sermons is not always a practice that preachers undertake. But to walk through a text and experience it with a sister or brother in the ministry is often a helpful way to learn as we go. No preacher worth his or her salt is ever a finished product. We all continually learn from others and from our own small victories and large mistakes.

In addition to the weekly worship themes, calls to worship, and prayers intended to help "prime the pump," *The Abingdon Preaching Annual* furnishes a series of twelve meditations. These meditations focus on a theme titled "Twelve Pillars of Abundant Christian Living." The meditations find their source of inspiration from Exodus. In a text from Exodus, we find Moses erecting an altar and twelve pillars as a monument to the Lord God (Exod. 24:4). These meditations have the preacher's mind in mind. As such, the meditations are for a preacher's devotional use and a pastor's quiet contemplation time.

David N. Mosser

SERMON SERIES

FACIAL EXPRESSIONS: FACING THE GOSPEL IN LIFE

FACING OUR FEARS

EXODUS 20:18-21

Did you know that The National Geographic Society has a magazine called *Adventure*? In the July 2002 issue there is an article titled "The Joy of Fear." Five people wrote about the adrenaline rush they got from doing extremely dangerous things, for example, racing at the Bonneville Salt Flats in Utah at 417 miles per hour, paddling a canoe through Iceberg Alley in Greenland, or dangling off a white-faced rock cliff in a remote Mexican jungle. We now have people in the United States and around the world for whom normal life is so boring and tedious that they need the surge of excitement that a death-defying experience provides to make them "feel" alive. This kind of human behavior has spawned a new field of study called adventure psychology.

Likewise, researchers tell us that "about 3.7% of the U.S. population ages 18 to 54—approximately 5.3 million Americans—has social phobia in any given year."

> Social phobia, also called social anxiety, is a disorder characterized by overwhelming anxiety and excessive self-consciousness in everyday social situations. People with social anxiety have a persistent, intense, and chronic fear of being watched and judged by others and of being embarrassed or humiliated by their own actions. Their fear may be so severe that it interferes with work or school—and other ordinary activities. While many people with social phobia recognize that their fear of being around people may be excessive or unreasonable, they are unable to overcome it. They often worry for days or weeks in advance of a dreaded situation. (National Institute of Health, National Institute of Mental Health, *Facts About Social Phobia*. Online: http://www.nimh.nih.gov/anxiety/phobiafacts.cfm.)

So whether or not fear is self-induced or given to us by our peculiar psychological makeup, we must all face fear one way or another. Our biblical writers recognized this fact of human life and comprehensively addressed it. In fact, in our Bible's sixty-six recognized canonical books the terms *fear, afraid,* and *dread* occur 498 times (NRSV). Our lesson today concerns the Hebrews' fear of God and death at God's hands if the Lord speaks directly to them. Hear the scripture text:

> When all the people witnessed the thunder and lightning, the sound of the trumpet, and the mountain smoking, they were afraid and trembled and stood at a distance, and said to Moses, "You speak to us, and we will listen; but do not let God speak to us, or we will die." Moses said to the people, "Do not be afraid; for God has come only to test you and to put the fear of him upon you so that you do not sin." Then the people stood at a distance, while Moses drew near to the thick darkness where God was. (Exod. 20:18-21)

The people were so afraid of God that they asked Moses to be their mediator so that the Lord God would not need to speak to them directly. It is odd but predictable that people often ask their leaders to do things that they fear to do for themselves, then later cast off the guidance when it is no longer needed.

Here now is the good news about our fear of God. This fear represents a real concern with the Creator of the universe. While the concept of God is not too fearsome, the reality of God's presence is something that we ponder, as Paul puts it, "with fear and trembling" (Phil. 2:12). In other words, our fear represents our awareness of God's greatness and power. However, only by seeing both the awesome and the loving sides of God can we come to a full awareness of the greatness of God.

"The fear of the LORD is the beginning of wisdom," both Psalm 111:10 and Proverbs 9:10 tell us. The "fear of the Lord" basically describes the awe that people ought to have before God. Although it does carry overtones of judgment, those who fear, or better respect, the awesomeness of God are those persons who have a grasp of the Lord's providential power for God's creation. The wisdom book of Ecclesiastes puts it appropriately at the end of the writer's musings on life and death. He writes: "The end of the matter; all has been heard. Fear God, and keep his commandments; for that is the whole duty of everyone" (12:13).

Fear is a part of every human life. Fear energizes us. Fear helps us stay alert to danger. Fear, thereby, is a necessary emotion or sensation for survival. Yet, as we have seen already in our mention of "social anxiety" fear can debilitate people. We all fear different things. Most of us fear our money running out before our life does. Some people fear retirement while others fear for their current jobs. People are in constant worry about their loved ones, and this is doubly true for our anxiety about our children, regardless of their ages. We all have worries, but they do have an effect on our lives. They can paralyze us into inaction, or worse, they can even spur us to inappropriate and unfortunate action. If you don't believe me, think back to some of your community's anxiety created by the prediction of our neighbors and friends concerning the self-induced apocalypse we called Y2K.

For most of us it all comes down to trust. Either we trust that the Lord will provide or we don't. For Christians, there is no other alternative. Only by trusting the God who created all and will bring all to its final completion can we forge our way through this life that is given as a great and wonderful blessing. To trust in God or not to trust in God: That is the question!

Fear is real and has been with us at least as far back as Aesop who once told a fable that goes like this:

> Long ago, the mice held a general council to consider what measures they could take to outwit their common enemy, the Cat. Some said this, and some said that; but at last a young mouse got up and said he had a proposal to make, which he thought would meet the case. "You will all agree," said he, "that our chief danger consists in the sly and treacherous manner in which the enemy approaches us. Now, if we could receive some signal of her approach, we could easily escape from her. I venture, therefore, to propose that a small bell be procured, and attached by a ribbon round the neck of the Cat. By this means we should always know when she was about, and could easily retire while she was in the neighbourhood."
>
> This proposal met with general applause, until an old mouse got up and said: "That is all very well, but who is to bell the Cat?" The mice looked at one another and nobody spoke. Then the old mouse said: "It is easy to propose impossible remedies." (Joseph Jacobs, "Belling the Cat," in *The Fables of Æsop: Edited, Told Anew and Their History Traced* [London: Macmillan, 1910], pp. 159-60)

On the other hand, a healthy fear keeps us alert to the great risks that make creative life possible. Our remedy for fear is simply our faith and hope in the love of God, who loved us enough to create us but also loved us enough not to leave us like we are. To live the "fear of the Lord" is to have wisdom that the creator will sustain us to the end and then receive us into our eternal and divine home. Fear drives us to become the people God created us to be. Amen. (David N. Mosser)

FACING OUR ENEMIES

Near the end of chapter 4 the writer of the Epistle to the Ephesians reminds his readers that they are leaving their old lives and entering into a whole new world made possible by the gift of God in Christ Jesus. Ephesians tells its readers, "Clothe yourselves with the new self, created according to the likeness of God in true righteousness and holiness" (4:24). The overall intent of this six-chapter letter helps recently converted believers get a sense of what exactly their new baptism does for them. Beyond God's gift through baptism, the letter provides guidelines of what they are now free to become in light of God's action in Jesus Christ. Hear our morning's lesson:

> Finally, be strong in the Lord and in the strength of his power. Put on the while armor of God, so that you may be able to stand against the wiles of the devil. For our struggle is not against enemies of blood and flesh, but against the rulers, against the authorities, against the cosmic powers of this present darknesss, against the spiritual forces of evil in the heavenly places. Therefore take up the whole armor of God, so that you may be able to withstand on that evil day, and having done everything, to stand firm. Stand therefore, and fasten the belt of truth around your waist, and put on the breastplate of righteousness. As shoes for your feet put on whatever will make you ready to proclaim the gospel of peace. With all of these, take the shield of faith, with which you will be able to quench all the flaming arrows of the evil one. Take the helmet of salvation, and the sword of the Spirit, which is the word of God. (Eph. 6:10-17)

Standing against our enemies, and in this case the ultimate enemy, the devil, our writer gives us striking images with which we can compete against those evil forces that we all sense conspire to defeat us in life.

An odd thing about the Bible is that sometimes it seems to speak to people far away and about issues that never enter our realm of experience. For example, Deuteronomy 14:21 tells the faithful, "You shall not boil a kid in its mother's milk." This idea might never have crossed my mind if I had not read it in the Bible. Or, what about the admonition to the Hebrew faithful in Deuteronomy 22:5: "A woman shall not wear a man's apparel, nor shall a man put on a woman's garment; for whoever does such things is abhorrent to the LORD your God"? Clearly, no one in our society today takes this caution to heart. Yet the Bible, wherever it happens to fall open, knows us better than we know ourselves.

The Bible says much about the issue of human enemies. One of the reasons that the children of Israel ended up with their long bondage in Egypt was simply because the Egyptians feared what might happen if the Hebrews joined their enemies to fight against them (Exod. 1:10). Later, after the entrance into the Promised Land, we read that "the sun stood still, and the moon stopped, / until the nation took vengeance on their enemies" (Josh. 10:13). The Psalms have at least seventy-seven individual verses that address the issue of "the enemy." When we think about our national interests, have we, too, not been absolutely preoccupied with the concept of enemies since September 11, 2001?

Usually we can count on Jesus to guide us as to what to think and how to act in our journey toward and with God. Yet, on the issue of enemies, Jesus throws us something of a curveball. Jesus does not say what the Old Testament says. Jesus does not gratify our own conventional wisdom. Instead Jesus says things like:

> "You have heard that it was said, 'You shall love your neighbor and hate your enemy.' But I say to you, Love your enemies and pray for those who persecute you." (Matt. 5:43-44)

> "But love your enemies, do good, and lend, expecting nothing in return. Your reward will be great, and you will be children of the Most High; for he is kind to the ungrateful and the wicked." (Luke 6:35)

However, even if most of us don't like what Jesus says about the enemy, at least he acknowledges that in life we will all encounter enemies. I think Jesus assumes enemies as a part of human life. What is important to us is not whether we have enemies, but how we deal with them. As Sally Kempton wisely noted, "It is hard to fight an enemy who has outposts in your head." She knows that most of the damage that an enemy does to us comes as something of a self-inflicted wound. Like an African proverb suggests, "When there is no enemy within, the enemies outside cannot hurt you." Practically, what does this mean?

The Reverend Norman Neaves related a television interview with the University of Oklahoma football coach, Bob Stoops. The University of Oklahoma (OU) had been a perennial contender for the NCAA national football title for decades. However, in the late 1990s, OU football had fallen on hard times. The reporter named several tough teams scheduled to go up against OU and asked Stoops how he felt about the schedule facing his team.

Neaves then went on in his sermon to praise Bob Stoops's answer. Stoops said, "I can't really worry about those teams at all, not one of them. I can't change who they are, I can't change the talent they have.... All I can do is to make sure we take care of our own business and that we execute our own game plan.... If we'll do that, ... everything will take care of itself" ("Don't Worry About the End of the World," Church of the Servant, Oklahoma City, December 5, 1999).

Plainly, football is not life. Yet, this youthful coach from the University of Oklahoma grasped the situation that he and his team faced. In fact, in the subsequent season, they went on to win college football's national championship. This accomplishment, I suggest, had a lot to do with the realism that the leader, in this case a very young head coach, possessed and his ability to help his team apply themselves to the things that they could control. When we focus our lives on the things that we can manage and ignore those elements that are beyond our ability to influence, then we can be satisfied that we have done our best.

To conclude our look at Ephesians, what is most interesting about the list of the "weapons" is that they are not merely weapons of human warfare, although they do evoke these images. In fact, these weapons are not even mere human virtues. Rather, each of these images is an extension of God's own might. Many of these elements are those that allow us to fight against the evil, and often invisible, forces in our world. So, the next time you get dressed for the day, imagine that you gird your loins with some of these divine designer clothes:

- the belt of truth
- the breastplate of righteousness.
- shoes that make you ready to proclaim the gospel of peace
- the shield of faith
- the helmet of salvation
- the sword of the Spirit, which is the Word of God.

The writer could have also added "forgiveness" to our arsenal. Oscar Wilde advised, "Always forgive your enemies; nothing annoys them so much." This sounds like Paul when he wrote to his beloved community in Rome:

> Beloved, never avenge yourselves, but leave room for the wrath of God; for it is written, "Vengeance is mine, I will repay, says the Lord." No, "if your enemies are hungry, feed them; if they are thirsty, give them something to drink; for by doing this you will heap burning coals on their heads." Do not be overcome by evil, but overcome evil with good. (Rom. 12:19-21)

Amen. (David N. Mosser)

FACING OUR SUCCESSES

PSALM 118:24-25

Winston Churchill surely knew of what he spoke when he quipped, "Success is the ability to go from one failure to another with no loss of enthusiasm." But, just as true may have been what Tennessee Williams said: "Success and failure are equally disastrous." This sermon concludes our three-part series. We have explored in brief what scripture said about fear and enemies. Today we tackle success. This is not a sermon that a preacher can preach just anywhere. Sermons like this one can be preached only to congregations who understand what it is to achieve. Yet, I am absolutely confident that virtually everyone in our sanctuary would be considered a success by the citizens of our towns. Occasionally this reality intimidates people. Perhaps they feel that a church house full of accomplished people will rebuff them. Of course, nothing could be further from the truth. Yet, success does carry a certain stigma.

For many people, the idea and ideal of success is that target at which they aim their whole life. For those who have been frustrated time and time again, success becomes merely one more aspiration that has eluded them. Some folks simply give up and have no long- or even short-range life goals. Edward Butler said, "One man has enthusiasm for 30 minutes, another for 30 days, but it is the man who has it for 30 years who makes a success of his life."

Generally, most people would agree that success is a good thing. We strive for it. We work for it. We dream of it. Even scripture extols success. Hear Psalm 118:24-25:

> This is the day that the LORD has made;
> let us rejoice and be glad in it.
> Save us, we beseech you, O LORD!
> O LORD, we beseech you, give us success!

Psalm 118 is a communal hymn of praise for which the people give thanks to God for all that God accomplishes among them. It also reiterates a request that God continue to "give us success!" The success it summons no doubt depends on the one who prays it.

Despite all the positive aspects of success, however, we are obliged as Christians to recognize and explore success from the perspective of the Christian faith. Nothing we, as believers, think or do should be thought or done in a vacuum. Rather, scripture calls us to "have the mind of Christ" (1 Cor. 2:16). One of the troubles with success is that it is so seductive. Success breeds more responsibility and this, in turn, breeds more success. Success can be like a merry-go-round where no one can ever jump off. As Henry Kissinger remarked, "Each success only buys an admission ticket to a more difficult problem." Thus, the issue for us today is simply, How can we be successful and Christian at the same time? It is worth noting that from the world's judgment Elvis Presley, Howard Hughes, and J. Paul Getty had "successful lives." Yet, biographies of these individuals read more like tragedy than success. Getty said, "The meek shall inherit the Earth, but not its mineral rights."

Success is seductive in the same sense that a kettle of cool water seduces a frog. If you throw a frog into a kettle of boiling water, the frog senses the danger and skips right off the surface seeking safety. However, if you put the frog in a kettle of cool water and gradually turn up the heat, the frog will remain in the kettle until it boils to death. The frog's survival instinct detects sudden changes, but not gradual change, which, of course, proves the frog's ultimate undoing. Sometimes successful people are lulled into a false sense of authentic life because of the work and effort necessary to achieve success. In other words, they miss the reason that they strive in the first place, which is to build a meaningful life, a life full of value and relationship and connection.

When the psalmist sings of success, it isn't reflective of the images we think of: cars and houses and prestige and all the rest of the modern images that success conjurses up. Success from a biblical point of view means the same thing as faithfulness. It means trusting God to provide for us. It means that God grants us success in our earthly pursuits. The prayer of Jabez puts it like this: "'Oh that you would bless me and enlarge my border, and that your hand might be with me, and that you would keep me from hurt and harm!' And God granted what he asked" (1 Chron. 4:10).

Success in the biblical sense means something completely different than our autonomous, Western, capitalist, American ideas of success. In fact, one of the dangers of living in modern America is that we may be seduced away from God by our own sense of success. Do you want to live in a world where all knowledge, insight, and experience is self-generated? Some critics of modern culture suggest that us moderns are naive.

We assume that everyone in America is a Christian. We feel confident that we live in a Christian nation and a Christian culture. But, sometimes things happen to us that jar that confidence. The last time that I was the senior-high dean at a church camp about fifteen years ago, I assumed that all the kids at camp were good kids who came from good homes. I got a rather rude and abrupt awakening one night.

On the third night of camp, about 2:00 A.M. one of the counselors came to me and said, "We have a problem." I got up and the counselor produced seven inebriated teenagers who had also been smoking pot. I asked them what church they were from and they said, "The big one in Temple." Then I asked, "Who is your pastor?" They didn't have a clue. I later discovered that these youngsters had never even been to a Methodist church. They had come to camp thinking that they could blend in and party without any obstacles whatsoever. But, they did not blend in, and, as far as I was concerned, their party was over.

I called one teen's father and asked him to come immediately. The father replied, "It's 2:00 in the morning. I will drive over tomorrow." To which I said, "Well if you get to the camp in the next two hours you can pick up these seven kids. After that, just drop by the police station."

He said, "I'm on my way."

I had thought that everyone at camp was a Christian, but there were some who evidently were not, or at least did not act like it. Each of us who wants to be successful as a Christian contributes to the whole community of faith. Some teach; some are generous givers; some know how to help with mission projects like the youth mission trips or a soup kitchen. However, we all have a part to play. This is the essence of success from the Christian point of view. Helping others find Christ—that is the real success in the household of faith.

During our last revival, on Monday and Wednesday nights, we had first twenty-nine and then thirty singers in the chancel area as choir members. They sounded beautiful, and they looked like they were "in the spirit." I wondered, "Why does this not happen on Sunday, the Sabbath of God?" If you want to be successful as a Christian, then help someone come to faith. Maybe it is by singing in choir or by mentoring in a confirmation program. But please do something.

Do you remember when the children of Israel left Egypt for the land of promise? Everyone went. Not some, but all. The ironic thing about Christian success is that we are never successful unless those around us also succeed. We need one another, and we need to reach out to others. This is what real success is all about. In the Psalm for today, notice the wording; it is intentional: "Save us, we beseech you, O Lord! / O Lord, we beseech you, give us success!" (Ps. 118:25). (David N. Mosser)

REFLECTIONS

Introduction to the Monthly Meditations

Tucked away in a little corner of the book of Exodus careful readers will find the statement: Moses "rose early in the morning, and built an altar at the foot of the mountain, and set up twelve pillars, corresponding to the twelve tribes of Israel" (Exod. 24:4). Those who know the Exodus story well recognize that this text relates part of the Sinai narrative. This element of the Exodus story recounts Israel's covenant ceremony with God. However, what may catch our attention is Moses' small and seemingly insignificant act of erecting "twelve pillars." Clearly, the biblical writer tells us that the twelve pillars correspond to the twelve tribes of Israel. Our question concerning Moses' actions in setting up the pillars, however, is why.

In truth, Exodus does not tell us why Moses sets up the pillars. Perhaps this leads us to casting about for possible answers. Why would Moses erect pillars at this momentous time in Israel's story? We assume that if the pillars represent the twelve tribes of Israel, as the story tells us, then the altar may represent God's part in the enacted sacred covenant. A few verses further in the story, Moses uses blood to seal the covenant in an act faithful to the instructions provided in Leviticus (see, for example, chapters 4 and 8). All these ritual acts solemnize the covenant to be sure, but why the pillars? What could the pillars' significance be?

One guess we could propose is that the pillars visually reminded the people of Israel, as the altar also did, about the sacred covenant they had entered into with God. As humans, we all need help remembering the things that are of sacred worth to us. It is not because we cannot remember but rather because forgetting is so easy. Few American people need reminding of the horror our nation and the whole world endured by the events of 9/11. But the fact remains that people do forget. Perhaps we forget the horrific out of a kind of psychic self-survival. Whatever the reason, we humans do tend to forget.

In terms of faith, however, remembrance fosters a positive connection between God and us. Remembrance also connects us with one another. Remembrance connects us to our past and helps us anticipate the future in hope. Thus, we anticipate our future with God as we remember God's providence for us in the past. As we know from the events of 9/11, one day can make a lot of difference. No matter how much we encourage one another by saying, "May we never forget," we are people, and people do forget.

The ancient art of public speaking, termed rhetoric, applied a memory method called mnemonics. Mnemonics helped students and speakers remember important details that they might otherwise have forgotten—especially important in public speeches. For an example of mnemonics our high school math teacher gave us a little phrase that reminded us that "Lucky Cows Drink Milk." This silly phrase supplied students with a way to remember the ascending order of Roman numerals: LCDM. Another teacher, this time in history, helped us remember two dates by using an old rhyme: "In 1492, Columbus sailed the ocean blue. / In 1493, Columbus stole all he could see."

These examples from mnemonics furnish students with a way to remember details from math or history that they might otherwise forget. I want to suggest that the pillars that Moses set up were likewise helpful to the Israelite community of faith in first remembering and then abiding by the holy covenant that God made with them at Sinai.

Our series of twelve meditations for pastors in the 2005 edition of *The Abingdon Preaching Annual* addresses the necessity of remembrance. Like Israel, we will use as our point of reference the twelve pillars of Moses (see Exod. 24:4). But rather than claim that each pillar represents one of the tribes of Israel, we dedicate each of the twelve pillars as a symbol that characterizes traits of abundant Christian living. These monuments to right living are each traits by which we pray that God will nurture us. Jesus told the first partakers of the Eucharist in the upper room, "This is my body, which is given for you. Do this in remembrance of me" (Luke 22:19). God, too, calls us today to remembrance.

There is no ulterior utilitarian purpose for the meditations other than for preachers to read and ponder. I have not written the meditations so that shrewd pastors may mine sermon illustrations. Rather, these meditations are to pray over, consider, and absorb as gifts. May we spend our set apart and spiritual time with God each day. May these meditations help us explore more deeply that sacred relationship God has forged with each of us. God continues to fashion our faith connections through our baptisms and calls to ministry. All we must do is nurture these ministry gifts from God as we receive them as precious gifts to use for the upbuilding of the realm of God. (David N. Mosser)

REFLECTIONS

JANUARY

Reflection Verse: *"You are witnesses, and God also, how pure, upright, and blameless our conduct was toward you believers."* (*1 Thessalonians 2:10*)

RIGHTEOUSNESS: A CODE WORD FOR THE PURE, UPRIGHT, AND BLAMELESS
1 Thessalonians 2:1-13

We preachers sometimes forget things. After all, we are human. Immersed in the daily tasks of ministry, we do forget many matters that few parishioners might suppose we forget. In the constant handling of sacred things it is easy to take our holy calling for granted. Whether our inattentiveness pertains to our daily devotions, life of prayer, or scripture reading, we are capable of neglecting those disciplines that give our life meaning and purpose. Our monthly devotions in *The Abingdon Preaching Annual* remind us of those disciplines that not only allowed us to first discern God's call into the ministry but also formed the very foundations that sustain us in that ministry.

January often promises a vision of a better year ahead. The year in front of us seems apparently as clear and clean as a new year's calendar. The pillars that Moses sets up as part of the Exodus 24 covenant ceremony can remind us of things that we too often forget. Our intention for a new year is to remain faithful to our call to ministry. God laid this call on our hearts and quickens it through Jesus' teaching and example. To Jesus' power in our lives, God adds the gift of the Holy Spirit. Perhaps we might designate the first pillar as a faith memory aid. This pillar reminds us to reclaim a little used, but highly significant, theological idea: the idea of righteousness.

Our first characteristic, a key to abundant life, derives from the venerated biblical word *righteousness*. Unfortunately, in our culture, *righteousness* is a word that we have let lapse into disuse. It is a rare day when we hear people use the words *righteous* or *righteousness* in conversation. Yet, for people of faith, *righteousness* is a well-appointed term that believers might want to reclaim, understand, and use. *Righteousness* originally meant "straight" or "right." Today we might use the term *righteousness* to mean "to be just" or "to act with justice." For Christians, this means that we act within all our relationships, both human and divine, with equity and fairness. We follow God's dictate to live in peace and harmony with others, always giving "the other" due consideration in all circumstances.

Righteousness was such an important biblical characteristic that when Paul writes about "justification by faith," the same Greek words could just as easily be translated "[God] makes people righteous by faith." The concept of righteousness is so central to our relationship with God that Paul informs the Corinthians: "Even Satan disguises himself as an angel of light. So it is not strange if his ministers also disguise themselves as ministers of righteousness" (2 Cor. 11:14-15).

I want to offer what, I believe, Paul would have us understand as aspects of righteousness. In one place in the Epistle to the Thessalonians, Paul writes,

> You remember our labor and toil, brothers and sisters; we worked night and day, so that we might not burden any of you while we proclaimed to you the gospel of God. You are witnesses, and God also, how pure, upright, and blameless our conduct was toward you believers. As you know, we dealt with each one of you like a father with his children, urging and encouraging you and pleading that you lead a life worthy of God, who calls you into his own kingdom and glory. (1 Thess. 2:9-12)

The defining phrase for Paul's understanding of righteousness comes from verse 10: "pure, upright, and blameless." Paul and his fellow workers display these characteristics among the people of Thessalonica. As Paul defends his behavior among them, he also recommends these qualities to the people there. These traits of purity, uprightness, and blamelessness specify the first pillar of abundant life and describe by other words what righteousness looks like when believers embrace it. "If you do this, then you will live," Paul seems to say. This idea of righteousness is vital to faithful ministry.

Our church celebrated a wonderful wedding recently. We as a faith community helped God unite a widow and a widower in holy matrimony. One of these happy and blessed people was the congregation's eighty-eight-year-old associate pastor. The Sunday before the wedding this octogenarian pastor said something important from our church's pulpit. He remarked, "I never dreamed that when I was this congregation's pastor back in 1974 and as we constructed this magnificent sanctuary that I would ever get married in it." He articulated perhaps a deeper truth than he knew. The tracks we make yesterday may be the tracks we later walk in again. Thus, people who live the life of righteousness are never anxious about how well they will later be received by people who encountered them earlier in life. Believers who live in righteousness by consistently demonstrating purity, uprightness, and blamelessness have little to fear. They are people who are always welcome wherever they go. The matrimonial pastor's insight reminded me of an old rabbinic story that I heard a minister relate during a funeral in the 1980s.

One day a good, rich man noticed the miserable conditions in which a certain poor carpenter lived. He decided to help the poor man and commissioned the carpenter to build a beautiful house. He told the carpenter, "I want this house to be ideal. Use only the best materials, employ only the best workers, and spare no expense." The rich man informed the carpenter that he was going on a journey, and he hoped the carpenter would complete the house before his return.

The carpenter saw this as a great opportunity to gain a financial advantage. Therefore, he skimped on materials, hired inferior workers at low wages, covered their mistakes with paint, and cut corners on the building of the house at every opportunity. In fact, the carpenter pocketed the cash difference wherever and whenever he could during the house's construction.

When the rich man returned from his journey, the carpenter brought the rich man the key and said, "I have followed your instructions and built your house as you told me to." The rich man replied, "I am glad," and handing the key back to the carpenter, he continued, "Here is the key. It is yours. You built this house for yourself. You and your family are to have it as my gift." The life God offers us has a number of daily options from which to choose. We can either do the right thing indicating righteousness or we can conform to the world's standards, and this option is unrighteous.

For pastors, the ministry journey can be difficult. Yet, all of us, if true to the upward call of Jesus Christ, are assured that God is with us. God has given us all the materials we need to be effective in the ministry. Perhaps we have different skills, but one thing God calls us to become and remain is righteous. Each of us may conjure a different image of a "righteous pastor." Like a beautiful painting, we may not be able to explain why it holds beauty for us, but we know beauty when we see it. *Righteousness* as a pillar in our memory can become a reminder of one of the many qualities God calls forth from us. Faithfulness in God's service is to be a servant who hungers and thirsts after righteousness.

People who live in the Lord's righteousness have nothing to fear. Righteous people are pure, upright, and blameless. If we need a reminder of one of the foundational characteristics of abundant life then there is a pillar with the word *righteousness* inscribed on it. Amen. (David N. Mosser)

JANUARY 2, 2005

New Year

Worship Theme: Time is a gift of God which is to be used in the service of his kingdom. Time is like a moving river in which the landscape is in a constant state of change. There is a time for everything.

Readings: Ecclesiastes 3:1-13; Revelation 21:1-6*a*; Matthew 25:31-46

Call to Worship (Psalm 8:1*a*, 3-6, 9)

> *Leader:* O LORD, our Sovereign, how majestic is your name in all the earth!
>
> *People:* **When I look at your heavens, the work of your fingers, the moon and the stars that you have established;**
>
> *Leader:* What are human beings that you are mindful of them, mortals that you care for them?
>
> *People:* **Yet you have made them a little lower than God, and crowned them with glory and honor.**
>
> *Leader:* You have given them dominion over the works of your hands;
>
> *People:* **You have put all things under their feet.**
>
> *All:* **O LORD, our Sovereign, how majestic is your name in all the earth!**

Pastoral Prayer:

Dear God, in whose kingdom time as we know it is relative, we who are always in a hurry come seeking some glimpse of your timely and timeless kingdom. As we reflect on the year that has just ended, we pray to be forgiven the sins we have committed; as we think of the year that lies ahead, we pray to be strengthened with godly determination to do those sins no more. Show us, O God, as much of your purpose as we can stand to know. Grant us the kind of faith we need to be able to live into life's mysteries. Help us to be able to live comfortably with the unknown. We do not pray for unlimited knowledge, but we do pray for enough knowledge to save us from unlimited ignorance. We offer this prayer in the name and spirit of your Son, and our Savior, Jesus. Amen. (Thomas Lane Butts)

SERMON BRIEFS

THE SEASONS OF LIFE

ECCLESIASTES 3:1-13

Wouldn't it be great if there was a person who could tell you what to expect out of the next year of your life? Most people who make predictions seem to miss them, including financial analysts on the stock market and the meteorologists about rain. However, there are some predictions we can make about our lives that will come true. Do you think it is possible? The wisest man who ever lived, according to scripture, wrote these predictions many years ago. Solomon formed his predictions into seasons of life that fall into two categories.

There are seasons of blessings, and there are seasons of testing, and we will experience each. If we believe that life for the coming year will be a time of blessing without testing, then we are going to have difficulties. Life is filled with tests.

What is a test? A test is a time when we need to move slowly. It does not mean that the ground is going to open up and swallow us. It means that we go through struggles and difficulties that may be dangerous. An example of this is our teenage years. We all go through some serious testing, and if we are not careful, we can make serious mistakes that follow us into adulthood.

Some of these seasons occur because we bring them on ourselves by our actions. Other seasons come and we have no control over them. There is a time to be born, and a time to die. We do not have anything to do with birth and will have less to do with death. There are seasons that just simply happen. There is a time to weep and a time to laugh. Many of the things that make us weep we did not bring on ourselves. Many of the things that make us laugh we did nothing to bring on ourselves either.

Nobody is happy if they think life is only going to be a blessing, but a person also cannot truly live well if they think life is only a big test. Life is both, and they come in seasons. The tests get mixed up with the blessings, and the blessings get mixed up with the tests. The seasons vary in length. Sometimes the blessings come in the middle of a test. Sometimes terrible things come in waves one after another. Sometimes seasons of blessings last a few weeks, and then a season of testing appears from nowhere and lasts a few months. The length has nothing to do with what happened in the last season. Many people today are in the midst of a season of testing, and they need to hang on during those seasons because there is a future season of blessing. The psalmist affirms this promise: "Weeping may remain for a night, / but rejoicing comes in the morning" (Ps. 30:5 NIV).

There are many seasons in life. The best news is that there will be a time, it is to be hoped many years from now, when we will experience a new season. It will be a season of blessings without any tests. It will be a great, unending gift. Christians often talk about this gift in terms of heaven. Solomon tells us, "[God] has also set eternity in the hearts of men" (v. 11 NIV). There will be a time of blessing that will never end. Jesus promises, "In my Father's house are many rooms; if it were not so, I would have told you. I am going there to prepare a place for you" (John 14:2 NIV). God placed in our hearts the understanding that there is something more than this world. Our hearts' true home and true season is eternity. God's eternity will never end and will be an everlasting blessing. (Tim Roth)

WHAT DO YOU SEE?

REVELATION 21:1-6*a*

Most of us have had the experience of coming upon a person or two who was looking up into the sky for an unknown reason. Almost without thinking, we ourselves have stopped, looked up, and asked, "What do you see?" As we begin this new year, more than one of us looks to see what lies ahead. We hope it is good, but perhaps there is some anxiety that it is not.

What do you see as you begin this new year? You would do well to let your vision be informed by the vision of God's long-ago servant named John in our text from Revelation 21:1-6*a*. This description and the promises it offers can clarify our own vision.

John first said he "saw a new heaven and a new earth" (v. 1). This verse may be picking up on the theme of Isaiah 65:17-25. That passage speaks of a time of joy, abundance, peace, and safety that would replace the sadness, poverty, war, and insecurity that the people in Isaiah's time had known. Both Isaiah and John saw God making life new and good again. Paul had foreseen something similar when he said, "I consider that the sufferings of this present time are not worth comparing with the glory about to be revealed to us" (Rom. 8:18). This vision of a new heaven and a new earth promises us that good things lie ahead. God will make life new and good again. Even more, God can make our lives new and good again.

Next, John "saw the holy city, the new Jerusalem, coming down out of heaven from God" (v. 2). What was John seeing when he saw this "new Jerusalem"? What did the vision mean? One thing it meant was that God was victorious and that God's ways and God's purposes were vindicated. God had won in the great struggle of good versus evil, God versus Satan. Sometimes as we survey our world and our lives, we may question whether good and God will be victorious. The Christians, for whom John originally wrote the Revelation, likely were concerned about God's victory. Under the pressure of persecution, they needed assurance that God would be victorious. What John saw here and in the rest of the Revelation offered believers assurance of God's victory and called for their faithfulness. That message is for us, too.

We now come to the greatest, most important part of what John saw. He saw God. God overshadows even the vision of "a new heaven and a new earth" and "the new Jerusalem." Verse 3 states:

> the home of God is among mortals.
> He will dwell with them;
> they will be his peoples;
> and God himself will be with them.

John saw unbroken fellowship between God and human beings. John portrayed God's near presence as the greatest blessing people could experience. Throughout the Bible and embedded in human experience is the desire, hope, and quest that people might have rich, unbroken fellowship with God. Verse 4 and also verse 6 speak of the blessings of God's presence—no more sorrowing, no more death, no more pain, but fullness of life.

As we move into the new year, are we seeing as clearly as we need to? We would do well to look through John's eyes and see what he saw: an opportunity to start afresh, a recognition of God's victory even as we face immediate difficulties, and an experience of God's presence. God's presence means blessing for us now and in all the future. (Ross West)

HOW WILL YOU MEASURE YOUR YEAR?

MATTHEW 25:31-46

"Five hundred twenty-five thousand six hundred minutes. / How do you measure—measure a year?" So begins the song "Seasons of Love" from the Broadway musical, *Rent*. These powerful lyrics touch the heart even more when one realizes that their young author, Jonathan Larson, died just prior to opening night. His search for significance in his life spills over into the song.

How do we measure a year? The question seems particularly appropriate this Sunday, as we begin a new year. What will be the standard by which we judge ourselves in 2005? Our world offers us many methods for evaluation. We can gauge our success in material standards: our amount of money, the kind of car we drive, the size of our house. Certainly, this is one of the most prevalent ways of looking at things in our society. We may also be tempted to measure the year by what we accomplish in our occupations: the raises we receive, the deals we close, the number of children who pass our class. Perhaps we have more artistic guides: the number of songs sung or enjoyed, the pages of books read, the quantity of good food eaten.

We may choose numerous ways to assess our year, but as disciples of Christ, our ultimate measuring stick must be the instructions Jesus gave us. Nowhere does Jesus make his requirements clearer than in our scripture today. We are to give food and water to those who are hungry and thirsty, clothes to the naked. We are to welcome strangers into our lives. We should visit those who are sick or in prison. This, according to Matthew's Gospel, is what we will be judged on; this is how Christ the king will determine who inherits the kingdom prepared for them from the foundation of the world.

Jesus' requirements are not just about what we do, however. They go much deeper, to the heart of who we are. The sheep, those who fed, clothed, and welcomed Jesus, did not do this because they knew they would receive recognition for it. In fact, they were as amazed as the goats Jesus rebuked. "Lord, when was it that we saw you?" (v. 44) they ask. They did not perform these acts of kindness in order to receive rewards from their king. Instead, their love for him had so transformed them that sharing love with others was a natural part of their existence. They could not see another person hurting or in need without stopping to help. This unconditional help is the standard by which we will be measured—love that has no choice but to act. As we begin the new year, let us search for Jesus in everyone we meet. As we continue to do this, we will eventually begin treating everyone this way without stopping to think about it. We will become the sheep of this story.

How will you use your 525,600 minutes this year? It has never been easy to live a meaningful life, but Christ provides the secret in this scripture. How can we measure a year? Love is measured in love demonstrated as we feed the hungry, visit those in prison, care for the sick, and welcome the stranger. (Melissa Scott)

JANUARY 9, 2005

Baptism of the Lord

Worship Theme: Jesus was authenticated as the Son of God by the prophets, and also on the occasion of his baptism. Our baptism in Jesus' name marks us as accepted by God.

Readings: Isaiah 42:1-9; Acts 10:34-43; Matthew 3:13-17

Call to Worship (Psalm 29:2-6a, 10-11)

> *Leader:* Ascribe to the LORD the glory of his name; worship the LORD in holy splendor.
>
> **People:** **The voice of the LORD is over the waters; the God of glory thunders, the LORD, over mighty waters.**
>
> *Leader:* The voice of the LORD is powerful; the voice of the LORD is full of majesty.
>
> **People:** **The voice of the LORD breaks the cedars....**
>
> *Leader:* He makes Lebanon skip like a calf.
>
> **People:** **The LORD sits enthroned over the flood; the LORD sits enthroned as king forever. May the LORD give strength to his people! May the LORD bless his people with peace!**

Pastoral Prayer:

Dear God, father and mother of us all, we come today to reflect on the baptism of our Lord. We pray that we may so vividly envision that occasion that it will inspire greater meaning in our own baptism. When we hear again the affirming words,

45

"this is my Son, the beloved, with whom I am well pleased," may we rejoice in our own baptism in the sure knowledge that in our baptism we are also affirmed and owned by God. We know there are those who have lost the assurance of your affirmation. Restore them, and all of us, to the joy of our salvation. As we confess our sins, we pray that the dividing wall of separation between you and us may come tumbling down. In the name of Jesus we pray. Amen. (Thomas Lane Butts)

SERMON BRIEFS

TEMPLATE OF A SERVANT

ISAIAH 42:1-9

I had never heard of a template. It's what my engineer father used when he made my twelve and one-half inch stainless steel mouthpiece for my brand-new trombone. The mouthpiece was unique, could not be dented, and was better than the original from which he made the template. A template is a pattern.

I've always loved patterns. I've always had my heroes after which I have sought to pattern my life. I have always loved to read biographies and find characteristics in others that I would like to duplicate in my own life. I became hooked when I was in the fourth grade and read *Lou Gehrig, Boy of the Sandlots*. Of course, my greatest hero, and the one after which I have humbly sought to pattern my life, is Jesus of Nazareth.

Then I wondered, What were Jesus' patterns? Who were his heroes who influenced him and after which he sought to pattern his life? John the Baptist, his cousin, forerunner and "greatest prophet in Israel"? No doubt! Mary and Joseph? Of course! How unique these two must have been! God? Jesus spent all that time in prayer for a reason. But there was at least one other influence and pattern Jesus used, the Old Testament.

But, in the Old Testament there were at least two views concerning the nature and ministry of the Messiah, as there were in Jesus' day. One view was that of a strong, militaristic messiah who would free Israel of the hated Roman yoke and restore her to the former glory known under David. But there was another view, the one Jesus chose as a pattern for his own life and ministry. It is found in the wonderful servant poems, at least four in number, that we find in Isaiah 42–53, the first of which serves as our text for the day.

Verse 1 introduces the servant chosen of God. The next verses describe this chosen servant. He is modest and quiet. The servant is considerate and compassionate. Here, the original language describes one who sits with the brokenhearted. This servant will not be discouraged or dismayed from this task of bringing justice, equal treatment for all, to all the nations.

Verses 5 and 6 strike the powerful image that God not only calls his servant but also empowers him to the point that he takes his hand and goes with him to every task. For this servant not only proclaims the covenant, the servant is the covenant. This servant personifies and embodies the covenant to bring light, sight, and freedom to any and all who are in bondage, even the Gentiles. This servant, who brings about God's new way of dealing with all humankind, embodies this covenant in manner, words, and spirit. As many have said, "I'd rather see a sermon than hear one." In Jesus, we see the fulfillment of the covenant and that to which every covenant person aspires.

I had read Harvey Cox's work for thirty-five years, but I learned more by observing Harvey and how he treated people with graciousness and that ever-present contagious smile than from all his books. I learned more about prayer from listening to Samford University's Mabry Lunceford, as he opened each class session with a word to heaven, than from any material on the subject. I have learned more about generosity by observing my wife, Sharlon, than I could learn in ten seminars. I would rather see a sermon than hear or read one.

Years ago, I was privileged to have a well-known university professor conduct a Bible study in the church of which I served as pastor. One of my deacons invited the professor to tour one of his farms on Sunday afternoon. Later, as the professor prepared for the evening service, notes in front of his face, he felt something happening to his feet. Removing his notes, he was astonished to find the owner of the farms, a leader in our community and member of a university board, on his knees, polishing the professor's shoes. No matter how high a position one attains in life, service to God and to others always places us on the top shelf. (Gary L. Carver)

EXCLUDED ANYONE LATELY?

ACTS 10:34-43

My personal commitment to mission ministry continues to call me to serve the abandoned children of Romania. My heart is broken as I look at infants who were left behind at the maternity hospital and see ten-year-olds doing their best to live on the city streets of eastern Europe. Most of those children are doubly impacted by their society. They are destined for difficulties because of their abandoned status. But, they are also separated from the world because they have Gypsy heritage.

Gypsy people have little or no standing in many eastern European societies. They are the ultimate outcasts. They are seen as untouchable and unreachable. Church leaders often ostracize pastors who seek to develop ministry among the Gypsy population. It is a pattern of discrimination that continues to destroy life and hope.

But we don't really need to travel to Romania to find discrimination and oppression. It happens in our own pews. People are not accepted because they don't dress right, or because they are in the wrong age group, or because they are poor, or because— you fill in the blank.

The church that we love as the Body of Christ stands guilty. Peter stood among a group of amazed people as he reflected on what God was teaching him. Peter's vision of unity (Acts 10:9-15) challenged the way he saw the world. Now it was his turn to share this powerful spiritual insight with those who were gathered with him in the home of Cornelius.

Peter's words were radical. For some, they would become fighting words. Peter spoke with great conviction when he said, "I now realize how true it is that God does not show favoritism" (v. 34 NIV). Even Abraham received a similar message in Genesis 12:3. He heard that all people on earth would be blessed through his family. Micah 6:8 refreshes the image by inviting God's people to do what is right. We are called to act with justice, to love mercy, and to walk humbly with God. The teachings parallel Peter's new-found insights. God has a place for everyone in the Body of Christ.

Peter doesn't mention the Great Commandment but the connection is strong. Love God and love your neighbor; those are the guidelines for walking faithfully with God. Peter connects this powerful teaching to the beginning of the earthly ministry of Jesus that came with the message of John and his gift of baptism. Peter retells the life of Jesus beginning with the Jordan River and moving through the Resurrection.

Peter's message is messianic in nature. Peter wants the people to realize that Jesus was indeed the anointed one spoken of by the prophets. Isaiah 61:1-3 became the character marker for Jesus as Jesus claimed his identity. He stood before his home synagogue in Nazareth to proclaim the prophetic words of Isaiah.

> The Spirit of the Sovereign LORD is on me,
> because the LORD has anointed me
> to preach good news to the poor. (v. 1 NIV)

Jesus was the Messiah, and the gospel message was targeted to those outside the boundaries of polite society.

The messianic message closes with a reminder of the blessing that is in store for those who are faithful: the power of forgiveness. Forgiveness is perhaps the most significant theological need for the life of the church today. How many times do we forget the message of the Messiah and the teaching of the apostles? How often do we exclude people and then stand in need of the forgiveness of God before we are able to move forward in mission and ministry? (Randy Jessen)

HEARING A VOICE

MATTHEW 3:13-17

Our world is full of voices. There are voices that speak to me continually. There are the voices of my parents that still ring even in my adult ears. They are voices that tell me I am loved and that I am to be the responsible person they raised me to be. Then also there is the voice of my wife that shows both her love and her expectations of me as a husband. There are the voices of my children that demonstrate everything from love and compassion to frustration and rebellion.

Then, of course, there are the voices that we hear in the rest of the world. There is the voice of our consumer-based world that demands that we produce more so we can spend more. There are the voices of our peers that entice us to act on values that we know are contrary to our faith and our upbringing. There is the voice of advertising that tells us that it is all about feeling good and having more. Wherever we go, we are surrounded by voices.

Then there was that voice that was heard at Jesus' baptism. It was a voice that sounded foreign amid the other voices that the people were accustomed to hearing. It was a voice that affirmed something few had yet to affirm. It was the voice of a holy parent affirming and revealing to the world the real identity of this holy child. "This is my Son, the Beloved, with whom I am well pleased" (v. 17).

Stop and think for a moment about this voice. This is the voice that spoke creation into being. This is the voice that called Moses and delivered the children of Israel. This is the voice that called and then spoke through the prophets. This is the voice of which the psalmist spoke: "The voice of the LORD is powerful; / the voice of the LORD is full of majesty" (Ps. 29:4). If ever there was a voice to be heeded, this would be that voice.

I have sought to remind my children, from the time they were small, of something very important. When I drop them off at school or when they leave the house, I leave them with the admonition to remember who they are and who loves them. I know that in the course of a day they will hear many voices. They will hear voices that will invite them to do what the popular kids are doing. They will hear voices that invite them to forget their moral underpinnings. They will hear voices that invite them to use drugs or alcohol. Amid these voices, I want them to hear my voice each day reminding them who they really are.

If we will listen, the voice of God is sounding yet again. This is Jesus, the Beloved, and Jesus is here to remind us to listen for that same voice. We, who are the Body of Christ, are also beloved, and when we function as that body, certainly we must know that God is pleased. Amid all the voices we hear in our world, this is the best voice to hear. It is, after all, the voice of our salvation! (Jeff Smith)

JANUARY 16, 2005

Second Sunday After the Epiphany

Worship Theme: The God who has known us from before we were born calls us to witness to the truth. The mission to which God calls us is not confined to the small circle where we are. Rather, God has called us to be in mission to all, everywhere.

Readings: Isaiah 49:1-7; 1 Corinthians 1:1-9; John 1:29-42

Call to Worship (Psalm 40:1-5c, 16)

Leader: I waited patiently for the LORD; he inclined to me and heard my cry.

People: **He drew me up from the desolate pit, out of the miry bog, and set my feet upon a rock, making my steps secure.**

Leader: He put a new song in my mouth, a song of praise to our God.

People: **Many will see and fear, and put their trust in the LORD.**

Leader: Happy are those who make the LORD their trust, who do not turn to the proud, to those who go astray after false gods.

People: **You have multiplied, O LORD my God, your wondrous deeds and your thoughts toward us; none can compare with you.**

All: **But may all who seek you rejoice and be glad in you; may those who love your salvation say continually, "Great is the LORD!"**

Pastoral Prayer:

Dear God, from whom we came, we thank and praise you for your call. May we be a light to all people, beginning with those nearest. We know there are many wounded around us every day whose lives appear outwardly calm and normal. We see people, and we may be people, who laugh on the outside, but weep on the inside. Help us to be sensitive to that kind of duplicity in ourselves and others. Be near those who have sustained great losses in life that they can't seem to get over. Bless those of us who more and more hear "time's wingéd chariot hurrying near." Bless us as we rearrange our lives to accommodate the illnesses and changes that come in the waning years of life. And we pray, here in the presence of the living, for the dead—there are so many of them—and since they cannot speak to us, we pray that we may live in such a way as to take good news to them when we join them. Hear our unspoken prayers, the prayers we just don't know how to say, but which we feel so deeply. In the name of our Lord. Amen. (Quotation from "To His Coy Mistress" by Andrew Marvell.) (Thomas Lane Butts)

SERMON BRIEFS

IN THE SHADOW OF HIS HAND

ISAIAH 49:1-7

While in seminary I was privileged to have Dr. Clyde Francisco for the study of Isaiah 40–66, or Deutero-Isaiah. Dr. Francisco was the consummate preacher. He always sought, even amid the criticism of some that he was not "scholarly enough," to apply exegetical study of Holy Writ to practical applications of a sermon for a local congregation. He would agree with the late Tip O'Neill that all "politics are local" in that he felt that focused inquiry and thorough investigation of scholarly research had no point unless it was practically applied to the local congregation. Dr. Francisco felt that study should lead to a sermon and that a sermon should be shared with a local fellowship of believers by a minister who lived with and loved those believers. Dr. Francisco died where he wished to die, where he had spent his life—in the pulpit! Jesus chose this servant of God from Isaiah as a pattern for life and ministry. It was also the pattern that Dr. Francisco so beautifully embodied.

The ideal servant is predestined from the womb. God called his spokesperson even before birth and entrusted that voice to a human agent for rearing. While we have made some progress, Protestants still de-emphasize the ministry and influence of Mary upon Jesus, God's ultimate servant. According to Luke, Mary personified the ideal servant and was steady in the task before her.

The ideal servant's mouth is like a sharp sound. The servant's voice is sharp, not destructive or harmful. The servant's words are sharp, pointed to the present issue because of his seclusion and time alone with God, hidden "in the shadow of his hand" (v. 2). The servant's word is also sharp and piercing because it is like a polished arrow, prepared and polished by God.

Still the servant is a human agent, not immune to failure, disillusionment, and weariness. Yet the servant is revived by the assurance of the guarantees from the God who called. The servant has the personal assurance that what God began, God will complete. God has been and will continue to be the servant's strength, enabling him to fulfill the mission for which he has been called: to bring restoration to Israel and to be a light for the Gentiles. The servant's work shall not be in vain. Even the kings of the earth shall hear, heed, and hasten to bow at the Holy One of Israel, the one who has chosen the servant. It is little wonder that the Ideal Servant patterned his life and death after such an image—the One of whom it is said:

Your attitude should be the same as that of Christ Jesus:

Who, being in very nature God,
   did not consider equality with God something to be grasped,
but made himself nothing,
   taking the very nature of a servant,
   being made in human likeness.
And being found in appearance as a man,
   he humbled himself
   and became obedient to death—even death on a cross!
Therefore God exalted him to the highest place

and gave him the name that is above every name,
that at the name of Jesus every knee should bow,
in heaven and on earth and under the earth,
and every tongue confess that Jesus Christ is Lord,
to the glory of God the Father." (Phil. 2:5-11 NIV)

Amen. (Gary L. Carver)

THAT PILE OF HOLIDAY GREETING CARDS IS WAITING

1 CORINTHIANS 1:1-9

Think about the holiday greeting cards you received this year. You probably still have some late arrivers trickling. They may be hanging nicely in one of those wreath-shaped card holders, or perhaps they are stacked in a pile still waiting to be carefully read. But usually, there are a few that come that are eagerly anticipated, opened with care, and read slowly and intentionally. Perhaps this kind of card comes from a mentor, a former teacher, or a wise friend. You know the words inside will be handwritten and chosen with love and insight. The sender knows you. They love you. They care about you. The card will, without a doubt, be filled with words you will long to read over and over again.

Paul establishes his mentorship to or authority with the Corinthians in the first few words of the letter as Paul calls himself an "apostle of Christ." With such a title, his words are to be respected, and his instructions should be heeded. For us, it is like seeing the return name on the corner of a treasured greeting card. Upon identifying whom the card is from, we can either toss the card in a pile to be read later or, as the Corinthians would have done with Paul's letter, eagerly anticipate the words to come when the letter is opened.

This letter to the Corinthians begins with intimate words, yet words that are distinctly Pauline. He consistently opens his letters affirming his readers. Paul writes, "I give thanks to my God always for you" (v. 4). Beginning a letter in this way makes the readers feel cherished, appreciated, and affirmed.

In the same way that holiday greeting cards come only once a year, Paul's letters to the Corinthians would not have been viewed as commonplace. They are eagerly anticipated, celebrated upon arrival, and read with the utmost concern and honor.

In the true form of a mentor, Paul does not disappoint readers. He gives thanks for them and then reminds them who they are. They are the saints of Corinth, called to be the Body of Christ. Paul reminds them of their uniqueness. The Corinthians are enriched by God, and the word of Christ is strengthened in them. To help them avoid discouragement, Paul tells them they are not lacking in spiritual gifts, but rather God is faithful in having called them into the fellowship of Christ.

It is as if we were to open a card and read the words, "I know things get rough sometimes, but I know who you are, and I know you are strong. You are on the right path. You are doing the right things. You have been chosen to do what you are doing for a specific purpose. I know you will triumph in the end." Wow! What a great message to receive. What an intimate relationship must be behind such words.

The message contained in the words Paul wrote to the Corinthians can hold the same encouragement and affirmation for us today. We are called to be the saints of our towns and communities. We have a special purpose in the fellowship of Christ. Our strength stems from the same source as the Corinthians, we are nourished and enriched by God.

Go back through that pile of greeting cards. They were sent for a purpose. Someone who knows you and loves you took the time to write to you. Do not just open the important ones, open them all. Use them as a source of strength as the Corinthians used Paul's letter. Cherish the messages within, for those who sent them know you well and want you to succeed. (Victoria Atkinson White)

THE BREATH OF PASSION

JOHN 1:29-42

John the Baptist is one of the stranger figures in the family tree of the New Testament. I suspect that should John appear at one of our churches on a Sunday morning we would not feel very comfortable. First of all, there is his dress. Camel hair girdles are definitely out of style. And his diet—locusts and honey—hasn't caught on at the weekly Wednesday night supper in the fellowship hall.

Perhaps most disconcerting about John the Baptist is the way he always seems to be looking for someone. Engage him in conversation and he looks past you as though he is expecting someone or searching for someone.

One thing you have to say for John the Baptist, however, is that when he sees what he is looking for he is not shy about pointing it out. "Here is the Lamb of God!" John exclaims (v. 29).

It is easy to be put off by John, with his strange habits of dress and diet. But, at the same time, there is something compelling about him. The attraction may have to do with his passion. John is a man on a mission. He believes there is something stirring in this world, and he does not intend on missing it. He is looking for nothing less than God's visitation. And when John sees that presence of holiness in the form of Jesus, he is bold to declare it: "Here is the Lamb of God who takes away the sin of the world!" Reading John's words in the Gospel is not unlike listening to someone who is breathless with excitement as they tell you what they have seen, what they have found.

I wonder, is passion what the church of Jesus Christ needs as it lives its life in this new year? Are we compromised by lethargy? Today is the second Sunday after the Epiphany. The Epiphany. Do you remember the Epiphany? That wonderful moment of manifestation when an old man declares that he is ready to die because he has seen it all, literally seen God's salvation, and now he can go. Simeon is at peace.

And what of us? It is just the second Sunday after the Epiphany. Have we become dulled so soon? Has the glow of that manifestation worn dim already? It was only days ago that we were all so excited by the lights of Christmas and the candles on Christmas Eve. Has it all left us so soon? It can happen, but, God help us, we must not let it.

In these days, we are asked to remember our baptismal vows. As we walk further and further away from the manger we need the manifestation of God more than ever. Christmas is over, but the Christ lives on. The gifts have all been opened, but God keeps giving. The world's observance of Christmas concludes, but the church still celebrates the light that the darkness cannot overcome.

Henry van Dyke once wrote, "Are you willing to believe that love is the strongest thing in the world—stronger than hate, stronger than evil, stronger than death—and that the blessed life which began in Bethlehem ... is the image and brightness of Eternal Love? Then you can keep Christmas. And if you keep it for a day, why not always?" ("Keeping Christmas," in *Six Days of the Week: A Book of Thoughts About Life and Religion* [New York: Charles Scribner's Sons, 1924], p. 347.)

Passionate John the Baptist is a good model for the church to be guided by in these postholiday days. John's passion, his witness, his declaration are the church's charter: "Here is the Lamb of God who takes away the sin of the world!" May we be boldly passionate as we proclaim this message in word and deed! (Chris Andrews)

JANUARY 23, 2005

Third Sunday After the Epiphany

Worship Theme: Jesus came to set us free from oppression and fear, to heal the divisions among us and unite us as people of one mind and purpose.

Readings: Isaiah 9:1-4; 1 Corinthians 1:10-18; Matthew 4:12-23

Call to Worship (Psalm 27:1, 11, 13-14)

Leader: The LORD is my light and my salvation;

People: **Whom shall I fear?**

Leader: The LORD is the stronghold of my life;

People: **Of whom shall I be afraid?**

Leader: Teach me your way, O LORD, and lead me on a level path because of my enemies.

People: **I believe that I shall see the goodness of the LORD in the land of the living.**

All: **Wait for the LORD; be strong, and let your heart take courage; wait for the LORD!**

Pastoral Prayer:

We come before you today, O Lord, with the smell of life fresh upon us. We come like sweaty children, with smudges on our faces and grass stains on our knees, straight from the playground. Some of us did not really want to come today. We are not here against our wills, but we are not all here. There are pieces of us in other places. Some parts of us are still in bed, at the beach, in front of the TV, behind the newspaper, or at work, or at the site of some unfinished job of last week, or hanging around an old hurt, or a recent put-down, or embarrassment. We are absorbed in a nagging anxiety that we cannot identify. We confess that we are here, but we are not all here, and we feel the fragmentation. Help us today—right now—to get ourselves together in this one place so we will have a better chance of leaving here one whole person. We do not ask to have our problems removed, but we pray that you will help us get them into manageable units. We pray for strength to negotiate life successfully and some sense of joy and meaning in what we do. Touch whatever part of ourselves we were able to bring to church today and bless whatever parts of us that never made it to church in the name of Jesus. Amen. (Thomas Lane Butts)

SERMON BRIEFS

LESS THAN IDEAL CONDITIONS

ISAIAH 9:1-4

After a long period of peace and prosperity under the rule of King Uzziah, Judah was plunged into decades of tumult by the westward drive of the Assyrian armies. Into this cauldron of history came the prophet Isaiah. Following him in his long ministry is unsettling. Isaiah is at once fatalistic and hopeful.

Isaiah brings his message into clear focus in chapter 5:1-7, as he tells the parable of the vineyard. God had chosen to establish his own people like a vineyard in a very fruitful land. God did everything possible to ensure the people's welfare and their safety. Nothing prevented them from bringing forth a rich harvest. Yet, the vineyard produced nothing but wild grapes. What else could God do but allow it to become uncultivated and over-grown? God looked for justice and discovered oppression; God sought righteousness and found nothing but injustice.

Still, this is not the final word the prophet has for the people. Despite Isaiah's severe words of judgment, his prophecy does not end on a note of despair. Isaiah believes there will always be a faithful remnant, whose trust is in God and whose desire is to walk in God's ways. This hope of final restoration is never extinguished. The prophet foresees a restoration of the land, when all the nations shall go to Jerusalem to be taught of the Lord and when men and women will learn of war no more (chapter 2:1-4).

On this third Sunday after the Epiphany, we are blessed to have one of Isaiah's hopeful images to consider. Isaiah pictures the light breaking on the land and the universal joy of the redeemed nation at the coming of God's salvation through the gift of a Messiah who will deliver the nation from its distress. The verses of Isaiah 9:1-4 are among the Bible's most hopeful words. A regenerated human society that lives in accordance with righteousness and faithfulness is dawning. Beyond judgment there is the revelation that God will save God's people.

Isaiah speaks in a way that can guide today's church. Similar to the prophet of ancient days, we work in less than ideal conditions. There is much to condemn and much that causes us to wonder if there is any hope for a different future. These are not easy times to be a community of faith. It is tempting to speak only words of doom and gloom, to draw people to the inevitable "turn out the lights, the party's over" sentiment which seems so practical and predictable as we look on a world of war, poverty, alienation, and oppression. Certainly the people of God must always acknowledge present conditions.

Yet, God's people are energized by something else: an undying hope. No matter how great the darkness of sin, God's people witness to a light that is stronger than that darkness. No matter how despairing the world may be of a new way of living, God's people witness to the joy that comes from deliverance of their burdens.

The circumstances for our ministry are always less than ideal. With brutal honesty we acknowledge such. However, despair is not our last word, for we are people of the light. We are people who have been brought to our feet as we sat in the gloom of deep darkness by the possibility that this Light will point us to a new way of living and being, even in the midst of less than ideal conditions! (Chris Andrews)

THE BIG PICTURE

1 CORINTHIANS 1:10-18

Just a few short weeks ago, we gathered together for the Christmas Eve service. The sanctuary was dark. Our voices joined together in several rounds of "Silent Night, Holy Night" as the light from our candles spread throughout the room. At the close of the service, it sounded as if we were one voice. It looked as if each individual candle came to be one solitary light.

Now the hype of Advent is over. The decorations have been put away until next Christmas. Our celebration of the coming of the Christ Child is complete and a sense of normalcy somehow returns to our church activities. There are meetings about curricula and building concerns to attend. Sunday school teachers must be recruited and nursery workers must be screened. There is a different kind of busyness in the air.

We find the Corinthian church in a similar place as Paul writes to them in 1 Corinthians 1:10-18. At one time, the Corinthians were acting as a single unit, propagating the gospel message. But, it appears that the novelty of unity has worn off and division has seeped into the church. As we recall from our Christmas Eve service, it is much easier to be in a spirit of oneness for special occasions or in times of celebration. Those are the times we feel the least different because we are gathered to celebrate the same cause, or in our case, the birth of the same child.

In Corinth, the unity is disrupted by claims of allegiance to those who performed baptisms. Perhaps some were claiming superiority because of who baptized them and thus trying to prove their higher worth in the community. At this point it is important to note that baptism is a worthy subject for discussion and even disagreement within Christian communities. Healthy dialogue can bring about greater understanding and appreciation for variations of baptismal beliefs. So Paul is not telling the Corinthians that baptism is not a valuable discussion topic, but rather he is making the case that baptism is not the most valuable object of dialogue. It is quite important to be baptized in the name of Christ, but what brings one to the place of baptism is what unifies all Christians. Thus, the baptismal spirit of unity should be the crux of the Corinthians conversations.

The Corinthians' belief in the crucifixion of Christ is what brought them together and will never allow them to be separated. The divisions Paul writes about are mere squabbles, which lessen the power of their proclamation of the gospel message. The lessening of the message of the cross should be the source of their concern, not upon what authority they were baptized.

Perhaps the divisions among us are not about who baptized us but about the color of the carpet in the new wing of the church, or what size bulletins we print, or where our budget surplus should be spent. These are all important issues and worthy of discussion because they obviously matter to someone. But, think about what would happen if we took the energy we expend on discussing sizes, or colors, or surpluses, and expended that energy on spreading the gospel message. What if in that time we visited the shut-ins in our congregation or went down to the community soup kitchen to talk with some homeless folks? Eventually, we would stop caring as much about carpets or bulletins or budgets because our focus would be on the bigger picture of what the Body of Christ is all about. May this season of Epiphany be one in which we may stay focused on the big picture we saw on Christmas Eve, on the gift we were all given, not because we deserve it or because we have earned it, but because God sees the big picture of our lives. Thanks be to God. (Victoria Atkinson White)

FISHING IN THE KINGDOM

MATTHEW 4:12-23

I'm not much of a fisherman, but I enjoy fishing when I have the chance. One thing I know about fishing is that it takes a good bit of time to get the equipment together. Once the equipment is assembled, then we have to get to where the fish are biting. Once, at the fishing location, we have to set up the equipment and bait the hooks. Then we have to wait. Usually, I end up having to untangle the line from something I snagged in the water or (on very unlucky days) in the boat or on the bank behind me. Fishing is fun, but it is so much work.

The disciples knew this reality of the hard work of fishing. While I just fish for recreation, they fished for a living. It is interesting that when Jesus called Peter and Andrew, they were casting their nets into the water. James and John weren't fishing when Jesus came by; they were mending their nets, which would have been a frequent task given the kind of nets they used. Fishing was hard work.

When Jesus asked them to follow and fish for people, surely they hoped it would be much easier work than fishing for fish. If not, at least perhaps it would be more rewarding.

The truth is that the task of following Jesus was more daunting than they at first imagined. When they started following Jesus, it was just around a very large lake that we know as the Sea of Galilee. The people they saw in the villages on that northern shore were people they probably already knew. They would share the good news of the kingdom of God, and people would welcome them warmly. They thought this would be a breeze of a job; but they had no idea what was in store for them in the days ahead.

What the disciples didn't know was what Matthew had already described for readers in the verses preceding their calling. The land known as Galilee is not here described as just another Jewish settlement. The area southeast of the Sea of Galilee was a Gentile area known as the "Ten Cities," or Decapolis. Our text quotes Isaiah describing this area as Galilee of the Gentiles (see Isa. 9:1). It is important that Jesus' ministry doesn't start in Jerusalem. Matthew makes an announcement that Jesus' ministry is going far beyond the walls of Judaism, and Jesus sets the stage for a radical movement that will change countless lives.

The message of Jesus is a radical message. It is not the provincial message of nationalistic hope propagated by the Jewish leaders of that day. It is not a message that is intended only for a friendly audience. It is not a message that is proclaimed to an audience that understands what faith in God is all about. No, this message is proclaimed to people who sit in darkness. The message is for the people who are outcast and cut off. It is a message foreign to most belief systems in the Gentile world, and a message that ultimately becomes a threat to the Jewish leaders themselves.

It is the message that the kingdom of God has come near, and it is a call to repentance. It is a message of deliverance and healing and hope. It is a message that God has come to the most unlikely people. Above all, it is a message that, when the nets are cast, even those doing the fishing might be surprised by what they catch. (Jeff Smith)

JANUARY 30, 2005

Fourth Sunday After the Epiphany

Worship Theme: The ways of the Lord are not the ways of the world. God is subtle yet abundantly vivid to true seekers.

Readings: Micah 6:1-8; 1 Corinthians 1:18-31; Matthew 5:1-12

Call to Worship (Psalm 15)

Leader: O LORD, who may abide in your tent? Who may dwell on your holy hill?

People: **Those who walk blamelessly, and do what is right, and speak the truth from their heart;**

Leader: Who do not slander with their tongue, and do no evil to their friends, nor take up a reproach against their neighbors;

People: **In whose eyes the wicked are despised, but who honor those who fear the LORD; who stand by their oath even to their hurt;**

Leader: Who do not lend money at interest, and do not take a bribe against the innocent.

People: **Those who do these things shall never be moved.**

Pastoral Prayer:

Dear God, we confess that we are broken people who live in a broken world. We pray for whatever ingredient we need to cope with brokenness in ourselves and in our world. We pray for all of the people we know who are living in dangerous territory and who are pushed from time to time into the zone of desperation. We pray for those who have illnesses that are not amenable to any medical procedure of which we know and who hope for a miracle to save them. We pray for those who love too much, and in whom love has become an illness. We pray for those in whom hate has become malignant. We pray for those in whose lives something that was once an answer to their problem has become an addiction more frightening and destructive than the problem it once solved temporarily. We pray for those who were wounded in childhood and who are still nursing a wound that has never healed. Have mercy on all of us who were abused, neglected, unloved, loved in wrong ways, or who grew up in some circumstance that hurt and still hurts. Help us to be set free from guilt about things that have happened to us over which we had no control. And, give us the courage and strength to take charge of our lives. We pray for these and all other ills, named or unnamed, that haunt the lives of the people we know. In Jesus' name. Amen. (Thomas Lane Butts)

SERMON BRIEFS

THE ETERNAL DANCE WITH GOD

MICAH 6:1-8

It is a dance as old as the hills and in this case, the mountains. God's love for us is constant and constant toward God are those times when we wander far from God's path. In this session of the eternal dance with God, Micah is the caller, the one who knows the dance and, here particularly, the Lord of the dance. Micah calls out to the people of God an invitation to be made right once again with God. How easy it is to be swayed away from God by the tunes that attract us with empty promises and almost immediate pleasures, thus the case of God's people, Israel. Micah in his role as dance caller calls out to the people to return to God. The first two voices ask the question, what do you have against God? God is as near to you as the natural surroundings of your land. If you have a case against God, plead it

THE ABINGDON PREACHING ANNUAL 2005

before the mountains and the hills. You will be heard. That's the enduring quality of God; no matter how angry we may be with God, God is always attentive to us. We may think God is at fault having caused our lives to experience something unexpected and unwanted. But that does not mean that God closes us off. No, God is near, and God can hear. Yet, God is also known as one who will deal justly with the people. Justice is God's. How God defines justice is for us to accept. However, God is a listening, caring God. In Micah's question to the people of Israel God asks, "What have I done to you? In what have I wearied you? Answer me!" (v. 3). Although sounding much more like the questions we ask to friends from whom we are alienated, the questions convey God's concern for God's people. The first question asks for reflection. What has caused us to wander from God? What is a good reason? The second question asks if we have tried hard enough to do what God required initially, and should we have given up so easily? The statement, "Answer me," is that invitation again. God invites us into honest dialogue with God and ourselves.

God has done great things for us as God did for the people of Israel. We are called to remember. That remembrance is why we have different celebrations that invite us to recall our baptism and membership vows. Where did God pull us from when we came to know the saving grace of God? Don't we consider these great things of God done by God on our own behalf?

Humanity's response many times is like that of the people of Israel: How much more can I do to worship God? How do I prepare myself to go before God to once again dance with God in that dance of life and love?

God's answer is that external things do not matter as much as the internal, those things from the heart: "To do justice, and to love kindness, / and to walk humbly with your God" (v. 8). God's invitation for us is to live our lives on the outside in ways that are pleasing to God because on the inside, in our spirits and in our hearts, God is in residence, sharing that which we need to please God and to serve each other. Shall we dance? Let God lead! (Eradio Valverde, Jr.)

66

SIMPLE MEANS

1 CORINTHIANS 1:18-31

We work so incredibly hard five, sometimes six or seven days a week to achieve what the world is telling us we need to do, have, own, or look like. We want the latest, the newest, the fastest, and the most efficient of everything. Our lives have become not only about consumption but also about who can consume things in the best and most extravagant ways. We spend so much time trying to obtain so much. Paul explains so simply in 1 Corinthians 1:18-31, that a life lived according to the world's standards is considered among the least pleasing in the eyes of God.

God works on an entirely different scale of judging what is worthy and what is not. It is almost as if God laughs at our standards because God's measures are, according to Paul, exactly contrary to ours. Why then, do we spend our time and effort trying to live up to what the world deems significant or important if those things are in direct conflict with what God believes to be of the highest value?

Too often, we place ourselves in the judge's seat and decide who is worthy of our time and energy when we should be judging ourselves. God chose us, without all of the improvements we are trying to make for ourselves that the world says we need to make. God chose us without those things. What a mind-boggling concept! God chose us just as we are. Why then, do we run ourselves to the point of exhaustion trying to improve what God has already deemed acceptable in God's sight? From this point of view, we truly are wasting our time conforming to the world's standards because the highest rank of success has already been granted to us by the only one who is worthy to sit in the judge's seat. We are children of God.

This passage concludes with guidelines for the only way to boast, which is a key action when one has reached worldly standards. Yet, boasting, according to Paul, can only occur when one boasts in the standards contrary to the world; that is, one can only boast when one boasts in the name of God. Therefore, the only way to boast is to choose God's standards, those which may make us cringe or want to turn the other way, for they are not the same paths the world screams for us to choose.

The only way to boast is to choose God's way, and what a relief! We no longer have to work ourselves into frenzies trying to succeed according to what the television, the magazines, or the shopping malls tell us we need to buy, wear, or do. We no longer have to decipher what we have time for and what will have to wait. God's plan is already laid out for us in Paul's words in 1 Corinthians 1:18-31.

Our self-proclaimed methods of wisdom are not part of God's plan, Paul says. For was it not in the midst of foolishness and craziness that the Christ Child was born? Jesus was born in a place for animals and waste in the midst of the chaos of a census in what would be, according to our standards, the most primitive of conditions. Yet in the simplicity of a young mother and in the faithfulness of some shepherds and upon the intuition of some wise astrologers from the East who chose to follow a chance, we have the story we celebrate in Advent. We continue to celebrate this story in Epiphany. This is not a story of worldly standards of success. In fact, it is a failure. Yet it is in this story, this simple story, that God evokes the means to save us, just as we are. (Victoria Atkinson White)

GOALS AND GRACES

MATTHEW 5:1-12

When Jesus returned from the wilderness, he went to his hometown synagogue. Jesus stood up to read. The scroll was given to Jesus and he read from Isaiah 61 (Luke 4:14-21). When Jesus saw the crowds, he went up the mountain. He sat down to preach. Jesus' disciples came to him and the text was Isaiah 61.

There is good reason to interpret the Beatitudes in light of Isaiah 61, and consequently seeing Jesus' Sermon on the Mount as the definitive interpretation of the prophet. Thus, while the temptation in our culture is to privatize and even sentimentalize these statements, their significance is far more essential and revelatory. In fact, just as Luke has positioned Jesus' sermon in Nazareth to set the tone for his subsequent ministry among "the last, the least, and the lost," so does the Sermon on the Mount generally, and the Beatitudes specifically, provide the palate of colors for Matthew's portrait of Jesus' work.

As we begin this dense, if familiar, section of materials, some introductory words are in order. In the first instance, we must remember that Jesus is, among other things, the Teacher. Greater than Moses or the other prophets, and certainly greater than the religious leaders of the day, Jesus teaches with astonishing authority. Five sections of material in Matthew's Gospel are offered as instruction for the disciples, each one ending with a characteristic formula: "When Jesus had finished saying these things." Furthermore, Jesus will reserve this teaching role for himself for as long as he lives on earth. Indeed, when Jesus commissions the disciples, granting them authority to heal, cast out demons, and preach, he will not give them authority to teach. Only in the last verse of Matthew's account, at the end of the Great Commission, will Jesus command the disciples to teach.

Still, Jesus is much more than a teacher. This gospel truth is communicated both explicitly and implicitly as here. Jesus' "position" on the mountain suggests not so much Moses giving the Law, as the King enthroned on Zion. Jesus' disciples are, in effect, the court officers, receiving instruction and commission—gracious imperatives.

It has long been debated as to whether the Beatitudes should be read as indicatives or imperatives, as promises or commands. Some read these verses, and in fact the entire Sermon on the Mount, as something on the order of "entrance requirements" for the eschatological kingdom. This reading seems cogent when one hears the call to be "poor in spirit" or a "peacemaker," even to set one's appetites on the right things. It is less obvious, however, as to how one is to go about "mourning" or to ensure "reviling and persecution." If being "pure in heart" is a requirement for entering the kingdom, then the blessing is beyond us all. If the Beatitudes are not grace, they are not gospel.

In a similar manner, the Beatitudes cannot be mere indicatives or promises. There do appear to be "goals" for discipleship here, both in our lives and in the world. It is precisely by "showing mercy" and "being meek" that our light—and more to the point, the light of Christ—is evidenced in the world.

Perhaps the reason that the debate as to the exact nature of the

Beatitudes shows no signs of waning is that there is truth on both sides. There are graces here and goals. Jesus is commanding and promising. Jesus marshals his disciples for their work and supports them with strength and comfort. When Jesus had finished speaking, the disciples were "blessed" indeed. (Thomas Steagald)

REFLECTIONS

FEBRUARY

Reflection Verse: *"[Love] bears all things, believes all things, hopes all things, endures all things." (1 Corinthians 13:7)*

LOVE: IT BEARS ALL THINGS
1 Corinthians 13:1-13

To modern people, few biblical texts are as familiar as Paul's hymn praising love. In 1 Corinthians 13 we possess one of the truly beautiful songs in the history of literature. It is a hymn to love that praises a concept melting the hearts of even the most cynical among us.

Everyone is in love with love. Love, apart from its more amusing sides, is serious business, and scandals that involve love can bring powerful people down from high places. In this month's meditation I would like to turn our attention to the issue of love in its more serious aspects. In ancient Greece there were three primary words for what we modern Americans call "love." Since we have amalgamated the three terms, perhaps it would be a good idea to at least touch on the three lightly. We will try to separate each peculiar use of love as the Greeks first understood them. As we all know from the father of the bride in the popular motion picture, *My Big Fat Greek Wedding*, all words originally take their derivation from Greek. However, this is truer than most people know.

In its most innocent sense the Greek word *phileo* means "to love" or "to fall in love." From this word *phileo* we derive terms like *philadelphia*, which means "city of brotherly love" or the word *philosophy*, which means principally a "love of wisdom." In the New Testament books of Luke and Acts, the writer addresses a person or group of people named Theophilus meaning "love of God." Often, when Americans say that they love this or that, they are using *love* in the sense of *phileo*, or friendly love, as we might say.

A second meaning of love is denoted by the Greek word *eros*, as in erotic love. Plainly, readers understand the sense of this term for love without me having to paint a picture for you. *Love Connection* and *The Love Boat* are two formerly popular television programs that employ eros when they use the word *love*. There are many comments that I could make about erotic love and its detrimental effects on our society. As much as erotic love is used and abused in modern culture, however, erotic love does have an appropriate place in human life. It is erotic love that often is the catalyst for deeper and fuller expressions of love that come with more mature relationships.

A third understanding for our American use for the word *love* is *"agape."* The Greeks, and especially the New Testament writers, used agape for the highest and most devoted kind of love. This is the kind of love symbolized by the person willing to lay down his or her life for another. Agape love is a mother's love for her children. Agape is the sort of love we speak about when we are talking of love in its loveliest form. Jesus specifically mentions this kind of love often, but most pointedly when he said, "This is my commandment, that you love one another as I have loved you. No one has greater love than this, to lay down one's life for one's friends" (John 15:12-13).

First Corinthians 13 has been terribly misunderstood over the years. Poets, playwrights, and musicians derive inspiration from Paul's hymn to love. These artists have offered this inspiration back to our general culture. Perhaps people would rather hear, see, or read something lofty than something that underscores our despair over violence and war. However, the church itself may be one of the greatest culprits in fostering confusion about what Paul means when he writes about love. Again and again, the church primarily uses 1 Corinthians 13 at weddings. This may be well and good, but it is not Paul's intention. Rather, we might take our signal from the chapter's context.

Paul's discussion about the spiritual gifts surrounds the hymn to love. Beginning with chapter 12 and continuing into chapter 14, Paul offers his theological insights into "spiritual gifts." The love-hymn interrupts, in fact, as something of an interlude. If we pasted the end of chapter 12 to the beginning of chapter 14 it would read like this:

> But strive for the greater gifts. And I will show you a still more
> excellent way. . . . Pursue love and strive for the spiritual gifts, and
> especially that you may prophesy. For those who speak in a tongue
> do not speak to other people but to God; for nobody understands
> them, since they are speaking mysteries in the Spirit. (1 Corinthi-
> ans 12:31, 14:1-2)

Thus, when Paul writes about love, he writes strictly in the context of the spiritual gifts, which apparently are a point of contention for those in the Corinth church. Time and again the Corinthian conflicts center on the use and abuse of spiritual gifts. But Paul does not suggest that love is greater than the spiritual gifts. Rather, Paul advocates that a spirit of love governs the spiritual gifts. In other words, for Paul, these spiritual gifts are merely expressions of authentic Christian love.

Thus, as righteousness is one of the pillars of abundant Christian living, then so too is love. Paul teaches that love is not so much a feeling or an attitude as *agape* love is a commitment to live and to abide in a community that we call the church. To love in the *agape* way is a method of putting into practice what God gives people in Jesus Christ.

Interestingly, Paul does not discuss Christ's resurrection—although he could have—in this section on the spiritual gifts. We certainly could ask, Why not? The most evident answer is that Paul assumes resurrection faith is a given for believers. "If Christ has not been raised, then our proclamation has been in vain and your faith has been in vain" (1 Corinthians 15:14). Without this resurrection plank in our doctrinal understanding, our faith, like the faith of those in Corinth, "would be in vain."

When we look at people's methods and motives in the church, Paul, I am certain, would suggest that we need to look no further than the method and motive of love. The next time you hear someone make a suggestion in the church about doing this or that, check the love motive. If the love motive is there, then the idea may be worth entertaining. If not, then it is simply another idea. Will the idea build up the community of faith, or will it tear it down?

If we ever need a reminder of one of the foundational characteristics of abundant life, then there is a pillar with the word *love* inscribed on it. Amen. (David N. Mosser)

FEBRUARY 6, 2005

Transfiguration Sunday

Worship Theme: God has, in time, spoken with abundant clarity to humanity. God may, from time to time, speak to some individually. In any case, we know all that we need to know to live as God's people from what God has already said.

Readings: Exodus 24:12-18; 2 Peter 1:16-21; Matthew 17:1-9

Call to Worship (Psalm 99:1-4a, 5)

> *Leader:* The LORD is king; let the peoples tremble!
>
> **People:** **He sits enthroned upon the cherubim; let the earth quake!**
>
> *Leader:* The LORD is great in Zion; he is exalted over all the peoples.
>
> **People:** **Let them praise your great and awesome name.**
>
> *Leader:* Holy is he! Mighty King, lover of justice. . . .
>
> **People:** **Extol the LORD our God; worship at his footstool. Holy is he!**

Pastoral Prayer:

Almighty God, you have spoken to us in days of old through the law and the prophets, and in more recent times you have spoken to us through your son, Jesus, the Christ. We pray today to be forgiven of the sin in our lives, not only the sin we see but also the sin that is so much a part of our lives that we do not see it. We are grateful for your word, which has come to us in so many ways. Give us insight to see how your word can guide the development of our lives. We do not pray for exotic experiences every day, but we do pray, O Lord, to be taken to the top of the mountain now and then, so we may be assured of what we already know. Could today be the day? Amen. (Thomas Lane Butts)

SERMON BRIEFS

GOD'S FUTURE IS OUR FUTURE

EXODUS 24:12-18

On this Transfiguration Sunday, this story in Exodus connects with the gospel. In both, we experience a dramatic revelation of the presence of God and the gift of an enduring covenant.

Chapter 24 opens with Moses revealing the laws and ordinances of the covenant. The people declare their intention to do all that God has told them to do. What follows is a ritual of worship and celebration.

In verse 12 Moses is called to go up the mountain into the presence of God while the elders wait below. Aaron and Hur are designated as those who are to settle disputes as they arise. To anyone familiar with the stories, this is not good news, foreshadowing the unfaithfulness of Israel later.

The promise that God makes to give the tablets of stone with the law and commandments is a significant one. On the one hand, it represents the promise of God's instruction in establishing patterns of behavior that will guide the people's life together. But on the other hand, the promise also represents a future toward which God directs them. God's promise becomes another installment of God's care and provision for those who have been led out of slavery and through the Red Sea. The covenant is extending beyond God's gifts of manna and water to include the guidance of the spiritual life of this newly formed and forming community.

Verse 15 begins a narrative of Moses' experience on the mountain. For six days he waits, and on the seventh day the voice of God calls to Moses. In a cloud that covers the mountain and in the appearance of a devouring fire Moses experiences the presence of God. God is not seen directly, but the glory of God is revealed as the sign of the presence.

This also is a sign of hope for the people. God's will, known in laws and commandments, exists within the presence of an abiding relationship. The seventh day of creation is the Sabbath; the Sabbath is the time when day to day details are put aside in favor of worship and adoration. Sabbath is the day through which the sense of God's presence is renewed. In this theophany (a manifestation of God), the covenant is known in the nearness of God that enlivens and empowers the laws and commandments given to the people. Moses becomes a sign of that presence as he mediates the glory revealed.

What is revealed in the "glory" of God? How could one describe it? Here it seems to be that moment when past and future become one in the presence of a love so great, a mercy so deep, a goodness so powerful that all creation seems to sing for joy.

In this passage we find that the past can only be helpful for those who believe they have a future. God continues to open doors of the future for us through the revealing of God's grace in Christ and the guidance for life we receive. Our worship stirs the memory of a past lived in God's saving work. Our worship quickens our awareness of the presence of Christ continuing to reveal itself to us in countless ways. (Bob Holloway)

DISCERNING THE TRUTH

2 PETER 1:16-21

Peter's account of the transfiguration provides many options for preaching on this Sunday. Although it is difficult for us to reconstruct exactly what Peter's opponents were arguing within that early Christian community, it is clear that they raised some questions about the reliability of Peter's teaching. We are able to gain great wisdom through Peter's thoughtful responses to the questions that arose about the return of Christ and the nature of Christian hope. Peter offers us a historical basis for our hope in

Christ, based on his own experience. He also offers us some wisdom about the discernment of other issues within the Christian community.

First and foremost, this passage provides an opportunity for the preacher to reflect on the way that Jesus' identity as the Messiah is revealed through the transfiguration. The main concern of Peter's writing was to defend the Second Coming of Christ. The Parousia was being called into question by those who were frustrated by its apparent delay. Peter defends the parousia by recounting Jesus' glorification at the transfiguration "For he received honor and glory from God the Father when that voice was conveyed to him by the Majestic Glory, saying, 'This is my Son, my Beloved, with whom I am well pleased'" (v. 17). By emphasizing the apostolic witness to this event, Peter relies on some of the strongest testimony he knows to validate Jesus' status as Lord over all creation. Peter's personal story of encountering God through Jesus is one of the most powerful ways he has of defending the honor and glory of God. Peter knows that God will be true to his word because he has already seen God at work in and through Jesus.

There are also interesting parallels that can be explored by comparing the account of the transfiguration with that of Jesus' baptism in the Synoptic Gospels. In all of these texts, Jesus is proclaimed to be the beloved Son of God. By reflecting on the divine sonship, we are able to better understand the transfiguration and its importance for understanding the role of Christ in the judgment. As Duane F. Watson noted, "The transfiguration provided the historical basis for the proclamation of the parousia, when Jesus returns as eschatological king. The parousia hope is not false" (*New Interpreters Bible*, vol. 12 [Nashville: Abingdon Press, 1998], p. 342). Jesus has been named the Messiah, and he will return to rule over God's kingdom.

Verses 19-21 provide us with an opportunity to reflect on prophecy and its role in the Christian tradition. We are reminded that "no prophecy ever came by human will, but men and women moved by the Holy Spirit spoke from God" (v. 21). The central issue in Peter's community was the discernment of true doctrine, and this continues to be an issue in today's church. As noted earlier, apostolic testimony is one method of discerning truth. We rely on the witness of scripture and the stories of lives transformed through God's grace to lead us to the discernment of truth. We are also reminded, however, that true prophecy originates through the action of the Holy Spirit. We are called to always be discerning, looking for the ways that any new prophecy is in line with God's revealed will. We are encouraged to be "attentive to this as to a lamp shining in a dark place" (v. 19). God will continue to reveal God's self to us. We must continually seek to be in relationship with God, however, so that we might be ready to hear the divine word through the leadership of the Holy Spirit. (Wendy Joyner)

HEAR YE HIM!

MATTHEW 17:1-9

Many of us are familiar with the old parable of the six blind men and the elephant. Each blind man happened to grab a different part of the elephant's body, so each had a very different idea of what the elephant was like. The man who got hold of the leg described the animal as being like a tree. Another discovered the trunk and explained that the elephant was more like a big snake. A third blind man wound up with the tail and insisted the elephant was actually as thin and flexible as a rope, and so on. The point is that all the men were right, but because they were all blind, none of them grasped the full picture. The wisest approach to understanding the mystery would have been to put all their impressions into a composite and learn from one another.

This is a lesson we should heed in our world of competing "religious truth" claims. Each of the great world religions contains truths that deserve a hearing. In the text for this week we find the following words attributed to God, "This is my beloved Son, in whom I am well pleased; hear ye him" (v. 5 KJV). That is the most important line in the passage, and one of the most important lines in the Bible. The glorious and nostalgic details surrounding this profound declaration were God's way of saying in the clearest possible terms that Jesus deserves a hearing. If

Jesus is indeed the Son of God, then what he had to say about God is of extraordinary significance. It has been suggested that all church signs should bear the inscription, "important if true." The transfiguration was God's way of emphasizing both the truth and importance of Jesus. Jesus' teaching was for more than the mere speculation of a sincere blind man. It was actually "that which I have seen with my Father" (John 8:38 KJV) declared unto us. A truth claim such as this places Jesus in a category all by himself, for there is nothing else like it in all of religion.

This is either the most wonderful opportunity ever made available to humanity, or it is the biggest lie to ever hit the planet. As Christians, we need not apologize for believing in the uniqueness of Christ. If I did not believe it I would need to rethink my choice of professions. I would need to sort through the impressions of the world's greatest religious teachers (including Jesus) accepting what seemed most reasonable and rejecting that which did not. After all, they are only well-meaning blind men who touched a reality too big to comprehend.

According to our text, Jesus is far more than just another of the world's great religious teachers. This is not to negate or criticize the contributions of other spiritual leaders. Like the characters in the old parable, some really have grasped the trunk or the tail, but Jesus was the elephant of which they all had hold and just could not see. Jesus is the one who most deserves our hearing. "Hear ye him!" (Lance Sawyer)

FEBRUARY 13, 2005

First Sunday in Lent

Worship Theme: Temptation to disobedience and expediency always hangs around the margins of life waiting for some crack in our spiritual resolve. The grace of the Lord, Jesus Christ, is the solution to all sin.

Readings: Genesis 2:15-17; 3:1-7; Romans 5:12-19; Matthew 4:1-11

Call to Worship (Psalm 32:1-6c)

Leader: Happy are those whose transgression is forgiven, whose sin is covered.

People: **Happy are those to whom the LORD imputes no iniquity, and in whose spirit there is no deceit.**

Leader: While I kept silence, my body wasted away through my groaning all day long.

People: **For day and night your hand was heavy upon me; my strength was dried up as by the heat of summer.**

Leader: Then I acknowledged my sin to you, and I did not hide my iniquity.

People: **I said, "I will confess my transgressions to the LORD," and you forgave the guilt of my sin.**

All: **Therefore let all who are faithful offer prayer to you; at a time of distress.**

Pastoral Prayer:

Dear God, we have been told that you are all-powerful, that you made everything, including ourselves, and that it was you who gave us the capacity to wonder who we are, and who you are, and why we are here. We confess, O Great and Mysterious One, that in our experience, this capacity is almost as often a curse as it is a blessing. We wonder why you gave us the capacity to ask questions that we cannot answer and the ability to think thoughts that are larger than life. We confess that our hearts and minds rise up to heights of grandeur, but our feet are mired in the clay. Are we broken angels in need of divine repair? Have we just not tried hard enough? Or, did you make us to be like this, to live in constant tension between what we think we should be and who we are? Did you intend from the beginning that faith in what we cannot see and trust in you should be the ingredients that compensate for our ignorance? Forgive us, O Lord, if our hearts and minds carry us beyond where we should try to go. "Lead us not into temptation, but deliver us from evil." In the powerful name of Jesus we pray. Amen. (Thomas Lane Butts)

SERMON BRIEFS

UNSCRAMBLING AN EGG

GENESIS 2:15-17; 3:1-7

"Humpty Dumpty sat on a wall, Humpty Dumpty had a great fall. All the king's horses and all the king's men couldn't put Humpty together again." This nursery rhyme began actually as a riddle, asking the question: "What, once broken, can never be repaired, not even by strong or wise persons?" Regardless of how hard we try, a broken egg can never be put back together again; a scrambled egg can never be unscrambled.

There is a Humpty Dumpty story in the Bible. We call it the Fall.

God places Adam in the Garden of Eden with the opportunity to work it as a partner. With that responsibility comes the freedom to enjoy God's provisions and unfettered fellowship. The only prohibition is to avoid the tree of the knowledge of good and evil. The tree is not about academic knowledge. It is knowledge in the Hebraic sense: personal, intimate experience. The tree's purpose is to provide a genuine choice for Adam and Eve. They can choose to trust and obey God, or they can choose to disobey. Either way, they will demonstrate their own free will. To help Adam exercise the appropriate restraint, God articulates the consequences for violating the prohibition: death. Evil leads naturally to destruction, and God lovingly warns Adam of the dangerous results.

The shrewd serpent (see also Rev. 12:9; 20:2) enters the scene. His lack of reverence and respect for God is evident by his refusal to refer to the "Lord God" rather than simply "God." The title "Lord God" reflects the revealed personal name for God and reflects his character as trustworthy, responsive, gracious, and knowable. However, the serpent uses only the generic title of "God" in his conversations with Eve. His vocabulary does not recognize any personal relationship; it denies God his rightful character and role as provider, protector, friend, and sovereign. He does not unload a direct attack against God or engage in hostile argument. Instead he uses ambiguity, suggestion, distortion, nuance, and indirect implication. By omission, he twists God's instruction to Adam (cf. 2:16 with 3:1).

Through the serpent's scheme of spinning the truth into half-truth, the seeds of doubt take root and bear fruit. Adam and Eve choose the creature rather than the Creator, impression rather than instruction, self-fulfillment rather than divine purpose, independence rather than interdependence, pride rather than humility. One minute, they are able not to sin; the next minute, they are not able not to sin. Sin changes trust into fear, innocence into shame. It takes us farther than we want to go, costs us more than we want to pay, and holds us longer than we want to stay.

If one football player jumps offside, the whole team is penalized. So it is with sin. Because one man, Adam, sinned, the whole human race is penalized. And make no mistake, the responsibility is our own, not simply the serpent's.

At the base of the Tetons in Wyoming lies Jackson Lake. Sometimes, early in the morning when the lake is perfectly calm, the reflection of the Tetons is magnificently mirrored on the lake's surface. However, if you take one little flat stone and skip it across the surface of the lake, the image of the Tetons becomes distorted and marred. In the same way, when Adam committed one sin, God's image in us became distorted and marred.

As Brent Philip Waters wrote in *The Christian Ministry* (January 1983), "Wherever we step we hear the crunch of fragile [egg] shells beneath our feet." (Dennis L. Phelps)

WHERE DOES LIFE BEGIN?

ROMANS 5:12-19

Philosophers refer to a "genetic fallacy" as an error in logic. It is the presumption that you can explain something by tracing its origin. The apostle Paul would not have agreed with this theory. He believed that it was important to know and understand the origin of all things. In this passage, Paul seeks to explain the origin of sin, death, and life.

Paul's letter to the Romans is one long, sustained, theological argument. That makes it difficult for a preacher to deal exclusively with one short passage in isolation from the rest of the letter. To do so, one must constantly be looking back to earlier passages in order to understand the one under study. This is made clear by Paul's frequent use of the word *therefore*. Paul reminds readers to review what he has already written. In this passage (5:12-19) the *therefore* refers to his claim in 4:11 that Jesus has brought reconciliation to God for human beings.

In light of this reality, Paul begins an explanation of why this reconciliation was necessary and how Jesus was able to affect it. He traces sin back to the first human being: Adam. Although the Mosaic Law had not been introduced, Adam's sinful choices introduced sin into the world. This introduction of sin resulted in the introduction of death, the punishment for Adam's sin. This punishment was exacted on all human beings, even those who had not disobeyed one of God's commands as Adam had.

This pattern—one man's act leads to consequences for others—was a precursor of Jesus' act of redemption. Paul contends that Jesus' act was greater, not because it was more inclusive but because it was an act of grace.

Paul's astounding claim is that one man, Adam, introduced death into the world and that one man, Jesus, provided justification not only for Adam's sin but also for the sins of all humanity. It is a cosmic view of universal atonement. We are put right with God through the obedience of Jesus Christ to God's will and purpose.

There is a great temptation to eliminate Adam's story from the explanation of reconciliation. After all, Adam's story is enveloped in the mists of the ancient past. We must accept the biblical stories as they stand because we cannot investigate the Garden of Eden. This does not mean that these stories are unimportant or irrelevant to our theological discourse. We cannot make sense of Jesus' life-giving actions and teachings apart from an understanding of the origins of sin and death.

There is an important moral corollary that follows from this passage: Our actions affect the lives of others. When we break God's commandments or ignore God's commands, we contribute to the web of sin that catches all of humanity. Conversely, when we act in Christlike ways, we affect the lives of others, and through them, we affect the wider world. In other words, the origin of the good and evil in our world may trace its origin back to us. (Philip D. Wise)

PROVING IT!

MATTHEW 4:1-11

If you're such a good swimmer, then jump in and prove it! Since you're such a good batter, step up to the plate and see if you can hit this! If you're really the manager you think you are, then let's see you get us out of this mess! Since you're such a good investor, let's see you make money in today's economy! Such are the challenges we get in a world where we are put on the spot to prove ourselves worthy.

Jesus, likewise, has a challenge put before him. It is a challenge to prove himself to the tempter. It is interesting to note that in Matthew's Gospel, Jesus is referred to as the "Son of God" in various places, but in at least three instances, the words come from the devil or demons. It is also worth noting that the word

Matthew uses for *if* can also be translated "since." The devil is not doubting Jesus; the devil is tempting Jesus.

The temptations are not temptations to do evil things. Jesus is tempted to turn the stones into bread, to jump from the pinnacle of the temple, and to be Lord of all the earth. Many people consider these things to be bad, but remember we are talking about the same one who turned water into wine, fed the multitudes with five loaves and two fish, rose from the dead, and is now proclaimed as "King of kings and Lord of lords." The temptation wasn't to do bad things; it was to do the right things for the wrong reasons. In other words, it became a matter of Jesus' focus and his motives.

In the passage immediately preceding our text for today, God affirmed Jesus, at his baptism, as God's own son, and in that passage, we are already told that God was "well pleased" with Jesus (see Matt. 3:17). In the temptation story, Jesus is tempted to please someone other than God. He is tempted to please his followers, leaders of nations around the world, and even himself, but his focus is singular, and he has no need to please anyone except God. Since God is already pleased, the devil is defeated and sent away.

So often this passage is preached in such a way that we are warned of temptations to sin and to fall into moral decay. It would be easy to focus our attention only on sins such as drugs, promiscuous sex, or corporate greed, but such an approach leaves those of us who successfully resist those evils in a state of self-righteousness and pride. This passage doesn't let us off the hook that easily; if we focus on how good we are, we miss the point entirely. The point is that God is the one who is good, and our job is to do only those things that are pleasing to God. To do something good just to show off or satisfy our friends, our families, our superiors, or ourselves is insufficient and fails in the mandate to worship God and God alone.

As Christians, we will often be challenged to prove ourselves worthy, and we may be tempted to take the plunge. However, if we remain focused on what it means to be a Christian, the test will be easy and the journey through the wilderness will be made joyous by the angels we will meet along the way! (Jeff Smith)

FEBRUARY 20, 2005

Second Sunday in Lent

Worship Theme: When we try to understand where our spiritual forebears found their strength, it appears that obedience, faith, and confidence in God's grace are primary factors. Listen to God's call, move from the physical to the spiritual and leave the rest to God.

Readings: Genesis 12:1-4*a*; Romans 4:1-5, 13-17; John 3:1-17

Call to Worship (Psalm 121:1-6, 8)

Leader:	I lift up my eyes to the hills—from where will my help come?
People:	**My help comes from the LORD, who made heaven and earth.**
Leader:	He will not let your foot be moved; he who keeps you will not slumber.
People:	**He who keeps Israel will neither slumber nor sleep.**
Leader:	The LORD is your keeper; the Lord is your shade at your right hand.
People:	**The sun shall not strike you by day, nor the moon by night....**
All:	**The LORD will keep your going out and your coming in from this time on and forevermore.**

Pastoral Prayer:

Almighty God, whose way is mercy and whose name is love, we pray for an awareness of your presence with us as we make the Lenten journey with Jesus to the cross. We have done so little to deserve your mercy and love. We have done things we ought not to have done, and left undone things we ought to have done. The specific recollection of our sin lingers like a dark specter in the back of our minds. We pray that as we make this journey of faith that we may unload the things and thoughts that hinder us. We remember how the Bible teaches us that you forget our confessed sins and remember them against us no more. More specifically, we are told on biblical authority that "as far as the east is from the west," so far have you removed our transgressions from us. Help us to set aside what you have set aside. Take away from our minds the oppressive thought that we have to work some more to be forgiven of what you have already forgiven. In the graceful name of Jesus we pray. Amen. (Thomas Lane Butts)

SERMON BRIEFS

A MIGHTY SLENDER THREAD

GENESIS 12:1-4*a*

Truth is often packaged in paradox. Paradox is something that appears to hold together apparent contradictions. Paradox is at the heart of mature Christianity.

Many of the teachings of Jesus were paradoxical, such as, "many that are first shall be last; and the last shall be first" (Matt. 19:30 KJV) and "those who lose their life for my sake will find it" (Matt. 10:39). In the season of Lent we brood upon the meaning of crucifixion so that at Easter dawn we might be prepared for the stunning, paradoxical, reversal of fortunes. Resurrection life has its roots in suffering death.

The doctrine of the Trinity is a paradoxical formulation; God is one, yet three. The Nicene Creed proclaims Christ is both God and human. We say we are body and spirit, and so on.

Paradox often trips up the truth seeker. Our limited human brains prefer our truths neat and tidy, fitting into well-ordered, completely manageable patterns. We secretly (or not so secretly) want to believe we can have God pretty well figured out. We can learn the rules. We can teach the rules. We can own the rules. We can rule. And this would be fine if only the truth weren't so paradoxical, so seemingly illogical, so ultimately mysterious. If only God didn't slip out of our neatly defined boxes and become, well, so godlike.

The story up to this point: God created the world and all living things and called all of it very good. God created man and woman and even called them good. They sinned; remember the "fruit incident," the sending out of the garden, and then the fratricide between Cain and Abel. Things really go downhill after that, so shortly God allows the primordial waters to overwhelm the land, wiping out most of humanity with the exception of a faithful remnant. True to its fickle form, humanity's hubris advances again, and they build a tower believing they might take heaven by force. God, being God, will have none of it, and scatters them abroad.

What is to become of this good creation? The message in the mystery seems to have something to do with God's relentless attempt to make "good" with humanity. That seems to be God's motivation when he tells Abram (soon to be Abraham, meaning "ancestor of a multitude") to pick up and leave what he knows for that which he doesn't know. God makes a one-sided promise with this anonymous man who doesn't know his apples from his serpents and hangs the whole of the future on his response.

Quite frankly, it doesn't make a whole lot of sense. It really doesn't seem like much of a plan at all. At this early point, it reeks of failure. And who is this Abram? We know nothing about him. There's nothing stated to especially commend him for the task at hand. Indeed, we're told he's already seventy-five years old and childless. As the story unfolds, we'll even discover that he doesn't possess a special moral rectitude. Many centuries later, Paul, writing to his friends in Rome will refer to Abram as "good as dead" (Rom. 4:19). This is God's plan? A mighty slender thread.

Yet here's the truth of it: Slender threads provide the paradoxical strength of God's covenant. Another slender thread—stretched upon a cross—appearing for all the world "as good as dead" will prove the climax of the story begun with Abram. And, in between their stories and following, many other slender threads will bear the weight of God's promise to make good with humanity. (Stephen Bauman)

FAMILY RESEMBLANCE

ROMANS 4:1-5, 13-17

In small towns all over the world, a child is often asked, "Who's your daddy?" The implication is clear; if you know the daddy, you know the child. As a Jew and a Christian, the apostle Paul wanted to claim Abraham as his spiritual father. However, Jewish critics were challenging him. They claimed that Abraham was the spiritual father of those who obeyed the Mosaic Law. Paul's rationale employs a new concept: justification by faith.

The phrase "justification by faith" has become a slogan for many Christians. It is a shorthand explanation of their understanding of the Christian faith. Luther's interpretation of this biblical concept became the linchpin of the Protestant Reformation.

Unfortunately, the frequent usage of the phrase has led to widespread misunderstanding. Preachers have assumed that their hearers understood the meaning of the phrase. This was brought home to me recently when my own twenty-eight-year-old daughter asked me, "What does 'justification by faith' mean?"

This passage from Paul's letter to the Romans is the classical explanation of this Christian teaching. However, this passage is only one part of a sustained argument about how human beings become justified before God and reconciled to God. In the process, Paul explains how Abraham is the spiritual father of all who put their trust in God.

The argument begins with an explanation of human sin and the need for justification before God. Chapter 3 explains that this is made possible by Jesus' sacrificial atonement (3:24). Paul imagines a cynic asking, "Are you saying that Abraham was justified by Jesus? Wasn't he justified by keeping the Mosaic Law?"

Paul answers that the Scriptures are clear. Abraham was justified before God not because of his goodness, but because of his faith and trust in God. Further, Abraham did not earn righteousness. It was a gift from God. Paul cites Genesis 15:6 as his proof text.

In the second part of the text (vv. 13-17), Paul talks about the promise that God made to Abraham that his seed would be blessed. The promise was given to Abraham as a result of Abraham's faith, not through his adherence to some rules. In fact, Paul says, trying to justify oneself by keeping God's rules is a recipe for judgment since human beings have never been able to successfully keep them.

The way to become a child of God is through faith in God, not the mere adherence to divine rules. This is good news because everyone—not just Jews—can trust God and thus become children of God. When we have faith in God, Paul concludes, Abraham becomes our spiritual forebear.

This conclusion has important spiritual and theological ramifications. If Abraham is our spiritual forebear, we can leave our comfort zones and follow God's call wherever it may lead. We can trust God to do the impossible in our lives as God did in giving Isaac to Abraham and Sarah. Also, we can trust our children and our children's children into God's hands because he has made the same promise to us that he made to Abraham about his offspring. Paul was justifiably proud of his Jewish heritage. I can envision him telling his Jewish questioners, "Abraham is my daddy." (Philip D. Wise)

I FOUND IT!

JOHN 3:1-17

"I Found It!" These bumper stickers were everywhere in the late 1970s. As a child, I always wondered what "it" was. This popular saying was to let others know that this person had been "born again." It was a way to share one's faith, to get other people's attention. From 1976 to 1980, the "I Found It" campaign rallied thousands of Christians from around the United States in an organized evangelistic effort. What was "it" that they had found? "It" was salvation through Jesus Christ. Symbols and slogans have always been popular ways for Christians to identify themselves in the world. Early believers used the sign of the fish to recognize other believers as they traveled. Some individuals created billboards throughout the United States with such sayings as "Yes, I do love you. —God," "What part of 'Thou Shalt Not' don't you understand? —God" and "I love you so much I died for you. —God." How many times have we seen a poster at some sporting event declaring, "John 3:16"? In John's Gospel, Jesus tells Nicodemus he must be born anew. He gives us one of the favorite expressions that individuals use to describe Christians, "born again." As I grew up in the South, many times people would ask me, "Are you born again?" Often these people used "born again" in the derogatory sense. "John, oh he's born again; he's not as fun as he used to be." Perhaps this is why I became uncomfortable with the term "born again."

Yet, that is exactly what happens to us when we give our life fully to follow Jesus Christ. When we rely on the Spirit to guide our lives we are born anew. Jesus uses the wind to describe to Nicodemus those who are "born of the Spirit." One can see the effects of the wind on various objects, but one cannot see the wind. Likewise, one can see the effects of the Spirit on an individual, but one cannot see the Spirit. It is perhaps our greatest witness to the world. When we allow the Spirit to guide our lives then others will see its effects and experience the living Christ in the world today. Faith is born again in the world when we live life according to the will of God.

John 3:16 may be the most quoted scripture verse of all time. Simply put, God loves us. God loves us beyond all human circumstances. Many are unable to accept the fact that God's grace is freely given. Immanuel, God with us, came into the world to show us the way so that we "might be saved through him" (v. 17). Jesus came to save. Jesus came to lift us up. I am always amazed at how quickly we want to judge others in the world. John tells us that Jesus did not come to condemn, but to offer eternal life. We can do no less than to offer eternal life through Jesus Christ and allow condemnation to someone more qualified for the job—God. If Jesus did not come into the world to condemn people then why are we so quick to do so? Similar to Nicodemus, Jesus challenges us to see the positives and reject the negatives. We may see the power of the gospel of Jesus Christ as it transforms sinners offering us a second chance. Similar to Nicodemus, we may ask, "How can these things be?" (v. 9). The answer is simple. God loves. Jesus saves. I found it! (John Mathis)

FEBRUARY 27, 2005

Third Sunday in Lent

Worship Theme: Adversity causes many to question God and ask for a sign. We should have stayed in Egypt? Show us a sign. Is God still with us?

Readings: Exodus 17:1-7; Romans 5:1-11; John 4:5-42

Call to Worship (Psalm 95:1-4, 6-7)

Leader: O come, let us sing to the LORD; let us make a joyful noise to the rock of our salvation!

People: **Let us come into his presence with thanksgiving; let us make a joyful noise to him with songs of praise!**

Leader: For the LORD is a great God, and a great King above all gods.

People: **In his hand are the depths of the earth; the heights of the mountains are his also....**

Leader: O come, let us worship and bow down, let us kneel before the LORD, our Maker!

People: **For he is our God, and we are the people of his pasture, and the sheep of his hand.**

Pastoral Prayer:

O God of power and patience, we come before you with a wagon load of doubts and misgivings, looking for an easy way out of adversity that will not only save us but also make us look good.

We are such strange creatures—even to ourselves—capable of

gaining heaven or creating our own hell. We confess that in times of trial, when we cannot see beyond our proverbial nose, we sometimes ask "why" in the strange hope that you will give us an answer that exonerates us of responsibility for the shape we are in, but in our best and most reflective moments, we know that you have placed the tools of heaven or hell within our grasp and always in equal balance.

We confess that we are beggars, but we pray that our begging will be for things that will make our lives purposeful instead of arrogantly proud. Save us, above all things, from the delusion of thinking that we know everything; and save us even from the limited delusion of thinking we know anything about very much. Save us from thinking we know enough on our own to tell people what they should think and do.

For all our problems and puzzles, it isn't the way *out* that we seek, O God, it is the way *through*. It isn't for control of life that we pray. We pray for a hand in it, but we want your hand on it. Save us from ourselves and all our petty misunderstandings of reality. In the dear name of Jesus. Amen. (Thomas Lane Butts)

SERMON BRIEFS

THE CURE FOR COMPLAINING

EXODUS 17:1-7

A man seeking a deeply spiritual life joined a monastic order of extreme silence. In fact, the members were allowed to speak only two words every five years. In his first meeting with the abbot, the man was invited to speak and said, "Bed hard." After the second five-year period, the meeting with the abbot was repeated. When given permission to speak the man said, "Food bad." Another five years passed and in the review with the abbot the man said, "I quit." The abbot looked at him for several moments and then replied, "I am not a bit surprised. All you have done since you have arrived is complain."

Once again we find the children of Israel complaining about their lot in life and blaming Moses. There is no indication that they remember the horrors of slavery, nor the mighty acts of God in leading them through the Red Sea. It is ironic that the geographical location of this incident is the wilderness of sin. Could it be that one of the symptoms of the presence of sin in our lives is a short memory when it comes to gratitude? In our difficulty, we fail to recognize the ways in which God has been present. Perhaps one of the symptoms of sin is in the lack of trust in God evidenced in our complaining about our circumstances instead of offering them to God in prayer and supplication. Could blaming others for our circumstances and our feelings about them be a sign of the presence of sin in our failure to take responsibility for our actions?

This habitual response by God's people is memorialized in the names for the place where the water is given. Massah and Meribah mean "because the Israelites quarreled and tested the LORD, saying, 'is the LORD among us or not?'"

Complaining and blaming is contagious. Even Moses is affected. He begins to complain to God about these troublesome people.

The wilderness is hard. Water is necessary for life. The distress and unhappiness is real. Their hardships are not the product of their imaginations.

Our challenges are significant as well. This passage has much to teach us. First, we learn that God's grace is God's grace. Even when we are contentious and stubborn, God is at work to help us. Mercy flows through our wilderness time. God is faithful to the covenant that God has made.

Second, we can ask questions of our memory. Where have I experienced God's help in unexpected ways? What blessings in my life have come to me without my having earned them? What do these memories teach me about the resources I already have that I have overlooked? What do I need? Am I willing to trust in God to answer?

The habit of complaining is one that characterizes our lives as much as it did the lives of the Hebrews. It is so much easier to diagnose the faults of others than it is to admit to either our feelings of being helpless or our own role in the creation of our circumstances. But there is another way. There is the way of deciding not to be helpless, not because of our confidence in ourselves but because of what our memory teaches us. We can take the way of deciding to walk and act in faith and trust in God.

Those choices help us discover that the wilderness is not our destination, only the place we must pass through. (Bob Holloway)

THE JOY OF CHRISTIANITY

ROMANS 5:1-11

Every Christian preacher has prepared a "serious" sermon that seeks to explain one of the mysteries of the faith. An experienced preacher knows that it is a good idea to insert some humor or a good story to "lighten" such a sermon. Parishioners, it seems, have a limited tolerance for heavy sermons. The apostle Paul understood that.

Perhaps this is the reason he inserts this passage from Romans in the middle of his most theological New Testament letter. This passage is a minisermon on why Christians should be joyful. It stands in stark contrast to the preceding chapters, which focus on sin, death, atonement, and justification.

However, this passage isn't separated from those earlier chapters. It is based on them. That is why Paul begins with a "Therefore." Although the first two verses of chapter 5 are convoluted in Greek and English, Paul's point is a simple one: Christians should be joyful because God has provided a way for them to be justified and reconciled. That way is the way of faith, specifically, faith in the son, Jesus Christ, who has died to redeem all humanity. "He was delivered over to death for our sins and was raised to life for our justification" (4:25 NIV).

Because of God's act of grace in the life, death, and resurrection of Jesus, Christians can look forward to the day when God's glory will be fully revealed. That day will come at the end of history when God's plan for humanity will be made clear. Some critics of Christianity have criticized Christians for being too future-focused. Some say, "Christians are too heavenly minded to be any earthly good." Their charge is that Christians ignore the challenges of living in this world of tears. Paul vigorously counters this criticism.

Paul acknowledges that life is full of suffering. Christians do not ignore the suffering or pretend it does not exist. Instead, they rejoice in their suffering. This is not masochism. It is the recognition that suffering is necessary for the development of joy. Paul sees the development of joy as a progressive experience: We suffer; this suffering develops perseverance; our perseverance through suffering develops character; character produces hope; hope results in joy. In addition, Paul points out, even when Christians suffer, they do not lose hope because God has given us his Holy Spirit, who encourages us. The Holy Spirit is a harbinger of joy.

The second part of this passage (5:6-11) is an explanation of this strange anomaly. Christians can rejoice in the face of suffering, Paul explains, because of what Christ has done for us. Christ has died for our sins. Since God loved us when we were his enemies, it is obvious that his love for us is even greater now that we have turned to God. We are saved by Christ's death, but we are also saved by Christ's life. The risen Christ gives us reason to hope. Also, Christ has shown us how to redeem suffering and turn it into joy. Christians then live a life of ongoing joy, joy now and joy in the life to come. (Philip D. Wise)

FORGET THE JAR; GET THE WATER

JOHN 4:5-42

First, a word of caution. This story doesn't really need preaching! One of the worst things we can do is to read a long, powerful story like this, one that provides its own commentary, as the Gospel lesson, and then retell it as preaching. Our retelling of the story is almost always dull and lifeless or shallow theatrics compared to the story itself.

So, don't read the story as a scripture and *also* retell it as a sermon. Do one of two things: Read it and then preach on some moment within it, with the story as context. An example of a moment is verse 24. Or, combine scripture reading and sermon into one gospel event. This can be very effective. You don't need "three points and a poem" to make it a sermon. This story is its own sermon and provides its own outline and "stinger." (That exclamation point single note at the end of a Sousa march.) In every scripture story, there is a general context, a specific context, and an application. Applications can come out of either context or both.

The *general* context in this story, and for the whole gospel, is moral acceptability. In every age, we divide people into the morally acceptable and those who are somewhere between morally ambiguous to downright unacceptable. At Jacob's well, these two groups meet. (The location is fascinating, for Jacob himself was a morally ambiguous character.) Jesus was a male Jew who lived a moral life and kept the Law (although his detractors claimed the latter was not true). The woman was female, Samaritan, and lived a life of questionable morals (six husbands).

Jesus refuses to accept the two-group division. To him, there is only one group, children of God, and *anyone* who worships God in spirit and in truth can drink of the living water. (An excellent commentary on this context in modern life is Stephen G. Ray, Jr.'s *Do No Harm: Social Sin and Christian Responsibility* [Minneapolis: Fortress Press, 2002].)

In our day, as traditional outward signs of unacceptability [race, gender, national origin] are obviated, the general context for our preaching is the equation of moral acceptability with wealth. Persons who have money are acceptable, regardless of how they got it, and persons who do not have it are unacceptable, regardless of why they don't have it. (The exceptions, such as the arrests of Enron officials, do more to prove the rule of the morals-money equation than to disprove it.)

The *specific* context is respect by one individual for another, the respect of listening. Good pastoral counseling is doing what Jesus did with this woman, listening to a person's story and letting him or her know it's okay. He didn't say that everything she had done or was doing was okay, but that *she* was okay. Her identity was not as a member of an unacceptable group. Her identity was as a child of God. All she had to do was ask, and she would receive living water, the same as anyone else.

The *application* in this story is Jesus' consistent call to new life, to come to drink of the living water, to worship God in spirit and in truth, regardless of who you are, and to extend that invitation to all, regardless of who they are. The woman was so excited by this that she forgot her jar, the divider between what's inside and what's out, and ran off to tell about the water. (John Robert McFarland)

REFLECTIONS

MARCH

Reflection Verse: *"Endure trials for the sake of discipline."*
(Hebrews 12:7)

DISCIPLINE: STRENGTHEN YOUR WEAK KNEES
Hebrews 12:7-13

During March, a time that moves the church through the days of Lent and toward Easter, discipline seems like an appropriate topic. Therefore, our series of meditations for preachers, "Twelve Pillars of Abundant Christian Living," adopts this timely theme of discipline. As Moses builds an altar and sets up twelve pillars representing Israel's twelve tribes (Exodus 24), the pillar image signifies for us traits of faithful Christian living.

Behind the local hospital there exists an outbuilding with the name "Wellness Center" posted over the door. However, if you have ever been inside and watched what went on in this structure full of exercise equipment, you might consider a better name for the building: "House of Pain." Few people go to the Wellness Center unless a doctor sends them. Or, perhaps, people go so that a doctor will not later send them. The Wellness Center is no doubt a place where more discipline occurs than at any other place in our town. Clearly there are other establishments that also have fitness as their primary purpose. These places have telling names: Curves, Body Works, Total Workout, and Busy Bodies. Although many of these labels sound like names for auto repair businesses, physical fitness regimens are as close as many people get to authentic discipline. Our text from Hebrews addresses the subject of discipline.

Hebrews is not trying to furnish a full-blown theological explanation of suffering, trials, or affliction. Rather, Hebrews attempts to place the human enduring of suffering into a faith perspective.

In fact, the writer employs the image of endurance to make the concept of discipline clearer. Further, the writer uses an analogy of a parent's discipline of a child to emphasize God's discipline for believers. If we accept the discipline of our human parents, then how much more should we be subject to the discipline of God?

This statement about discipline is the classic Greek rhetorical argument of "the lesser to the greater," similar to an argument that Jesus uses in Luke's Gospel. Jesus argued rhetorically, "Is there anyone among you who, if your child asks for a fish, will give a snake instead of a fish? Or if the child asks for an egg, will give a scorpion? If you then, who are evil, know how to give good gifts to your children, how much more will the heavenly Father give the Holy Spirit to those who ask him" (Luke 11:11-13).

God's discipline surpasses that of parents, but as parental discipline exists for a short time, God intends for divine discipline to endure so that believers may share in God's holiness. Discipline always seems painful at the time, but later it yields righteousness as a fruit of discipline. The text's argument boils down to the assertion that discipline eventually leads to healing. Most pastors can predict which elderly patients will respond to rehabilitation and which ones will not. Those with willpower and discipline will prosper; those without discipline will not thrive. It is no different in rehabilitating the faithful life of the spirit.

No doubt, discipline involves pain, but, as this text reminds its readers, "what is lame may not be put out of joint, but rather be healed" (Heb. 12:13). Thus, in the long run, the pain of discipline promotes good health in both the physical and the spiritual realms. Discipline is the ability an individual calls on to do what Stephen Covey suggests by the phrase "putting first things first" (one of Covey's book titles). "First things" promote health and wholeness in our lives. It is to this end that discipline aims.

But the self-discipline of self-mastery we urge on ourselves includes actions that we are not naturally inclined to do. We might describe this "inertia" from the point of view of physics. A limited definition of inertia is that objects at rest tend to remain at rest until acted on by an outside force. When I was a child, I could play basketball from early in the morning until late in the afternoon and still have enough juice left over to argue with my parents about my bedtime. Yet, when my mother took me shopping for school clothes once a year, I was totally worn out after a mere hour.

Recently, I went on a family shopping trip. After walking through various stores for only thirty minutes, I was exhausted. So I sat down on an opportune bench I encountered. It felt so good just to sit. I believe I could have remained there all day. Getting off that bench—changing my inertia—took major motivation, or discipline. Much of our lives mimic this circumstance. We grow so comfortable even in the pursuit of nothing that it is easier merely to sit than to get up and do something.

In terms of self-mastery, discipline is required to change our inertia, to get us moving in a positive direction. Generally, self-discipline is not a once in a lifetime heroic effort. Instead, discipline is a series of constant, consistent habits of doing the right things the right way over time. This particular condition is the heart of discipline. The only way to get off the bench and do something is to let discipline exert itself on us. Spiritual discipline is what Christians do to put themselves in God's arena. Perhaps this is why John Wesley so often addressed the spiritual disciplines.

In the Wesleyan bands and classes (that is, the small groups intended to foster the spiritual disciplines), believers asked each other this question: "How is it with your soul?" Wesley saw community as vital to the practice of spiritual disciples. Among these spiritual disciplines is Bible study, prayer, worship, fasting, meditation, and works of service. Richard J. Foster aptly described spiritual discipline as "the detachment from the confusion all around us is in order to have a richer attachment to God" (*Celebration of Discipline: The Path to Spiritual Growth*, rev. ed. [San Francisco: Harper & Row, 1988], p. 21).

A disciple is a learner. We learn from the disciplines we impose on ourselves—and for the less mature, from the discipline others impose on us. Perhaps the mode of discipline is from our parents, or God, as suggested from this Hebrews passage. But could our discipline be derived from the law, or a policy manual, or even promises we make to one another? Each of these modes of discipline serves to help us become the person God wants us to be, as well as the person we want ourselves to be. But, to begin on a path of spiritual discipline, many of us need a community to encourage us.

In college, I had a friend who was an avid runner and ran every morning. He thought it was a good discipline for his health, at least for the first month of college. Soon, however, he fell out of his good habit. One morning about 6:30 another jogger knocked on his door. He explained later, "I could not get myself out of bed anymore, so my buddy promised he would come by and get me. Now I am back in the habit." Other people can help us get, and stay, disciplined. Discipline is one method by which we can, as Hebrews advocates, "strengthen your weak knees." If you don't believe me, then ask them down at your local fitness or wellness center.

If we ever need a reminder of one of the foundational characteristics of abundant life, then there is a pillar with the word *discipline* inscribed on it. Amen. (David N. Mosser)

MARCH 6, 2005

Fourth Sunday in Lent

Worship Theme: God's ways are not our ways. God looks upon the heart and not upon outward appearance.

Readings: 1 Samuel 16:1-13; Ephesians 5:8-14; John 9:1-41

Call to Worship (Psalm 23)

> *Leader:*   The LORD is my shepherd, I shall not want.
>
> ***People:***   **He makes me lie down in green pastures; he leads me beside still waters; he restores my soul.**
>
> *Leader:*   He leads me in right paths for his name's sake.
>
> ***People:***   **Even though I walk through the darkest valley, I fear no evil; for you are with me; your rod and your staff—they comfort me.**
>
> *Leader:*   You prepare a table before me in the presence of my enemies; you anoint my head with oil; my cup overflows.
>
> ***People:***   **Surely goodness and mercy shall follow me all the days of my life, and I shall dwell in the house of the LORD my whole life long.**

Pastoral Prayer:

Almighty God, whose kind care has been made known to us in the person of Jesus Christ and in the lives of the saints, hear us as we lay our lives before you to be blessed.

Help us to know ourselves through godly introspection, that in seeing ourselves as you see us, we may more readily revise and correct our lives. Save us from vain comparisons of ourselves to others, and save us from seeking identity in the approval of others. We know that you have made us, but we have never accepted or used all that you gave us in creation. May we exploit for good the best and the most of what you have built into us. May we see in life something of the holiness of beauty so that some of the beauty of holiness may rub off on us. We remember in our hearts today the cares and concerns of those whose lives have intersected our life this past week. We pray for the sick, those who are ill in any way that infirmity may strike someone. Give us ears to hear your voice in the people and circumstances we encounter each day. In Jesus' name. Amen. (Thomas Lane Butts)

SERMON BRIEFS

HOW GOD'S GRACE TRANSFORMS THE ORDINARY INTO THE EXTRAORDINARY

1 SAMUEL 16:1-13

In 1 Samuel 16:1-13 we have the wonderful story of David's anointing at the hand of Samuel to become the next king of Israel. It's a story of how God chooses the most unlikely vessel to make a difference in the world. Samuel has come to Bethlehem, a town that is not known for great things, to a family that is without reputation, to choose the youngest (not the oldest) of eight sons, who is a shepherd, to become the next king of Israel!

The wonderful thing about God's grace is that it can transform all of us into people who can make a difference. It was in November of 1998 that Terry Tuszynski was watching the NBC evening news when she saw a report from their Moscow correspondent, Dana Lewis. Lewis was standing outside a Russian orphanage two hundred fifty miles northeast of Moscow. Lewis explained that the building was one hundred years old, there were fifty-three children who had no shoes, little to eat, and no coal for the furnace, and the first snows of winter were already on the ground. The question Dana Lewis asked was how were these children going to make it through the winter (see Foundation for Russian Orphans: www.RussianOrphans.org).

Terry and her husband, Tom, had one child, Zeke, who was five years old. While doing the dishes that night, she looked out through the window at the $4,000 jungle gym they had bought for their son. Then she thought of those fifty-three children who would not have enough to eat, who would not have heat for their building or even shoes to wear. She felt God's call in her life to do something. Tom and Terry were normal people living an ordinary life in Seattle. But four-and-a-half years later, through their own gifts, and through the gifts of friends, they had totally refurbished the orphanage. All the children had shoes, clothes, beds, food, and a good environment in which to live and grow up. Beyond that, they have been finding families in Russia and America to adopt these kids.

Recently, when Terry was interviewed, she was asked what one thing would she want people to learn from her story and she said, "If you have something to do that at first seems impossible, but you feel it deeply enough, you can get it done. Make a plan, pick up the phone, get started. I saw a story on national TV about children who needed help on a different continent. At the time, I didn't know for sure *how,* but I knew I had to do *something.* Even if you are just one or two people, you *can* make a difference!" God can use the most ordinary of us to do extraordinary things when we commit ourselves to serving him (Mark Reiman, "Terry Tuszynski: 'You Can Make a Difference'" [2003], online: www.incrediblepeople.com). (Robert Long)

LIVING IN THE LIGHT

EPHESIANS 5:8-14

One of my least favorite creatures in God's creation is a cockroach. I don't like to look at them, step on them, or hear them scurrying across the floor. We seldom see cockroaches during the day because they don't like the light. They live and do most of the things cockroaches like to do at night. On occasion I have walked into a room, turned on a light, and seen a cockroach scurrying for a dark crevice to hide. In today's passage Paul encourages his friends in Ephesus to expose the deeds of the disobedient. What does Paul mean by this? How should we expose those who are walking in darkness? Should we turn a light on them just like a cockroach in a dark room? Or is there a better way?

Paul quotes a passage from Isaiah 60:1 comparing light and darkness. "Wake up, O sleeper, / rise from the dead" (NIV). The prophet Isaiah urges Jerusalem to wake up from the night to let its light shine before the nations because God's glory was with them. They had been asleep by not wholeheartedly honoring God with their lives. Paul was urging those in Ephesus to be aware of the sleepy and dark condition into which they were slipping.

Many of us go through life as if we are half asleep. We get up, go to work, eat dinner, watch television, take care of the kids, go to church, then do it all again the following week. During the ho-hum routines of life, we may not be living in the darkness, but we are not living in the light either. We are half awake and half asleep. We miss the joy of letting our light be visible to others.

How then do we live in the light? In this passage, Paul defines living in the light as walking in goodness, righteousness, and truth and finding out what pleases the Lord. Living in the light calls Christians to imitate Christ and love others as he first loved us.

It is most important that we seek to live in the light during those seasons when we are tempted to live half asleep. It is in these times of living in the world that we can expose the deeds of darkness that Paul writes about in this passage. Jesus teaches this concept in Matthew 13 where wheat and the weeds were growing together in a field. The owner of the field instructed his servants not to pull up the weeds because some of the wheat may also be pulled. Instead, he told them to wait until the harvest when the wheat would be brought into the barn, and the weeds burned. Jesus used this parable to illustrate that it is not our job to pull up the weeds. It is God's job. We instead are to live among the disobedient as God's faithful, people representing the light.

People will notice that children of light are different. Those persons living in the darkness may be won over to the light through character that emulates Christ. This is why we must leave the holy huddle of our Christian friends and church. We do need to spend time in the huddle to learn the plays and come together as a team. But, after coming together, we need to get out on the field and into the action. The action happens out in the world where the darkness and light exist together. Jesus directly instructs us to live this concept in Matthew 5:16. "Let your light shine before men, that they may see your good deeds and praise your Father in heaven" (NIV).

Paul does not mean that Christians are to expose the disobedient by calling them out and telling them they are evil. Paul even says our conversation should be gracious, effective, and pleasant without accusation. "Let your conversation be always full of grace, seasoned with salt, so that you may know how to answer everyone" (Col. 4:6 NIV). Instead of rooting out the evil, we are to expose the evil with our light shining before others. (Tim Roth)

WHAT ARE YOU WORTH?

JOHN 9:1-41

The general context of this story is defilement. In every society, some people are considered "unnecessary" to society. Their right to exist is not absolute, apart from what they do or don't do. A glaring example is the Jews in Nazi Germany. They contributed a great deal to the cultural, moral, and financial well-being of Germany but were still considered "unnecessary." Their marginal right to exist could be taken away by those who had an absolute right to exist.

A more recent example is that hideous term, "ethnic cleansing." There are many other examples, such as the "untouchables" in the Indian caste system or Gypsies in many countries.

Sometimes people are defiled because of their activities or their condition. A leper can be a highly moral person, can write great essays or music, but is still, in the eyes of many, defiled, unnecessary, one who must be avoided. In some societies, people who handle dead bodies, even though it is a necessary function for society, are considered defiled.

In "the new global economy," where the single moral value is money, the homeless or welfare recipients come dangerously close to defilement, regardless of uprightness of life. The assumption by the general society is that defiled people, "unnecessary" people, cannot be moral, cannot live upright lives, anyway. The very nature of their existence makes it impossible for them to, in the Judeo-Christian context, "keep the Ten Commandments." It goes in a circle: They cannot be moral because they are defiled, thus they are defiled because they cannot be moral. Therefore, they are unnecessary.

In a society where wealth is the definition of value, being poor is defilement. Activity is useless unless it leads to money. Winning the lottery—gaining much money by not working—is a higher and more worthy goal than earning a little money, or even a lot, by honest hard work.

When someone dies, we ask, "What was he worth?" All that means is, "How much money did he have?" It has nothing to do with what he or she was worth in relationship to family or friends. The poor are defiled; they cannot be moral.

The specific context of this story is a presentation of a visual impairment as defilement. The physically and mentally disabled are considered unnecessary and, thus, incapable of virtue. The man blind from birth was the product of sin, either his own or his parents'.

But it is not the absence of sight that defiles but the absence of light, the light of the world. Jesus' purpose for the man who was blind is not sight but healing, wholeness. Wholeness has nothing to do with having two working eyes, two walking legs. You can be whole in a wheelchair or broken on a racing bike. Sight without light, the light of the world, can be misleading. Many of us have good eyesight but poor soul-sight; we're always looking at the wrong things.

Recently we have begun to learn that sight in itself is not a virtue. Cameras do lie. Eyewitnesses to crimes often identify the wrong person. Sight that is made whole by the light, the light of God in Christ, makes us whole, whether or not we have eyes. The real defilement is in claiming to be the ones who see, the righteous ones, while living in the dark, claiming others are defiled by their worldly condition instead of living in the light of Christ that makes all whole.

The application is doing the works of God while the light is with us. (John Robert McFarland)

MARCH 13, 2005

Fifth Sunday in Lent

Worship Theme: The words and witness of Jesus are our source of security in a world where death is universal. As we become conscious of God's Spirit in our world and in ourselves we will no longer fear death.

Readings: Ezekiel 37:1-14; Romans 8:6-11; John 11:1-45

Call to Worship (Psalm 130:1-6*b***, 7***bc***)**

Leader:	Out of the depths I cry to you, O LORD.
People:	**Lord, hear my voice! Let your ears be attentive to the voice of my supplications!**
Leader:	If you, O LORD, should mark iniquities, Lord, who could stand?
People:	**But there is forgiveness with you, so that you may be revered.**
Leader:	I wait for the LORD, my soul waits, and in his word I hope;
People:	**My soul waits for the Lord more than those who watch for the morning....**
All:	**With the LORD there is steadfast love, and with him is great power to redeem.**

Pastoral Prayer:
   Almighty God, by whose will we were created and sent to live in this time and place, we pray for a deeper insight into the

meaning of our lives and a more profound trust in the ways of Jesus for living.

Bless the beautiful people who have come here today looking for some light, some encouragement, and some love. May the acts of worship that we perform together and privately open our eyes to new visions of personal possibilities. We pray for such understandings of healing and health that we may not be afraid to grow old or be terrified of being sick, and grant us, O Merciful God, such trust in the ways of your created world and such trust in the words of Jesus, that we finally will not be afraid to die. In the good name of Jesus, we pray. Amen. (Thomas Lane Butts)

SERMON BRIEFS

THE GLORIOUS IMPOSSIBLE

EZEKIEL 37:1-14

Can dry bones live again?

I sat in a circle of approximately sixty ex-offenders who were participants in a program called Project Return. Located just outside of New Orleans, Project Return helps the recently paroled prisoner transition back into society. Early returns suggest a remarkable success for this innovative initiative.

Project Return uses some traditional methods such as reeducation and mentoring, but the founder locates its real success in a process of mutual self-help and spiritual encouragement called "community building." Sitting in a circle for a number of hours several times a week—much the way an especially serious Quaker meeting might be organized—these prisoners spill out their stories, share their defeats, celebrate their victories, and generally engage the long hard process of rebuilding their identities and place in the world.

The stories were severe. The twenty-one-year-old sitting next to me, tried as an adult at the age of fourteen and released just six months ago. The forty-five-year-old woman who became an addict at the age of nine. Their stories recalled brothers killed by guns, parents dead by overdose, and the devastations of poverty.

These stories were not thrust out in angry tirades for the benefit of a few naive visitors. They more nearly leaked out as these courageous women and men told of how their lives had been transformed by the love and care they found in this program. Their gratitude was palpable for the second, maybe even third chance they found here. One man spoke simply and eloquently for the group when he said that what the program had given him—something that he had thought was gone forever—was his dignity.

Tears dripped from my eyes for a good part of the session. At some point I realized these tears were not about the suffering. Instead, they captured the joy of resurrection. Through these people's surrender to a spirit far larger than their own and their own willingness in turn to reach out to one another under the umbrella of this spirit, these friends who now thought of themselves as family had made the plain industrial room in which we met a sacred space. From the moment I walked through the door and first experienced their respectful silence, I felt that space was far holier than many churches I had been in over the years.

Like Ezekiel, in that circle I heard the rattling and clattering of bones coming together. "I looked, and there were sinews on them, and flesh had come upon them, and skin had covered them .... and the breath came into them, and they lived" (37:8, 10).

Ezekiel goes into exile with his people in the sixth century B.C.E. Being with them he knows their state. The people say, our bones are dried up, and we have no hope. Their God resides elsewhere. They have been cut off at the root. Can dead things come to life again?

Ezekiel preaches a powerful word about the "glorious impossibility" of God's animating spirit. God's breath (Heb. *ruah*, meaning "spirit," "wind," "breath") enters the dry bones and brings them to life. Remember Genesis 2: God "formed man from the dust of the ground, and breathed into his nostrils the breath of life; and the man became a living being" (v. 7).

What is impossible for hopeless humanity to imagine is, for God, but a simple exhalation. Where God breathes, life springs up. This "life-giving" is God's nature. Ezekiel's vision of a desecrated valley—by biblical standards a place of great impurity—fully restored, provides a powerful foreshadowing of what God

110

accomplishes with another set of lifeless bones in first-century Palestine, and what is in fact possible for anyone who might believe at any moment that one is part of the company of the walking dead. (Stephen Bauman)

THE CORPORATE CHARACTER OF THE BODY OF CHRIST

ROMANS 8:6-11

Paul is speaking here to the communal nature of the church. Far from expounding any individual psychological dualism, Paul is carefully drawing a picture for the congregation at Rome about the distinguishing mark of our corporate character in the Body of Christ: a desire to abide in the Holy Spirit. (See Gordon D. Fee's excellent discussion of this topic in *Paul, the Spirit, and the People of God* [Peabody, Mass.: Hendrickson Publishers, 1996], pp. 126-32.) This abiding is clearly opposed to being conformed to the world around us. For Paul, the most prevalent image that captures this goal is the tension between flesh (Gk. *sarx*) and spirit (Gk. *pnuema*). No doubt Paul intends this idea to apply to the gathered community of believers and not solely to individual believers.

This kind of understanding, then, completely alters how we might hear this passage, does it not? Paul's theological thought here will necessarily lead our congregations to examine their collective identity and witness. Such an examination is often uncomfortable at best and threatening at worst. What shall we do?

One of the images I sometimes like to use is that of a mirror. When I'm dealing with a potentially troublesome text such as this, I often lead into the passage by holding up the Bible, saying, "This text is like a mirror: I might ... or I might not ... like what I see, but either way, I know I have an accurate picture." Having said something along this line assures the congregation that I have had as much difficulty wrestling with the text as they will have had in hearing it preached. Perhaps this can open the way for God to speak a fresh word that the congregation can hear without feeling as if I am unjustly attacking them.

Given this point of view, then, what is an appropriate way to shape the sermon? I would allow the flow of Paul's argument to guide the flow of the sermon. After setting up the contrast between a mind set on the flesh and a mind set on the Spirit, Paul goes on to apply this analogy directly to the congregation at Rome. His key statement in this text is his charge to the community: "But you are not in the flesh; you are in the Spirit" (v. 9). This is at once a positive yet challenging imperative, spoken as a standard for the congregation to always strive toward and to measure themselves against. Paul goes on to provide a means of knowing whether they meet this standard: If the Spirit is truly in them, then the same God who raised Jesus from the dead will use that Spirit to make their spirits alive "because of righteousness" and "give life to [their] mortal bodies."

Especially as we lead our congregations through the wilderness of Lent and toward the glory of Easter, a text such as this can be an invitation to collective examination. Paul does not categorically assure the congregation at Rome that they live in the Spirit; he only provides them the means to measure whether they do or not. In a similar vein, this text can prompt us to ask ourselves as local congregations, Are we truly living in the power of the Spirit, and thus standing distinctly for Christ in the world, or are we living out of the meager strength of our flesh, and thus conformed to the culture around us? The answer to such questions provides opportunity for pause, but it's a necessary answer to hear in order to decide whether or not we truly represent the Body of Christ as Paul envisioned. (Timothy S. Mallard)

HAS ANYONE BEEN LISTENING?

JOHN 11:1-45

For me, the account of the raising of Lazarus is one of the most remarkable stories in the Bible. Over the course of the forty-five verses that tell this story, the character of the disciples, Mary, Martha, and even Jesus is explored. The story begins just on the heels of Jesus' narrow escape from the Jews who were trying to stone him. Jesus and the disciples receive word from

Bethany that Lazarus is ill. Although it seemed likely that Jesus would visit his good friend, for some reason Jesus waited two days before leaving for Bethany. After the second day, Jesus announces to the disciples that indeed they will travel to visit Lazarus. The disciples balk at this idea! Verses 7-16 explore their reaction to Jesus' decision to return to Bethany, a journey that would increase their vulnerability to the Jews once again. Probably afraid for their lives, the disciples were less than optimistic or insightful. They seem to ask, Why would we return to a region where the Jews will want to stone you? After alluding to the impending miracle in verse 11, the disciples, failing to recognize Jesus' foreshadowing, suggest that since Lazarus is sleeping, there is no need for a visit. Realizing their failure to catch his hint, Jesus tells them outright that Lazarus is dead and they must go to Bethany. The disciple segment of the story concludes with Thomas's somewhat sarcastic comment that they should go to Bethany so they could die with Lazarus.

After this discourse with the disciples, Jesus is no doubt frustrated. After all that they had been through together, probably at least two years by this point, the disciples were reluctant to follow Jesus in perilous situations. Expecting what was ahead, it must have been terribly difficult for Jesus to accept their lack of faith. Jesus must have wondered who would understand him and his message if even his own disciples did not.

In the next phase of the story, Jesus encounters the sisters of Lazarus. In typical fashion, Martha, upon hearing that Jesus was close by, went out to meet him. Her greeting is desperate. "If you had been here, my brother would not have died" (v. 21). What follows is a theological conversation with Jesus telling her that Lazarus will indeed rise again, and Martha completely misunderstanding and assuming him to talk about the Jewish understanding of resurrection in the last day. Martha then fetches Mary. Mary greets Jesus saying the same thing as Martha, "If you had been here, my brother would not have died" (v. 32). Jesus is deeply moved by Mary and the others who were with her because of their grieving and asks to be led to the tomb. Verse 35 is one of the most famous in the Gospels, "Jesus began to weep." We all know the wonderful ending to this story. Jesus goes to the tomb, against the protests of the sisters, orders the tomb open, and calls Lazarus out. Miracle of all miracles, Lazarus walks out of the tomb alive.

This event is a pivotal one for Jesus. It is definitely the most amazing of Jesus' miracles. More than that, however, it is the moment perhaps that we find the greatest vulnerability in Jesus. As chapter 11 unfolds, the Jesus in the Gospel of John has a good sense of himself as the Christ. This same Jesus has spent his ministry thus far teaching his disciples and others that he is indeed the Christ, the one whom God has sent to change the world. In verse 35, as mentioned above, Jesus wept. I have often thought that Jesus was weeping out of grief for his dear friend and compassion for Mary. I think that it is more likely that Jesus was weeping out of frustration. I think that Jesus was anticipating the future, and the kind of leadership it would take for his disciples and followers. In chapter 11, neither his disciples nor his closest friends seem to understand the person of Jesus. They are too bound by their own earthly fears and doubts. With the Christ right before them, they still do not get it. Jesus must have wondered how they would understand when he was gone.

What John 11 is really about is more than just a great miracle. John 11 is about faith. Jesus was noticeably disappointed by the shaky faith of those closest to him. I think that the application for us is the issue of where our faith is when we find ourselves in difficult situations. When we are afraid or grieving, do we acknowledge the power of God or ignore it? As for me, the image of my Lord weeping over my faithlessness will serve as a powerful reminder. (Tracey Allred)

MARCH 20, 2005

Passion/Palm Sunday

Worship Theme: In the consummation of the act of "emptying himself," Jesus walks faithfully into the eye of the storm, knowing there is no one upon whom he can depend save God alone.

Readings: Isaiah 50:4-9*a*; Philippians 2:5-11; Matthew 26:14–27:66

Call to Worship (Psalm 31:9-12*b*, 14-16)

Leader: Be gracious to me, O LORD, for I am in distress; my eye wastes away from grief, my soul and body also.

People: For my life is spent with sorrow, and my years with sighing; my strength fails because of my misery, and my bones waste away.

Leader: I am the scorn of all my adversaries, a horror to my neighbors, an object of dread to my acquaintances; those who see me in the street flee from me.

People: I have passed out of mind like one who is dead; I have become like a broken vessel....

Leader: But I trust in you, O LORD; I say, "You are my God."

People: My times are in your hand; deliver me from the hand of my enemies and persecutors.

All: **Let your face shine upon your servant; save me in your steadfast love.**

115

Pastoral Prayer:

Dear God, we know you have known the noise of a thousand Palm Sundays and the disappointment of even more crucifixions. We come into your presence in confession for how we have participated in all that pains your heart. We pray to be delivered from false values, selfish desire, and the worship of things, that we may not waste our lives in the pursuit of things with no eternal significance. Guard us this week from betraying our Christ, as Judas did, for a few pieces of silver, or a promotion at the office, or a quick thrill, or a cheap victory over an enemy, or not attending church because we are angry at someone.

Lead us daily to our place of prayer, that we may empty ourselves and know your will and have the courage to do it. Strengthen us for the betrayals and crucifixions we face, that we may triumph through faith and love and that we may know in our hearts and minds the power of your resurrection.

Grant health to the sickly and wholeness to the broken. Let grace overflow like a fountain in our lives, nurturing our affection for mercy and peace and goodness. And guide us into ministries of healing and response to the needs of all your people. In the name of Jesus, who died for us. Amen. (Thomas Lane Butts)

SERMON BRIEFS

WHEN GOD WHISPERS IN YOUR EAR

ISAIAH 50:4-9*a*

It is easy for us to see that this is a messianic passage of scripture since we have the advantage of the Gospels as a perspective from which to look back on it. I doubt that those who first heard or read Isaiah were so readily persuaded. Isaiah's words do not fit into the mainline Jewish theology of his day. Most Jewish people would have looked upon such ill treatment as punishment for some known or unknown sin. The attitude of the three friends who came to "comfort" Job in his distress would more likely represent how Isaiah's hearers would have considered this suffering servant passage (see Job 2:11–37:24). This attitude was a new, if not foreign, idea. Isaiah prefaces the passage with the explanation that what he is saying comes directly from God. Four times in the passage he invokes the powerful name of God—Adonai, Sovereign Lord—to give authority to the message.

Whatever meaning Isaiah's first hearers may have drawn from this passage, the real meaning was yet to be revealed. It is revealed and fulfilled in Jesus who suffered all these indignities. He was beaten, spat on, and insulted; yet he was steadfast in his purpose. He had "set his face like flint." Jesus was confident of the ultimate outcome because God—Adonai—had whispered in his ear.

No doubt Jesus was familiar with this passage from Isaiah because Jesus was deeply learned in the scripture. When Jesus went to the synagogue in his hometown of Nazareth, early in his ministry, Jesus read to the congregation from "the scroll of the prophet Isaiah" (Luke 4:16-19).

Jesus set his face toward Jerusalem knowing that he was going into a hostile environment and had already warned his disciples of the coming conflict and his imminent death. When Jesus rode into Jerusalem on that first Palm Sunday, he knew what lay ahead. Jesus was greeted with dignity and adulation, and his followers were encouraged by the fine reception he received. Jesus, however, was not fooled by the superficial festivities. Jesus knew! Jesus had read Isaiah. The Lord God had whispered in his ear. He knew that suffering and death lay ahead, but he was undeterred from his purpose because he had word from on high. Jesus must have drawn comfort from his knowledge of the lonely struggle of Isaiah's suffering servant as Jesus sought to survive with his integrity intact in a hostile environment.

Jesus is best known to us as "Savior." There are various theological understandings of exactly what that means. The efficacy of our salvation in Jesus, the Christ, is not dependent on our theological correctness but on our simple faith in his having acted (as he still does) on our behalf. Isaiah's suffering servant, whose identity is made known to us in Jesus, is a proper model for us in our own personal struggles to survive suffering and insults, some of which come to us all. The key to suffering without the loss of integrity and faith is not to be found in conventional wisdom regarding power. It is not by worldly power and strength. It is not by unusual stamina and grit. The power to endure to the end is given to those who have heard God whispering in their ear. The besieged suffering servant is a source of encouragement to the weary. One would think that little energy would be left to consider the needs of others, but there is great power in even a wordless witness of one who is obviously in touch with God. We have all seen people (and we may be people) who have suffered great hardship, who have endured great pain (physical and emotional), and who have suffered harsh insults.

The survivors are those who have seen Jesus and have heard God whispering in their ear. Listen! (Thomas Lane Butts)

ONE NAME: JESUS, THE NAME ABOVE ALL NAMES!

PHILIPPIANS 2:5-11

Elvis. Sting. Bono. Cher. Madonna. Eminem. Most of you know these celebrities just by knowing the one name associated with them. For most of the names you can name an incident or a recording that goes with them. Some of you are even startled that I would mention their names in church! How about this name: Jesus? This is the Sunday when Jesus entered into Jerusalem as the new king. We know the story well, many of us having heard it since our childhood. Although today we celebrate a triumphant entry into the holy city, we know that it is but the start of a week that ends with a horrific Friday. Paul tells readers, This is why it happened. This is also the Sunday when we prepare ourselves to remember the passion of Christ as he suffered and died for us. Today's epistle tries to explain Christ's death to us. Paul says, It was all because of Jesus.

To understand the passion of Christ we ask ourselves, "Why would anyone die for me?" An even harder question would be to ask ourselves, "Would I be willing to die for someone else outside of my immediate family?" Paul writes that Jesus chose to live his life in a way that would bring redemption to the world. It's explained in John 3:16, "For God so loved the world that he gave his only Son." The verse ends with "so that everyone who believes in him may not perish but may have eternal life." Jesus' act was a selfless act of total obedience and love toward God and God's creatures. It was a selfless act of love just for you and me.

Paul equates the seriousness of Jesus' obedience in comparing his life to that of a slave. A slave did not own his or her own life. A slave's freedom was not his or hers to choose; even the slave's fate was in the hands of his or her master. Jesus' master was also his parent. But unlike a slave/master relationship, this one was based solidly on love and obedience. Jesus knew that for the sins of the world someone had to die and out of his obedience to God, Jesus was "obedient to the point of death—even death on a cross" (v. 8). The victory of today is nothing compared to the victory on that Friday on our behalf. The humiliation of that Friday pales with the victory won by Jesus because of his obedience to God. Why do you think it's now called Good Friday? It's good because it was on that day that Jesus defeated death and sin once and for all. Here's that one name again: Jesus. What a powerful result that Paul writes that just to hear the name of Jesus "every knee should bend, in heaven and on earth and under the earth, and every tongue should confess that Jesus Christ is Lord, to the glory of God the Father" (Phil. 2:10-11). What a name! Our realization of the great price Jesus paid on our behalf because of his great love for us should humble us. It should bring us to the type of obedience that Christ had toward God. The bending of the knees was to pay homage to someone of a higher or royal status. Here indeed is the king of kings, Jesus the Lord. Just the mention of Jesus' name should bring us joy, the kind of shared joy that lets others know of the relationship we enjoy with Jesus. Say that name with me. Jesus. Let your heart leap for joy at the mention of the name that spells our freedom and victory. Jesus: a name above all names. (Eradio Valverde, Jr.)

NOT I, LORD!

MATTHEW 26:14–27:66

"Surely not I, Lord?" Jesus must have shaken his head, wearing a bittersweet smile as he heard these words repeated by each disciple sitting at the table with him. Jesus had just told them that one of them would betray him. Their distress showed in their faces and in their words, "Not I, Lord? I would never betray you. Surely, you must mean someone else!"

"Surely not I, Lord!" The words attempt to answer their own question. I would never betray my teacher and master, would I? Scripture tells us enough about some of these disciples that we can imagine their responses. At one end of the table sat Thomas. We learn later that he is the resident skeptic. Only the evidence of his own eyes will convince him of anything. Perhaps that is why he began following Jesus in the first place; Thomas needed to see for himself whether the claims he had been hearing were true. As he heard Jesus' words, Thomas must have felt certainty for a moment, only to have it undermined by the questions that constantly whispered in his mind. "How can you be so sure? You cannot know what your response will be until it happens."

Peter sat closer to Jesus; he always wanted to be as close to the action as possible. His response was probably the first, and the loudest. In fact, he comes back to the subject later. "Though all become deserters because of you, I will never desert you.... Even though I must die with you, I will not deny you" (vv. 33, 35). Blustery, confident Peter surely believed that he would never abandon Jesus. That is what makes the rooster's crow—and the realization that accompanies it—so devastating.

Finally, Judas speaks up. "Surely not I, Rabbi?" He cannot even call Jesus "Lord," because Judas knows what he is about to do. Judas's disillusionment and anger have caused him to betray the one he has followed for three years.

"Surely not I, Lord!" These words echo in our own minds today. We want so much to live our lives for Christ; we would never want to be guilty of betrayal. And yet, despite ourselves, we are as reproachable as the disciples. Maybe it is because we do not feel deserving of such love, and so we doubt like Thomas. Perhaps our enthusiasm gets in the way, and we trip over our own good intentions, as Peter did so often. Perhaps we have been disappointed by God, and we act out of our anger, frustration, and fear, as Judas did.

Whatever the reasons for our doubt, we can find hope in this: Although Jesus knew that he would be betrayed and deserted by these special friends, Jesus gave them an incredible gift that night. As they ate together, Jesus took the bread, blessed it, broke it, and said to the disciples, "Take, eat; this is my body" (v. 26). Jesus also shared a cup of wine with them, too, saying "this is my blood of the covenant, which is poured out for many for the forgiveness of sins" (v. 28). Jesus knew that, despite their brave words, each of the disciples around the table would forsake him in some way. Jesus knew that they needed the gift of his forgiveness and love and even the sacrifice of his life, and Jesus gave all of that willingly, not only to them but also to us.

"Surely not I, Lord?" we ask. The reply comes, "Yes, it is you. But do not worry. You are forgiven already. Eat this bread, drink of this cup, and remember—I love you." (Melissa Scott)

MARCH 27, 2005

Easter Sunday

Worship Theme: We live with confidence because we believe in the resurrection of Jesus, the Christ. We do not fear death because we believe that in resurrection we have life eternal.

Readings: Acts 10:34-43; Colossians 3:1-4; John 20:1-18

Call to Worship (Psalm 118:1, 5-9, 29)

Leader: O give thanks to the LORD, for he is good; his steadfast love endures forever!...

People: **Out of my distress I called on the LORD; the LORD answered me and set me in a broad place.**

Leader: With the LORD on my side I do not fear. What can mortals do to me?

People: **The LORD is on my side to help me; I shall look in triumph on those who hate me.**

Leader: It is better to take refuge in the LORD than to put confidence in mortals.

People: **It is better to take refuge in the LORD than to put confidence in princes....**

All: **O give thanks to the LORD, for he is good, for his steadfast love endures forever.**

Pastoral Prayer:
Dear God, it is Easter, and we are still alive, and because of your Son, Jesus, we believe we will be alive forever, even after we die.

We pray today for all conditions of human ill manifest in the lives of people. We pray for those into whose life loneliness has come, in whatever form it may be found. We lift up the lives of those who have been separated from someone they love, in one of the many ways in which separation can take place, especially for those who are struggling with the emptiness that death has left in their lives. We remember as well those who know the emptiness of lost communications, betrayal, broken relationships, and unfulfilled hopes and dreams. We pray for the people here today who have loose ends in their lives, which they find hard to gather into new beginnings.

We pray for the dear departed dead, who once brightened our lives with their presence but who are with us today only in memory. May their memories inspire and guide but also save us from getting tied down spiritually and emotionally to a place in time that is no more and will never be again.

Hear these and all our unspoken prayers for ourselves and others, in Jesus' name. Amen. (Thomas Lane Butts)

SERMON BRIEFS

MAKING HIS STORY OUR STORY

ACTS 10:34-43

Christ the Lord is risen indeed! We have heard the stories again today. About the disciples and their struggles to remain faithful. About Mary and the others weeping, preparing their Lord for burial. We know their stories.

The story, however, does not stop. In Acts, Peter argues passionately that the story is for all people, not just for Israel. Peter was right, for there are millions of others who have made Jesus' story their story.

In eighteenth-century England, a young man, John, had no interest in spiritual things. After forced service in the British Navy, he deserted and captained his own merchant ship, becoming a renowned slave trader. It was a hard business, and it left John bitter, unhappy, and angry. One night, caught in a violent storm at sea, John feared he would die. He cried to Christ and found God's grace.

Many of us make commitments we don't really mean in the midst of dire circumstances, but John held true to his word. He gave up slave trading and sailing, entering the ministry. He became an influential leader, convincing politicians to end the international slave trade thirty years later. John's most famous words have encouraged millions, "Amazing grace! How sweet the sound that saved a wretch like me!"

Cassie Bernall seemed an unlikely person to make Jesus' story her story. By her freshman year of high school she was involved with the wrong crowd, defiant at home, and failing school. Her parents moved her to a Christian school and forbid her from seeing her former friends. Cassie fought them tooth and nail until 1997 when she met Christ on a weekend youth retreat. Later, Cassie returned to public school, partly so she could share her new faith with others. In April 1999, she wrote to a friend, "I want to live completely for God. It's hard and scary, but totally worth it." Her words were prophetic. The next day as she was studying in the library at Columbine High School, two gunmen began a random shooting spree. One asked Cassie if she believed in God. Her simple answer, "Yes." The gunman asked her why, but ended her life with a bullet before she even had the chance to respond.

Often it is children who make Jesus' story their story. Jeremy was born with a disabled body and a slow mind. At age twelve, he was only in second grade and in failing health. That spring, the teacher explained the story of Easter to the children and gave them a plastic egg. She instructed them to bring it back filled with something that showed new life.

The next day, the children piled their eggs in the basket and waited eagerly for the teacher to open them. The first several contained signs of new life—a plastic butterfly, a flower, a piece of new moss. The children proudly claimed their contributions. The next egg was empty. The teacher assumed it was Jeremy's and that he had not understood the assignment. She set it aside. Suddenly, Jeremy spoke up.

"Teacher, aren't you going to talk about my egg?"

"But, Jeremy, your egg is empty!"

"Yes," Jeremy replied, "but Jesus' tomb was empty, too!"

Three months later, Jeremy died. At the funeral, there were nineteen Easter eggs by his casket provided by each of Jeremy's classmates—all of them empty.

You and I are somewhat like John Newton, Cassie Bernall, and Jeremy. We may never write famous hymns or be martyrs for our faith. Yet, we are all invited and called to make Jesus' story our story. The message of Easter is that God's love is for all of us. The journey of faith is not always an easy one. However, God promises God's faithful presence with us, guiding us and giving us strength, peace, and hope. Christ is risen for all, indeed. (Tracy Hartman)

REAL FREEDOM

COLOSSIANS 3:1-4

Easter is always better when you've gone out of your way to experience all of Holy Week. I find Communion on Maundy Thursday and my home church's three o'clock service on Good Friday to be especially necessary. While I've always been critical of those among us who say they're looking forward to death and meeting the Lord, it is a simple truth that to experience resurrection, you need to die first. That's why we need Good Friday. Yet Easter is here, and where I live and worship, we've said very little about death.

As individuals and as a culture, we are more interested in prolonging life. For example, look at the money we spend annually on health care. Go to any gym or health club around 6 P.M. on most weekdays and wait in line for the treadmill. Turn on your television and look at all the products that claim to restore your hair or trim down that waistline. We want to stay young, and death?—well, death needs to remain where it is, lurking in that corner near the back of your mind. We want it to remain an idea, not a reality.

Even in the church, where we claim victory over the grave, death is not something Westerners want to deal with. I once asked a South African minister who came to teach while I was a student at Duke Divinity School how he liked the United States. He responded, "I'm

125

still getting used to a culture that thinks it's more important to go to worship on Mother's Day than it is to go on Good Friday."

Yet, Paul says in Colossians 3 that we have already died. Of course, many will say that "died" here means only that, as Christians, we have set our sights higher than others, that we ignore worldly things and ponder spiritual things. Paul's word is an exhortation, however. Paul implies that we have experienced death and resurrection by being united with Christ. Helpful for my understanding is baptism, where God buried my "old self," and then raised me to charge into the future as a new creature, a fearless witness for Christ, and a witness to the hope that only a risen Christ provides.

Fearless. We've been buried with Christ and raised to "walk in newness of life" (Rom. 6:4). Yet how can we live for Christ fearlessly if we're so frightened of death that we can't even talk about it. In 1956 in Montgomery, Alabama, a young pastor named Martin Luther King, Jr., said that the fear of death holds us hostage and that we must conquer this fear before we can be truly free.

This year, I hope you've looked death in the eye on Good Friday and have come away with the knowledge this Easter morning that resurrection is real and joyous. Of course, a healthy respect for death must be maintained! Even in this text we are told that there is much we cannot know, and the unknown is frightening. Yet consumed by death we are not, for we have much to do here for the kingdom of God, and we must do it boldly, without fear. Thanks be to God that we have been "raised with Christ" this Easter Day, to go into the world and serve the very God who raised this Jesus from the dead. (Scott Bullard)

UNEXPECTED GLORY

JOHN 20:1-18

How do you handle unexpected events? Unexpected deaths are never easy to accept. We cannot help asking why. As we watched the towers collapse in New York, it did not seem real. Officials say it is difficult to get good eyewitness reports from people when unexpected tragedies occur. As the adrenaline begins to flow, people tend to see things that are not there. When we find out about something we did not expect, we might begin to see and believe things that are not there. Mary Magdalene confronts the unexpected. As Mary reports what she has seen to Peter and John, they may have believed that she was seeing things that were not there. John sprints to the tomb. Perhaps John believes that Mary is distraught by her grief. They must have had to wipe their eyes as they entered the tomb to find the body of Jesus missing. They went from a state of shock at his crucifixion to a state of shock at Jesus' disappearance. Jesus has done the unexpected. Jesus has conquered death. It is the unexpected glory of the Easter story. "O Death, where is thy sting? O grave, where is thy victory?" (1 Cor. 15:55 KJV). It is not easy for us to understand the world. So much in our world is unexpected.

Mary continues to search for her Lord while the disciples return home. John tells us that they did not understand the scripture, but it is obvious that they also did not understand many things in these days surrounding Jesus' arrest, death, and resurrection. We can only imagine that the disciples returned home to continue grieving and to figure out what happened to Jesus' body. Mary, on the other hand, stays at the tomb to grieve. She did not want to contemplate Jesus' disappearance; she wanted to find her Lord. She needed to know what happened to Jesus. Jesus appears to Mary in the midst of her grief. Jesus appears to us in the midst of our grief, to share in our burdens. It is easy to imagine that the presence of the risen Lord comforts Mary. Jesus instructs Mary to go and spread the news of the Resurrection. Mary goes and tells the disciples all that she has seen and all that Jesus has said to her.

At Easter, we celebrate the unexpected glory of Jesus' resurrection. We gather as a community of believers to share this amazing story. Our proclamation is little different today than when Mary proclaimed her story to the disciples. They bury Jesus in a borrowed tomb. Jesus' friends came to the tomb on the first day of the week. Jesus was not there. Jesus appears to Mary. Mary follows Jesus' calling to tell her story. From that day, Jesus has been calling men and women to share their stories, to preach the good news of the resurrection of Christ. Are we willing to look for God working in the world in surprising ways? How can we on this Easter Sunday experience the resurrected Christ anew? As the morning sun rises in the east, let us remember that wonderful day when Mary and the disciples arrived at the empty tomb. Jesus called Mary to share in the unexpected glory of that first Easter. Jesus is still calling us today to share in Christ's unexpected glories. (John Mathis)

REFLECTIONS

❦

APRIL

Reflection Verse: *"The fear of the LORD is the beginning of wisdom; / all those who practice it have a good understanding."* (*Psalm 111:10*)

"THE FEAR OF THE LORD": RECIPE FOR WISDOM
Psalm 111

Easter is not just a liturgical day but also a season. Thus, we consider those first believers who encountered Jesus' empty tomb. We also consider the fear produced. For these reasons, "the fear of the Lord" seems a fitting topic for preachers to meditate on during this April, part of the liturgical season of Easter. One of the "Twelve Pillars of Abundant Christian Living" is clearly a healthy, godly fear.

We find the phrase "fear of the Lord" regularly in our Bible. For example, we read this phrase in the books of 2 Chronicles, Job, Psalms, Proverbs, Isaiah, Acts, and 2 Corinthians. "The fear of the Lord" is a phrase sprinkled throughout scripture.

Constructively, fear is a biological part of the makeup of God's creatures. Fear provides an organism an internal warning to be on guard. Fear functions as a catalyst for the survival instinct. Fear prompts organisms to either take flight or stay and fight. Either way, fear helps creatures preserve life. Fear alerts responsive creatures to unsettling distress and arouses alarm when danger challenges.

In human life (and who can know whether or not this is constructive) fear furnishes people an adrenaline rush. This surge of adrenaline is often a pleasant feeling. If not, then why do people pursue such otherwise inexplicable behaviors as bungee jumping, skydiving, or roller coaster riding? Films also scare us in supposedly exciting and enjoyable ways. Such movies include *Psycho, Halloween, Carrie, Rosemary's Baby, The Exorcist, The*

Haunting, A Nightmare on Elm Street, The Birds, The Silence of the Lambs—well you get the point. Fear makes us feel alive and retrieve many feelings that we rarely have the opportunity to access. For most of us, these neglected feelings merit sidestepping. Most people avoid feelings of fear whenever possible because we know that fear has a darker edge to it than mere thrill-seeking.

Thus, for most people, fear is not something they seek out, for fear, while intended to be constructive, too often becomes destructive in many circumstances. There is enough anxiety in daily living that most folks do not need to artificially stimulate themselves in this fearful fashion. Fear is anxiety raised to the nth power. Fear is a natural human response to danger, financial ruin, disease, the breaking of relationships, and good old-fashioned war. Although tough talking among world leaders intends to create fear in the enemy, anyone with a brain knows all too well what is in store for people and nations who engage in warfare. Stage fright too is a symptom of our fear of people sitting in judgment over us. We all are afraid of having "been weighed on the scales and found wanting," as Daniel 5:27 tells us. Fear is not an emotion or human response that many of us seek. Fear is destructive when it locks us up emotionally and paralyzes our more productive responses to the authentic danger that life throws at us.

Unfortunately, the phrase "the fear of the Lord" has too often assumed negative connotations, at least in the church. Although it does on occasion conjure associations of God's judgments, I propose that "the fear of the Lord" is nonetheless a positive image in the Bible's teaching. "The fear of the Lord" is one way to confess adherence and loyalty to God. When a believer possesses a proper fear of the Lord, then that person subjects herself or himself to God and God's realm.

Fear of the Lord summons us to God's sovereignty. We worship God because we recognize a gulf between worshipers and the object of worship—God. We who fear God respect God and hold God in holy awe. God is God, and we are not. God is worthy of devotion because it is God who protects us. I want us to consider this constructive side of the biblical understanding of that troublesome phrase, "fear of the Lord."

The "fear of the Lord" implies protection as suggested by 2 Chronicles when it tells readers, "The fear of the LORD fell on all the kingdoms of the lands around Judah, and they did not make war against Jehoshaphat" (17:10). The phrase also suggests justice when we read, "Let the fear of the LORD be upon you; take care what you do, for there is no perversion of justice with the LORD our God, or partiality, or taking of bribes" (2 Chron. 19:7). Wisdom also is part of the fear of the Lord. The wisdom book of Job relates this understanding when the character Job says, God

> said to humankind,
> "Truly, the fear of the Lord, that is wisdom;
>   and to depart from evil is understanding." (28:28)

We could continue in this fashion, but rather let us simply suggest that throughout the Bible we see that the fear of the Lord offers purity (Ps. 19:9), the beginning of knowledge (Prov. 1:7), the hatred of evil (Prov. 8:13), the lengthening of life (Prov. 10:27), confidence (Prov. 14:26), riches and honor and life (Prov. 19:23; 22:4), and delight and judgment and treasure (Isa. 11:2-3; 33:6). From the Bible's perspective, these gifts are always positive and not negative. These gifts are constructive for abundant life and not destructive of it.

When we hear the phrase "the fear of the Lord," we understand this phrase as the blessing God intends. Those who do not fear the Lord clearly risk the possibility of God's judgment. For believers, this fear is a blessing, not a curse.

The words "fear not" and "be not afraid" are prominent in both the Old and New Testaments, and especially in the Gospels. God notifies Abram in a vision, "Do not be afraid, Abram, I am your shield; your reward shall be very great" (Gen. 15:1). Moses tells the Israelites, "Do not be afraid, stand firm, and see the deliverance that the LORD will accomplish for you today; for the Egyptians whom you see today you shall never see again" (Exod. 14:13). The psalmist sings to the people of Israel, "With the LORD on my side I do not fear. / What can mortals do to me?" (Ps. 118:6).

Jesus himself taught, "Do not fear those who kill the body but cannot kill the soul; rather fear him who can destroy both soul and body in hell" (Matt. 10:28). Luke launches the Gospel bearing the evangelist's name with a series of comforting words that contain the phrase "do not be afraid" to Zechariah, Mary, and the shepherds (1:13, 30; 2:10). Acts tells us that the Lord said to Paul in a vision, "Do not be afraid, but speak and do not be silent; for I am with you, and no one will lay a hand on you to harm you" (18:9-10). Revelation recounts Saint John the Divine's utter fear and the Lord's reassurance: "When I saw him, I fell at his feet as though dead. But he placed his right hand on me, saying, 'Do not be afraid; I am the first and the last'" (1:17).

In summary let me say as clearly as I can that the fear of the Lord for believers is a blessing. But for those outside God's realm the lack of fear becomes pure judgment. God blesses those who worship God with the awe and reverence due God. God judges those who do not respect God's holy otherness.

If a believer wants to live abundant life, then he or she will "fear the Lord." If we need a reminder of one of the foundational characteristics of abundant life, then there is a pillar with the phrase "the fear of the Lord" inscribed on it. Amen. (David N. Mosser)

April 3, 2005

Second Sunday of Easter

Worship Theme: When doubts dog our tracks, and our confidence is held together by thin hope, looking for additional factual evidence will not help. Faith that abounds is not based on research of the facts but trust in the promises of Jesus. Remember Jesus.

Readings: Acts 2:14*a*, 22-32; 1 Peter 1:3-9; John 20:19-31

Call to Worship (Psalm 16:1-2, 5-9 RSV)

Leader:	Preserve me, O God, for in thee I take refuge.
People:	**I say to the LORD, "Thou art my Lord; I have no good apart from thee."**
Leader:	The LORD is my chosen portion and my cup; thou holdest my lot.
People:	**The lines have fallen for me in pleasant places; yea, I have a goodly heritage.**
Leader:	I bless the LORD who gives me counsel; in the night also my heart instructs me.
People:	**I keep the LORD always before me; because he is at my right hand, I shall not be moved.**
All:	**Therefore my heart is glad, and my soul rejoices; my body also dwells secure.**

Pastoral Prayer:
Dear Lord, God, Father, and Mother of us all, hear us as we pray. For reasons that lie beyond our limited knowledge, it appears that

you did not intend for us to have perfect knowledge in this world. But, you have called us to perfect trust in you. We come from a past we cannot remember, and we are moving toward a destiny we cannot see. Darkness enshrouds so much that we would like to see. Mystery meets us at every turn. There is something in us that will not let us believe that the darkness is empty, or that we are ever really alone, or that at the end of a life of faith there is a blank wall or a drop into nothingness. Forgive us the shallowness of our faith that causes us to ask for a sign, but we do ask a sign, for some tangible indication that we are at least moving in the right general direction. Forgive us our slowness to transfer our blind faith in material possessions, which in our better days we know will ultimately fail us, to a blind faith in spiritual values, which in our hearts we know will be with us forever. In Jesus' name. Amen. (Thomas Lane Butts)

SERMON BRIEFS

WHAT DO YOU REALLY BELIEVE?

ACTS 2:14a, 22-32

The day of Pentecost must have been an electrifying event to witness. Peter's powerful address to the crowd recalls the character of Peter, which, for modern-day Bible readers, is legendary. Legend and myth can be so close to one another that their boundaries may become blurred.

Today's text evokes the image of Peter, which is both legend and truth. Peter, the bold man who is always running, acting, speaking, pushing, defending, is the person who addresses the crowd. Peter, the one who only weeks ago had denied the same Jesus whom he had proclaimed "the Christ," is now the Peter we have come to know early on in the Gospels. Peter now publicly, courageously, unflinchingly proclaims his belief in what God has done through Jesus, the Christ.

We see in this text the Resurrection faith and the Resurrection story condensed into twelve powerful verses. What power words have. Peter's words of faith and conviction sway a doubting crowd, and three thousand persons are baptized in a day (v. 41)!

More than mere words compel us; personal witness puts power into words. Personal experience, when shared with conviction, has passion, purpose, power, and persuasion. This is the power of Peter's address and is a powerful lesson for any who fail to understand that the Christian faith is never only personal.

Two years ago I was called to testify in a civil trial involving a family in a former parish where I had served as pastor. The trial was in the state of Washington, while I lived in Texas. Yet the family's attorneys were insistent that I fly to Washington in order to testify in person. They had already come to me to take a deposition of my testimony, so they knew what I was going to say. They could have read my words to the jury or even handed out copies of my deposition to all the parties involved, but they wanted my personal witness. Personal experience, when shared with conviction, has passion, purpose, power, and persuasion. The same is true for believers in sharing Christ with others.

Faith in Christ is about relationship. Christianity is not merely belief about a god, it is a belief in the God revealed through Jesus Christ. Faith in Christ is not simply knowing *about* Jesus, but *knowing* Jesus through a spiritual journey that leads to an encounter with the Christ. The Christian faith is never only personal, it is meant to be shared.

What do you really believe? Belief informs our journey, influences our response to life, and impacts how others perceive us. Belief is a reflection of our true self, our inner being, our very soul. Belief transforms us, empowers us, encourages us, uplifts us, and saves us. Belief can also limit us, weaken us, discourage us, burden us, and destroy us. That is why the content of our belief is as important as the conviction of our belief. When we place our faith in that which is not of God, we are not only sadly misled but also ultimately disappointed.

The nonbelievers who acted to bring about Jesus' crucifixion were people of faith. Their faith was in the wrong things and misguided them to ignore God's mighty acts through the Messiah. They did not examine their beliefs or consider other possibilities. Their focus was on religion rather than relationships, law rather than love. What we believe matters. Being so comfortable with religion that we neglect relationships can have disastrous consequences for others and for our very own soul. (Gary G. Kindley)

A GLORIOUS HOPE

1 PETER 1:3-9

On the second Sunday of Easter, it is so tempting to stay with the Gospel text, yet this opening from 1 Peter deserves careful consideration. Written possibly as a baptismal address for new Christians in a time of persecution, 1 Peter magnificently lays out what it means to live as a follower of the resurrected Jesus.

We note three things. First, the opening verse is a blessing addressed to God. Second, in swift order the following verses lay out the great themes of the letter. Third, this passage is shaped by worship. Numerous scholars have pointed out its clear liturgical character. It should be read in the language of transcendent praise. We are given new birth through a living hope. We have "an inheritance that is imperishable, undefiled, and unfading, kept in heaven" for us (v. 4). We are protected by God "through faith for a salvation ready to be revealed in the last time" (v. 5). All this is put in the context of persecution reflected in verse 6. Furthermore, despite trials, the theme of joy and rejoicing pervades the passage. Verse 8 is presented as a shout of praise. We are an Easter people who live with a "glorious joy." In our darkened, sin-stained world, this is a triumphant word of faith that needs to be heard. The whole passage is grounded in the resurrection of Christ. It demands that the preacher not move too quickly away from the joy of Easter morning but, instead, use this text as an opportunity to lay out the full meaning of the Easter event.

The passage itself suggests an outline for the sermon. It should begin with lifting up what is meant by a living hope. This is a hope that is not passive but vigorous and active, motivating the life of the believer. It should not be confused with optimism. It is not based on human ability to conquer trials but on God's greater triumph over evil that is assured in Christ's resurrection.

The second point should be developed on the lines of inheritance suggested in verse 4. All human aspirations and projects ultimately fade and fail, but not God's great divine plan of salvation. Each day is to be lived under the protection of God's power in which the church and individual Christians place their full and final hope. Verse 6 allows the preacher an opening to acknowledge the reality of sin and suffering in the world today but demands that life's struggles and problems be faced in the joy of God's ultimate triumph. The testing we all face is seen, then, in its proper perspective as something that brings forth praise, glory, and honor to God.

I remember visiting a man in the hospital who was dying of cancer. The end was approaching when I visited him. He said to me, "You know, in a strange way this has been a blessing." He went on to explain how it had brought him closer to God and others whom he loved. Tested severely, his faith had grown into a witness of glorious joy.

Verses 8 and 9 should govern the closing part of the sermon both as a call to faith for us and as an invitation to enter into the joy of the Lord this day regardless of our situation. We may have a glorious joy precisely because "you are receiving the outcome of your faith, the salvation of your souls" (v. 9). However unclear it may be to us, the triumph of Easter dramatically changes the very way we look at the problems of life and the world. Our ultimate trust, hope, and joy is with God. (Mike Lowry)

PEACE, LOVE, AND UNDERSTANDING

JOHN 20:19-31

Our story continues from the Easter appearance of Jesus to Mary Magdalene. Later on in the evening as the disciples were hiding, Jesus appears to them. John is quick to tell us that the disciples locked the doors of their house. They were afraid that the Jewish leaders may do to them as they did to Jesus. In their state of fear, Jesus appears to the disciples and offers peace. Earlier in their ministry on a lake in Galilee, Jesus had appeared to them, walking on the water, to offer comfort in their frightening situation. Jesus offers peace and comfort to those who are afraid and terrified by the world around them. Jesus offers comfort to see us through hardships, heartaches, and difficult circumstances. Jesus comes to disciples who are afraid, confused, and without hope. Jesus equips disciples to go forth and spread the gospel message with less fear and full authority. The disciples receive an indwelling of the Holy Spirit and the power to forgive sins. Many people saw the disciples throughout Jerusalem and Judea proclaiming the resurrected Christ to all who would listen.

Can our faith grow without a little doubt? Thomas always seems to get a bad rap when it comes to the subject of faith. Thomas's doubts are no greater than the other disciples' doubts. His absence from the first appearance allows Jesus one more opportunity to teach the disciples. Thomas is a person who needs to experience. Some people learn better by doing something than by reading about it in a book. Thomas must experience the risen Savior for himself, with all of his senses. It is not so much that he did not believe the other disciples, but he must see for his own sake for his faith to grow. Again, John emphasizes that the door is locked yet Jesus appears. Although Jesus offers Thomas what he requests, to touch his wounds, Thomas immediately proclaims, "My Lord and My God!" (v. 28). Thomas is the only disciple of the eleven that we read about, as Jesus appears, who announces the deity of the risen Lord. His little doubt has led to a mighty faith.

Verses 29-31 speak to all believers in Jesus Christ, from the early church to those yet born. God blesses us by giving the Scriptures to read. God blesses us by the gift of the many saints who have gone before and preserved the faith. God blesses us as we experience the living Christ in new ways each day. We do not see all that Jesus did here on earth but experience the living Christ through the Holy Spirit. John does not even attempt to tell all that Jesus did in his earthly ministry. Did not John write enough about what Jesus did in his earthly ministry? It would be foolish for us to attempt to write down all that the Holy Spirit does in the world today. Do we take for granted the miracles of our life? Let us be awake to all that the Lord does for us and listen for that still, small voice inside to guide us in all that we do. We can experience the living Christ through the Holy Spirit. "Blessed are those who have not seen and yet have come to believe" (v. 29*b*). Jesus comes into our life to grant us peace, to show us his love, so that we may understand and believe in him. (John Mathis)

APRIL 10, 2005

Third Sunday of Easter

Worship Theme: All that we need to know awaits us at the feet of the resurrected Jesus. Repent and believe.

Readings: Acts 2:14*a*, 36-41; 1 Peter 1:17-23; Luke 24:13-35

Call to Worship (Psalm 116:1-6, 12, 17-18 RSV)

Leader: I love the LORD, because he has heard my voice and my supplications.

People: **Because he inclined his ear to me, therefore I will call on him as long as I live.**

Leader: The snares of death encompassed me; the pangs of Sheol laid hold on me; I suffered distress and anguish.

People: **Then I called on the name of the LORD: "O LORD, I beseech thee, save my life!"**

Leader: Gracious is the LORD, and righteous; our God is merciful.

People: **The LORD preserves the simple; when I was brought low, he saved me.**

Leader: What shall I render to the LORD for all his bounty to me?

People: **I will offer to thee the sacrifice of thanksgiving and call on the name of the LORD.**

All: **I will pay my vows to the LORD in the presence of all his people.**

Pastoral Prayer:
Lord Jesus, we confess that so many circumstances in life keep on triggering weaknesses within us, which brings sorrow to your heart as well as our own. We have not given attention to the necessary disciplines of faith, and our spiritual life has grown threadbare. We have become so enamored with power and position and possession and personal privilege that we have forgotten or neglected those disciplines and achievements of the Spirit, which make for true and lasting happiness. We have adopted ideas and philosophies of life, which are convenient and nonthreatening, at the expense of those understandings of life that would cause us to grow and change and become strong persons. The truth is, O Lord, we have been so mentally and spiritually lazy that we would be horrified if that same degree of laziness were exercised in our daily work and our household responsibilities. Forgive us, and lead us to new beginnings. Amen. (Thomas Lane Butts)

SERMON BRIEFS

DOES YOUR FAITH CHANGE YOU?

ACTS 2:14*a*, 36-41

An encounter with Jesus Christ has an effect on you. It can have a profound effect on your feelings, thoughts, perspective, choices, actions, words, even the direction of your life's journey. It can transform those who hear the message.

The Christ's presence is reflected in what Dr. Tex Sample, professor emeritus at St. Paul School of Theology, defines as "good preaching." In many lectures and presentations, Sample has often described what he terms "good preaching" as "a message that comforts the afflicted and afflicts the comfortable."

Do we hear the message? Are we open to the possibility of Christ's message changing us? Are we open to the possibility of change? Do we arrive for worship with any expectation of something significant occurring? Do we approach biblical study with the prayerful hope of an encounter with God? Do we enter into prayer listening for a word from God, a nudge from the Holy Spirit, or a deepening awareness of the presence of God in our lives? Are we available to ever hear the message of the Christ for our journey?

A pastor was arranging a guest speaker for a special event. Due to various circumstances, she had never spoken directly with the keynote speaker. In desperation, she called his home the night prior to the event and, once again, found him to be away from the phone. Instead, she spoke with his hearing-impaired mother. After confirming with her that he was indeed planning to attend, she ended the call by saying, "I'm glad he's coming." The man's mother misheard her and said, "You're Gladys Cummings, I'll tell him to look for you when he arrives." Then she hung up the phone before the pastor could correct her. The next day, the pastor arrived early at the event. She wore a nametag which read "Gladys Cummings." Sometimes, we do not hear the message.

When change occurs, we may be changed for better or for worse. Perhaps, in part, it is this uncertainty of change which leads us to avoid it. Mark Twain once said that the only thing that likes change is a wet baby.

When change occurs, the change may be enduring or short-lived. We may backslide into apathy or old patterns. Change is not transformative unless it is lived out and allowed to take root in our daily existence, routines, habits, and relationships.

Does your faith change you, make you different, impact your life and your choices? Does it ever step on your toes, bring chills to your spine, move you to tears, put a lump in your throat, or cause you to give it all up—whatever "all" may be?

Faith in Christ changes those who believe. As we read on to verse 42, we discover that being Christian is not a transformation into morose and stoic religious behavior. Being Christian is a transformation that leads to a life of relationships, devotion, fellowship, and celebration of the bread of life for body and spirit. (Gary G. Kindley)

LIVING UNDER GOD

1 PETER 1:17-23

The triumph of Easter beckons followers of Christ to take a fresh look at how life is to be lived. This text designed for the third Sunday of Easter directs our attention to holy living. The opening clause sets the context for the consideration of the rest of the passage, "If you invoke as Father the one who judges all people impartially according to their deeds" (v. 17*a*). Traditionally, Christians are those who invoke God as Father. Because father may be difficult for some people, God as parent or mother can be more helpful in finding the intimacy with God that we all seek. Christians are a people who operate "under God" as the divine parent. Calling upon God as Father reminds us of the familial relationship we have with God. The implication of intimacy should not be missed. We are a part of the family and, as such, are expected to act accordingly. We should also not miss the implication of God as Judge. Judgment is a function of love and holds up for the Christian the expected standard of behavior.

The last half of verse 17 begins a string of imperatives implied in living under God. We are to live in "reverent fear." The actions of each day are to be taken in awe of God and obedience to the Lord.

Verses 18 and 19 invoke Old Testament imagery of those ransomed from slavery. The Christian is reminded that the cost of our liberation was more than mere silver or gold. The cost was the sacrifice of Christ. This ransom price frees us from slavery to sin for service to God. We are no longer captive to "the futile ways inherited from your ancestors" (v. 18).

Verses 20 and 21 complete the implications of life under God. Verse 20 reminds us that God is acting in and through history for salvation. We are not merely the pawns of human history but the children of God in history. Through Christ, we are to put our trust and hope in God. These actions of reverent fear, liberation from sin, and placing our ultimate hope and trust in God form the basis of living under God. The sermon might well be developed along the fault line of these three points as aspects of what it means to live under God.

It is significant that the passage for today's lesson does not end with verse 21. In the first part of verse 21, Christ's followers are noted as those purified through obedience to God. This purification is to lead to a "genuine mutual love" for one another (v. 22). The reader cannot help but note the way the passage has delivered us to the great command of Christ: to love God and each other. The entire theme of life lived under God is summed up in verse 23 by the notion of being born anew through the living Word of God—Jesus Christ. The Easter triumph is not just about resurrection hereafter but carries sharp moral implications for living today. To be Christian is to wear the label of Christ followers in all our relationships.

There is an old story told of a rebellious soldier who was brought before Alexander the Great. The soldier had been unruly and disobedient. Alexander asked him his name and, with a smirk, he replied, "Alexander." With one swift blow, Alexander the Great knocked him to the ground. As he stood over him he said, "Either change your name or change your ways." So it is with the Christian. We are the resurrection qualities of a people of God. Through Christ, we are purified for obedience. (Mike Lowry)

CHRIST KNOWN IN THE BREAD

LUKE 24:13-35

Luke 24 raises an interesting question: Why didn't the individuals on their walk to Emmaus recognize Jesus? Luke hints that in some supernatural way, their eyes were prevented from identifying Christ. Or perhaps they had never seen Jesus up close. Perhaps they were simply disciples from afar. Maybe Jesus appeared cosmetically different in his glorified, resurrected body. And they weren't expecting to see Jesus, thinking he was dead. This might explain why Mary did not recognize Jesus at the tomb and why the disciples were slow to recognize the risen Christ standing on the shore of Galilee.

A more timely question is, Why don't more people recognize and acknowledge the risen Christ today? Again, we speculate:

perhaps some do not look for God. Perhaps some are not expecting God to appear in human form. Even these devout followers of Jesus did not fully understand the concept of a Messiah who was God in the flesh. This brings us to another question: Why was Christ's identity made known to the men in the breaking of the bread (v. 35)? Yet again, we guess: a supernatural "opening" of their eyes? Some mannerism or style that Jesus had used previously when breaking bread? Or something more? Here we see an allegory for the sacrament of communion. We cannot fully grasp the nature of God and the mystery of the incarnation, but through the breaking of bread—through the communion ritual—the reality of God is revealed in fresh ways. One message of communion, and of the Emmaus account, is that we find Jesus in both the miraculous and the ordinary.

The breaking of bread is an everyday, mundane act. Jesus made it a supernatural act when he took the loaves and fishes from a little boy and fed five thousand. Jesus made it especially holy at the Last Supper, by connecting the image of his impending sacrifice with the symbolism of the Jewish Passover.

Sacraments and holy symbols are, as Lawrence Stookey puts it, "God's message mediated through the created world." All of us need a palpable image or symbol to help our imagination "see" the invisible. Flowers to my spouse are an attempt to make visible my love for her. The "Stars and Stripes" is a visible banner of intangible patriotism. The bread and the cup evoke many images: the joy of family meals and togetherness, passover and manna in the desert, the broken body and blood of Christ.

The sacred mystery of Jesus is not a riddle meant to be solved, but we are allowed a wider experience and knowledge of the Divine Mystery through the sacraments. As the divine came into the human in the person of Jesus, similarly, the supernatural comes visually into the physical world through the sacraments.

A final thought about communion and a related word, community: At Emmaus, the opening of the men's eyes came only *after* they invited Jesus in to share a meal with them. When you share the table in peace and harmony with your Christian sisters and brothers, you should feel bonded to God's community and can thus see Christ more clearly. When you are reminded of Christ's miraculous acts of feeding the five thousand or of the manna falling from heaven, you can see Christ more clearly. When at the Lord's table and you receive God's forgiveness, you can see Christ more clearly. When you remember his shed blood and broken body, you can see the love of Christ more clearly.

So may Christ be made known to you in the breaking of the bread! (Lance Moore)

APRIL 17, 2005

Fourth Sunday of Easter

Worship Theme: Jesus is the "Good Shepherd." We can depend on him in life and in death.

Readings: Acts 2:42-47; 1 Peter 2:19-25; John 10:1-10

Call to Worship (Psalm 23 RSV)

Leader: The LORD is my shepherd, I shall not want;

People: **He makes me lie down in green pastures. He leads me beside still waters; he restores my soul.**

Leader: He leads me in paths of righteousness for his name's sake.

People: **Even though I walk through the valley of the shadow of death, I fear no evil; for thou art with me; thy rod and thy staff, they comfort me.**

Leader: Thou preparest a table before me in the presence of my enemies; thou anointest my head with oil, my cup overflows.

People: **Surely goodness and mercy shall follow me all the days of my life; and I shall dwell in the house of the LORD for ever.**

Pastoral Prayer:

Almighty God, Creator of all things, great and small, we rejoice that we are a part of your creation. We are glad to be alive and connected with so much that counts in life. Hear us as we search for our proper place in your world, so that our lives will have maximum meaning.

We confess that we are sometimes puzzled by the strange and unexpected turns that life takes. We feel wounded by the hard and unfair aspects of life, when the good die young, and evil triumphs. We pray for courage and strength to meet the changing fortunes of life. When circumstances are such that we just do not understand, help us to trust your wisdom for the ultimate outcomes that we cannot see. When the day is over, O Lord, help us to pick up our part of the load and walk with courage into the night. We pray in the name of Jesus, the Good Shepherd, who loves and cares for us all. Amen. (Thomas Lane Butts)

SERMON BRIEFS

LIVING NOW LIKE WE CLAIM WE'LL LIVE THEN

ACTS 2:42-47

The Christian life is different. The spirit of the Christ infuses our communion and community. I would be hard-pressed to pick only one of the countless inspiring hymns as our theme song of Christian community. If I had to select only one, the hymn "They'll Know We Are Christians by Our Love" wouldn't be a bad nominee. The issue of religion and love is at the heart of why some folks question the validity of faith and spirituality. Both critics and skeptics can confuse being loving with being religious. So can many pew sitters.

Acts 2:43-47 is a microcosm of Christian community. It is how faith and life in the early church were, but it is also a compelling testimony of how wonderful faith and life in Christian community can be. There is generosity and sacrifice, an outward focus rather than merely self-serving mission.

The look-what-we've-accomplished syndrome often focuses on self-centered motivation or institutional glorification rather than healthy self-affirmation. True Christian community, as reflected in Acts 2, is not likened to corporate America with profit margins,

performance goals, spin doctors, and a success-at-any-price philosophy. Christian community that is described in scripture is a
communion of unconditional love, selfless service, sacrificial
sharing, and Christlike commitment. Deeds are based on devotion to God and others. Actions and agendas are focused on
Christlike love, justice, service, and response to human need.

In his book *Courageous Leadership*, Bill Hybels shares the
story of a young couple who brought their infant child to him for
prayer. When he took the child in his arms and lifted the blanket
that was covering her face, he saw a horribly deformed child. The
parents told him that she did not have very long to live, perhaps
only six weeks. After he prayed with the parents and their fragile
infant, he asked if there was anything the church could do. The
parents responded that their small group was already doing all
they could to support them. They had prayed for this compli-
cated pregnancy. They were there at the hospital when the child
was delivered. They were with them the night the couple got the
bad news of their baby's prognosis. This small group of loving,
caring, Christian disciples cleaned their house, prepared their
meals, and were helping them to plan their precious daughter's
funeral (Bill Hybels, *Courageous Leadership* [Grand Rapids:
Zondervan, 2002], pp. 22-23). This is what it means to be church.

Christian community is not simply about a people awaiting
their heavenly reward. It is not merely about living life with the
hope that things will be different in the "sweet by and by." It is
about hope that is now, faith that is for today, and a life of discipleship that is a journey, not just an end. If we believe that
heaven is such a wonderful place of peace, joy, love, and care,
then why not live now like we claim we will live then? What a
wonderful world this would be if Christians everywhere made the
conscious choice to do just that. (Gary G. Kindley)

THE CHALLENGE TO FOLLOW CHRIST

1 PETER 2:19-25

This epistle reading continues the Easter readings in 1 Peter
and is also a continuation of the so-called household duties found

in 1 Peter 2:13–3:17. Many scholars believe that verse 18 should be considered a part of this passage. Verse 18 places the context of the passage in a set of instructions for a slave who is Christian. A wider reading sees this section as a continuation on the theme of being under the authority of God in our relationship with others. This passage recalls the teachings of Jesus with regard to those who persecute Christians and reminds us that an attitude of love is to pervade all relationships as a reflection of Christ living in us and through us. Jesus' teaching in the Sermon on the Mount and Paul's phrase in 1 Corinthians to "have the mind of Christ" are instructive (2:16). Simply put, relationally, we are to follow the model of Jesus.

The Christian life should be determined by our relationship with God and not by others' attitudes toward us. Thus, the passage opens with a call to endure unjust treatment in a matter that reflects credit to us as followers of Christ. In an age governed by fairness, claiming your own rights, and getting even, this scriptural teaching runs contrary to conventional wisdom. There should be no attempt to soften its true impact. Jesus instructed his followers: "But I say to you, Do not resist an evildoer. But if anyone strikes you on the right cheek, turn the other also" (Matt. 5:39). Verse 21 makes explicit the call to follow in the steps of Christ.

The image from verse 22 comes from Isaiah 53:9, the suffering servant. It is followed in verse 23 by direct reference to the way Christ handled persecution and suffering. Verse 24 ties his suffering directly to redemption in the cross and our call to live by righteousness. Verse 25 completes the instructions by once more reminding us that Jesus is the shepherd and guardian of our souls.

There can be no doubt that such a passage flies in the face of much modern thinking, but that is also the reason it so desperately needs to be lifted up and preached on. The Christian ethic and way of life is a radically different ethic that calls us to reach out in love even to those who abuse us. Historic examples like the peaceful resistance of the Civil Rights movement and Martin Luther King, Jr., readily come to mind. God's strength is made known in weakness, and we are challenged to be truly Christ followers. (Mike Lowry)

THE GATE

JOHN 10:1-10

I live among many gates in my home. As a matter of fact, there are approximately 4 gates or barriers that I have erected throughout our house. Contrary to how it may sound, I neither live in a dangerous area nor am particularly paranoid. I live in a "gated home" because I am the mother of a toddler. I have gated my home not to keep someone out, but to keep my little one inside of the boundaries that I have set for her. If you have ever spent much time around a toddler, you know that parents set up gates to protect their children because they love them.

Throughout the Gospel of John, both the person and divine nature of Jesus is explored. Unlike the synoptic, more narrative accounts of Jesus' earthly ministry, John delves into the theological implications of Jesus' teachings and miracles. In John 10, Jesus uses a parable of a shepherd, his sheep, and the gate that keeps the sheep in place to explain his own divine role. The shepherd imagery is familiar throughout the Scriptures. It was, after all, an image that most people at that time would have understood. In this parable, Jesus describes himself as a shepherd who loves and cares for his sheep so much that he is willing to die for them. Although others may claim to be the shepherds of those same sheep, they are false, and their real intent is to harm the sheep. The sheep, however, would recognize the voice of their true shepherd and follow his leadership alone. Although this is the first time that this imagery is used in John, this scenario is familiar to us as we recall similar descriptions of God as our shepherd throughout both the Old Testament and the New Testament. A new element of this parable is the concept of Jesus as not only the shepherd but also the gate. In verses 7-11, Jesus describes himself as the gate by whom all those who will be saved will enter. Likewise, the gate will prohibit those who approach the sheep out of malevolence. What a wonderful dual image of Jesus not only as the loving shepherd, but also as the protective gate ushering us into abundant life, while protecting us from those who seek to harm us.

Perhaps there is no time of year more than Easter that we

acknowledge the depth and sincerity of Christ's love for us. It is a love that is willing to sacrifice, endure tremendous suffering, and overcome even the grave. This parable teaches us that this love is also a protective love. This parable reminds me of the gates in my home. I did not place them so that my daughter will be restricted from living her life. I did not intend to keep her from exploring or learning. I did not install them to show her who was in control. The gates are placed out of my love for her and my desire to keep her from dangers she is not ready to face. Perhaps most important, the gates ensure that when my daughter is ready to go through them, I will be there to go with her. This is the message of the parable of John 10. The love of Christ is a boundless love, an enduring love, and yes, even a protective love. As both the shepherd and the gate, Jesus is not only our entry point into abundant life but also our partner along the way. During this season, embrace this love and the abundant life that Christ so freely offers. Hear Jesus' call. Enter the gate. Embrace the shepherd. (Tracey Allred)

APRIL 24, 2005

Fifth Sunday of Easter

Worship Theme: When we come to that place in life in which all things fade into mystery, when what we know no longer explains what is happening, the wonderful words of Jesus are our source of security.

Readings: Acts 7:55-60; 1 Peter 2:2-10; John 14:1-14

Call to Worship (Psalm 31:1-5, 15-16 RSV)

Leader:	In thee, O LORD, do I seek refuge; let me never be put to shame; in thy righteousness deliver me!
People:	**Incline thy ear to me, rescue me speedily! Be thou a rock of refuge for me, a strong fortress to save me!**
Leader:	Yea, thou art my rock and my fortress; for thy name's sake lead me and guide me.
People:	**Take me out of the net which is hidden for me, for thou art my refuge.**
Leader:	Into thy hand I commit my spirit; thou hast redeemed me, O LORD, faithful God.
People:	**My times are in thy hand; deliver me from the hand of my enemies and persecutors!**
All:	**Let thy face shine on thy servant; save me in thy steadfast love!**

Pastoral Prayer:

Gracious and Holy God, from whom our lives take their beginnings, and in whom we find our home at last, we gather at this
time and place to listen once again to the music of eternity. We
confess that we have argued with the hard edges of providence,
and we have doubted things we thought we knew when we have
walked in the gray areas of uncertainty. Help us to look past our
doubts and fears and see Jesus and hear his voice when we are
going through the valleys of life. Save us from discouragement
and doubt. Show us where we may most profitably invest our
lives, so that we will gain the greatest meaning as we pass
through this transient world. In the name of Jesus. Amen.
(Thomas Lane Butts)

SERMON BRIEFS

DYING TO LIVE

ACTS 7:55-60

Martyrdom is not all that it is said to be. Some cults glorify it,
some major religions speak glowingly of it, many Christians
accept it as a possibility, as long as they are not the one being
martyred. How much are we willing to risk for our faith? How
strongly do we hold fast to what it is that we believe? Is the love
of God, revealed through the Christ, worth dying for?

A member of my congregation, who travels extensively for his
company, shared a news account from a city that he had visited.
It seems that a passerby saved the life of a little boy at the cost of
personal injury to himself. A very young boy was playing in his
driveway, when he wandered too far out into the street. The
"good Samaritan" who was walking down the sidewalk, saw that
the boy was in the path of an oncoming car. The driver of the
automobile either did not see the boy or could not react in time
to stop. Without thought of his own personal safety, the passerby
dove out into the street, pushing the boy out of the way. The driver of the car, unable to stop in time, struck the man, fracturing
his leg.

The hero, recovering in a hospital bed, was interviewed by the news media. When asked why he did it the man simply said, "I am a father. Anyone who has kids would understand. You do what you have to do for the sake of a child." Because this man, this father, believed in the sanctity of children and their well-being, he was willing to put his life on the line for his beliefs.

Firefighters, police officers, public safety officers, military personnel, pilots, flight attendants, and other professionals all put their lives on the line, knowing that their duty might call them to great personal sacrifice. The events of 9/11 certainly etched that truth on our minds. When we know what we believe, what we stand for, we are willing to take a stand. With deep faith and commitment comes courage.

The Acts account of the stoning of Stephen is told many years after the event. As the Christian disciple that history records as the first martyr of the faith, there is much glorification and adoration surrounding the story. It is hard to discern historical fact from reverent embellishment as the story was passed down before being recorded for our own inspiration. What is clear is that Stephen believed that God had revealed the Way through Jesus Christ.

The Way was the path of salvation, a life of love, a devotion to Christ and all God's people. Stephen did not merely know about Jesus, he was one who had a spiritual encounter with the Christ. It was a Christ encounter that changed his heart, deepened his faith, strengthened his courage, and anchored his resolve. Stephen knew what he believed. Stephen was willing to witness the good news to persons who were not ready nor willing to hear what God might be saying to them. Like so many prophetic souls who came before, and who will follow, Stephen laid his life on the line for love.

Although we may not need to hang on the cross or stand in the midst of a stone-throwing crowd, our faith is still tested and our beliefs challenged. Love demands a response. We have been loved by God and shown the Way through Christ and Christ's disciples. The choice for us is simple: Believe and act, or ignore and move on. The direction that our journey takes is up to us, but there are no roads or detours as fulfilling as the Way of the Christ. (Gary G. Kindley)

FINDING GRACE IN EAST TEXAS

1 PETER 2:2-10

The letter of 1 Peter was written to a group of Gentile Christians in Asia Minor. In the past they had experienced ridicule and persecution. Now the future was uncertain and hard times were likely to come again.

The author wanted to remind the church of two important things. First, he tells them they have experienced the gift of God's amazing grace; they have been blessed and called to be God's people. "You are a chosen race, a royal priesthood, a holy nation, God's own people" (v. 9).

> Once you were not a people,
>   but now you are God's people;
> once you had not received mercy,
>   but now you have received mercy. (v. 10)

Second, even though the times were difficult, they were still called to share the good news of God's grace with others. "You are a chosen race ... in order that you may proclaim the mighty acts of him who called you out of darkness into his marvelous light" (v. 9).

Proclaiming as a chosen race is not always easy to do when times are hard. Yet, if we remember what it felt like when we received grace, then we would be inspired to share that good news with others.

One day I was driving home to Houston, on some back roads through little towns in east Texas, when I was pulled over by a police officer. When I rolled down my window he said, "Your inspection sticker has expired." Sure enough my inspection sticker had expired three days before. I wasn't worried. I figured he would give me a warning ticket and tell me to get it fixed. But instead, he gave me a ticket for sixty-eight dollars. A sixty-eight-dollar ticket for a five-dollar inspection sticker that was expired by three days! It was true I had done wrong, but I didn't think the crime was that extreme. I took the ticket home, tossed it on my desk and thought that I would take care of it soon but I forgot. One month later I received a certified letter saying, "You failed to pay your fine and did not show up for your court date. The fine is now three hundred fifty dollars. If you do not show up in the next seven days, a warrant will be issued for your arrest." Three hundred fifty dollars for a five-dollar inspection sticker. A warrant for my arrest for an inspection sticker that was three days overdue. I immediately called and got a court date. When I arrived at court, I found that the building was set out in the middle of a cornfield, and it wasn't a courthouse at all but rather a dance hall. There were folding chairs sitting on a concrete floor. Behind a high bench sat a judge who wielded complete control with the law. I watched as the people approached the bench. They would confess their sins, and then the judge would slam down the gavel and pronounce their sentence. Justice was dispensed quickly and completely.

There was no question I had made a mistake and now I was getting worried about what the judge might say about my failure to pay my ticket. Suddenly, the court clerk called my name. When I went over to her desk, she said, "We've lost your paperwork." "I brought you the letter you mailed to me," I said. "I know," she said. "You did everything right but we've lost your paperwork." "Well, what does that mean?" I asked. She said, "It's like nothing ever happened. Your crime is forgotten. You're free to go. Good night and good-bye." I ran for the door, jumped in my car, and took off in a cloud of dust before they could change their mind.

Free to go. All is forgiven. It felt so good. Then I remembered, that is what grace is like. Although we are guilty, we are forgiven and we are free to go—go "in order that you may proclaim the mighty acts of him who called you out of darkness into his marvelous light." (Robert Long)

MORE THAN JUST GOOD-BYE

JOHN 14:1-14

Good-byes can be excruciating. There is a very distinct pain that accompanies a "good-bye." It is a pain that we all hope to avoid, but a pain that by virtue of loving others, we all will face.

There are both very temporary farewells (a short trip away from a family member) and very permanent farewells (the death of a loved one). My family recently moved to another state, and thus, had a series of farewells to good friends and church family. Perhaps, one of the most difficult parts of bidding farewell is finding words to express your feelings. In today's text, Jesus begins a farewell to his closest friends.

John 13 is perhaps one of the tenderest scenes between Jesus and the disciples. This chapter includes their last meal together, Jesus' washing of the disciples' feet, his prediction of his own death, and the likely even more painful predictions of Judas's betrayal and Peter's denial. I can imagine the feelings that must have been present in that upper room. There must have been both fear and incredible love. I imagine the disciples' amazement as Jesus, the Son of God, humbled himself to wash their feet. I imagine a sense of dread as they savored their last peaceful moments together while anticipating the unknown evil that was ahead for them. Although the Gospel of John reiterates the divine nature of Jesus consistently, Jesus' tender human feelings toward his disciples and friends are evident in chapter 13.

As John 13 described the poignant farewell setting of the Last Supper, John 14 recapitulates Jesus' deep emotions at both his own impending death and his love for the disciples through a passage known as the farewell discourse. Although the farewell discourse continues through chapter 17, chapter 14 begins this richly emotional discourse with some familiar texts. "Do not let your heart be troubled. Believe in God, believe also in me" (v. 1). Recognizing the distress of the disciples, Jesus encourages them to not be troubled. What a remarkable encouragement from a person mere hours away from his own death! As Jesus offers support and reassurance, he also acknowledges his divine nature. Jesus teaches even in these last hours that God is indeed his parent, and that his role is more than just one as a great teacher. In verse 6, Jesus answers the ever-questioning Thomas with a powerful theological statement. Jesus states that he is "the way, and the truth, and the life" (v. 6). Jesus was more than their mentor and leader; he was their salvation. In verse 11, Jesus describes his oneness to God, a concept that would be a challenging issue for the early Christian church. In verse 14, he describes the power of

157

merely the mention of his name in prayer. In but a few verses, Jesus not only gives words of comfort for his disciples but also establishes important theological teaching for generations of believers. I think it is significant that in this last conversation with his disciples, Jesus is reiterating and explaining the complex issues of incarnation and salvation.

In many ways, through this passage, he is passing the torch to his disciples. As Jesus' own death impends and the disciples deal with the implications of life without Jesus, he makes sure that they really understand what his ministry and life have been about. This passage, which so passionately bids farewell, also ordains the disciples for the next phase of their ministry. They must realize that he will not physically accompany them on their journey, so they must once and for all grasp the truth of the Christ. We, too, must grapple with this text as more than a beautiful good-bye. It is a text of instruction that for the writer of this Gospel so encapsulated the message of the Christ that it is specifically remembered as part of his last words. May his words this season affect us as profoundly. May our hearts embrace like never before the truth of the Christ. (Tracey Allred)

REFLECTIONS

MAY

Reflection Verse: *"Open your hand to the poor and needy neighbor in your land." (Deuteronomy 15:11)*

OPENNESS: COMPASSION EXTENDED
Deuteronomy 15:1, 7-11

In our series of meditations for pastors, "Twelve Pillars of Abundant Christian Living," we now raise the topic of openness. Moses builds an altar and sets up twelve pillars representing Israel's twelve tribes (Exodus 24). The pillar images are to signify qualities of authentic Christian living. The characteristic "openness" is this month's focus.

Horatio Alger, Jr. (1832–99), best known as an author, wrote one of the first American boys' adventure series. Alger published more than 120 novels and included heroes who invariably succeed in life through a mix of courage and good fortune. The heroes are lucky, in part, because they create their own luck. The young protagonists make their own luck through their own dedication to, among other things, hard work, private study, speaking the truth, personal grooming, frugal living, loyalty, and courtesy to all people. These young heroes always expect success.

"Bootstrapping" is a modern way we speak of the Horatio Alger philosophy. Bootstrap means to succeed through our own enterprise without relying on any outside help. Bootstrapping means if we are going to achieve something, then it is up to our self-generated hard work, ingenuity, and resolve. Today, few people argue with such a philosophy. It is the soil from which we all grow. Yet, despite our agreement with the notion that we are responsible as individuals for life's success or failure, we do know that life's circumstances regularly make it problematic for all people to prevail over negative circumstances no matter how hard they try.

With this said, we might remember that Israel continually understood itself as a community or people of God. Israel rarely contemplated a perspective such as individuality or pulling oneself up by the bootstraps. Instead Israel identified itself as primarily a community. Hence, when there was a social or economic problem, it was up to the community to solve it.

Deuteronomy 15:1, 7-11 seizes upon the idea of the land's release for a year and gives it both a social and an economic twist. It may be a twist that we neither understand nor like, but for Israel it was important to convey theological meaning. God owns all!

I am not a social historian, but I know enough of human social evolution to recognize that people first provided food for themselves by hunting and gathering wild vegetables, nuts, and berries. Sporadically throw in a decent-sized mammal and one had the makings of something of a feast. In due course, people began to settle. Soon the settlers discovered that they could cultivate food. Thus originated elementary farming. Certainly, these early farmers noticed that rain helped crops thrive and that weeds had a deleterious effect on cultivated food. Perhaps the idea of crop rotation was a later farming development. Somewhere in the midst of all these agricultural discoveries was the discovery that fields needed to rest on occasion for a growing season. Consequently, farmers in due course adopted the strategy that a field occasionally remains unplanted.

Later, Israel formally codified in its sacred law that a field must rest from production for a year: "For six years you shall sow your land and gather in its yield; but the seventh year you shall let it rest and lie fallow, so that the poor of your people may eat; and what they leave the wild animals may eat. You shall do the same with your vineyard, and with your olive orchard" (Exod. 23:10-11).

Deuteronomy 15:1, 7-11 extends the Exodus law of the release of land from cultivation and applies the same idea economically to a family's debt over generations. The law of a field going fallow for one year means that the land belongs to God and not to individuals. It follows then that the release of debts means essentially the same thing: The wealth humans possess is not theirs alone, but God's wealth. People are merely the stewards of God's prosperity. Thus, the community shares its wealth and provides for the community's needy. The Pentateuch's legislation pertains not only to the land but also to a broader concept of the Israelite Jubilee Year. In the Jubilee Year, every fiftieth year, the land goes uncultivated, slaves are freed, and debts forgiven. Does this strike you as oddly impractical?

A woman, after a lecture on the Jubilee Year concept, once asked Walter Brueggemann, a respected Old Testament scholar, "Sir, is there any evidence that Israel actually practiced the idea of Jubilee?" Brueggemann replied, "My dear friend, the Bible is full of things that have never actually been practiced." Brueggemann's quip suggests the difficulty of this Jubilee Year concept in modern America, what with our complex economy and multifaceted social structure.

We all understand the downside of implementing something like Jubilee Year in our society. I remember an episode of *Law & Order* a few years ago that focused on a successful woman's husband who ran up incredible gambling debt. The creditors expected her to continue paying for her husband's many indiscretions. Eventually, she had enough and arranged his murder. She was a sympathetic character, despite a jury finding her guilty of murder for hire. Who among us wants to bear responsibility for irresponsible people?

Although we may never propose to practice the idea of the Jubilee Year, what does it suggest? I think the idea of Jubilee's release of debts recognizes that not all people are in fact responsible for the debts they incur. Sometimes bad decisions or unfortunate circumstances carry over from generation to generation. Numbers 14:18 acknowledges this reality:

> The LORD is slow to anger,
> and abounding in steadfast love,
> forgiving iniquity and transgression,
> but by no means clearing the guilty,
> visiting the iniquity of the parents
> upon the children
> to the third and the fourth generation.

To be open to others means we use discernment when we reach out to those who, through no fault of their own, find themselves in need of open hearts, open minds, and open doors.

Perhaps forgiving debt is, for all intents and purposes, unworkable in our complex economic world. President Truman purportedly responded to the contradictory reports from the world's best economic advisors by saying, "[the economists say] 'On the one hand . . . , but on the other hand. . . .' What I need is a one-handed economist!" However, it is worth considering Israel's suggestion that when people opened themselves and relaxed their hands from around the throats of those in debt, maybe God could also fill those empty, open hands with good things.

The problem is that when people are open to others, especially in other's need, then we become vulnerable, exposed, and at risk. In other words, when we put ourselves in a place to be taken advantage of by another human being, then we look a lot like Jesus did on the cross. After all, playing it safe means playing it by yourself. If we need reminding of one of the gateway qualities to abundant life, then perhaps we can see a pillar named "openness." Amen. (David N. Mosser)

MAY 1, 2005

Sixth Sunday of Easter

Worship Theme: We need not despair when we come to the hard spots in life, or even when we stand in the valley of the shadow of death. Jesus has already been wherever we may be. He stands on the other side of sorrow and pain, darkness and doubt to show us the way.

Readings: Acts 17:22-31; 1 Peter 3:13-22; John 14:15-21

Call to Worship (Psalm 66:8-9, 16-20)

> *Leader:*   Bless our God, O peoples, let the sound of his praise be heard,
>
> **People: who has kept us among the living, and has not let our feet slip.**
>
> *Leader:*   Come and hear, all you who fear God, and I will tell what he has done for me.
>
> **People: I cried aloud to him, and he was extolled with my tongue.**
>
> *Leader:*   If I had cherished iniquity in my heart, the Lord would not have listened.
>
> **People: But truly God has listened; he has given heed to the words of my prayer.**
>
> *All:*   **Blessed be God, because he has not rejected my prayer or removed his steadfast love from me!**

Pastoral Prayer:

Dear God, Creator and Preserver of life, we come to dedicate ourselves today to the mighty propositions of faith and lifestyle to which you have called us. We remember that you have counseled us to seek no more security than daily bread, so help us with our unreasonable worry about tomorrow. We remember, O Lord that you called us to seek no greater stature, and power, and place than that of a servant, so help us deal with unrighteous ambition and the struggle for power over the lives of others. We remember, O Lord, that you have warned us not to attach ourselves to the things of this world, lest we come to the end of our lives having accumulated things we cannot take with us, and that we will leave to loved ones whom we have ignored in order to accumulate. We remember, O Lord, that you told us that it is all right to die, because we will be perfectly safe in your hands, so save us from unhealthy fears about when and how we will pass through the gate through which we all will someday pass. In the name of Jesus. Amen. (Thomas Lane Butts)

SERMON BRIEFS

WILL THE REAL GOD PLEASE STAND UP?

ACTS 17:22-31

It seems that religions and gods are a dime a dozen these days. An Internet search of the term *religions* yielded more than two million websites. And people are searching. In these uncertain times, people are looking for answers, for help, for something to believe in. In a time when scripture is seen as archaic and irrelevant and mainline churches are declining, what can be said of Christianity? Why would or should anyone choose Christ from among the vast list of choices? Is our God the real god? If so, how can we proclaim this god with integrity and faithfulness?

We are not the first to ask these questions and share this struggle. Our text for today finds Paul in similar circumstances. Paul, a missionary who started churches all over Asia Minor in the first century, was not always a Christian believer. Originally named

Saul and born and raised a faithful Jew, he was one of Christianity's earliest and most vigorous persecutors. Early in his life it was his passionate goal to wipe out this group of Jesus followers. How did he go from persecutor to proclaimer and why?

For Paul, it began with a personal experience with the living God. One day, as he was traveling, a light from heaven flashed around him, and he heard the voice of Jesus speaking to him. Temporarily blinded by his encounter with God, he was led to Damascus where he waited for three days. God called Ananias, a frightened but obedient follower of Jesus, to go and minister to Paul. During this encounter, Paul regained his sight and was baptized into the faith. After a time of learning and study, the unlikely convert began traveling, proclaiming the gospel to anyone who would listen.

Paul had been changed by his encounter with the Lord. Not all of us have such dramatic experiences, however, as it was with the group of academics. These philosophers Paul encountered in Athens, a city full of diverse religions. This group was curious about a "new religion" Paul proclaimed. In order for a new god to take up residence in Athens, three things were required. First, the sponsor must claim to represent a deity. Second, he must provide evidence that the deity wants to live in the city. And finally, the deity's residence in Athens must benefit the Athenians (Robert Wall, *Acts–First Corinthians*, vol. 10 of *The New Interpreter's Bible* [Nashville: Abingdon Press, 2002], p. 245). The philosophers wanted to know about Paul's god and his intent for their city.

Paul's response is a classic piece of rhetoric. First, he complements his hearers, "You are so religious you even worship unknown gods!" Then, he lays out a reasoned argument that God, as made known to us through Jesus Christ, is the god that they seek. This god is transcendent, so a residence in Athens is not necessary. But this god is also imminent, wanting instead to reside in the hearts of all who are willing. The text tells us that some scoffed at Paul, but that others believed.

So it will be with us, those of us who have come to know Christ and wish to share the gospel with others. In some instances, classical arguments such as Paul's may be appropriate. In other cases, more innovative approaches may be needed. But the truth remains, no matter how convincing the argument or how innovative the method, committing to Christ is a matter of faith. The real God will not stand up in the way that we would like. We are called to trust and believe by faith. The real God will not solve all of our problems or make our lives easy as many would wish. Instead, the real God promises love and grace and strength for the journey. This we can claim with integrity and faithfulness. (Tracy Hartman)

CONSTRUCTIVE REVENGE

1 PETER 3:13-22

The Gentile Christians of Asia Minor were undergoing persecution and slander even though they were trying to live a good life as disciples of Jesus. The author of 1 Peter encouraged the early Christians to stand strong in their faith even though they suffered for it.

But how do you respond to evil when you have suffered wrongly? "With gentleness and reverence" you make your defense (v. 16). From the beginning, Christians have been called to "turn the other cheek," rather than repay evil for evil. But that does not mean when evil is aggressive we should just accept what happens to us. We are called to speak up in truth and with love. We resist evil, but with "gentleness and reverence." There is no better example of this kind of response than the Civil Rights movement in America led by Martin Luther King, Jr. and the movement led by Mohandas K. Gandhi in India. Both called for people to stand against evil, but not return evil for evil.

Laura Blumenfeld says that the way to respond to slander and persecution is with "constructive revenge" (Laura Blumenfeld, *Revenge: A Story of Hope* [New York: Simon & Schuster, 2002]). Her father was an Orthodox rabbi who, in 1984, was shot in the old streets of Jerusalem by a Palestinian. He was a random target of terrorism. Fortunately, the bullet only grazed his head, and he received a superficial wound. However, Laura wanted to respond to what had happened to her father. Ten years later she went to Israel and found the family of the man who had tried to kill her father. She did not tell this Palestinian family who she was or that she was Jewish. The man, Omar Katib, who had tried to assassinate her father was now in prison. Over the next year, Laura got close to Omar and his family and got to know them as human beings and let them get to know her. She posed as a reporter doing a story about the oppression of Palestinian people. She told the family and Omar about David Blumenfeld, the man he had tried to assassinate, without letting on that he was her father. She wanted them to get to know more about her father as a person. It would be Omar who would later say, "People are so different when you get to know them from near." Laura would finally reveal her true identity to Omar and his family when Omar was standing trial. The judges were deciding if Omar should get out of prison early, and Laura and her mother went and spoke on Omar's behalf. Through the experience, the Blumenfelds and the Katibs have not just reconciled, they have become friends. The way of love is stronger than hate and is our only hope for a world of peace. (Robert Long)

MORE THAN A MEMORY

JOHN 14:15-21

A good friend of mine lost her father when she was very young. She scarcely remembers him. Consequently, when she had her own children, one of her greatest fears was that her own children would have to grow up without her. She feared that if something happened to her, her children would not remember her, just as she did not remember her own father. Thankfully, her children grew up and her fear never became reality, but as a young mother, it was terrifying for her to consider this possibility. She realized that perhaps even as great as the pain of losing someone is, it is even worse to not remember.

Today's text is part of the farewell discourse of Jesus to his disciples. By this time, he had already eaten the Passover meal with them, washed their feet, and even predicted Judas's betrayal and Peter's denial. He had comforted them with the early verses of chapter 14. Verses 15 and following give the first teaching regarding the coming of the Holy Spirit. Throughout this farewell cycle, Jesus is sensitive to the disciples' sadness and fear over his impending death. Inasmuch as Jesus had been their teacher and leader, he had also been their friend. They were affected greatly by the reality that they were not going to be together on earth much longer. Mindful of their feelings, Jesus acknowledges in this passage that, though he is leaving them in this life, there will be one to follow him who will be with them forever. Jesus tells them that he will send them an Advocate. The term *advocate* takes on various meanings including support, counsel, comfort, and exhortation (Gerald L. Borchert, *John,* in *The Gospels.* Vol. 6 of *Mercer Commentary on the Bible.* Edited by Watson E. Mills and Richard F. Wilson [Macon: Mercer University Press, 1996], p. 207). Jesus was assuring them that, though he would not be there with them any longer, they would not be alone. God was going to be with them in a way like never before. In this passage, Jesus divulges very little specific detail regarding the Holy Spirit, although the latter part of this chapter explores a second Advocate saying.

It is hard to imagine how receptive the disciples were to this concept. It would not be long of course until they received the life-changing Holy Spirit. Although the concept of the Holy Spirit is a familiar concept at least in some form to most mainstream Christians, it is not without mystery. The disciples probably experienced that same mystery. Yet, this is what Jesus offered them in his place. Jesus offers this Advocate or Paraclete as a source of comfort and presence for the disciples. They would not be alone. They would not worry about their memories of him, because through the Spirit, Jesus would be present with them. What a wonderful gift!

I think that many Christians are intimidated by the Holy Spirit. Affected by the various interpretations of the Spirit, its manifestation, and purpose, it is no wonder that many Christians nearly ignore this part of the story altogether. Yet, the Holy Spirit was an intentional part of Jesus' message. It was the final wonderful part of his story. You see, he did not come to change this world for that one certain time period. Jesus' presence is not just experienced by those select few two millennia ago. On the contrary, his life changing message and presence are timeless gifts through the

Holy Spirit. We have access to Jesus in a personal, tremendous way, although we will never experience him in the flesh. During this season, do not ignore the whole story. Do not bid the Christ farewell at the end of the Easter season only to reintroduce yourselves at Advent. This year, grasp the real Christ and feel his life-changing presence through the great Advocate. (Tracey Allred)

MAY 8, 2005

Seventh Sunday of Easter

Worship Theme: We are members of the family of God. God is on our side. Do not fear the ultimate outcome of things in this world or the next.

Readings: Acts 1:6-14; 1 Peter 4:12-14; 5:6-11; John 17:1-11

Call to Worship (Psalm 68:1-6 RSV)

> *Leader:*   Let God arise, let his enemies be scattered; let those who hate him flee before him!
>
> **People:**   **As smoke is driven away, so drive them away; as wax melts before fire, let the wicked perish before God!**
>
> *Leader:*   But let the righteous be joyful; let them exult before God; let them be jubilant with joy!
>
> **People:**   **Sing to God, sing praises to his name; lift up a song to him who rides upon the clouds; his name is the LORD, exult before him!**
>
> *Leader:*   Father of the fatherless and protector of widows is God in his holy habitation.
>
> **People:**   **God gives the desolate a home to dwell in; he leads out the prisoners to prosperity; but the rebellious dwell in a parched land.**

Pastoral Prayer:

Dear God, Father, Mother, Parent of all Creation, we know that we belong to you and are beloved to you as if there were no other. We pray for the families in our church, and the many families in our lives, as well as for the family to which we so intimately belong. We confess the ups and downs, the tensions and struggles that characterize any growing family. Save us from shame that we are not perfect, and help us to find in the struggle to adjust to one another the grace to grow beyond littleness with those we love. Save us from discouragement with our families. Save us from the fear that we have made mistakes of such magnitude with our children that they will not recover from our errors. Save us from giving in to the feeling that important relationships have drifted too far or have been broken too badly to ever be repaired again. May this be a day of joy for families everywhere. In the name of Jesus. Amen. (Thomas Lane Butts)

SERMON BRIEFS

PLUG INTO THE POWER

ACTS 1:6-14

Have you ever had that dream? You know the one. It is Saturday night; you go to bed with a convoluted message jogging through your head. Suddenly you wake up and realize that the sun is shining brightly and all the clocks are flashing. It is that flashing clock that will get you every time. We all know what that means. The power has been out sometime in the night, the alarm was not able to function, and the early service has already started. Does that happen to you?

It finally became a reality for me. The power went out. I woke up from my typical fitful Saturday slumber only to discover the clocks flashing 1:29 A.M. Fortunately, it was actually 4:30 A.M., and I still had plenty of time to get to church, but my heart still could stand a good jump start. Don't you just hate it when the power goes out?

When the resurrected Christ appeared to the disciples outside Jerusalem, he was only interested in one thing. He wasn't interested in talking about the restoration of Israel. He didn't want to discuss the days and the hour when the kingdom might arrive.

171

But he did want to talk about power. At the heart of the conversation was this message: Don't let the power go out!

He wanted the disciples to receive the full power of the Holy Spirit so they would be empowered to be the most effective witnesses possible. The kingdom will come, but Jesus is more interested in the transforming influence of a witness plugged into the power.

In fact, Jesus describes the process of kingdom development through the outward movement of the gospel. His core message that the kingdom is near will become reality through the faithfulness of this hub of faithful disciples.

Jesus' ascension into heaven adds an exclamation point to the message. Jesus will be exalted to the right hand of God (Heb. 1:3) leaving the disciples to carry the message to the ends of the earth.

The disciples regroup. They gather together in a spirit of worship and prayer to consider their experience with Jesus. Through the avenue of prayer, God launches them on the mission of increasing circles of ministry. The prayer experience plugs them into the power.

The same process is necessary today. God calls on faithful disciples to spread the word. But the word will not move forward on human energy alone. It is the power of the Holy Spirit that mobilizes and validates the message.

Our task today is to help ordinary people discover that same power that was available to the original disciples. We must point one another in the direction of the world. The task is clear but the method is sometimes elusive. At the heart is the spiritual reality that we cannot give away something we have not received. Where is your source of power? Are the lights flashing? Do you need to take time to reset and to be renewed? (Randy Jessen)

YOU'VE ALREADY BEEN BLESSED

1 PETER 4:12-14; 5:6-11

Times were hard for these new Gentile Christians in Asia Minor. They were trying to live as they felt Christ would have them to live, yet they were being slandered and persecuted by others.

Life was not easy and the author of 1 Peter knew that when times are bad it is easy to be overcome with fear. Then, as you start to worry you become paralyzed, and you stop doing the things you need to do. It becomes a negative spiral. Hard times cause us to worry and become depressed, which leads us to be tired and weak, and before we know it, we quit.

Thus the author reminds us, "Discipline yourselves, keep alert" (5:8). Don't worry, rather "cast all your anxiety on him, because he cares for you" (5:7). If we will look to God in these difficult times, Christ "will himself restore, support, strengthen, and establish you" (5:10).

Alvin and Calvin Harrison were identical twins. They were born in Orlando, Florida to a very young mother. Before long it was their grandmother who took them in and raised them. When they became teenagers, they decided to move out on their own, and they went to Salinas, California. They thought they had a job lined up, but it fell through and before long they found themselves homeless, out on the streets with no where to go. They became hungry. They had to sleep in their car. The first night they didn't think it was a big deal, surely something would work out soon. But one night turned into two and then into five. By the end of the third week, they began to give in to despair. They felt so alone, hopeless, tired, and broken. Calvin began praying that someone would come along and kill them because he just didn't feel like he had enough energy to try again. But before they left home, their grandmother had given them a New Testament, and since they had so much time on their hands, they started to read. Life had been hard, and now they felt defeated. But as they started to read the Bible, it was Calvin who said they had a reality check. The reality was that God had already blessed them. They were young; they were healthy; and they had good hands and good arms and good feet. They were blessed. They decided to trust God more and at the same time become disciplined, stay alert, get up and do something. It was that night that they began their journey back to life. The very next day they were looking at the want ads in the paper, and they found a job house painting. With money coming in, they soon had food to eat and a place to stay. Then they went and found a track coach. They had always enjoyed running track in high school and now they asked Coach Gary Shaw at Hartnell College to train them. After Coach Shaw saw them run, he agreed.

They worked during the day and trained at night. Five years later, Alvin and Calvin Harrison were on the United States Olympic Track Team in Sydney, Australia. They were on the 4 x 400-meter relay. The other members of the team were Andrew Pettigrew and Michael Johnson. When they came into the stadium for their race that night, everyone knew their story. It was the first time in history that twin brothers had run on the same relay team.

In the race Pettigrew and Johnson gave the United States a good beginning. The American team was in the lead when Calvin took the baton and ran the third leg. It was a tight race but the United States was still in the lead as he began to approach his brother, Alvin, to hand off the baton. Immediately one hundred twenty thousand people came to their feet all at once. They were shouting and screaming as Calvin handed that baton to Alvin, who ran for the gold. Five years earlier they were homeless and living in the back of a car. But Alvin and Calvin will tell you, that in the race back to life it all started when, in spite of hard times, they discovered that God cared for them. They became disciplined and trusted that Christ himself would restore, support, and strengthen them (Robyn Stern, "Go to Your Destiny by Alvin and Calvin Harrison," online: www.freshangles.com/xpressions/litbitz/articles/58.html). (Robert Long)

PRAYER FOR BRIGHT LIGHTS

JOHN 17:1-11

Whom does Jesus pray for in the seventeenth chapter of John's Gospel? Is it just for his twelve disciples? I do not believe it is a stretch to say his prayer is for all believers in Christ, not just the disciples. Jesus is returning to God. He is nearing the end of his earthly ministry. Soon, Judas will betray him and the events of his last week will quickly pass. With all that he will soon face, Jesus takes time to pray for those who will remain behind and follow his example.

Prayer is essential in our spiritual life to tune in to God's presence in our lives and the world. We should follow Jesus' example by praying for those around us that God will bless them and keep them. Too often, we pray and tell God what we want or what we need. We take our shopping list to God as if we were going to the grocery store. In addition, we may pray to God then continue with our busy lives not taking time to listen for God to respond. As I entered my first year of seminary, Dr. Glenn Hinson talked about the motions of prayer. He described us as radar receivers intercepting God's love rays. Hinson continued to say that we should become transmitters of God's love. "Ideally, you should become, as it were, a step-up transmitter. . . . To become a step-up transmitter of God's love energies, you as a human being made in the image of God would need to let God's love energies flow through you in your prayers and work and to add some of your own love energies to God's" (E. Glenn Hinson, *Spiritual Preparation for Christian Leadership* [Nashville: Upper Room Books, 1999], p. 41). Jesus is praying for his followers to receive his teachings and to pass these teachings on to others.

Jesus says, "I have been glorified in them" (v. 10). John 1:5 states, "The light shines in the darkness, and the darkness did not overcome it." In John 8:12, Jesus proclaims, "I am the light of the world." The light has come into the world through Jesus, and Jesus passes the light to the disciples. The amazing truth of Christianity is that the light of the world has continued to burn brightly in the hearts of the faithful for more than two thousand years. Throughout history, people have tried to extinguish the light, but they have not been successful. The light of the world glorifies believers in Jesus Christ so that they shine brilliantly in the world. The light passes down from believer to believer as God continues to work in the world. Like prayer, the light of the world increases as we add our love to God's love and share the light with the world. A match lit in a very dark forest shines brightly, but only for a short time. If that match lights a few logs, that light may last a little longer. When we ignite a few trees, we begin to start a bigger light. Scientists say that satellites in outer space can see forest fires. Let us share God's love with the world. Let the light of Christ shine bright in the darkness. (John Mathis)

MAY 15, 2005

Day of Pentecost

Worship Theme: Pentecost is a timely reminder to all who trust in their own power and skill that the Bible teaches us: It is "not by might, nor by power, but by my spirit, saith the LORD" (Zech. 4:6 KJV). "They that wait upon the LORD" (Isa. 40:31 KJV).

Readings: Acts 2:1-21; 1 Corinthians 12:3*b*-13; John 7:37-39

Call to Worship (Psalm 104:24-27, 31, 33-34 RSV)

Leader: O LORD, how manifold are thy works! In wisdom hast thou made them all; the earth is full of thy creatures.

People: **Yonder is the sea, great and wide, which teems with things innumerable, living things both small and great.**

Leader: There go the ships, and Leviathan which thou didst form to sport in it.

People: **These all look to thee, to give them their food in due season.**

Leader: May the glory of the LORD endure for ever, may the LORD rejoice in his works,

People: **I will sing to the LORD as long as I live; I will sing praise to my God while I have being.**

All: **May my meditation be pleasing to him, for I rejoice in the LORD.**

Pastoral Prayer:

Dear God, Father and Mother of us all, we confess how we have trusted too much in our own knowledge, skill, and power in the work of your kingdom in the church. We have believed if anything good happens in our lives and in the life of the church, it will be because of human effort. Forgive us our illusions of power and competence. Save us from the failures that come when we place our confidence in human effort and forget the power of your Spirit in and among us. We confess that in our better moments we realize that we are channels of power, not the source. May we have more frequent "better moments," for the sake of your kingdom on earth. Amen. (Thomas Lane Butts)

SERMON BRIEFS

IT'S PENTECOST! BUT WHAT DIFFERENCE DOES IT MAKE?

ACTS 2:1-21

Today is Pentecost Sunday, but what does that mean for us? Churches and denominations everywhere have disagreed for centuries over the importance of Pentecost, but it is one of the three major holidays in the church year, along with Christmas and Easter. In fact, it's the oldest of the three. Yet many Christians are frightened of, or virtually ignore, this celebration of the gift of the Holy Spirit. We see in Acts 2 that strange things happened on that first Day of Pentecost. Surprisingly, we have the uneducated disciples breaking into foreign tongues.

Admittedly, Pentecost is not very bourgeois, and many withdraw from it, perhaps in reaction to others who insist Christians speak in tongues to demonstrate their giftedness. Yet, as Christians, our calendar is *full* of improbable celebrations. Throughout the year, we talk a great deal about resurrection from the dead, eternal life, virgin births, and God coming to earth in the form of a servant. In light of the other bold claims of the church, why should Pentecost shock us?

177

Pentecost's relative obscurity plays out in the rest of society, too. Of all the places I like to visit, I'm most attracted to New York and the many things to do and see there. I love New York so much that I don't even think twice about the commercialization of Christmas while I do my December shopping at Macy's. Last May, as I was on vacation, I sat in a Manhattan coffee shop while writing a sermon for Pentecost Sunday. As I watched the New Yorkers scurry past the window, I wondered if these busy folks had any idea that Pentecost was approaching. There were no signs in store shops about Pentecost sales, no special lights decorating midtown, no giant tree at Rockefeller Center.

No one, in all the churches I've served, has ever given me a gift in order to celebrate our oldest Christian holiday. I often point out that many in our society spend a great deal of time mocking the church and its bold claims about resurrection and virgin births. Yet, when Christmas and Easter roll around everybody seems to want to jump on board. But who wants to jump on board at Pentecost? Certainly, "the world" that we are so quick to critique and its lack of reaction to Pentecost can be linked to *the church*. Do *we* know what to do with it? So many names—Paraclete, Comforter, Holy Ghost, Wind, Fire, and Guide—have been used to describe this elusive third person of the Trinity. God, in and through the Holy Spirit, does so much, and we understand and comprehend so little. Yet we believe that the Spirit has enlightened us, and so do those who celebrated the first Pentecost.

Most of us have attempted to learn a foreign language, and perhaps that is why we are so intrigued with what so many ordinary people experienced on that day in Jerusalem. But, returning to the text, we return and find that speaking in tongues is not the only miracle that occurred there. The second miracle, the one more of us can relate to, is sometimes forgotten because of the power and impossibility of the first. Pentecost is also about the miracle of twelve ordinary people who spoke a message of boldness. The disciples, who had been excited but frightened since Easter, spoke bravely and publicly about the grace and love of God. They challenged people to dream, to have visions inspired by God, and to proclaim these visions—to pour them out as liberally as the Spirit was poured out to them.

This is why we celebrate Pentecost. Through God's Holy Spirit, we who are ordinary have been empowered to do marvelous things. As Acts proclaims, the elderly and the young can ponder what it might be like to live in a world of harmony. We can take the gospel of Jesus to the busy streets of New York. We can take the love and hope provided by Jesus to the apartment complex behind our sanctuary.

We don't need a seminary degree or ordination to love our neighbors. As Christians, we have the gift of the Holy Spirit to embolden us, to empower us to do what we might not do otherwise. (Scott Bullard)

THE GIFTED!

1 CORINTHIANS 12:3*b*-13

Throughout the book of 1 Corinthians, the apostle Paul addresses a hurting, struggling church. As he moves through his instructions and insights, he comes to a three-chapter segment, chapters 12, 13, and 14, in which he delves into the topic of spiritual gifts. Often we just read the thirteenth chapter. Yet for Paul, that is only the centerpiece and not the sum of the whole. With steadily mounting force, his argument is that you and I are the gifted! It is not based on our goodness or our merit but on God's gracious giving.

While our passage begins at verse 3, it must be read in the context of verse 1. "Now concerning spiritual gifts, brothers and sisters, I do not want you to be uninformed." Most of us would rather be called sinners than ignorant, yet it is easy to miss an essential biblical truth about being Christian. Simply put, according to the Bible, if you confess "Jesus is Lord," you are gifted!

The first point of a sermon might well focus on an understanding of the work of the Holy Spirit in our lives. Through the Holy Spirit, we confess that "Jesus is Lord." We are not gifted based on our goodness, merit, or hard work but through the Spirit's grace.

Verses 4 through 7 forcefully draw our attention to the reason for spiritual gifts. They are for the common good. Verse 7 acts as a summary. "To each is given the manifestation of the Spirit for the common good." In a deeper sense, there is a twin focus here. Each of us is gifted, and the gifts are for the common good. In this one seminal verse, a blow is struck against low self-esteem (which would believe everyone else is gifted but me), and a blow is struck against any pretensions that spiritual gifts are given for private enjoyment.

I suspect we often fail to perceive ourselves as gifted, because we mistakenly apply this notion of ministry and spiritual gifts only to the clergy. The British army even exempted the clergy from enlistment on their recruiting poster for World War I. We laugh, but all too often the reverse perception is mistakenly held that ministry belongs to the clergy. Biblical reality is far different. Jesus used a number of parables to speak of everyone using their talents or gifts for the work of the Lord. Enshrined in the Protestant Reformation is the principle of the priesthood of all believers. "Now there are varieties of gifts, but the same Spirit; and there are varieties of services, but the same Lord" (vv. 4-5).

In the following verses, each gift is explicitly described as a gift of the Holy Spirit. Thus verse 8 reads: "To one is given through the Spirit the utterance of wisdom, and to another the utterance of knowledge according to the same Spirit." Furthermore, the list of gifts in verses 8 through 10 is only the beginning. There are a number of other biblical lists of spiritual gifts. Some scholars are convinced that Paul deliberately leaves the list open-ended by way of demonstrating that there are many gifts and that all of God's people are gifted.

One afternoon while viewing Boston Harbor from an overlook, I was fortunate to watch a race of large sailing ships. As they rounded a buoy marking the course, the wind caught the vessels directly from behind. With precision, accuracy, and speed, the crews unfurled a sail on the bow, which billowed outward catching the wind. Such was the power of the sail catching the wind that the ships almost leaped forward in the water.

This is a reflection of the image Paul unfolds for us in this passage. All are gifted! That means all of us are gifted for the work of ministry! This is the presence, the manifestation or making known, of the Holy Spirit's presence in our lives both individually and as a community of faith.

One of the ancient symbols for the Christian church was a ship with its sails unfurled. Such is the image for any church when we employ our spiritual gifts properly. We surge forward catching the full wind of the Holy Spirit. It can only happen with the helmsman and the crew working in graceful precision as they accomplish the mission entrusted. We know the helmsman; it is Jesus our Lord. Jesus' wind, the wind of the Holy Spirit, gusts across our community calling us to unfurl our sails.

Using verse 7 as the key verse, a sermon could be built on three points: (1) Spiritual gifts are a work of the Holy Spirit; (2) All are gifted; (3) Our gifts are to be used for the common good. (Mike Lowry)

THE GREAT DAY

JOHN 7:37-39

In preaching about the Holy Spirit we must not give the impression that there is more than one God or that God is divided in any way. It's easy to make the Spirit sound like a lesser version of Christ or a loose cannon on the deck of God's covenant ark. Spirit is simply a convenient way of speaking of the post-resurrection active reality of God in our world, the same reality that indwelled Jesus, Emmanuel. It would be best not to make it sound like the Spirit is Jesus-lite or God's email.

Augustine said that within each person is a God-shaped void. Only God can fit there, and a person is not whole unless that empty place is filled. This void is not completely filled without all the pieces of the Trinity: Creator, Christ, and Spirit. The gift of the Spirit rounds out the soul.

The Spirit gives life. That's the main preaching point of this text. Just as the body cannot live without water, the person cannot live without Spirit. Water is an especially powerful symbol in an arid country. Water figures often and prominently in the Gospels, as in the story of the woman at the well in John 4. Because water is so important, Jesus refers to himself as water for the soul, the one who quenches the thirst of human need.

We must be careful not to overdo a metaphor, even a sacramental one like water. In spiritual matters, water is a symbol. Too much water creates a swamp or a flood. I heard this story from George Buttrick and I think he told it on himself. Someone once told a pastor, "Your sermons are like water to a drowning man." Not good!

The sin against the Holy Spirit is the one unforgivable sin because it is the very refusal to accept life. We shall surely die if we refuse the Spirit.

Receiving the Spirit is simple: Believe in Jesus, come to Christ and drink. There are many different ways to receive the Spirit. The purpose of the Spirit is not to make us the same but to make us whole, to give us a bucket so we can drink from the well of Christ. Jesus dealt with many different types of people, but he didn't change their personalities. The only way he changed them was to make them whole.

In *The Hoosier Schoolmaster,* Edward Eggleston tells of how the town bully got saved at a revival meeting. He came to the schoolmaster and said, "I don't know what to do now. I always prided myself on getting my best licks in. That's who I am." The schoolmaster told him, "Now you put your best licks in for Christ."

This is an important preaching point because there will be people who think they can't or have not received the Spirit because they haven't had a particular kind of experience. Don't limit the Spirit by saying one doesn't have it without certain experiences or vocabularies.

Filling the bucket: How does one receive the gift of the Spirit? There's no simple or magical way to fill the bucket; you just do it one spoonful at a time. Read the Bible, especially the Gospels. Pray. Actor Dick Van Dyke says he conquered alcoholism by praying. Meditate. Worship. Learn from others, in reading or song or in person. (John Robert McFarland)

MAY 22, 2005

Trinity Sunday

Worship Theme: We are fragmented persons, living in a fragmented world, but we find security and wholeness in the perfect unity of God as Parent, Son, and Holy Spirit.

Readings: Genesis 1:1–2:4*a*; 2 Corinthians 13:11-13; Matthew 28:16-20

Call to Worship (Psalm 8:1, 3-9 RSV)

> *Leader:* O LORD, our Lord, how majestic is thy name in all the earth!
>
> *People:* **When I look at thy heavens, the work of thy fingers, the moon and the stars which thou hast established;**
>
> *Leader:* What is man that thou art mindful of him, and the son of man that thou dost care for him?
>
> *People:* **Yet thou hast made him little less than God, and dost crown him with glory and honor.**
>
> *Leader:* Thou hast given him dominion over the works of thy hands; thou hast put all things under his feet,
>
> *People:* **All sheep and oxen, and also the beasts of the field, the birds of the air, and the fish of the sea, whatever passes along the paths of the sea.**
>
> *All:* **O LORD, our Lord, how majestic is thy name in all the earth!**

Pastoral Prayer:

Holy, invisible, and all-powerful God in whose kingdom time, as we know it, is relative and sometimes without meaning as we understand it; we, who are always in a hurry, come today, seeking a glimpse of your timely and timeless kingdom of truth. With a boldness born of at least a casual acquaintance with Jesus, we, who are such powerless, earthbound creatures, shackled with ignorance and of limited vision, pray for some meaningful contact with you, the unknowable God of a universe beyond our imagination and our knowledge. If we are brash, it is not because of irreverence, it is because we are friends of a savior who has convinced us that he not only knows you well but also is your son. It is in his name that we pray today. Show us, O God, as much of your purpose as we can stand to know. Include us in your mysteries so that we may participate even in things we do not understand. We do not pray for unlimited knowledge, but we pray for enough knowledge to save us from unlimited ignorance and for faith to fill in our empty spaces. Amen. (Thomas Lane Butts)

SERMON BRIEFS

GOATS-ON-A-ROPE

GENESIS 1:1–2:4*a*

In 1999, scientists in Tokyo were attempting to "create a viable artificial womb, a system to sustain a developing infant," by using a fetal goat and an acrylic tank. At the time, they were able to "keep their goats-on-a-rope alive for up to ten days" (Natalie Angier, "Baby in a Box," *New York Times,* Sunday, May 16, 1999, sec. 6, p. 86).

A *Star Trek* episode of forty years ago might have wondered about such children, ripened in mechanical wombs. Would they be materially different in their humanity from their genetic parents? And suppose they had no true genetic parents. Suppose, instead, their genes were individually chosen from a catalog at the baby farm. It's not quite so far-fetched a scenario as it once was. Indeed, it's very near to possible within the lifetimes of many of us. And the question this impending "advance" begs has never been more relevant: What does it mean to be human?

After creating everything else, our tradition thunders that

> God created humankind in his image,
> in the image of God he created them;
> male and female he created them. (Gen. 1:27)

The echo resounds within church walls and human hearts: We have been created in God's image, the *imago dei*. Among the ideas theologians have posited for this remarkable insight include humanity's ability to reason with intellectual faculties, our knowledge of self, and our originative powers. Whenever we engage our creative capacities we participate in reflected divinity. That is part of God's own self: creative power. We share in that, and it is part of our glory.

Years ago I heard a minister paraphrase the theologian Pierre Teilhard de Chardin: "We are collaborators in creation. What you and I are becoming, the world is becoming." This has the ring of truth. And it has the ring of grave danger.

We are not the prime originators. We take what has already been given and manipulate it through talents that have also been given. We are the beneficiaries of a surfeit of riches. Precisely because we are so clever with the bounty set before us, we are easily distracted from our truest work, that is, consciously reflecting God's glory. As Genesis puts it, God said the whole of creation was originally very good. Unfortunately, what has become very bad in the world seems most often to wear a human face.

While God's creation was decisive, it was not conclusive. In other words, as the story is told, the work of creation once begun is yet to be completed. We enter the picture after the beginning and before the end. So our work is creation work, but it is creation work that already has a model, intended movement, and direction.

Entering these early years of the twenty-first century, one has the feel of standing on the edge of "the final frontier" in many arenas of human endeavor. At the least, each one of us who reads these words stands at the frontier of our individual lives. The future rushes in on us at an alarming rate. Never have the stakes seemed so high and the responsibilities so awesome. Our birthright is too magnificent to squander or misapply. (Stephen Bauman)

ONE GOD, ONE PEOPLE

2 CORINTHIANS 13:11-13

Trinity Sunday is always one of the most difficult Sundays to preach. As important as it is to educate congregations on the theological doctrines that form the heart of the Christian faith, I find myself struggling with how to make this doctrine relevant to everyday life. It is so easy for me to get swept up in the intellectual arguments and explanations, that I lose sight of the gifts that are bestowed to us in this rich understanding of the Godhead.

In Paul's letters to the Corinthian church, his primary concern is for the internal health of this congregation. There were apparently many tensions within the church body and some divisiveness had arisen over time. Paul writes these Christians to help resolve some of these differences, reminding them of the call of Christ on their lives. Paul encourages them to treat one another with love and respect, and in these closing lines of Second Corinthians, he offers them a blessing or prayer for their restored unity.

Many scholars have noted that this blessing is the longest and most detailed of Paul's benedictions. This extended benediction can help guide the preacher toward a more concrete, pastoral understanding of the importance of the Trinity. As Ernest Best notes, "It is not a deliberate theological construction intended to teach the threefold nature of God and the relation of the Father, Son, and Holy Spirit to one another. The emphasis lies on grace, love, and fellowship as three things for which Paul prays for the Corinthians" (Ernest Best, *Second Corinthians, Interpretation: A Bible Commentary for Teaching and Preaching* [Louisville: John Knox Press, 1987], pp. 136-37).

Perhaps the best way for us to approach a sermon about the Trinity is to reflect on how this understanding of God helps us to better understand ourselves and how God works in and through us. In the three persons of the Trinity, the Godhead is most fully revealed. We can reflect on God, who created us and sustains us in love. We can reflect on Jesus, who came to reveal God in the fullness of time by offering us redeeming grace through his death. We can reflect on the Holy Spirit, God's indwelling presence in each of us, which brings us into a closer relationship with God and one another. Each of these persons of the Trinity highlights an important component of who God is, has been, and will be in the lives of those God loves.

Perhaps the unity of God within the Trinity speaks to the unity that the people of God should have within their communities. By reminding us of the gifts God has given to us, we are encouraged to focus on those things that unite us rather than divide us. In a world currently divided over cultural, ethnic, and doctrinal differences, what more healing words can the church offer than love, grace, and peace? Do these not belong to us all in the fullness of God?

Paul blesses his community and reminds them that they are God's beloved children. They have received the grace of Christ in their lives. Each is called to live in the peace through the gift of the Holy Spirit. The fullness of these gifts is a persuasive argument. It covers every possible division with a reminder of those things that we must agree upon in our common life. Sometimes the most pastoral response to a troubled congregation is a reminder of who we belong to and who we are called to be in light of God's goodness. (Wendy Joyner)

A PROMISE FULFILLED

MATTHEW 28:16-20

A promise is made. Children are born to the old and barren. People are delivered out of captivity. A nation is born. A prophet speaks of hope and light amid a world of despair and darkness. A messiah is born. Yet the promise seems to remain largely unfulfilled. The final fulfillment of the promise continues to challenge our thinking. The promise is of something phenomenal. Even today, we still cannot fathom what it would be like if it were fulfilled.

The promise is the one made to Abraham: "Now the LORD said to Abram, 'Go from your country and your kindred and your father's house to the land that I will show you.... I will bless those who bless you, and the one who curses you I will curse; and in you all the families of the earth shall be blessed'" (Gen. 12:1, 3).

It is not just the promise of land or national identity; it is a promise that the entire world will be blessed through Abraham. Matthew tells us that it is now time. In many ways, the partially fulfilled promise had become little more than a fond memory in the museum of the human mind. But Jesus, the descendant of Abraham, took the promise from the shelf, breathed new life into it, and sent his followers into the world to fulfill the promise.

We are those sent into the world to make disciples and invite people into a relationship with this God on whose promises we rely. We are to baptize people "in the name of the Father and of the Son and of the Holy Spirit" (v. 19). This baptism brings with it an initiation into a new fellowship and a new place of belonging. We belong to this multifaceted God whose plan of salvation is now being worked in us.

We are also challenged to teach and instruct people in the ways of Christian living. We do not bring people into a fellowship of faith and then set them loose without thorough instruction on precisely what it means to be a disciple. It is important that this commission is not asking us to establish just one more Bible study or class on Christian discipleship. It is challenging us to be in relationship with people and let our relationships themselves foster the environment where the new believer (or sometimes even the old believer) eagerly soaks up the teachings of this Messiah of hope.

I heard a United Methodist missionary once address this issue. When asked how it was that she found ways to effectively share her faith in a place heavily influenced by the Muslim faith, she responded that she did so by being in relationship with people and listening as they were given a place to tell their own stories. When people feel they have been heard and are in relationship, then they are much more receptive to hearing the witness of their new friend.

Do not be deceived, however, into thinking that the promise is wholly contingent on us. Jesus' final words remind us that it is not by our own power that disciples are made. Disciples are made by the power and authority of Christ himself. The ultimate fulfillment of the promise made to Abraham comes in Christ himself. Christ is the blessing to all the world, and it is finally through Christ that we hear the voice of the psalmist: "O LORD, our Sovereign, / how majestic is your name in all the earth!" (Ps. 8:1). (Jeff Smith)

MAY 29, 2005

Second Sunday After Pentecost

Worship Theme: God is always gracious, reaching out to save us from the mess into which we have gotten ourselves. It is by faith, the gracious gift of God, that we are saved.

Readings: Genesis 6:11-22; 7:24; 8:14-19; Romans 1:16-17; 3:22*b*-28 (29-31); Matthew 7:21-29

Call to Worship (Psalm 46:1-7 RSV)

Leader: God is our refuge and strength, a very present help in trouble.

People: **Therefore we will not fear though the earth should change, though the mountains shake in the heart of the sea;**

Leader: Though its waters roar and foam, though the mountains tremble with its tumult.

People: **There is a river whose streams make glad the city of God, the holy habitation of the Most High.**

Leader: God is in the midst of her, she shall not be moved; God will help her right early.

People: **The nations rage, the kingdoms totter;**

All: **He utters his voice, the earth melts. The LORD of hosts is with us; the God of Jacob is our refuge.**

Pastoral Prayer:

Almighty God, by whose hand all that is came to be, and by whose inspiration good people of every age have been motivated to seek the common good by moving beyond the circumscribed boundaries of their own lives to touch the lives of others; we are grateful for the strength to love in the midst of hostility and indifference. We celebrate the sensitivity you have given us to hear the cries of others above the selfish bickerings of our own souls. We confess that we have sinned against the best that is in us. We have exploited for our selfish ends the gifts and talents that you gave us. Our sins are too numerous to name, but neither their number nor magnitude put them beyond forgiveness. We pray that when you have pronounced your forgiveness upon our sin that we will be as willing to let go as you are to forgive. Forgive us for not being willing to put as much distance between ourselves and our forgiven sin as you are willing to put, "as far as the east is from the west." In the name of Jesus. Amen. (Thomas Lane Butts)

SERMON BRIEFS

A TERRIFYING CHILDREN'S STORY

GENESIS 6:11-22; 7:24; 8:14-19

The account of Noah and the ark is one of the best-loved stories in the Bible. It is especially popular among children, in whose nurseries and picture books we see images of the ark and the "two-by-two" animals. Our culture—even the Christian culture—has made the story of Noah cute and appealing to people of all ages. Unfortunately, all of this hype makes Genesis 6–9 a difficult passage to preach. It is always hard to preach the popular texts, but it's especially challenging to preach a story that has been diluted and sugar-coated by the culture.

When we return to the story itself in Genesis 6–9, we remember how tragic and bleak life really is. We learn that humankind and their violent ways have broken God's heart (6:6). We witness not a God of second chances but a God who gets fed up, not a

191

God who creates but a God who destroys. We see all of humankind and all of life on the earth (including innocent plants and animals) blotted out. The only exception made to this destruction is Noah's family and two members of every animal species.

Where, then, is the good news to be found in this story? Certainly, the ark is good news to Noah and his family, but to no one else. Are we supposed to be happy for Noah and to rejoice in the destruction of so much life? Does the story encourage us to rejoice in our own salvation and not to care about the destruction of others? Does it teach us that God gives up on sinners? Do we come away believing that God has a short fuse?

Each preacher will have to seek the good news in this passage in his or her own way. Some may find it in the fact that God protects the righteous. The ark might be seen as a metaphor for God's care and providence as we navigate through a violent world, through temptation, or through tumultuous times in our own lives.

Others may focus on Noah and his righteousness. Genesis 6:9 tells us that Noah was a righteous man who "walked with God." What does it mean to walk with God? How do we nurture a daily relationship with God in our lives? What kind of spiritual disciplines can help us do that? Not only did Noah walk with God but he also remained faithful in a time of great wickedness in the world. How might we stay close to God when the world around us seems consumed with violence and corruption (6:11-12)? What believers need is the courage and commitment to follow the ways of God. How do we help our listeners find that faith?

In the search for good news in this passage, some preachers might look to what caused God's anger in the first place. God was grieved by the wickedness and violence of humankind. To be sure, it is not difficult to find examples of corruption and violence in our world today. Are there times even now when our ways break God's heart? What in our individual lives or in our world causes God to grieve? This passage invites such soul-searching. And when we identify where and how we fall short—as individuals, as a church, as a planet—we can confess our sins and repent. Surely then we will find forgiveness and hope.

Perhaps the easiest place to find good news in the Noah story is 8:21, which is not included in the week's lectionary selection. In this verse, God resolves never again to destroy the earth. The promise continues in chapter 9, when God makes a covenant with Noah. One can't help but wonder whether God has repented. Does God regret the destruction of the Flood? The answer to these questions must come out of the preacher's own understanding of God and of scripture. No matter how one resolves these issues, we have an assurance at the end of this story that ultimately God does not choose to be a God of destruction. We are promised the rainbow as a sign that God will never again give up on humankind. It is remarkable how much people need to hear that message again and again: God will not give up on you. We also know from this story that, despite God's anger in the past, God is committed to the earth and all its creatures. God has high hopes for us and for this world.

If God will not give up on us, then we are called to live up to God's hopes. If we do not want to break God's heart, then we are called to the righteousness of Noah. If we love God, then we are called to walk with God and move the world around us toward peace and reconciliation. (Carol Cavin-Dillon)

BOLD BUT NOT ARROGANT RELIGION

ROMANS 1:16-17; 3:22b-28 (29-31)

Can we be too bold about our faith? The ordinary answer we expect to hear in church is, "Of course not. After all, didn't Paul himself say in this passage, 'I am not ashamed of the gospel'?" It sometimes seems so hard to get folks to profess and certainly to demonstrate their faith that encouraging any expression of faith is important. We would do well, though, to consider more carefully Paul's testimony that he was "not ashamed of the gospel" (1:16).

The fact is that we live in a world where religion is misused to justify great evil. All over the world great conflicts are occurring that involve people who say they are engaging in this conflict because of their religion. These conflicts involve adherents of the great religions of our world, including Judaism, Islam, Hinduism, and Christianity. We Christians are not exempt from fighting among ourselves, either. The conflicts of our world also involve Christians engaging in physical conflict with Christians of another viewpoint. Furthermore, conflicts among Christians do not happen only beyond our borders. Hardly a Christian denomination is not now in internal conflict over something. Citing these conflicts does not suggest that there are no matters of principle and justice that are worthy of struggle. It is to suggest that sometimes our boldness in expressing our religious faith is misapplied.

Note that Paul said, "I am not ashamed of the gospel." We might state this another way and say that Paul was *proud* of the gospel. Paul's pride, though, was in the gospel, what God has done in Christ to bring "salvation to everyone who has faith" (1:16). Paul's pride was not in himself or in his own expression of the gospel. Indeed, Paul saw himself as "the foremost" of sinners (1 Tim. 1:15). Paul included himself in the statement, "all have sinned and fall short of the glory of God" (Rom. 3:23). Paul did not brag on himself, his heritage, and his achievements, but on the gospel.

Furthermore, this gospel was not merely for people like Paul but for all people, Greeks as well as Jews. Thus Paul sought to share the gospel—the good news—with all people rather than to use a narrow view of religion as a club to attack people who did not adhere to a particular set of beliefs.

Nothing about the gospel meant that Paul was superior to other people. In Paul's bold expression of his faith, he never forgot how far God had to come to redeem him. Paul did not call people to see how he had been able to lift himself up by his bootstraps. Rather, Paul called people to stand amazed at the greatness of God's utterly undeserved gift. Paul believed he belonged to God, not through Paul's efforts, though, but solely through God's grace "in Christ Jesus, whom God put forward as a sacrifice of atonement by his blood, effective through faith" (3:24-25).

Paul calls us to ask this question with him: "Then what becomes of boasting?" The answer for Paul and for us is, "It is excluded" (3:27).

We who claim to follow Christ can easily succumb to the mentality of our world and come to think that putting other people down is the way to lift up our way of life. Nothing could be further from Christian truth. Let us learn to recognize that we, like all human beings, come before God as sinners who in no way deserve God's mercy. Let us then seek to relate to one another first and foremost on the basis of God's love and not the notion of our superiority. We are to be bold about our recognition of God's mercy but humble about ourselves. (Ross West)

LOCATION, LOCATION, LOCATION

MATTHEW 7:21-29

Our preaching professor used to remind us students that every sermon needs a strong conclusion. While we were inclined to labor long and hard on our introductions, thinking, I guess, that if we didn't "hook" the listeners early we would lose them, he said that every bit as important was the conclusion. "If you don't 'bring it home,'" he said, "the sermon itself is lost."

Jesus ends the Sermon on the Mount with a "strong conclusion," to be sure, and one that is, quite frankly, frightening. It has the power to make us nervous and guilty, addressed as it is not to the crowds but to disciples, to those who would speak in Jesus' name and reprise his work, to those, indeed, who would claim him as "Lord." But "not everyone who says to me 'Lord, Lord,' will enter the kingdom of heaven," Jesus says; "only the one who does the will of my Father in heaven" (v. 21).

What we call the Sermon on the Mount is but the first of five major sections of teaching that Matthew has Jesus, the Teacher, presenting. This first sermon, however, sets the tone for all his subsequent instruction. He has seen the crowds; he knows the world; and he offers this sermonic charge that his disciples might be, as it were, the light of the world.

The sermon is full of statements and statutes, blessings and commands, indicatives and imperatives. And at the end comes this terrifying—and surprising—word, all the more surprising and terrifying because it is addressed to those nearest him on the mountain. This warning is directed to those he has called and those who have answered, who know the name that is bestowed on him, which is above every name.

Lord, Lord, they say. And they have the right words but not

the right works. They have done works, to be sure—and great ones in their own estimation—they have preached powerful sermons and exorcised powerful demons; they have done mighty things, and all in the name of Jesus. But it seems as if they have not done the first work or answered the first call.

In Mark's telling of it, Jesus' first call to the disciples is to "be with him" (Mark 3:14). The phrase suggests intimacy and friendship—exactly what is lacking here among the condemned in Matthew. "I never knew you; go away from me," Jesus says (v. 32). The same formula, from plea to judgment, will appear in Matthew 25 in the story of the ten bridesmaids. It begs the question, When called to serve Jesus, how do we ensure that we know him and are known by him?

Richard J. Foster quotes Mother Teresa, "Pray for me that I do not loosen my grip on the hands of Jesus, even under the guise if ministering to the poor." Foster concludes, "That is our first task: to grip the hand of Jesus with such tenacity that we are obliged to follow his lead, to seek first his Kingdom" (*Freedom of Simplicity: Finding Harmony in a Complex World* [San Francisco: HarperSanFrancisco, 1989]).

The denouement of the sermon suggests that the basic problem of the excluded disciples is that they let go of the hand of Jesus, that they did works in his name but for themselves. In short, they built their houses in a bad location, on a bad foundation, and when judgment came, they were judged indeed. Wise disciples know that the first rule of discipleship is "location, location, location," in all our work staying near to the heart and hand and will of God. In that way our discipleship itself will have a strong conclusion. (Thomas Steagald)

REFLECTIONS

JUNE

Reflection Verse: *"Surely this great nation is a wise and discerning people!" (Deuteronomy 4:6)*

DISCERNMENT: A WISDOM OBSERVED
Deuteronomy 4:5-8

Our series of pastoral meditations, "Twelve Pillars of Abundant Christian Living," examines a shadowy concept that the biblical writers often describe as the gift of discernment. Evidently this gift is a dear gift because 1 Kings 4:29 tells readers "God gave Solomon very great wisdom, discernment, and breadth of understanding as vast as the sand on the seashore." That is some gift!

Paul also pictures discernment as a gift; he calls it a "gift of the spirit." Writing to Corinth, Paul advises that, "Now there are varieties of gifts, but the same Spirit; and there are varieties of services, but the same Lord. . . . to [one the Lord gives] the working of miracles, to another prophecy, to another the discernment of spirits. . . . All these are activated by one and the same Spirit, who allots to each one individually just as the Spirit chooses" (1 Cor. 12:4-5, 10-11).

Long before Paul, however, Moses taught the people of Israel God's ordinances and statutes. In other words, Moses lifted up the Torah. Today we often think of Torah as "law," but its wider meaning concerns the teachings of God or God's instructions for holy and faithful living. To think of Torah as merely law discounts the concept of Torah, at least as Israel understood it. Deuteronomy tells its readers that Moses teaches Israel,

> You must observe [God's ordinances and statutes] diligently, for this will show your wisdom and discernment to the peoples, who, when they hear all these statutes, will say, "Surely this great nation

is a wise and discerning people!" For what other great nation has a god so near to it as the LORD our God is whenever we call to him? And what other great nation has statutes and ordinances as just as this entire law that I am setting before you today? (Deut. 4:6-7)

Discernment is the ability to understand things that are often obscure and ambiguous. Spiritual discernment is the ability to differentiate between the voice of God and other voices that persistently play in our minds. Spiritual discernment is spiritual discrimination, deciding between alternatives. Frequently when we employ discernment, it seems as if we experience a conversation going on in our heads. To discern something is to distinguish the voice of God competing with other voices we may hear.

We all have little voices that play inside our heads constantly. There is the voice that tells us as we sit before our mealtime plates, "Clean your plate." Another voice tells us when we contemplate rough talk, "Nice boys and girls do not speak like this." There is the voice that tells us when we screw up our courage to try something new, "You can't do this. It is too hard for you." Yet another voice reminds us when we come up with a new idea that, "You're not that smart." Most of us have voices speaking to us persistently. Christians believe that God does speak to us, but the question is, How do we distinguish between God's voice and other voices that may not be from God?

One way to understand the voice of God involves our perception of God and our experience of God. Perhaps this perspective appears too subjective, but for many people psychology and theology seem to meet at this moment of discernment. If our theology suggests God is judgmental, then the voice of God we hear will be disapproving. However, if we understand God as eternally loving and just, then perhaps we will hear God's voice as a benevolent voice. If we believe that God loves us, then we will hear a voice that calls forth the best from us and for us.

A second way to discern the voice of God from among other voices is through the spiritual discipline of prayer. People who pray regularly and frequently put themselves in the proper spiritual position to be better able to hear God. Through prayer people come to know God. The Protestant Reformers believed that individual believers could pray directly to God and that God could and would answer them directly.

Third, and this idea builds on the spiritual discipline of prayer, the more we pray the better we attune our ears to God's voice. We call prayer a spiritual discipline because genuine prayer takes obedience and strength of will. The more we pray the better we become at it. The better at prayer we become, then the more we practice it. We might think of the discipline of prayer like the discipline required to play a musical instrument. We can be intimidated when we hear experts play the instrument that we want to learn. Yet, in time, with ample good instruction and constant focused practice we become more and more proficient. Like learning to play an instrument, we quickly lose heart and give up if we pray thinking that we can never pray well enough.

Thus for God to give us the gift of spiritual discernment we must first trust that God will give us the gift. Then we practice a prayer life that allows God to speak to us. Finally, we continue in a regular regimen of practicing spiritual discernment until it becomes second nature. As Jesus said, "Let anyone with ears to hear listen" (Mark 4:23).

For Israel, the guide to discernment was Torah. If Israel meditates, prays, and follows Torah's precepts, then Israel will become wise, and that wisdom will in turn help develop Israel into a discerning people, a nation of priests.

Often discernment means that we search out God's voice in practice much like we try to hear the underlying meaning in the voices of people. After all, discernment is not a science so much as it is a spiritual art. Max DePree is a writer and chairs the board of directors of the Herman Miller Company, a leading name in the furniture industry for many years. DePree's father founded Herman Miller and related a story about one of the employees to his son who, in turn, shares it in his book, *Leadership Is an Art*. In Herman Miller's early days, millwrights supervised the production of furniture and ran steam engines in the days before electric motors. The millwright made sure that the steam-run boiler produced enough steam to run a motor that operated the pulleys connected to the central drive shaft. The millwright was a key person in the furniture manufacturing operation.

One day a valued millwright in the company died, and DePree's father being just a young manager did not know what to do. So he went to the millwright's house to offer sympathy. As they sat in the family's living room, the millwright's widow asked DePree's father if she might read some poetry aloud. He naturally said yes. So the widow produced a bound book of poetry and read some selections from it. DePree's father remarked how beautiful the poems were and asked who the author was. She said that the millwright, her husband, was the poet. Max DePree writes that sixty years after the death of the millwright, people at the Herman Miller Company continue to ask the question, "Was he a poet who did millwright's work, or was he a millwright who wrote poetry?" (pp. 7-9). Only the most discerning person can make a judgment like this.

In a similar sense, when we attempt to discern the voice of God as God speaks to us, we must make distinctions carefully. Those who are called by God are those who can discriminate between the voice from on high and the many other voices that compete for our hearing's undivided attention.

One of the pillars of abundant life is the spiritual gift of discernment. It is a gift of God, but, like many human abilities, it is a gift that grows with use and practice. Similar to a muscle, if we have the gift of discernment, then it will only develop through exercise. If we exercise our spiritual listening, then God will grant us greater and greater degrees of discernment. If we ever need a reminder of one of the foundational characteristics of abundant life, then there is a pillar with the word *discernment* inscribed on it. Amen. (David N. Mosser)

JUNE 5, 2005

Third Sunday After Pentecost

Worship Theme: Radical faith in the efficacy of God's promises will enable any who believe to meaningful service and great spiritual rewards.

Readings: Genesis 12:1-9; Romans 4:13-25; Matthew 9:9-13, 18-26

Call to Worship (Psalm 33:4-7, 10-12 RSV)

Leader: The word of the LORD is upright; and all his work is done in faithfulness.

People: **He loves righteousness and justice; the earth is full of the steadfast love of the LORD.**

Leader: By the word of the LORD the heavens were made, and all their host by the breath of his mouth.

People: **He gathered the waters of the sea as in a bottle; he put the deeps in storehouses.**

Leader: The LORD brings the counsel of the nations to nought; he frustrates the plans of the peoples.

People: **The counsel of the LORD stands for ever, the thoughts of his heart to all generations.**

All: **Blessed is the nation whose God is the LORD, the people whom he has chosen as his heritage!**

Pastoral Prayer:

Most Holy Lord, God of the Universe, we confess that we really do not know what in the world you are up to. We confess our frustration at the imperfect and partial nature of our knowledge of who you are and what you are about, because we see only through a glass darkly. We are not only ignorant but also lonely for you. We treasure the glimpses of reality that you have given us. We are grateful that in time and history Jesus came to our world to give us a grand glimpse by which to measure all other fleeting insights that we have. May our faith in your great promises sustain and guide us in the dark days of doubt. Empower us to faithfulness in all things. In the name of Jesus. Amen. (Thomas Lane Butts)

SERMON BRIEFS

THE COURAGE TO ACT

GENESIS 12:1-9

There are approximately 3 billion people the world over who trace their spiritual lineage back to Abraham. Jews, Christians, and Muslims are all "children of Abraham" by their own reckoning. By default this makes his story among the several most seminal stories of Western civilization.

God covenants with Abram and his wife, Sarai, that he will be their God, and they and their descendants will be God's people. God promises that these descendants will be as numerous as the stars in a clear night's sky. Abram and Sarai pick up their household and follow the seemingly ludicrous vision for an elderly, childless couple. After all, Abram is seventy-five years old when he receives this call to follow a far path.

Three billion seems a reasonable return thus far.

Abram and Sarai did not know quite what they were doing or where they were going. They did not know what adventure lay before them or what series of decisions would be required of them. God established this couple as the biblical prototype for radical trust. This response we call faith. Abram and Sarai courageously acted in their present moment for an end that was larger than they knew, but rooted in divine intention.

Paul counts Abraham as the enduring model of faithful response to God's overture. "He did not weaken in faith when he considered his own body, which was already as good as dead . . . or when he considered the barrenness of Sarah's womb" (Rom. 4:19). Faith of this sort demands the courage to act, not certainty.

At the age of sixteen, emancipated slave Booker T. Washington determined to go to school. From Malden, West Virginia, he walked the five hundred miles to the Hampton Institute in Virginia.

> I presented myself before the head teacher for assignment to a class. Having been so long without proper food, a bath, and change of clothing, I did not, of course, make a very favourable impression upon her, and I could see at once that there were doubts in her mind about the wisdom of admitting me.
>
> After some hours had passed, the head teacher said to me: "The adjoining recitation-room needs sweeping. Take the broom and sweep it."
>
> . . . Here was my chance. . . . I knew that I could sweep.
>
> . . . When she was unable to find one bit of dirt . . . , she quietly remarked, "I guess you will do to enter this institution."
>
> . . . The sweeping of that room was my college examination, and never did any youth pass an examination for entrance into Harvard or Yale that gave him more genuine satisfaction.
>
> . . . The head teacher offered me a position as janitor . . . where I could work out nearly all the cost of my board. (Booker T. Washington, *Up From Slavery*, Oxford World's Classics, ed. William L. Andrews [New York: Oxford University Press, 1995], pp. 30-31)

Washington went on to graduate with honors. He then traveled a path to become the most influential black educator of his time. While more aggressive political actors displaced his early accommodationist style, there is no question that Washington's movement out of slavery was a great journey of faith—no certainty, but nevertheless, the courage to act.

I have an affinity for this story because I worked as a janitor of an elementary school while attending seminary. I did not know where or how those tentative steps would lead into my future. While cleaning the cafeteria floor or the first through fourth grade bathrooms, I could not have guessed the miles I would travel to the city I now call home and the work I refer to as "my call."

Anaïs Nin said, "Life shrinks or expands in proportion to one's courage." This captures an essential outcome of faith: Through the courage to act, our lives grow into their full glory.

Radical trust = the courage to act = faith = real life. (Stephen Bauman)

THE SEED OF PROMISE

ROMANS 4:13-25

The story of God's promise of grace to humankind really began even before creation, but most of us agree that we begin to understand that promise of grace with the story of Abraham. Because of Abraham's faith we begin a long line of people of faith who strive to allow God to work within them and among them. God's promise of offspring that would number as many as the stars in the sky came into being as Abraham trusted in God and left his familiar and secure surroundings to go to an unknown land. Abraham's faithfulness was in response to God's gracious acts. The willing faith of Abraham allowed God room to work within Abraham and his descendants.

Later, as the law was given, the people had instructions for living in the light of God's love. So often, however, the people made this law a demand rather than a gift of grace. Jesus often criticized the Pharisees and the teachers of the law for their rigid and unforgiving attitudes concerning the law. Some people mistake the law for faith. The keeping of religious requirements can be means of experiencing God, but so often, these laws and requirements become barriers in our faith.

Paul experienced the difference of living under the flesh of the law and living by the promise of the Spirit. When the practice of our faith leads to condemnation and works of the flesh, then we have missed out on the fruits of the Spirit. In Christ came unity and equality of Jews and Gentiles. In Christ, the seed of promise was fulfilled.

Wherever there is faith, there is life, and wherever there is life, we see a gift from God. From Abraham came the seed of promise in Isaac. Spirit breeds spirit, and the seed of promise is passed on to all of those who would have faith like Abraham. However, some of us try to take the promise into our own hands. This is where we see the law come into effect, for with the law comes transgression and wrath.

Remember, as Abraham and Sarah tried to take matters into their own hands, they gave Sarah's maidservant to Abraham, and Ishmael was conceived. They didn't wait for the fulfilling of the promise. We often try to take things into our own hands and do "good works" on our own, when we really haven't trusted God. Then, the results vary and eventually we find ourselves under the law and living in the flesh. But even while God often protects and even blesses the works of the flesh (Ishmael and his descendants), God desires us to live under the promise of the Spirit. All who have faith can live amid the fulfillment of the law, and by bearing the name of Jesus Christ we have the possibility of living in the Spirit. Let us give thanks to God for this promise of grace and to Father Abraham who modeled such trust in God. Those who display this type of faith come from the seed of promise and bear the fruit of the Spirit. (Ryan Wilson)

NAMING AND CLAIMING

MATTHEW 9:9-13, 18-26

Not long ago I preached the funeral of one of our saints. Martha was a registered nurse who, for long years, worked in the county health department. For years she made her rounds among the poorer of our neighbors, in the more rural corners of our world. She took medicine and compassion to those off the beaten path, visiting and seeing the poor as persons of sacred worth and dignity. In that way she surely shared in the ministry and purposes of the Lord, who healed the outcast and unclean.

A large part of Martha's work was tending to new mothers and their newborns. As she did, it was not at all unusual for the mothers to ask her to name their new babies. After the funeral, someone remarked that she might have named half the babies in the county since the 1940s. If that was an exaggeration, it was not much of one. Her daughter noted, "She always gave them biblical names, too, proper, biblical names."

Naming babies. Claiming babies, as it were, for God. Martha put a biblical stamp on those poor children before the world and its ungodly prejudice would name them something else. It was the sacrament in everyday life, and no priest or preacher could have done better, I think. In her service we were reminded of the text in Ephesians where the author maintains that every family on heaven and earth is, in fact, named by God, and it pleased us to think of Martha sharing in the work and purposes of God. Healing, helping, naming, and claiming, she was a minister and saint.

The Gospel text for today reminds me of Martha, or perhaps it is that in reading these three stories I am able to see the day-to-day work of Martha and people like her in a new way. No longer just in terms of their jobs, but in terms of their vocations. Martha was a sacramental presence in the lives of many of God's children, continuing the work of Jesus in the world.

For, what is Jesus doing for Matthew in our lesson of the day, really, more than naming him and claiming him for God? If Matthew is like other tax collectors, he has already been "named" with many other names by his contemporaries—most not flattering. Yet Jesus calls him to be one of his own. That night Matthew and others who were marginalized by polite society shared table fellowship with Jesus, whose healing presence claimed them for God. Jesus bestowed mercy in just that way. Of those Jesus bestowed it on: "Blessed are the merciful, for they will receive mercy" (5:7).

Similarly, Jesus' ministry to the woman with the hemorrhage, which is a miracle within a miracle, demonstrates not only healing but also naming: "daughter," Jesus calls her, and one wonders how long it had been since anyone was willing to see her as a person of worth and dignity or to associate with her in the presence of others.

What interests us about Jesus' healing of the child is how he sees her situation differently from all others. Just as Jesus saw Matthew differently, and the woman, Jesus sees the child as "sleeping." It is this different perspective that fuels his work of naming and claiming, of healing the sick and the sinful, of raising the dead and all his children into the newness of life.

Likewise, when we claim and name one another—not just with proper names but especially with biblical names such as friend, brother, sister, and saint—when we become a merciful and healing presence in the world, then we share in the very purposes and ministry of God. (Thomas Steagald)

JUNE 12, 2005

Fourth Sunday After Pentecost

Worship Theme: God enables us to do what he calls us to do. Problems that we envision, a power beyond ourselves will resolve.

Readings: Genesis 18:1-15; Romans 5:1-8; Matthew 9:35–10:8 (9-23)

Call to Worship (Psalm 116:1-2, 12-15, 17)

Leader:	I love the LORD, because he has heard my voice and my supplications.
People:	**Because he inclined his ear to me, therefore I will call on him as long as I live.**
Leader:	What shall I return to the LORD for all his bounty to me?
People:	**I will lift up the cup of salvation and call on the name of the LORD,**
Leader:	I will pay my vows to the LORD in the presence of all his people.
People:	**Precious in the sight of the LORD is the death of his faithful ones.**
All:	**I will offer to thee a thanksgiving sacrifice and call on the name of the LORD.**

Pastoral Prayer:

O Lord God, in whose hands rest the issues of life and death, we acknowledge you as the initiator and sustainer of life. We

208

believe that you will not leave us "hung out to dry" by all the evil and besetting circumstances which come into our lives. We trust that you will keep us here in this dimension until we have finished whatever you sent us here to do.

Dear God, life can get so tangled and confusing that we lose the vision of purpose and the grand design. Tell us again why we are here, not because we do not believe, but because we need to be reassured and called to remembrance by a voice that sounds like love. Speak to us, O Lord, in such ways as please you, and grant that in your word to us we may obtain courage for hard times, and strength for difficult places, and determination for challenging tasks. We pray in the strong name of Jesus. Amen. (Thomas Lane Butts)

SERMON BRIEFS

WHEN GOD COMES TO DINNER

GENESIS 18:1-15

Most pastors can share interesting observations about how people react when we are guests in their homes, especially during meals. Sometimes people are self-conscious, tense, or concerned about the children's behavior. But what if God came to dinner?

In the hottest time of day, God and two divine messengers surprise Abraham at his tent's entrance. We know it is God because throughout the story he is referred to by the unique, unpronounceable, divine name.

Abraham hurries to greet his visitors and humbles himself at their presence (similar to an act of worship). Maybe they bring special news. Maybe this visit will fulfill the divine promise made to him. His greeting of "Adonai" expresses profound respect and even possible awareness of God's presence. Later we are assured that Abraham realizes who visited him.

Abraham springs into action, making his guests comfortable, tending to their needs with unrestrained hospitality and servanthood (Heb. 13:2) even in the uncomfortable desert heat. He underpromises and overdelivers. He promises only a little water to wash their feet but actually provides them with yogurt and milk to drink. He promises only a morsel of bread but actually provides cakes of bread. He promises no entrée but actually provides meat from the fatted calf. Quite a contrast with the reception they get in chapter 19 in Sodom.

However, do not become too enamored with Abraham's hospitality, as kind as it is. Observe God during this visit. God is gracious, polite, and engaging. When the Lord is ready to reveal the timing of the promise's fulfillment, God comes in person and eats in Abraham's tent. Nothing could more significantly communicate their close relationship. Eating together is important for fellowship, peace offerings, and treaties.

The two messengers have not seen Sarah, although they know she has prepared their meal. They ask where she is. Abraham assures them she is in the tent. God then announces the timing of the coming of the promised son. It will be within the year (literally "about a life's interval," possibly referring to nine months). Sarah is at the tent entrance behind them, eavesdropping. This may be the first time she has heard about the divine promise. If it is not, she certainly has not yet been persuaded of its validity. Abraham and Sarah are both advanced in years, and Sarah is certainly past the possibility of conception.

At hearing the promise, Sarah laughs privately at the thought of such an impossibility. She describes herself as literally "worn out, like a garment." But before being too hard on her, remember that in the previous chapter Abraham himself laughed when he first hears the promise. However, she is surprised that their guest hears her secret laughter. God asks Abraham why Sarah laughed at the news. Does he assume that Abraham has already discussed the promise with her? God asks bluntly if anything is literally "too wonderful or miraculous" for the Lord. He repeats the promise. When she realizes that the guest knows she has laughed at his news, she becomes afraid and pleads innocence. Nevertheless, this unusual guest denies her plea and confirms the truth.

Within the year a son is indeed born of the laughter of Sarah and Abraham (Gen. 21:3, 6) and is given the name commanded by God—"laughter" (Gen. 17:19). Also within the year Sarah comes to know that the guest in their tent that day was more than just another bedouin (Gen. 21:6), and she trusts all his promises (Heb. 11:11).

When God comes to dinner, God arrives suddenly, deserves our humble service, engages us in relationship, knows the secrets of our hearts, and brings the gift of promised life (see Rev. 3:20). (Dennis L. Phelps)

ARE YOU AT PEACE WITH GOD?

ROMANS 5:1-8

Every generation has had "wars and rumors of wars." This generation is no different. Perhaps that explains the human quest for peace—both external and internal. Some have dubbed the twenty-first century as the "Century of Spirituality." That sobriquet is an indicator that this generation is seeking a spiritual solution for life's most perplexing questions. The answers provided by science and secularism have proved unsatisfactory. That has led to a new philosophy du jour—postmodernism. Postmodernism contends that there are no ultimate answers to life's questions. So, the quest for peace continues.

The apostle Paul was familiar with this human desire and quest. Paul exploited it to explain the attraction of Christianity. In his words, "we have peace with God through our Lord Jesus Christ" (v. 1). It is natural for a seeker to ask, "What does Paul mean? What kind of peace is being offered? How does one experience such peace?"

In this passage, Paul answers that the peace we experience with God allows us to have access to God. We can come into God's presence with confidence. We can do so, not because of our own merit, but because of the grace we have received from putting our trust in Jesus Christ.

This is an especially important concept for Paul and his Jewish readers. The separation between God and human beings, including God's chosen people the Jews, was made manifest in Jerusalem. The Jewish Temple was structured in such a way as to teach this truism: We are not able to stand before God. Only the high priest was allowed to enter the Holy of Holies, where God was thought to dwell. The high priest could do so only once a year. If others entered this holy space, they would die. Walls and curtains separated the ordinary person from God's presence.

Now, Paul writes every person can stand in the presence of God. Through Jesus' sacrificial death and resurrection, we have unlimited access to our creator. No longer do we have to wonder about our eternal fate. We can stand in God's presence with confidence and anticipate the final judgment with hope and joy.

Further, the peace that we experience with God can sustain the Christian in the vicissitudes of this life. Suffering is life's given, and Christians are not immune. They are not promised that they will not suffer. They are promised the presence of the Holy Spirit, who can and will comfort them as they deal with the "slings and arrows" that come their way.

Dietrich Bonhoeffer taught us that grace is not cheap. Paul reminds us in this passage that peace is costly, too. That is a lesson that history teaches. The peace between individuals, races, and nations is always costly. Paul teaches that the peace we have with God was bought at a great price. We did not pay the price, of course. Jesus Christ paid it for us. The most astounding fact concerning that payment is that it was made for those who did not deserve it. We can almost hear Paul's voice rise with amazement when we read the words, "While we were still sinners, Christ died for us" (v. 8 NIV). (Philip D. Wise)

THE IMITATION OF CHRIST

MATTHEW 9:35–10:8 (9-23)

Stuart Henry, late Professor of American Christianity at Duke University, once said that within these verses of Matthew there appeared, for him, the clearest evidence of Christ's divinity. He described a walk he took across the Duke quadrangle. The students were, at the time, celebrating something—a game, a break, a holiday—and doing so "riotously." They were loud and unrestrained, a good many of them drunk. Henry recollected that, as during other similar strolls, he was disgusted by what he saw: disgusted with the students, disgusted with their behavior, disgusted with a culture that blesses debauchery. When all at once he remembered these verses: "When [Jesus] saw the crowds, he had compassion for them, because they were ... like sheep without a shepherd" (v. 36). Henry said that his memory of those particular verses at that particular moment not only doxologized Jesus, as it were, but also both judged him in his own condescension and pique and summoned him toward a deeper sense of his call as a minister.

Indeed, the rich texts for today remind us that we who bear the name of Christ have as our vocation nothing less than continuing Christ's incarnation as we imitate Christ in the world. That imitation is not impersonation: We are not to think or act as if we are Christ, for there are many things Jesus would do that we cannot. Rather, we look to Jesus for inspiration with regard to both our attitudes and our actions. We work to see people as Jesus sees them and, as a consequence, minister to them as best we can in honor of Jesus' dying love for them. That does not mean disregarding obvious sin, and especially sin that is self-destructive. Neither, however, does it allow condescension and self-righteousness.

As Jesus emptied himself of everything but love for his children, Jesus' continuing call is for us to rid ourselves of all that keeps us from loving "the least of these," his "brothers and sisters" (25:40 NLT). Jesus calls disciples then and now to be about his business.

When Jesus saw the crowds, he saw a field unto harvest of shepherdless souls. "The harvest is plentiful," he said, "but the laborers are few" (9:37). Like many others, I grew up going to church camps whose culminating moment was a bonfire where we were invited to surrender to the call to full-time Christian service. Often this very text served as the basis for the camp evangelist's sermon. Indeed, as the list of the disciples was read, we were challenged to let our name become a part of the list. We were promised "authority" to preach and minister in Jesus' name. I cannot, however, remember hearing the camp evangelists emphasize Jesus' first command to would-be disciples: "Pray!"

Yet prayer lets us begin to see as Jesus saw, to love as Jesus loved, to serve, after a fashion, as Jesus served. Prayer opens our eyes to see fields white unto harvest with God's children: oppressed and harassed and shepherdless souls, not flint for our self-righteousness. It is prayer that opens our ears to hear whether God calls us into service of those souls or whether we might be listening to another voice. It is prayer that opens our hearts as well as our hands and gives us both the humility and the authority to continue the incarnation of Christ in a world so in need of a Savior.

It is prayer that gives us a memory of the Word, a hope for the kingdom, and the real presence of Christ in our work. (Thomas Steagald)

JUNE 19, 2005

Fifth Sunday After Pentecost

Worship Theme: Tribulation and evil circumstances are part and parcel of every life. Do not be distressed when darkness comes at noonday. God can transform any defeat into a victory.

Readings: Genesis 21:8-21; Romans 6:1*b*-11; Matthew 10:24-39

Call to Worship (Psalm 86:1-6, 11 RSV)

Leader:	Incline thy ear, O LORD, and answer me, for I am poor and needy.
People:	**Preserve my life, for I am godly; save thy servant who trusts in thee.**
Leader:	Thou art my God; be gracious to me, O Lord, for to thee do I cry all the day.
People:	**Gladden the soul of thy servant, for to thee, O Lord, do I lift up my soul.**
Leader:	For thou, O Lord, art good and forgiving, abounding in steadfast love to all who call on thee.
People:	**Give ear, O LORD, to my prayer; hearken to my cry of supplication.**
All:	**Teach me thy way, O LORD, that I may walk in thy truth; unite my heart to fear thy name.**

Pastoral Prayer:

Dear God of us all, we pray for those persons in our families who bear the responsibility of difficult decisions. Forgive us for

215

giving up on people because they do not fit our image of what they should be. Forgive us for berating ourselves when we have done our best and it did not seem to be enough. May the warmth of worship and the love of friends be a balm that reminds us of your great love that forgives all sin and heals all wounds. We pray for all who labor under impediments brought on by some particular stage or circumstance of life. Bless the elderly who are grieving the loss of youthfulness, vitality, and health and who face displacement and indignities they have dreaded for a lifetime. Bless the young who are struggling with temptations to be less than they could or should. We pray in Jesus' name. Amen. (Thomas Lane Butts)

SERMON BRIEFS

NO JOINT CUSTODY

GENESIS 21:8-21

The most heart-gripping divorce cases I observe involve children. The threat can be so destructive that joint custody is simply not a healthy option. The child cannot be halved in Solomon-like fashion. The adults must be separated from one another, and the child must go with one of them. Often the single parent and child struggle financially, personally, and emotionally. The anger, abandonment, and pain leave a wake of devastation. It is not an experience desired by anyone.

The Bible contains the stories of many single parents and their children. Even Abraham, the patriarch of faithful obedience, experiences failure of his blended family. The failure leaves behind a struggling single parent and a teenager. Still God's purpose prevails.

The impulsive acts in Genesis 16 bear bitter fruit. At a family celebration for the healthy weaning of Isaac, Sarah notices his teenage half-brother mocking him, possibly even making fun of his name (which means "laughter"). Maybe Ishmael resents Isaac's health and senses that he now is a threat to the inheritance. At the least, Ishmael remains true to his promised conflicted and troublesome nature (16:11-12).

Ishmael's cynical, malicious insults incur Sarah's wrath. If he perceives Isaac as a threat, Sarah now perceives Hagar and her son as the threat. Although Ishmael is the result of Sarah's own insistence, she now will not even say his name or acknowledge any relationship with him or his mother. Instead, he is called "the son of Hagar the Egyptian" or "the son of the maid or servant." Ishmael is a child of the flesh and the law; Isaac is a child of grace and God's promise. Sarah demands that Ishmael and Hagar be disinherited and thrown out of the family. This is the second time that she demands Hagar's expulsion (Gen. 16:4-6).

Sarah's bitterness toward Hagar and Ishmael distresses Abraham. He does not despise them. He loves Hagar and knows abandonment is not proper. Abraham is expected to be their provider; otherwise, his name will be shamed.

God intervenes. He instructs Abraham to allow Sarah's demand because God has chosen Isaac as the son of blessing. God repeats that he will still make a great nation from Ishmael, as he has promised from the beginning. However, Abraham must trust Ishmael and Hagar into God's care. What he does not know is that this is preparing him for a greater test. By trusting God with Ishmael now, he avoids having to choose between Ishmael and Isaac later. It heightens the indispensability of Isaac as the son of God's blessing. It removes any sense of a "Plan B" when the greater test of trust comes. Previous tests necessitated him primarily to watch and wait patiently. This period of deepening faith moves him to make difficult choices and take difficult actions.

Ishmael's name means "God hears"—indeed, God hears Ishmael's cries and again intervenes. After all, he has promised to make a great nation of Ishmael.

Hagar and Ishmael have no nourishment, no shelter and safety. There is no indication they believe God's promises or ask for God's help. However, an angel in heaven interrupts Hagar's helpless wailing, tells her that God hears Ishmael's voice, and instructs her to pick him up. God then opens her eyes and reveals a well. She fills the waterskin and gives Ishmael water. God graciously provides an abundance of water and the promise of life and posterity to Hagar and Ishmael. God is sovereign over all people, even those who do not trust him.

Like Hagar and Ishmael, we were once excluded, abandoned, doomed to death. Then God intervened through Christ. Those who trust God become adopted by grace and are made joint heirs through the Son of blessing; they are true children of Abraham but not according to the flesh (Rom. 9:6-8; Gal. 4:21-31). There is no joint custody. (Dennis L. Phelps)

THE LOGIC OF BAPTISM

ROMANS 6:1*b*-11

Much of Paul's theology flows out of his understanding of baptism. Baptism isn't magic. It doesn't have a divine power that operates independently of human will and cooperation. God does something in our baptism, but in order for us to benefit fully, we must lay hold of God's gracious act and make it a directing force in our lives.

The defining dynamic of our baptism is that we are "baptized into Christ Jesus" (v. 3). The phrase "in Christ," which describes our baptized state, becomes Paul's chief way of characterizing the Christian life. Those who live "in Christ Jesus" certainly can have no thought of living "in sin." Peter Gomes remarked about our union with Christ: "The most important truth in the whole world is that it is God's intention that we be united with Christ and that to know that truth makes a difference in how we live in and cope with the world. . . . Christ shares our destiny and we are meant to share his. We are at one with him" ("United with Christ," *Pulpit Digest,* Oct.-Dec. 2000, p. 84).

Many of us make our Christian journey in three stages: (1) As children we start out "in Christ"—with the wonder and trust of children. (2) Then certain forces pull us "outside of Christ." (3) Finally, whether through a radical and violent reordering of our will or through gentler means, we end up "in Christ." We discover with Paul, "It is no longer I who live, but it is Christ who lives in me" (Gal. 2:20).

The fact that we are joined to Christ has great implications. It means, in an overall way, that we have become different creatures and entered a completely new way of life. As Paul states in 2 Corinthians, "If one is in Christ, there is a new creation: everything old has passed away" (5:17). We stand in a new relationship to God, that of reconciliation. We become "ambassadors for Christ" (5:20) and "the righteousness of God" (5:21). Our lives are set in a whole new direction.

Another implication of our being "in Christ" is that we who are baptized share in Christ's resurrection. We are "united with him in a resurrection like his" (Rom. 6:5). Our destiny is linked to his. Our relationship to him is that of *union* and *participation,* not merely reenactment and imitation. We should not understand resurrection just to be what happened to Jesus at the end of his earthly life. Resurrection is a power that believers may and do experience here and now as they "walk in newness of life" (6:4). Just as Jesus healed and brought hope wherever he went, so do his disciples participate in the redeeming activity of God's kingdom. The dreadful powers of sin and death no longer have dominion over those who are united with Christ. These powers don't have the last word!

Still another implication of our being "in Christ" is that we, the church, are the body *of Christ,* not a body *of Christians.* When baptized, we are united to Christ and his church. We can't have union with one without the other. Everything is in the plural here. There are no "Lone Ranger" Christians. Ours is a thoroughly social religion, and we always have to think and act as those who are in community with others.

Here in chapter 6 Paul leads up to a final implication of our being "in Christ." This truth bursts forth two chapters later when Paul declares that absolutely nothing "will be able to separate us from the love of God in Christ Jesus our Lord" (8:39). This is the inevitable outcome of Paul's logic. To be in union with Christ is to be in union with love itself. This love will never fail us. Praise be to God! (Sandy Wylie)

GOD PHOBIA?

MATTHEW 10:24-39

Whom or what do you fear? Hollywood continues to capitalize on exploring and exploiting people's fears. Have you noticed how many films deal with unexplainable and unexpected events, and the fearful response?

There are television programs in which contestants, to win money, allow themselves to be vulnerable and completely exposed to their nemeses. People crawl into coffin-shaped containers filled with spiders or worms. Others dangle from the end of a rope ladder, suspended hundreds of feet by helicopter, to face their fear of heights—betting they will not black out or jump.

Linguists have even given names to our fears: agoraphobia, claustrophobia, ecclesiophobia, euphobia, and arachnophobia to name just a few. If one reads a list of phobias, these fears can seem absurd, like the fear of peanut butter sticking to the roof of your mouth (arachibutyrophobia) or the fear of writing in public (scriptophobia).

So what do we, as Christians, fear? Do we fear heaven (ouranophobia)? Do we fear death (necrophobia)? Do we fear hell (hadephobia)? Do we fear Satan (Satanophobia)? Do we fear God (Theophobia)?

The Message by Eugene H. Peterson paraphrases Matthew 10:28 as "Save your fear for God, who holds your entire life— body and soul—in his hands."

I am Navajo, and many of our elders do have a fear, a reverential fear, of God. The idea of Jesus being one's friend or buddy is foreign to them. They equate Jesus, the begotten Son of God, with the same awesome reverence they have for God. The early Israelite frame of mind—"Take off your sandals for you are standing on holy ground" (Exod. 3:5 NLT)—is present in their lives.

But how do present-day Christians "fear" God? Is there a difference between worshiping and fearing God? Is the fear motivated by love or terror?

Many times, as a parent, I remember cautioning my children about a dangerous object. "Don't touch. Hot! Hot!" Of course, many times my child ignored my warnings and reached out, testing and experiencing heat for herself. In my efforts to protect my daughter from harm, I did not mean to teach fear of a stove or a furnace, but to teach her respect for heat and fire. As she grew, her understanding of the possibilities and the necessity for respect also increased.

Just as there is a negative sense of the word *fear*, there is also the positive sense in which the word is used. Respect, awe, or reverence are positive uses of fear especially toward authorities to whom one is responsible. Perhaps it is exactly for this reason many of us have lost the sense of "fear" of God. In a country that prides itself on self-determination and individualism, to submit to another's authority can be seen as weakness.

Respect can also be given when we are reminded of acts or events that we are completely unable to accomplish by ourselves or have control of. Even insurance companies recognize and respect "acts of God," natural disasters over which all our technology and intelligence have no power. The fear of God is evidenced in the miracle of birth when one holds a newborn's delicate hand and sees a miniature finger complete with nail and fingerprints. The awesomeness of God's creation is seen in the grandeur of a mountain range or the stars at night.

Just as children grow in their understanding of fire and heat, so our understanding of revering God must also keep expanding.

What are your fears? From what do you run, and in your fear, whom do you run to? Save your fear for God, who holds your entire life—body and soul—in his hands. In a world full of fears and fearful people, may you be an example of strength in your fear of God. (Raquel Mull)

JUNE 26, 2005

Sixth Sunday After Pentecost

Worship Theme: When life requires something of us we do not understand, we may safely trust in the providence of God for ultimate outcomes.

Readings: Genesis 22:1-14; Romans 6:12-23; Matthew 10:40-42

Call to Worship (Psalm 13:1-2*b*, 3-6 RSV)

> *Leader:* How long, O LORD? Wilt thou forget me for ever? How long wilt thou hide thy face from me?
>
> **People:** **How long must I bear pain in my soul, and have sorrow in my heart all the day?**
>
> *Leader:* Consider and answer me, O LORD my God; lighten my eyes, lest I sleep the sleep of death;
>
> **People:** **Lest my enemy say, "I have prevailed over him"; lest my foes rejoice because I am shaken.**
>
> *Leader:* But I have trusted in thy steadfast love; my heart shall rejoice in thy salvation.
>
> **People:** **I will sing to the LORD, because he has dealt bountifully with me.**

Pastoral Prayer:

Dear God, whose Spirit searches all things and whose love bears all things, encourage us in our search to find what is best for our lives as we struggle with ourselves and the world around us. We sense that you, O God, have set us in a scheme of circumstances, and that it is your will for us, in this stern conflict, to find strength and triumph over all. We pray that you would not withhold from us the courage by which we can conquer. Save us from weak complaining against conditions over which we are called to conquer. May we obediently accept the conditions of our earthly pilgrimage so that we may come to possess our souls and achieve our destiny. Help us to grieve our losses when they happen and then pick up our share of life's load and keep moving on. In Jesus' name. Amen. (Thomas Lane Butts)

SERMON BRIEFS

WHAT GOD REQUIRES, GOD PROVIDES

GENESIS 22:1-14

Early in my ministry my wife and I depended on weekend offerings. One weekend the treasurer was unable to sign the check. With no money we made the long drive back to our seminary apartment. We did not know how we would buy food.

When we arrived home early Monday morning we unloaded the car quietly. We grabbed the mail and lay down to get some rest. When she flipped through the mail, my wife noticed something. As she opened an envelope her jaw dropped. We had been awarded some scholarship funds that already had been deposited at the business office. We were not aware such scholarship funds existed. The money could be used toward tuition, class supplies, or even groceries. It was a surprise answer to a desperate need. The seminary's motto as a "school of providence and prayer" proved more than advertising. It was reality. In God's providence God answered our prayers. God provided!

God is about to require something unusual of Abraham. It will be a defining moment. He already has lost Ishmael. Now he faces the greater challenge of losing Isaac. God's purpose is to perhaps prove Abraham's devotion.

This test originates with God. God instructs Abraham to take his only child, the son of his love, Isaac, and offer him as a sacrifice. But this flies in the face of all common sense, parental affection, and earthly ambition. Will the son of God's promise to Abraham now die at the hands of Abraham in obedience to God?

Abraham does not delay responding. He gets up early to prepare. For three days he, Isaac, and two servants hike to a mountain named Moriah. Upon arriving, he tells the servants that he and Isaac are going up to worship and assures them that they will return. Isaac carries the wood; Abraham carries the tools. Along the way, Isaac asks about the sacrifice. Abraham has not yet told him about God's request but reassures him that God will provide the need. As they reach the spot for worship, Abraham builds the altar and lays out the wood.

The serious nature of this crisis becomes evident. The offering will not be a lamb but a lad. Abraham binds Isaac (who does not resist) and lays him on the wood that will feed the fire.

The crisis climaxes. What will Abraham do? The loss of Ishmael was a loss of his past. The loss of Isaac will be a loss of his future. Will Abraham follow God without the motivation of a future and at the expense of this unique son? Clasping the knife, the father prepares to slay his son as a sacrifice. He withholds nothing from God. However, God intervenes. God wants Abraham's obedience, not Isaac's sacrifice (Jer. 7:31; 19:4-5).

The test results are announced. God stops Abraham from harming the child and confirms that his actions match his trust in God (James 2:21-22). Abraham's loyalty is to the Promise Giver, not the promise itself. He understands that the covenant depends on God, not Isaac (Rom. 4:16-25). Abraham reveres, worships, and obeys God (Heb. 11:17-19). God knows this now in an intimate, experiential way.

Abraham lifts his eyes and notices a ram stuck in the thicket. He offers it on the altar in worship and gratitude to God's grace (Lev. 1:4). Abraham names the spot "the LORD will provide."

As we trust and obey, we, too, can discover that what God requires, God provides. Even God's own son of promise takes wood on his back and offers himself as the sacrifice on the altar for our sin. It is God's nature. God has been doing it for thousands of years. (Dennis L. Phelps)

IN SEARCH OF A MASTER

ROMANS 6:12-23

In the hours preceding his execution on June 11, 2001, Timothy McVeigh left us a final written statement, the poem "Invictus" by the British poet William Ernest Henley. Henley wrote the poem in 1875 as an expression of the kind of heroic individualism that resonates to this day. The poem concludes, "I am the master of my fate: / I am the captain of my soul."

"Invictus" expresses our common human aspiration to live a life of proud autonomy. We mortals want to be our own master. We prefer not to be under any lordship outside our own ambitions.

This sentiment is not in harmony with the witness of the New Testament. Paul is more in tune with a song of Bob Dylan in which the singer declares, "You're gonna have to serve somebody." The plain fact is that all of us inevitably serve some kind of lord. We all choose a master. It is only a matter of *which* master it is.

Paul recognizes two general kinds of master. We will become either slaves of "sin" or slaves of "obedience," which is to say God. Although most of us serve both of these masters at times, we usually arrive at a basic orientation toward one or the other. The course that we chart always has consequences.

Paul understands sin to be a great realm of power that opposes God and enslaves people. It isn't just bad social form or occasional lapses in judgment. It is the "powers and principalities" of the world that continually harass us and strive to defeat God's purposes. We are engaged in a never-ending warfare with these powers, and the sooner we recognize this, the better. Thus, we can never take sin lightly.

Sin inserts itself into every area of life, even the most sacred. It appears in extreme ideologies such as that of Timothy McVeigh. Sin shows up in corporate greed, corrupt political power, institutional racism, oppressive nationalism, and many other social arenas as well as in individual indiscretions. Wherever it appears, it results in death.

But there's a way out of sin and into life. This way opens up for those who become "slaves of righteousness" and place themselves under the lordship of Jesus Christ. P. T. Forsyth said, "The purpose of life is not to find your freedom but to find your master." Those who choose Jesus as master find a path that opens into life.

In his parable, "The Rigorous Coachman," Søren Kierkegaard tells about a rich man who purchased a team of excellent, faultless horses for his own use. He, however, was not a coachman. After several weeks, the once proud horses were nearly unrecognizable. They were sluggish; their stamina was gone; and their pace was inconsistent. They displayed bad habits and odd quirks. So the rich man summoned the king's coachman, who knew horses. The royal coachman drove the horses for a month, and, as they became familiar with his voice, the transformation in the animals was amazing. They held their heads high; their eyes were sharp and bright; and their pace was magnificent. The capacities were in them all along. It all depended on whose voice they recognized and followed (*Parables of Kierkegaard,* ed. Thomas C. Oden [Princeton: Princeton University Press, 1978], pp. 59-60).

Those who follow the Lord Jesus Christ and heed his voice discover that wonderful capacities in them begin to emerge, even capacities they never knew were there. They feel strong and hold their heads high. The "powers and principalities" of the world harass them as before; they continue to be scarred by battle. But these pilgrims walk with increasing confidence because they hear a voice that is true and reliable. They have a master whom they can trust with their very lives. (Sandy Wylie)

START SMALL

MATTHEW 10:40-42

John Wesley urged us, as Christians, to strive for perfection. So we make decisions, go to work, live as responsible citizens, try to fulfill our commitments, and go to church as "good" Christians do. Right? When we get to our place of worship, we hope to be in the company of other saints, godly persons living godly lives. Never mind that your spouse didn't help get the children ready, the dog decided on that morning to track in mud, you couldn't find the car keys, and a cold front moved in while you dressed everyone for moderate temperatures. Finally, the Christian education director informed you that the nursery worker did not show up and she knew you wouldn't mind watching the nursery, after all, your children are in there.

Where are those "perfect" Christians? Are they in that new

church on the other side of town? Why do some in our fellowship appear to be gossipers, controllers, whiners, hypocrites?

We tend to look at ourselves with rose-colored glasses and others with a magnifying glass. The church is made up of human beings, each with their own weaknesses and strengths and with their own peculiar personalities. Personalities that we must work around, work with, and work against.

Yet it is precisely because of the other personalities of other Christians, other disciples that Jesus reminds us that "whoever gives even a cup of cold water to one of these little ones in the name of a disciple—truly I tell you, none of these will lose their reward" (v. 42).

I recently read a bumper sticker, "Want what you have. Give what you need." What a motto for us as disciples! Do we appreciate the gifts the Creator has given us, or do we wish we were different? We all need love, compassion, guidance, and acceptance; are we as generous in those gifts?

At times of war and rumors of war, may we be reminded that God created each one of us, even the Adolf Hitlers and the Saddam Husseins. Do we love them in the name of Jesus?

If we say yes, then the next step is to look at our motivation. Are we following the law, or are we so much in love with God that we can do nothing but love our enemies, those other human beings who do not live up to our standards or even society's standards? We are reminded that it is easy to love those people we admire, those we like, but as disciples we are to love everyone else also.

Jesus understood this, and his advice: start small. Just a glass of water. Jesus promises we will not lose anything. In the local setting, it may be listening—really listening—without judgment or solutions, but with a compassionate ear to the complainer. It may mean looking at the bigger picture, making up our mind to do what is right for the kingdom, not what is best for us. For those other disciples who do not think the same as we do, our energy might be better spent praying for them rather than criticizing or condemning them.

A good servant is willing to do big and small jobs. True power lies in the hands of a servant. Just look at Jesus. The more God uses us, the more one realizes it isn't us—it is God. If we are faithful with little, we will be blessed with more.

227

Where do we start? When do we start? The time is now! Look around you. Is there someone who looks lonely? Offer them your company. Is there anyone hungry in your midst? Give what you need: water, food, love, shelter.

Jesus sent his disciples into strange, foreign lands knowing that they would be rejected by some and embraced by others. In order for people to welcome them, they had to present themselves. The world awaits you, Christ's disciples, to present yourselves and give what you need to others in the name of our Lord and Savior. (Raquel Mull)

REFLECTIONS

JULY

Reflection Verse: *"So that you may know that the Son of Man has authority on earth to forgive sins"—he said to the paralytic— "I say to you, stand up, take your mat and go to your home."* (Mark 2:10-11)

FORGIVENESS: A BLASPHEMY TO COMMON SENSE
Mark 2:1-12

For preachers as well as lay folk, the notion of forgiveness is one of the hallmarks of the Christian faith. Yet, in practice it is one of the most difficult of all God's guidelines to observe. People do appalling things to one another. Sometimes parishioners do appalling things to the pastors who love and care for them. Sins against pastors are realities that only the most naive among us could discount. Clergy, moreover, sin against those people in their charge and under their pastoral care. We are all human, and all people sin against one another. Therefore, although forgiveness runs counter to our common sense—and more obviously against our natural inclinations—if we cannot forgive others, then we cannot live abundantly. Forgiving others is one chief portal into the blessed life that God offers us. It is through our God-given ability to forgive that we release our own lives from the bondage that results from refusing to forgive. Forgiveness allows us to receive the blessings God so willingly offers us.

Therefore, forgiveness is one of the Bible's substantial subject matters. For this reason, forgiveness emerges as one of the "Twelve Pillars of Abundant Christian Living." Realistically, however, the topic of forgiveness is one that begins long before the Christian faith developed in the New Testament. Indeed, in the Old Testament, almost from the beginning of God's relationship with God's covenant people, the idea of forgiveness occupies a prominent place.

One memorable story recounts the haggling between Abraham and God over the destruction of Sodom and Gomorrah (Genesis 18). In this account Abraham sounds similar to an auctioneer. By asking for mercy on behalf of the evil city of Sodom, Abraham asks God, "Shall not the Judge of all the earth do what is just?" To which the Lord answers, "If I find at Sodom fifty righteous in the city, I will forgive the whole place for their sake" (vv. 25-26). Abraham then barters with God as he might bargain with an open-market hawker of merchandise. In due course, the divine voice declares, "For the sake of ten I will not destroy it." Forgiveness is the key element. Genesis recounts that God cannot find ten righteous people. The account concludes: "Abraham ... looked down toward Sodom and Gomorrah ... and saw the smoke of the land going up like the smoke of a furnace" (19:27-28). So much for the cities!

Later, Moses likewise negotiates with God. Evidently the Lord was none too pleased that Israel went wild and that Aaron fashioned a golden calf. This unfaithfulness commenced as God and Moses worked out the details pertaining to the covenant's stone tablets. To slightly amend a well-known saying, "When Moses is away, the disloyal people will play." Upon Moses' return from the mountain and nearing the camp, Exodus tells us, "Moses' anger burned hot, and he threw the tablets from his hands and broke them at the foot of the mountain" (Exod. 32:19).

Nevertheless, Moses was a faithful leader, and he returned to the mountain and to the Lord. Moses said, "Alas, this people has sinned a great sin; they have made for themselves gods of gold. But now, if you will only forgive their sin—but if not, blot me out of the book that you have written" (Exod. 32:31-32). These stories from the life of Abraham and Moses remind us that from faith's initial stages, an aspect of the connection between God and God's people includes forgiveness. Wherever God and the people are, then the need for forgiveness looms large.

Forgiveness is also an essential part of New Testament faith. In Mark's Gospel, for example, we read no farther than the second chapter to find a story where forgiveness of sins occupies a central position. In Mark 2:1-11, some friends of a man who is paralyzed are trying to get him to Jesus. In order to get their friend into the house where Jesus is, they must dig through the roof.

Then something remarkable happens. Mark tells us that, "When Jesus saw their faith, he said to the paralytic, 'Son, your sins are forgiven'" (v. 5). Jesus did not seem to notice the faith of the man who needed healing as much as Jesus perceived the faith of the four friends. Perhaps the faith of the friends precipitated the forgiveness—and ultimately the healing.

Of course this forgiveness presses another problem. The watching scribes said in their hearts, "Why does this fellow speak in this way? It is blasphemy! Who can forgive sins but God alone?" (v. 7). It was a deeply held Jewish belief that God alone has the power and authority to forgive sins. Conceivably this story was Mark's way of telling the early church who Jesus was. By forgiving sins, Jesus revealed himself to be the Son of Man, a designation for Messiah. To put an exclamation point on the whole business, Jesus remarks, "'So that you may know that the Son of Man has authority on earth to forgive sins'—he said to the paralytic—'I say to you, stand up, take your mat and go to your home.'" And the man did! Of those in the gallery watching this confrontation between Jesus and the scribes, Mark tells the readers, "They were all amazed and glorified God, saying, 'We have never seen anything like this!'" Indeed, they had not!

Forgiveness is at the heart of the gospel. We read Mark 11:25 emphasizing forgiveness when it tells us, "Whenever you stand praying, forgive, if you have anything against anyone; so that your Father in heaven may also forgive you your trespasses." Not only that, but the centerpiece of clearly the most prayed prayer in all church history offers these words: "Forgive us our debts, / as we also have forgiven our debtors" (Matt. 6:12). The forgiving of debts is not only a monetary transaction, but also a transaction necessary in the give-and-take of all human relationships. Consequently, the prayer that Jesus teaches his disciples discloses that what is true of the divine-human relationship is just as true of strictly human relationships.

Regarding healing, I ask that you notice a diminutive detail from Mark's story. Jesus first forgives the man, and only then heals him. Could it be that forgiveness is at the heart of healing? In other words, I wonder if in order for healing to take place there must first be forgiveness? Does this make sense? I do not know, but the thought occurred to me when I read Mark's story of the paralyzed man.

Last week one of my best friends and a former part-time local pastor took his own life. In my experience he was a wonderful and multitalented person. There was nothing I know of that he could not do if he tried. Everyone who knew him loved him, and at least seven hundred people attended his funeral, but possibly many more. Why he did what he did I cannot say. However, I confess that I have had many angry moments with him since his death. Why did he not pick up the phone and call? How could he have left his family and friends this way? What did we do, what did I do, to deserve this horrible event? Can I ever forgive him?

Then Mark introduces Jesus, the great healer. I suppose this is the gift of faith given me in my time of need. After all, pastors are people too. We have the same struggles and questions everyone else has. Fortunately, Mark gives me a clue in the paralyzed man's story for my own soul's healing. Mark reminds me that on at least one occasion forgiveness precedes healing. Jesus first forgives the man and then heals him. Perhaps my forgiveness of my friend's suicide can help heal my anger. Perhaps Jesus can heal our broken relationship through forgiveness.

In God's mercy, forgiveness is beyond a doubt one of the pillars of abundant Christian living. Without forgiveness healing will never come to any of us. (David N. Mosser)

JULY 3, 2005

Seventh Sunday After Pentecost

Worship Theme: Whether we fall in love with another, like Isaac and Rebekah, or struggle with our own actions, like Paul, humankind can depend on the love and mercy of God reflected in the life, death, and resurrection of Jesus—the Christ of God. In Christ we find rest for our souls.

Readings: Genesis 24:34-38, 42-49, 58-67; Romans 7:15-25*a*; Matthew 11:16-19, 25-30

Call to Worship (Psalm 45:10-11*a*, 15-17)

Leader: Hear, O daughter, consider and incline your ear;

People: **Forget your people and your father's house, and the king will desire your beauty.**

Leader: With joy and gladness they are led along as they enter the palace of the king.

People: **In the place of ancestors you, O king, shall have sons; you will make them princes in all the earth.**

Leader: I will cause your name to be celebrated in all generations;

People: **Therefore the peoples will praise you forever and ever.**

Pastoral Prayer:

Gracious God of glory and of mercy, we come to you in our hour of need. Like Paul, our own actions often confuse us. At one moment we profess allegiance to you and those whom we love. However, in the next moment, we say and do things that reflect not the loyalty we profess but rather a violation of the sacred covenant you have given us as a blessed gift. Help us repent of our sin against you, O God, and our sin against our brothers and sisters. Too often we have failed to do unto others as we would have them do unto us. Give us strength of purpose and help us abide by the holy covenants we have made with you and with our fellow believers.

This day, O Lord, let us reaffirm the covenant that we made long ago with you and others so that our relationships remain disciplined within the boundaries of your divine love. Let us live for others as Christ has lived—and died—for us. It is in the name of Christ that we pray. Amen. (David N. Mosser)

SERMON BRIEFS

THE DYNAMICS OF PROMISE KEEPING

GENESIS 24:34-38, 42-49, 58-67

Vows and promises get little attention in our world these days. Whether it is within the contexts of marriage, vocation, friendship, or faith, the norm of breaking promises surpasses the norm of keeping them. Many things influence this breakdown in relationships. It is unfair to pinpoint any one cause as the singular, defining culprit. Many influences collide at the intersection of a promise between two people or two organizations, which result in one or both breaking commitment with each other.

Promise keeping has a rich and powerful place in the Bible. If one were to research the Old Testament from its beginning, one would find that promise keeping was a serious aspect between God and people and between people and people. It was taken seriously and contained certain powerful dynamics. Genesis 24:34-38, 42-49, and 58-67 encapsulate such dynamics and may provide ways in which we may learn to keep promises we make to ourselves and others.

The first dynamic of the divine-human relationship is epitomized in the human-human relationship. The person in the story is identified only as "the servant of Abraham." He knows the one who has commissioned him to carry out a command of finding his son a life companion. His character is directly related to his relationship with his superior. He has no problem with trusting Abraham. He is faithful because he knows that Abraham's relationship with God is a blessed one. He can act on Abraham's instructions because Abraham trusts God. As Charles Wesley put it, "To serve the present age, my calling to fulfill; / O may it all my powers engage to do my Master's will" ("A Charge to Keep I Have," *The United Methodist Hymnal* [Nashville: The United Methodist Publishing House, 1989], no. 413).

In my first career track, I was planning to become a manager for an internationally known electronics company. What I learned in a short stint of three years prior to entering ministry was that in order to be a successful manager, you have to trust the company. The first dynamic in the divine-human relationship is that you have to trust the company—of God. The "servant of Abraham" trusts Abraham because Abraham trusts God.

The second dynamic of promise keeping is that you have to take the risk of trusting God in order to carry out your commitment to another person. Note what the servant does: "When I came to the well today, I prayed, 'LORD, God of my master Abraham, please give me success in what I am doing'" (v. 42 GNT). Then he took the risk of formulating a plan to complete his mission. How many times have we just launched into some important work in the church, some extraordinary mission without framing the venture with the words, "Lord, God of my master, Jesus Christ, please give me success in what I am doing"? This dynamic of trusting God empowers us to take the necessary risks in being successful—on God's terms, of course—as we follow Christ's commands.

The third dynamic of promise keeping is allowing people choices. Rebecca had the freedom to choose whether to go with Abraham's servant or to remain where she was. We cannot deny others the right to choose to be part of God's great plan of salvation. Simply because we have been called to serve God does not give us the right to deny people the choice of accepting or denying God's plans for our lives.

These three dynamics of promising keeping call to us to take seriously who and whose we are and the ways we are to behave toward God and others. This story could help change our lives and our world the next time we make a promise. (Mike Childress)

THE STRANGE CASE OF DR. JEKYLL AND MR. HYDE

ROMANS 7:15-25a

The last decades of the nineteenth century were a time of buoyant optimism about the human condition. In the midst of this jubilation there appeared in 1886 a book from Robert Louis Stevenson called *The Strange Case of Dr. Jekyll and Mr. Hyde.* It was at heart a social commentary, a warning. It alerted the properly mannered, well-educated people of that day that there was lurking in every person a nether world populated by demons.

We cannot help seeing the evil in our world that the New Testament calls "sin." Hate and cruelty and war convulsed the human community all through the twentieth century. The worst deeds were done in the name of religion. Yet we live in a sin-denying time. Crime and terrorism are exploding in our face, and social unrest and addiction and moral failure are everywhere. But our age has no name for the evil that besets us. We have swept away the language of theology in favor of the language of psychology. There is no evil doing, only neuroses. There are no sinners, only victims.

As an old man, Karl Menninger figured he had one more good book left in him. In 1973 he unloaded his mind in a book called *Whatever Became of Sin?* He suggests that the New Testament might after all have something to say about the human situation. Its theological analysis of the human condition is as valid as any psychological analysis. Sin belongs in the human equation as much as any other factor does.

Paul also lived in a sin-denying age, and he played a role for his time that was similar to the one Menninger has played for ours. Paul knew that the conventional analysis of the human situation in his time was wrong. Paul's analysis flashes forth in the seventh chapter of Romans. Remember that this is the mature Paul, the Paul who is at the peak of his intellectual powers. Paul has met the Lord Jesus Christ; he has given himself to Christ; he has tried for many years to live an exemplary Christian life.

Paul starts with an analysis of his own behavior. "I do not understand my own actions. For I do not do what I want, but I do the very thing I hate.... I can will what is right, but I cannot do it" (vv. 15, 18). What's wrong? Paul tells us three times that sin is dwelling within him! Paul's whole self has been disrupted by sin. He does not have the will or the ability to give himself to God as he knows he ought to. Paul has realized, finally, that his is a permanent condition. No amount of social engineering is going to get this thing off his back.

The social engineers have always been busy. They have told us how we can pull ourselves up by our bootstraps and cure what ails us. They have said that the key is education or discipline or positive thinking or self-esteem or government programs. Paul will have none of this. He knows that he's plagued by what Carl Jung called "the shadow" of human personality, that is, the dark aspects of the personality that we push underground but that still have some control over us. We are harassed by demons that we can't always keep locked up.

In light of this situation, what we need is a savior—someone who will, in Paul's words, "rescue [us] from this body of death" (v. 24). Paul says there is such a one: Jesus Christ. Our salvation does not begin when we pull ourselves up by our bootstraps or become better than others or achieve this or that. Our salvation begins when we, in all honesty, own up to who we are and who God is. The key is not what we can do for ourselves, but what God can do for us and in us, if we will but allow it. (Sandy Wylie)

AN ANTIDOTE FOR EXHAUSTION

MATTHEW 11:16-19, 25-30

A pall seems to shroud the opening lines of the eleventh chapter of Matthew. John the Baptist is in prison. He sends messengers to Jesus asking "Are you the one who is to come, or are we to wait for another?" We are asking the same question. And yet, unlike John, we ask it not from the dank space of a prison cell, but from the dark uncertainties of our lives. We are exhausted from searching without finding while fussing at God for not answering our questions.

Jesus, listening to John's friends, seems exhausted. He listens carefully to their questions. You can almost see him wince. Finally, he sends John's disciples away with the answer they needed most. "Go and tell John what you hear and see" (v. 4). Jesus is the Promised One. John can die knowing he gave his blessing aright.

Jesus is exhausted, wearied by questions that seem blind to obvious answers. "To what shall I compare this generation?" Quoting a well-known saying of his day in verse 17, he says we are like whining children who play in the streets of our discontent. Nothing seems to satisfy us. We hear lively music but do not dance; we weep, and no one weeps with us. Whereas Jesus is exhausted by the fickle crowds that follow him, the crowd is exhausted from never finding soul satisfaction in the spiritual quest.

We are then told that "at that time," our Lord opened his life to God in prayer, thanking God for revealing God's will, God's heart to "infants" (v. 25). Here, Jesus reminds us that our search for answers, our quest for certainty can only be found in child-like trust, placing our lives in the care of the one who reveals God. It is only in trusting relationship with Jesus that we discover satisfying release from the haunting questions of life's meaning.

Our Lord now turns and addresses us. Jesus has answered John's disciples, he has voiced a prayer of gratitude to God. Here are words that have comforted seeking people for nearly two millennia. "Come to me, all you that are weary and are carrying heavy burdens, and I will give you rest" (v. 28). Burdens come in many packages. For John, the burden was wrapped up in confusion. He so much wanted Jesus to be the Messiah on his terms. At the end of his life, John found rest in Jesus' assuring words. Sometimes, we too are confused about Jesus' presence and work in our lives. For some, faith is a riddle to be solved with our minds rather than an action expressed through our work. For others, following Jesus requires the "letting go" of the heavy burden of prejudice so Jesus can give rest in uncommon acceptance. Like John, we want to know from deep within our souls.

One of the onerous burdens under which we live is this thirst for certainty. We search for answers from the dark cells of our doubts believing that if we had the right answers, we would find peace. To our amazing relief and surprise, Jesus gives himself rather than answers. He invites us to give him our burdens in exchange for his blessing. He invites us to take on ourselves his way of liberating life rather than our way of demanding life. He invites us simply to come to him with our soul's exhaustion and, in his presence, find our rest.

Here is an antidote for exhaustion. Like John, bring our Lord all your confusions, uncertainties, and pain. In so doing, you will both hear and experience a love that will never let you go. (Timothy L. Owings)

JULY 10, 2005

Eighth Sunday After Pentecost

Worship Theme: New life comes as a gift from God whether this new life is in the form of a baby or in the form of seeds bursting forth from dormant soil. Wherever there is new growth we can see the Lord's handiwork.

Readings: Genesis 25:19-34; Romans 8:1-11; Matthew 13:1-9, 18-23

Call to Worship (Psalm 119:105-106, 108-109, 111-112)

Leader: Your word is a lamp to my feet and a light to my path.

People: **I have sworn an oath and confirmed it, to observe your righteous ordinances.**

Leader: Accept my offerings of praise, O LORD, and teach me your ordinances.

People: **I hold my life in my hand continually, but I do not forget your law.**

Leader: Your decrees are my heritage forever; they are the joy of my heart.

People: **I incline my heart to perform your statutes forever, to the end.**

Pastoral Prayer:

The Word, O God, is what gives each of us hope and direction in life. It truly is a lamp unto our feet. Your light provides a guide for our journey. Our journey is not only an outward sojourn of faith but also an interior discovery of what it means to be human as well. Give us the wisdom and discernment to learn from you the ways to be fully human as well as a genuinely faithful people. May you, O Lord, grant our prayers as you did the prayers of Isaac as he prayed for his beloved Rebekah. Furnish us the will to grow in grace according to the dictates and precepts of the gospel. Help us find fertile soil in which to do ministry in the name of Jesus. Make him our morning star and grant us the good judgment necessary to follow him in the paths of righteousness. Forgive us where we have failed and open us to the abundant life made possible through Jesus, in whose name we pray. Amen. (David N. Mosser)

SERMON BRIEFS

WHEN FAITH HAS NO MORE VALUE THAN A HAPPY MEAL

GENESIS 25:19-34

When our children were young, in their toddler years, their favorite trip out of the house would always be a stop at McDonald's. Upon entering the restaurant, their eyes would glow with the expectation of getting what is still known to children today as a McDonald's Happy Meal. It is a minor array of a burger, small order of fries, a cookie, and always a little toy of some kind. Best of all, this instant-gratification meal is always packaged in a nifty, eye-catching little box decorated with some fanciful scene that would entice the children to want it. It is a modern version of what Esau called Jacob's "red stuff."

Hunger can have a ravaging effect on people. Esau was content on trading the most important thing he was given for the instant gratification a cup of soup and a slab of bread could offer him: the stilling of hunger pangs in his stomach. He thought no more of his birthright than equating it with an ancient fast-food meal.

We have been trading our most precious gift ever since that

fateful day when Esau traded his birthright to his brother Jacob. The gift of faith that God offers all people is being traded every day for things that have no more value than the quick-fix qualities of a Happy Meal dinner. No one is exempt from those things that threaten to have us trade our faith for something that would separate us from God and those within our own community of faith.

In the modern sense, the most alluring thing, the most threatening temptation is that we will forgo building a lasting relationship with God and try to apply the fast-food concept. Instead of the long road of developing faith in God, folks will opt for the short road. Instead of taking the time to learn of God's ways over the years, we will turn on the television and reach for the dazzling and enchanting messages of the religion brokers posing as modern-day prophets who sell God at the lowest market price. They peddle their religious wares for the minimum gift of a contribution, all the time making the listener think he or she is purchasing a relationship with God. And people will forgo the relationship with their local faith community so that they can "acquire" God through some easy, low-cost, quick-fix way. Even the computer world is offering what we are finding as the "virtual church." Without ever attending or stepping into the confines of a church community, one can go online into cyberspace and be a part of a church community without ever seeing or talking to a human being.

These are but several of the many ways God's family, the human family, is still bartering its most precious gift—a faith relationship with God—for the miniscule value of the world's plethora of Happy Meals. (Mike Childress)

A MATTER OF LIFE OR DEATH

ROMANS 8:1-11

In our text Paul is drawing a contrast between "flesh" and "spirit." He isn't using the word *flesh* as we might commonly understand it. He isn't referring to a kind of duality in human nature that we characterize as a lower and a higher nature. By *flesh* he isn't pointing simply to our physical bodies. Rather, Paul has in mind an orientation to our world or a lifestyle.

This lifestyle that Paul calls "flesh" is a life that is lived under the lordship of the sinful self. It involves the whole being. It's more a product of the mind and will than it is of bodily cravings. It's a life that is turned away from God and neighbors. And because this is so, this lifestyle is characterized by rebellion, sin, and death.

In our text Paul draws a line between two very different lifestyles. One life ("flesh") is under the dominion of sin while the other is under the dominion of God. If the line between the two seems sharp, that's because Paul intends it to be. In the end, people come down on either one side or the other, and the consequences are strikingly different.

Those who walk "according to the flesh" (v. 4) are hostile to God (v. 7) and cannot please God (v. 8). Because their orientation puts them in the service of sin, they are turned away from God and others. They are cut off from the highest good and headed in only one direction: toward death.

In his last book, psychiatrist Karl Menninger tried to bring us back to an understanding of sin that sounds very much like Paul's. He writes, "Sin has a willful, defiant, or disloyal quality; *someone* is defied or offended or hurt. The willful disregard or sacrifice of the welfare of others for the welfare or satisfaction of the self is an essential quality of the concept *sin*" (*Whatever Became of Sin?* [New York: Hawthorn Books, 1973], p. 19). Sin, says Menninger, is at heart a refusal of God's love and the love of others. It is such a harsh concept to the modern mind that we have put the word and concept aside in favor of euphemisms. We speak of error, weakness, infraction, mistake, delinquency, sickness, and so forth—anything but sin.

Menninger, like Paul, cautions us to see sin not just in terms of individual wrongdoing. Sin is a great field of energy that is directed against God's purposes. It has cosmic and social locations, and it reaches into every area of our lives. It tries to pervert all that is good. Nothing is beyond its reach. In his book, Menninger includes a chilling section on "groupthink" (pp. 96-98). He tells how groups and whole societies can unwittingly become captives of their own twisted ideologies and dissolve into a sea of self-righteousness.

Fortunately, there is a power greater than sin, and there is a deliverance from sin's consequences. That's what Paul is proclaiming here. Those who walk "according to the Spirit" have found that power and are claiming that deliverance. Any condemnation they felt is no longer hanging over them. They have set their minds on the things of the Spirit. Their orientation points them and others toward life and peace (v. 6). A favorite New Testament phrase for this life is "eternal life," which has to do with present life as much as it does life beyond the grave. It's not so much what happens when life ends as it is what happens when life with God begins. It has to do with quality of life as much as with quantity. It describes the lifestyle of those who turn away from sin and take rest in God. (Sandy Wylie)

FIELD OF DREAMS

MATTHEW 13:1-9, 18-23

The parable of the sower has been called the parable of parables. Like a marquee, it stands at the beginning of Matthew 13, the parable chapter of the first Gospel. The setting of the parable likewise suggests its importance. As if to hark back to the calling of the first disciples, Jesus tells this parable "beside the sea" to "great crowds gathered around him." So crowded is the shore that our Lord uses a boat as a pulpit.

Matthew tells us Jesus "told them many things in parables." At this moment, however, he tells them only one parable, the parable of the sower. The gravity of this parable in Jesus' thinking is accented by the use of the word "Listen!" Here is something very important, a must-hear story we could easily dismiss. So important is our listening that Jesus ends the parable with the admonition "Let anyone with ears listen!" So we shall listen.

As the story goes, a farmer sows his field with seed. Unlike modern farming techniques that plow and disk the ground before sowing, first-century farmers cast seed over unplowed ground and then turned the seed into the dirt. This farmer has a particularly pesky plot of land. Between plantings, as the field lay fallow, travelers wore paths across the length and breadth of the land. The sown seed on the path seemed as a served up meal to the birds who quickly devoured the seed with not so much as a "thank-you" to the farmer.

Other seed landed on "rocky ground" where it "sprang up quickly" but just as quickly "withered away." Still other seed "fell among thorns, and the thorns grew up and choked them." And yes, a portion of the seed "fell on good soil and brought forth grain, some a hundredfold, some sixty, some thirty." Here is a story colored by generosity but shaped by confusion. Who would seem to waste such precious seed and hard work knowing so much would be lost? We are greatly helped in understanding this parable by the fact that Jesus offers an interpretation in verses 18-23. Like a mirror held up to the story, our Lord's interpretation suggests that the four kinds of soils in the parable represent four kinds of people in the human family.

Is there another interpretation? In my judgment, our Lord's interpretation gives clear focus to the many kinds of people in the Gospel story who, having heard the word, respond in a variety of ways. But could the field represent just one person in which we find all four types of soil? It seems that we can find within all of us the path, rocky ground, thorns, and good soil. How so?

The path could represent the worn roads of life where, because we travel them so much, there is not much chance the word will grow. Jobs, hobbies, habits, long-term loyalties both political and social often find little place for the word. The rocky ground might well be those parts of our lives that quickly welcome the good news. Life has hardened us; we long for good things to happen where there has only been difficulty. The thorns may be the parts of our lives where sin, prejudice, indifference, or complacency simply choke out the good news.

But in all of us there is far more good soil than we first imagine. In that good soil, God can bring forth a good and bountiful crop. What's the parable saying? There exists within us all a field of dreams that, having received the gospel, can and will bring forth a bountiful harvest. Cultivate that soil and watch the gospel grow in your life. (Timothy L. Owings)

JULY 17, 2005

Ninth Sunday After Pentecost

Worship Theme: In God's realm the good seed grows along with the weeds that the evil one sows. In due time, God will harvest both the good and the bad and bring creation to fruition.

Readings: Genesis 28:10-19*a*; Romans 8:12-25; Matthew 13:24-30, 36-43

Call to Worship (Psalm 139:1-3, 7, 23-24)

Leader: O LORD, you have searched me and known me.

People: **You know when I sit down and when I rise up; you discern my thoughts from far away.**

Leader: You search out my path and my lying down, and are acquainted with all my ways.

People: **Where can I go from your spirit? Or where can I flee from your presence?**

Leader: Search me, O God, and know my heart; test me and know my thoughts.

People: **See if there is any wicked way in me, and lead me in the way everlasting.**

Pastoral Prayer:

Merciful Lord of all Creation, we pray to you because you are the author of everlasting life. To you, O God, we owe a great debt of gratitude for all that we are and have been and hope to become. Your abundance is too great for us to grasp or appreciate. Yet, like petulant children, thanksgiving does not come easily from our lips. Too often we believe that we are the products of our own talents and labor. Too frequently we believe it is by our own work that we have made ourselves what we are today. In this hour of worship, however, we pray that you might bring us to our senses. Help us take hold of the divine reality that you reveal in the life, death, and resurrection of Jesus. As our Messiah, Jesus teaches us humility of spirit and thankfulness of heart. Make us this day your grateful children so that we might become worthy heirs of your divine promise in Jesus. It is in Christ's name that we pray. Amen. (David N. Mosser)

SERMON BRIEFS

A UNIVERSAL PROMISE

GENESIS 28:10-19a

It occurred during those formative, early years of my professional ministry pilgrimage following seminary. It was a hectic time filled with both promise and skepticism. Pastor of a small, rural congregation, I was determined to build a small, sleepy congregation into a viable, thriving ministry. While visiting each church member and making a pastoral plea for support in helping build the ministry, one of the church members asked if I would make a visit to one member who had recently taken seriously ill and been admitted to a local nursing home. I learned that she had not been an active member for years. As busy as I was visiting the active members, I agreed to make the visit. That one visit turned out to be a series of visits that became a friendship until I would preach her funeral almost a year later.

Early in our friendship, the woman I visited in the nursing home made a passionate plea for me to release her from the care facility and take her home. Without exception, every visit I made would always be concluded with her plea for discharge. On one particular visit, she held my hand and said, "Reverend, I have nagged you to death about leaving and going home." Somewhat shocked at her admission, I was going to answer her when, gripping my hand more firmly and looking at me with a peaceful smile, she said, "Reverend, I don't have to go home any more. Everything is going to be all right!" I left that day both puzzled and relieved by her acceptance of the fact that she would never get to go home again. The next visit I made to the nursing home, was to meet the family. Margaret died. She had made it home after all.

"Remember, I will be with you and protect you wherever you go, and I will bring you back to this land. I will not leave you until I have done all that I have promised you" (v. 15 GNT). I still wonder if Margaret had ever heard about Jacob's story. I wonder if you and I have ever really heard it, especially whenever we find ourselves in faith's journey through uncharted territory. How often do we find ourselves feeling seemingly all alone and as though our journeys of life have no sense of God's presence? It probably happens more than we are willing to admit. But then something happens to wake us out of our spiritual stupor and we realize that God has never left our presence. What we realize is that God not being with us is really all about us not being with God. This is why Jacob was so marveled by his realization—God is not stymied by our unfamiliar territories. God is not even repulsed by our lack of acknowledgment. God waits until that timely and most opportune moment to remind us that no matter where we go in this life, be it in a faithful our unfaithful direction, God will bring us back to our senses, God will bring us back to God's self!

It would be a misguided rabbinical student who would come to his own senses along the dusty roads of Syria, Saul of Tarsus, and would later make the profession of faith that echoes the deepest truth of the gospel of Jesus Christ when he said: "There is nothing in all creation that will ever be able to separate us from the love of God" (Rom. 8:39 GNT). It was Jacob's realization, his coming to his senses that made him proclaim, "The Lord is here! He is in this place, and I didn't know it!" It was my sister in faith, Margaret, who came to her own senses in the midst of her life's greatest difficulty when she said, "Reverend, I don't have to go home any more. Everything is going to be all right!"

May we not ever forget the universal and eternal promise from God: "Remember, I will be with you and protect you wherever you go, and I will bring you back to the land. I will not leave you until I have done all that I have promised you." (Mike Childress)

A COSMIC CHRISTIAN FAITH

ROMANS 8:12-25

I often cringe at Christian attempts to adopt cultural symbols or language. At times in the history of the church, Christian appropriation of societal icons has produced a great reworking of ideas or institutions. Indeed, the key image of our faith, the cross, was once for ancient Rome a symbol of a slave's death. Still, I retain this uneasiness when Christians slip too comfortably into their cultural milieu.

To my mind, a prevalent symbol from American culture is space, as in stars, planets, galaxies, black holes, and so forth. Since the mid-1970s, *Star Wars* and its sequels have spawned an entire generation of movies preoccupied with encountering space and its mysteries. These films, as well as NASA's exploration of space and the moon landing, have made space a dominant modern cultural construct. Indeed, through them, space has become a symbol for humanity's belief in our limitless potential, for if we can conquer space (even notionally), then we conquer anything. At least in my estimation, space has gone from being an innocent setting for a movie to a symbol of our collective pride.

As a result, I'm somewhat uncomfortable with this text. Paul has just finished an analysis of what it means for the people of God to live in the power of the Spirit as opposed to walking in the desires of the world (Rom. 8:6-11). Now he moves to a description of what it means to be sons and daughters, even "heirs" of a God who allows us to call him "Abba! Father!" What a joyful privilege God grants those who truly desire to live in the power of the Spirit and in the light of the resurrection of Jesus Christ!

But Paul doesn't end his missive there. No, Paul further ties this glorious status of royal adoption to a concept we'd probably like to forget: suffering. You see, Paul loved the people at Rome too much to let them be blinded by any sort of triumphant notion of being prematurely drawn into glory. Paul reminds them that to gain the status of being God's children entails a capacity to suffer with the Christ who suffered for them.

Yet even here Paul has another surprise in store, because now he moves to tie in Christian suffering to a suffering world around us. Creation labors as it waits for Christ's glory to be revealed. This

249

travail that creation suffers is the same we endure as we wait for Christ to reclaim us in the Parousia. Do you see what Paul has done here? He has deftly tied in our status as God's children to that of the entire world, indeed the cosmos, as part of God's creation! In Paul's mind, the created order is looking for the coming of Christ to complete his redemptive mission! We, along with the creation around us, are bound together in hope as we await Christ. As members of the Body of Christ, we are a part of God's project to reclaim all of creation.

In the wake of Pentecost, this kind of truth lays open Christianity as a cosmic faith. At the inbreaking of the Holy Spirit in Jerusalem, God began to redeem all of creation, including the stars, galaxies, and planets around us. We are a part of a truly intergalactic struggle of good versus evil, but it's no fantasy in which we immerse ourselves for a few hours and then from which we reemerge. Rather, our faith is based solidly on the promise that God will not rest until he redeems the entire universe in Jesus Christ. (Timothy S. Mallard)

WEED CONTROL

MATTHEW 13:24-30, 36-43

The parable of the weeds presents no small problem to the Christian family. We who find ourselves on the gospel road, armed with generous and pointed invective against the ills of the world, hear Jesus offering a curious, even disarming response to the presence and reality of evil. To our amazement, even unbelief, we of faith are urged to let the weeds grow alongside the wheat "until the harvest."

Did I hear our Lord correctly? Let's listen carefully to the parable, eavesdropping on Jesus' insight into the presence of weeds among the wheat. Notice first of all that the story tells us some very positive things about the farmer. He "sowed good seed in his field." Of course he did. What farmer would do otherwise? And yet, we who wrestle with wrong, who know the "slings and arrows of outrageous fortune" in this life, who have been wounded by words spoken in anger question whether God cares for us (quotation from William Shakespeare, *Hamlet*, act 3, scene 1). This is the position of the household slaves who ask, "Master, did you not sow good seed in your field? Where, then, did these weeds come from?" Where indeed?

The shocking solution to the presence of weeds among the wheat redefines weed control for all time. Whereas a modern farmer would use herbicides or mulch to control the weeds, Jesus suggests in the parable the doing of nothing. In fact, Jesus says the best thing we can do is let both the weeds and the wheat grow together. What in the world gave him that idea?

It seems this radical approach to weed control is at the heart of Jesus' teaching from the beginning. Isn't this what our Lord meant when, in the Sermon on the Mount, he taught, "Do not resist an evildoer. But if anyone strikes you on the right cheek, turn the other also; and if anyone wants to sue you and take your coat, give your cloak as well; and if anyone forces you to go one mile, go also the second mile" (5:39-41)? More gospel grows on a turned cheek than a clinched fist. Always has, always will.

Through the great, and at times checkered, history of the church, we have found more sorrow from our feeble attempts to pull weeds than simply to let the weeds grow alongside the wheat. This is risky farming, risky living, risky discipleship. Weed control of this variety requires more thoughtful engagement of the enemy, more focused responses to the reality of evil rather than attacks on people caught in the grip of evil. Weed control as Jesus taught it demands that we of faith spend more of our energies nurturing the gospel seed, cultivating the gospel crop, believing in the gospel harvest.

The best way to prove a stick is crooked is to lay a straight stick alongside it. Would that we who follow Jesus in the twenty-first century would learn to be "salt and light" in the world without poisoning relationships with our salt or wilting the gospel crop with our light. Would that we could be patient and trusting, knowing that one day, God will bring about the harvest, gathering into the gospel barn the wheat that has come to maturity among the weeds.

Weed control. Not the kind of thing you'd practice in your garden in the backyard, but a powerful way to live out the claims of Christ. "Let both of them grow together until the harvest." A radical idea that we might practice and, in so doing, find an abundant harvest unlike anything we've seen before. (Timothy L. Owings)

JULY 24, 2005

Tenth Sunday After Pentecost

Worship Theme: Like a treasure hidden in a field or a pearl of great price, God's realm is worth the sacrifice of all earthly possessions. Like Jacob of old, today's believers serve God with their labor. For the faithful, God is the object of their love.

Readings: Genesis 29:15-28; Romans 8:26-39; Matthew 13:31-33, 44-52

Call to Worship (Psalm 128 RSV)

Leader: Blessed is every one who fears the LORD, who walks in his ways!

People: **You shall eat the fruit of the labor of your hands; you shall be happy, and it shall be well with you.**

Leader: Your wife will be like a fruitful vine within your house; your children will be like olive shoots around your table.

People: **Lo, thus shall the man be blessed who fears the LORD.**

Leader: The LORD bless you from Zion! May you see the prosperity of Jerusalem all the days of your life!

People: **May you see your children's children! Peace be upon Israel!**

Pastoral Prayer:

O God, you who justify and make righteous the handiwork of your creative imagination, give us a spirit of earnest gratitude for your mercy. We are the sheep of your pasture, therefore we turn to you in our time of need. Make us mindful of your manifold blessings that you shower upon us both day and night. Remind us that your hand, and your hand alone, furnish us the food we eat and the shelter from which we benefit. In our times of distress we count on you, as others rely on us to share the divine blessings offered to our world by your unsurpassed generosity. Give us the compassion necessary to pass along our material blessings to others who also stand in need of life's necessities. Make us a people known for benevolence and a spirit of loving charity. Most of all, O Lord, we offer our lives as a testimony of your divine love found in the teachings of Jesus. Jesus came to give us abundant life. Let us share this good news with the world. In Jesus' name we pray. Amen. (David N. Mosser)

SERMON BRIEFS

WHEN TRICKS BECOME TREATS

GENESIS 29:15-28

Many people grow up supposing that life is fair. And if life is not fair, nevertheless, we have to be fair in everything we do. Then comes along one of life's teachable moments. Moments like this teach us that life is not fair. When we have been doing our best to play by the rules, what is our response to those who have perpetrated the unfairness? Our response is no different than Jacob's response to Laban: "Why did you do this to me? I worked to get Rachel. Why have you tricked me?" (v. 25 GNT). What we can do is take Rachel's name out of the reply, and we realize what it is liked to be bamboozled.

One's first reading of this story of Jacob being tricked by Laban begs the question, Where's the anger? Why is Jacob not in Laban's face? Jacob worked seven years to marry his choice. Suddenly Jacob finds out that Laban duped him. Laban's plan was to marry off both of his daughters, and Jacob only bargained for love. Maybe seven years are but a day with God, but this chronological equation is not acceptable in the human realm. It is just not fair. Even after all the years following Jacob's experience, even after all the books like Harold S. Kushner's *When Bad Things Happen to Good People,* we still expect life and people to treat us fairly.

So what kernel of truth can we harvest from this story?

First, God has no problem working through our chicanery. Undoubtedly, Laban had failed to apprise Jacob of his community's wedding practices. Undoubtedly, Jacob had not inquired. The human penchant for manipulation cannot ultimately interfere with God's plan for humankind. And while this does not justify Laban's seemingly deceitful behavior, it does not prevent Jacob from fulfilling God's plan for his life.

Second, Jacob doesn't do the obvious, rather, he refused to give up. The story intimates that Jacob didn't get mad and quit. Jacob dug in and did exactly what was necessary to achieve his faithful end: marry the woman of his choice. In fact the text ends with a matter-of-fact response from Jacob when we read, "Then he worked for Laban another seven years" (v. 30 GNT). Rather than a resigned disappointment, Jacob simply resolves to do whatever is necessary to fulfill Laban's expectations.

Both of these qualities in Jacob's experience beg the question, What will you and I go through, to what extent will we go, and under what conditions will we work in order to fulfill God's will for our lives? Furthermore, what will we as a church go through, to what extent will we go, and under what conditions will we endure in order that the church will fulfill God's plan of salvation? If we are willing to apply what could be called the "Jacob principle," even the tricks perpetrated on us may actually treat us to some of the greatest blessings. (Mike Childress)

A CHRISTIAN VISION OF LIFE

ROMANS 8:26-39

As an army chaplain, I serve soldiers and their families as a means of serving God. A former chief of chaplains shared with me that, while student at the Army War College, he attended a class where the lecturer stopped in midsentence, closed his notes, and walked off stage. The lights were dimmed, the curtains were drawn, and the army chief of staff walked out on stage to talk to the students. He began by holding up his forearm, and then moving it ever so slightly, he said, "To change the Army, even one degree," and let his words trail off. The lesson was not lost on the students: Organizational change is difficult at best. Yet this general went on to say that no change is possible without a new vision. The first task of a leader is to create a vision that people can buy into and eventually adopt as their own.

Paul, I think, understood this facet of leadership. In today's text, he is coming to the conclusion of a major section of Romans: an analysis of what it means to live as a body of believers in the life of the Spirit. Many of the verses in today's passage are often quoted singularly or in small segments (e.g., vv. 26, 28, 31, 35, or 37-39). The problem is that, valuable as any of these texts are, there's an inherently cohesive quality to them when read as a whole. Together these verses constitute the summation of Paul's pastoral task to this congregation: Paul is providing them the vision that God has first given to him. Paul understands that it is this vision—God's vision—of what is happening to this threatened flock that will embolden them to face the future together.

What is this vision for the Christian life? Notice how the Revised Standard Version of the Bible groups these verses into paragraphs: the Spirit intercedes for us in our weakness (vv. 26-27); God's plan from eternity included our predestination to election, our call to faith, our justification by grace, and our future glorification in Christ (vv. 28-30); since God has so perfectly enacted our salvation, who can thwart his design (vv. 31-36); no one, for God controls all facets of creation and has perfected our redemption through his love in Christ Jesus (vv. 37-39). Note how eloquently Paul conducts the argument with a series of rhetorical questions (perfect for reading aloud in a congregation) in verses 31-36 followed by a definitive "No" in verse 37. Paul's intent is clear: He wants the congregation to understand that they are part of the grand scheme of God's design to redeem his creation, but that scheme is so perfect that it includes the regeneration and redemption of each saint in this struggling body of believers. Who could fail to be captured by such a grand vision and personal promise?

And that's exactly the point! A faithful reading and preaching of this text can incorporate this Christian vision for life. In essence, such a sermonic task can provide people today the timeless view Paul offered those early Christians. And perhaps that's as important now as it was then. Think of how fragmented our world is in terms of human relationships. How isolated many people feel even though they live in a sea of humanity. How hungry so many people are for genuine meaning and purpose. Paul's vision for the Christian life meets people at all these basic levels and assures them that an integral part of God's grand design is the nurture and strengthening of our collective and individual faith. Thanks be to God! (Timothy S. Mallard)

THE SURPRISING LIKENESS OF THE KINGDOM

MATTHEW 13:31-33, 44-52

There are times that Jesus doesn't make understanding him or his kingdom easy. Top on the list of difficulties is our Lord's tendency to use the word *like* rather than *is*. Why does he do that? It would be so much easier to understand, so much more "preachable," if you please, if he had simply said, "The kingdom of heaven is," rather than, "The kingdom of heaven is like." But that's what he said and that's what we have.

The Gospel text this week pummels our ears with, count them, six parables in which Jesus says "The kingdom of heaven is like." In each of these parables we gain a powerful insight into the reality and life that is God's kingdom revealed in Jesus Christ. Two parables deal with the growth of the kingdom (the mustard seed and the yeast), three parables describe the joy discovered in finding the kingdom (treasure in the field, the pearl of great price, and the net), and one parable defines the role of the preacher in sharing the message of the kingdom (the scribe).

In the parables of the mustard seed and the yeast, Jesus used two earthy pictures that open a window on the growth of the kingdom. In both parables, the emphasis is on small beginnings that lead to large endings. Sometimes we wonder whether what we are doing for Christ, be it ladling soup at an inner-city mission or tutoring a child, makes any difference to anyone. The mustard seed of love, the yeast of devotion, although measured in thimbles grows to measureless abundance. In God's economy, no small gift offered in service to Christ is lost.

The three parables of joy discovered remind us how good the good news of Christ is. To experience radical forgiveness undeserved and unexpected is like finding a chest of gold in a forgotten field. To receive the uncommon love of God's church is like finding one priceless pearl in an ocean of tiny round balls. To be accepted "warts and all" in the family of God is like being treated with respect and value when other relationships and groups of human beings have treated us with disrespect; it's being named "good" when we know we are far less.

Finally, the parable of the scribe reminds all who speak and live out the claims of Christ, preachers and laity alike, that God takes the "old" and the "new" and finds treasure in both. With God, nothing or no one is devalued, ignored, or forgotten. So it is with us who speak for God and represent God in this broken world. The Pentecostal Spirit of God enables us to be faithful sharers of good news.

Sometimes we want concrete, undeniable proof that the kingdom of God is in our midst. Such "big" proofs can be compelling, but are they rooted in the kingdom? The teaching of our Lord tells us that, more often than not, we will see and experience the likeness of the kingdom in the tiny mustard seed of faith germinating in a human life making it new. We discover the pearl of incomparable price in the company of people much like ourselves. We believe God takes what is old and what is new and weaves it into our life's story. Such is the work of the kingdom of God making all things new. (Timothy L. Owings)

JULY 31, 2005

Eleventh Sunday After Pentecost

Worship Theme: Modern believers seek, like Jacob, to see the face of God. Today we witness in Jesus' life and ministry the presence of God in our world. Our God has compassion on our world. God offers spiritual food for the hungry.

Readings: Genesis 32:22-31; Romans 9:1-5; Matthew 14:13-21

Call to Worship (Psalm 17:1-7, 15 RSV)

Leader: Hear a just cause, O LORD; attend to my cry! Give ear to my prayer from lips free of deceit!

People: **From thee let my vindication come! Let thy eyes see the right!**

Leader: If thou triest my heart, if thou visitest me by night, if thou testest me, thou wilt find no wickedness in me; my mouth does not transgress.

People: **With regard to the works of men, by the word of thy lips I have avoided the ways of the violent.**

Leader: My steps have held fast to thy paths, my feet have not slipped.

People: **I call upon thee, for thou wilt answer me, O God; incline thy ear to me, hear my words.**

All: **Wondrously show thy steadfast love, O savior of those who seek refuge from their adversaries at thy right hand. As for me, I**

shall behold thy face in righteousness; when I awake, I shall be satisfied with beholding thy form.

Pastoral Prayer:

O Lord, let this Sabbath be one of the Holy Spirit's presence among us. We worship you, O God, in a spirit of truth and justice. Let the righteousness that is yours bathe us. May the spirit come upon those who worship you. Let us wrestle with you, Lord, just as Jacob did so long ago at the Jabbok River ford. We remember that it was there that Jacob wrestled for a divine blessing. We today need that blessing that comes only from you just as much as our forebear Jacob did. Help us make peace with those with whom we abide in estrangement. Make us bearers of a peace, which comes only from our acknowledgment of you as Lord and Sovereign of the universe. Although none of us desires to limp away from our experience of the holy, yet remind us, O God, that Jacob's limp is indeed a mark of divine encounter. Help us bear Christ in our ministry to the world. In Jesus' name we pray. Amen. (David N. Mosser)

SERMON BRIEFS

A WRESTLING RELATIONSHIP

GENESIS 32:22-31

In this chapter of Genesis, we come upon the pivotal moment in Jacob's history, when Jacob wrestles all night with a mysterious figure and comes away with the name Israel. This story of Jacob's wrestling at Peniel is wrapped in mystery and has about it an almost dreamlike quality. When we read the statement, "and a man wrestled with him until daybreak," we are left with a thousand questions: What man? Was it a stranger? Was it Esau? Was it an angel? Was it God's very self? Indeed scholars have varying opinions about the wrestling match.

While some preachers may find the story's ambiguity frustrating, the mystery of it allows many interpretations and many perspectives for preaching. There is, of course, no harm in acknowledging the mystery of the story and in leaving the question unanswered for the congregation. They are perfectly capable of drawing their own conclusions and meaning. Before we explore these possibilities, it is important to note the pivotal moments in the wrestling match. The struggle goes on all night, and Jacob is wounded in the hip. Then, Jacob refuses to let go until his opponent blesses him. In response, the stranger gives him the name Israel. Finally, Jacob limps away a changed person.

As we consider who Jacob's wrestling partner might be, we might think that Jacob is wrestling with his conscience, since he had deceived his father, Isaac, and his brother Esau. It is also possible that Jacob is wrestling with Esau himself, since the two brothers will meet the next morning for the first time in years. In either case, the issue Jacob struggles with is shame and forgiveness. This image can be powerful for those in the congregation who are struggling with their past. This story reveals the very real, human experience of wrestling with oneself and seeking to be delivered. As the story unfolds, Jacob is blessed by persevering in the fight. We too can be blessed if we face our own past and risk the wounds that it takes to find healing.

Another possibility is that Jacob is wrestling with God or with an angel of God. In verse 28 Jacob's opponent renames him Israel because he has "striven with God and with humans and [has] prevailed." Jacob himself seems to believe that he has been wrestling with God, for he says at the end of the wrestling match, "I have seen God face to face" (v. 30). What a powerful image this text provides! It gives us the opportunity to affirm that it is okay for people to wrestle with God, to struggle with doubt, to engage God in hand-to-hand combat. That thought alone will be liberating to many listeners.

As Jacob wrestles, he wants to know his opponent's name. The stranger's reply is, "Why is it that you ask my name?" The stranger refuses to tell Jacob. This exchange mirrors our own experience. We want to know God's name, to have some control, to know the answers to God's mystery. But God won't be named or controlled.

Nonetheless, God will give us what we need. No matter how violent our struggles with God may be, if we persevere and continue to seek God, God will bless us. In fact, we are blessed by and through the struggle. Anyone who has struggled with doubt and has come through to the other side can testify to their deepened faith and hope.

In our wrestling with God, we may not come away with all the answers, and we may walk away limping, but God will bless us and give us a new name. (Carol Cavin-Dillon)

A FAMILY OF THE COVENANTS

ROMANS 9:1-5

One of the worst genocides ever to occur was the systematic execution of European Jews by the Nazis during World War II. As the state began its program of arresting, imprisoning, and murdering Jews (and other "undesirables"), the German church was almost wholly silent. (For a thorough treatment of this difficult subject, see Victoria Barnett, *For the Soul of the People: Protestant Protest Against Hitler* [New York: Oxford University Press, 1992], and the outstanding work of Wolfgang Gerlach in *And the Witnesses Were Silent: The Confessing Church and the Persecution of the Jews* [Lincoln: University of Nebraska Press, 2000].) There was little prophetic witness against this terror, even from members of the Confessing Church, because of latent anti-Semitism in many Protestant churches and because the Third Reich co-opted them through the installment of a *Reichsbischof* (Reich Bishop) and a concomitant state agency.

One of the few Germans to protest against the Holocaust was Dietrich Bonhoeffer. Known by Christians mostly for his martyrdom by the gestapo on April 9, 1945, Bonhoeffer early came to see the Nazi program as one designed not just to persecute Jewry but also to destroy the church. However, even for a noted theologian such as Bonhoeffer, it was only late in the game that he came, theologically, to be able to claim Jews as "children of the covenant." Prior to that, Jews had remained, for him as for many German Christians, neighbors and fellow Germans but distant spiritual cousins unknown or unwanted in the family of God.

This highlights the problem that Christians have faced since the crucifixion: How do we as people of the new covenant treat our brothers and sisters of the old covenant? Too often, like the *Landeskirchen* (regional churches) of prewar Germany, many Christians have misunderstood, disdained, or even actively repressed Jews. Paul faced this dilemma as well, although his problem was more personal. Born, raised, and educated a Jew, as he writes to the congregation at Rome, he voices a pathos that bespeaks of a family torn apart. He uses the language of a grieving brother as he describes his own "great sorrow and unceasing anguish" at the division in God's kingdom because Jews have not recognized Jesus as the Christ. Herein lies the key to Paul's thought: We misunderstand him if we think this issue is one of his own mere psychological conflicts. In essence, he is concerned not for himself but for the kingdom of God. Even as he affirms the gifts of faith that God has bestowed on them and affirms that the Christ stands as the fulfillment of these gifts, Paul is still unquestionably distressed that his people have rejected the most glorious of all God's blessings.

Perhaps Paul's thought, then, provides us the direction to follow as we face the issue of our own ecumenical interaction with Jews today. Not in a condescending or hypocritical way but with love and respect, we can open avenues for dialogue, understanding, and mutual cooperation with Jews in our communities. Like brothers and sisters long estranged within a family, perhaps we can remain true to our confession of Christ and even witness to them of Christ's resurrection glory while appreciating their particular and historical expression of faith. In this way, perhaps we can effect a measure of reunion with our fellow children of God's promise. In this way, perhaps we will open ourselves to understanding not only Jews but also others outside of our faith to which God might wish us to witness. In this way, perhaps such an opening of ourselves can lead us to a more full expression of what it means to be the church. As he sat in prison and contemplated his church's relationship to German Jews and its failure to actively love them, Dietrich Bonhoeffer penned these words that can prompt us today, "The Church is the Church only when it exists for others" (Dietrich Bonhoeffer, *Letters and Papers from Prison*, ed. Eberhard Bethge, rev. ed. [New York: Macmillan, 1967], p. 211). (Timothy S. Mallard)

DOGGIE BAGS FOR DISCIPLES

MATTHEW 14:13-21

Have you ever noticed that some things taste better the second day? This is why God created leftovers and restaurants offer doggie bags. Just when you can't eat another bite, the waitress says those four golden words: "Shall I wrap this?" You feign indifference. Then you mutter, "Oh, what the heck. Wrap it up. I'll take it to my dog." This story is about leftovers. Whether you think of it as "The Multiplication of Loaves and Fishes" or "Jesus Feeds Five Thousand," it is the only miracle recorded in all four Gospels. The details may differ, but most scholars assume one narrative.

But, back to the story. Jesus and the disciples need to get away. A crowd follows. Supper time comes. The disciples turn to Jesus and say, "Send 'em to the store." To which Jesus says, "Feed 'em yourself." But the cupboard is bare. In John's version, a youngster comes to the rescue. Suddenly a voice is heard above the crowd. "Over here, Lord. I've got a child with a lunch. Check it out."

If the situation sounds ridiculous, it's meant to. The author wants us to see how impossible things seem. So many hungers, so few resources. Jesus has five thousand sit on the grass. Grace is said. Food is passed. People eat beyond satiation. ("No thank you. Everything was wonderful, but I really couldn't eat another bite.")

How can this be? It's hard to say. But preachers have never lacked for theories. The answers may include:

- Stretching! A small amount of food is "stretched" to feed a large number of people. It's not unlike "watering the soup" when more show up than expected.
- Multiplying! Ironically, though this story is known as "The Multiplication of Loaves and Fishes," the word *multiply* appears nowhere in the text.
- Sharing! Someone says: "I have some oranges in my tunic." Another unpacks a kielbasa from his briefcase. And several others produce pita from their pockets. All told, a miracle in itself.

The fact of the matter is, the story doesn't tell us how the people get fed. So I can't, either. Your curiosity will have to go hungry.

But redirect your attention to the leftovers. Remember that when everybody has eaten their fill, there are food fragments left over. Jesus tells somebody to collect them. So somebody does. And when the fragments are gathered, there are twelve full baskets, which ought to suggest something. Twelve baskets of fragments. Twelve disciples. One basket per disciple. That can't be coincidental. The message is given to would-be disciples: "You can feed people. You have food. Always have had. Always will have. There are no Mother Hubbards among you. No bare cupboards. You do not come unprepared or empty-handed," which is a message I need as much as anybody.

Let me share my version of "the unpreparedness dream." It concerns preaching and my lack of readiness to do it. In one version of the dream, I am improperly dressed. It is time to preach, but I am in a sweatshirt. Or barefoot. Or tieless. In another version, I have the right clothes on my back, but no sermon in my hands. Either I didn't write it or I can't find it. And in the third version, I can't find the church. I have the right clothes and the right pages, but I can't find the sanctuary. I can hear the organ, but I can't find the door that leads to the pulpit. Or the door is locked. Thirty-eight years in the ministry and I can't outgrow the anxiety.

Or consider something closer to home, or closer to church. There's a job that needs doing. I figure you'd be the person to do it. So I call you up. You listen. You wrestle. Then you say: "Gee, Bill, in a church as big as yours (at such moments, it's always 'my church'), there must be somebody better than me." Somebody with more time, more talent, more treasure. Like the disciples, you think of yourself as underequipped to do what is needed.

This is why this is your parable. Sure your baskets differ. Some of you have a basket of lobster. Some, chunk tuna. And some have nothing but crackers and carp. But each of you has a basket. And yours is far from empty. So you need to be alert, aware, awake. For you never know when Jesus—or one of his friends—

> will need your basket,
> will need your lunch,
> will need you. (William A. Ritter)

REFLECTIONS

AUGUST

Reflection Verse: *"Now faith is the assurance of things hoped for, the conviction of things not seen. Indeed, by faith our ancestors received approval." (Hebrews 11:1-2)*

ASSURANCE: FAITH YOKED TO HOPE
Hebrews 11:1-7

An old saw has it that "there are no guarantees in life." Another quotation that often accompanies the one about guarantees is, "Nothing in life is certain except for death and taxes." How universal is this sentiment? A family I once visited had a refrigerator magnet with these words emblazoned on it: "Life is uncertain, eat dessert first!" What each of these concepts holds in common is a universal human tendency to desire an ironclad agreement between life and us. We want to know what we can count on so that we may leave the rest to chance. However, as the quotations suggest, between life and us there are few ironclad agreements made.

Truthfully, all people need a foundation from which to operate in life. Some things we seem to count on without much thought. For one, most of us upon waking do not worry much about whether or not our heart will beat throughout the day. We take this fact of our physiology for granted. Likewise, few of us have anxiety that suddenly the laws of nature, for example the reality of gravity, will somehow be other than we have always known it to be. Do you worry about whether or not the sun will come up? Do you persistently concern yourself about the ozone layer or the atmospheric pressure of the earth, or even the polar ice caps melting soon?

Clearly, there are a million and one things that could drive us absolutely insane if we worried about each of them constantly. Mercifully, however, there are things that we simply take for granted in living life. If we could not count on some things being constant, then we would go mad. Yet, in the wisdom of creation we can count on some things. We can have confidence that generally speaking we can rely on the sun rising in the morning—and in the east—and we can assume that our hearts will continue beating rhythmically and regularly until our cardiologists tell us otherwise. It is these kinds of assumptions we make that constructs a life bearable and worth the living. When these taken-for-granted realities are no longer in force, then we are all in trouble.

Where does faith fit into this picture? Some people settled their questions about faith in God and life long ago in Sunday school. For some, belief in God is not something to question. The reason: Once we begin asking the deep questions about God, our whole world view begins to unravel like a ball of twine. Indeed, the philosophical questions that life poses can so torture some people that they can literally go mad. The deeper mired in the questions these people become the nearer they move toward the edge of insecurity, anxiety, disbelief; all of which may eventually lead to insanity. Thus, is it better to just not ask? Our scripture seems to suggest that faith is far too important for people to take it for granted. Although, in truth, avoiding difficult questions of meaning and value often makes life easier to swallow.

Hebrews 11:1-2 tells its readers, "Now faith is the assurance of things hoped for, the conviction of things not seen. Indeed, by faith our ancestors received approval." Most people I know, and this includes pastors, need people and promises that they can count on. We also know that, in the church, however, there are two kinds of people: promise keepers and promise breakers. Preachers generally embrace the former and avoid the latter, however untheological it may be. After all, preachers are human too. We want to deal confidently with folks who are in ministry with us. Yet, we all know the all too human shortcoming of forgetting what we promise or simply refusing to do things that we had committed to earlier.

When I attended the University of Texas, I had a wonderful professor named James Kinneavy. Rhetoricians generally recognized Dr. Kinneavy as one of the world's two leading authorities in the academic discipline of rhetoric. I loved to meet with him and soak up all the wisdom and knowledge that he dispensed without even realizing it. He knew Plato, Aristotle, Isocrates, and Augustine backward and forward—and so many other great rhetorical scholars as well. The problem was that although he could cite any text in Aristotle's *Nicomachean Ethics* or *Rhetoric* by both chapter and verse, he could not remember lunch dates he made with me to discuss my reading assignments. We would make a lunch date, and three times out of four he would fail to appear. He always apologized, but, after a while, anyone might get gun-shy when setting plans for lunch with him. We all want to count on promises made by others. This is especially true about the promises God makes to us.

John Wesley was one of those great souls who spent much of his life looking for assurance, or what the book of Hebrews might call the "things hoped for, the conviction of things not seen." He searched Scripture, church history, the doctrines of the church, and the minds and hearts of all he respected. Yet, the peace and inner calm he sought continued to elude him. Finally, as Methodist lore tells the story, Wesley found that peace of mind in the assurance of God's love at a little church on Aldersgate Street, as he listened to someone read Luther's preface to the commentary on the book of Romans. As the *United Methodist Book of Worship* puts it: "On Wednesday, May 24, 1738, John Wesley experienced his 'heart strangely warmed.' This Aldersgate experience was crucial for his own life and became a touchstone for the Wesleyan movement" (Nashville: United Methodist Publishing House, 1992, p. 439).

Generally the feeling of assurance is a gift of the Holy Spirit. Some people get it immediately upon conversion, while others, like Wesley, search for it for many years. My guess is that assurance is like the missing remote control for the television. About the time we stop looking for it, it finds us.

Assurance is the calmness that people sense and feel when they know that God has sent Jesus to save us and redeem us. It is an inner testimony by the Holy Spirit that God loves us and offers us salvation in Jesus. But assurance is not an equivalent to knowledge. Rather, assurance is more like a promise that we wholly and fully believe, accept, and trust. This "faith" then gives us the confidence to lead lives that befit the gospel. As Paul himself says, "We walk by faith, not by sight" (2 Cor. 5:7).

As believers, the bedrock of our ability to live abundant lives is to have that certain confidence or assurance that God revealed in Jesus Christ. Every other idol, whether in nature or our own success, is a chimera. These objects of false confidence are fleeting and untrustworthy. Faith in Christ is the only trust in abundant life that we believers can grasp.

As people of faith we live between two alternatives. One alternative leads to countless questions that eventually bring us back to where we began. The other alternative is to live in faith until the Holy Spirit grants us that inner peace with God, which we call assurance. I like this second alternative because, after all, hasn't God already given us everything else? Maybe assurance, too, merits a pillar in abundant living. Amen. (David N. Mosser)

AUGUST 7, 2005

Twelfth Sunday After Pentecost

Worship Theme: The Word of God is near us, but in order for us to live God's Word fully we must receive it in faith. It is by faith in God's revelation that we can embrace our life as God's wondrous miracle.

Readings: Genesis 37:1-4, 12-28; Romans 10:5-15; Matthew 14:22-33

Call to Worship (Psalm 105:1-6, 45c)

Leader: O give thanks to the LORD, call on his name, make known his deeds among the peoples.

People: **Sing to him, sing praises to him; tell of all his wonderful works.**

Leader: Glory in his holy name; let the hearts of those who seek the LORD rejoice.

People: **Seek the LORD and his strength; seek his presence continually.**

Leader: Remember the wonderful works he has done, his miracles, and the judgments he uttered, O offspring of his servant Abraham, children of Jacob, his chosen ones.

People: **Praise the LORD!**

Pastoral Prayer:

O God, in whom we move and live and have our being, we praise you this day for the gift of Jesus Christ and the Holy Spirit.

Jesus as the Christ saves us from our sin. In the shadow of the Holy Spirit, Jesus saves us for the gospel's good news in which we stand. As ambassadors of the gospel we spread the good news of Jesus in our homes, our neighborhoods, and indeed, throughout our whole world. Let us take our mission task with utmost seriousness. Help us share the saving grace of Jesus wherever we go. Lord, you do not call all of us into the ordained ministry, but you do call all of us to ministry through our baptism in Jesus' name. Whether we teach, or manage a business, or practice law or medicine, or work with our hands, may we apply the dictates of the gospel to encourage and sustain the world as you, O God, first creatively imagined it. Make us a people vital to a world of justice and peace. In the name of Jesus we pray. Amen. (David N. Mosser)

SERMON BRIEFS

MEN BEHAVING BADLY

GENESIS 37:1-4, 12-28

This text from Genesis 37 presents a great challenge to the preacher because it portrays a bad turn of events all the way around. The story has a sad ending and leaves us hanging. Although many parishioners will know how the narrative turns out in the end, we don't get to that point until next week. As tempting as it may be to jump to the good and redemptive part (Genesis 45), perhaps we must challenge ourselves to stay within the text and wrestle with its messiness.

Here we have humans behaving badly on all sides. Initially we have Jacob, who plays favorites among his children. He not only loved Joseph more than his other children but also openly acknowledged it by giving Joseph a special coat to wear. This part of the story could very well resonate with persons whose own families have been torn by favoritism. This ancient family represents all human families and the politics that govern them. This story gives an opportunity to address families and to encourage healthy relationships.

Beyond Jacob's bad behavior, we have Joseph, the teenage tattletale, who enjoys the favoritism of his elderly father. Although Jacob sends him to be a helper to his brothers (v. 2), Joseph instead watches their bad behavior and reports them to his daddy. Although nothing can justify the brothers' malicious treatment of Joseph, we can certainly understand why they are angry and why they dislike him.

Of course, the obvious "bad boys" in this story are the brothers. When they see Joseph coming toward them in verse 18, they immediately conspire to kill him. Only Reuben and Judah show any compassion for their brother. In fact, their mercy offers us the only glimmer of hope in an otherwise bleak passage. Reuben talks his brothers into leaving Joseph in a pit, planning to come back later and rescue him. Reuben, then, is perhaps the hero in this story. He is willing to stand up to his brothers, to talk them out of their evil plan, and to restore Joseph to safety. Perhaps Reuben could be held up as an example of moral courage, one who stood up to peer pressure. Although Reuben himself may have disliked Joseph, he did what he could to save him and to do what was right.

Judah also stood up to his brothers in order to save Joseph from death. He reasoned that Joseph was his brother, his own flesh (v. 27), and therefore should not be killed. Judah also was looking after his own good when he asked, "What profit is it if we kill our brother" (v. 26). Although Judah spared Joseph's life, he was still anxious to get rid of Joseph and came up with the plan to sell Joseph to the Ishmaelites. It is more difficult, then, to hold Judah up as a moral example. He seems to be looking out for his own profit and is perfectly happy selling his brother into slavery.

How many of us are more like Judah than Reuben? We lack the courage to go against the crowd. We are happy to sell our brothers and sisters down the river in order to rid ourselves of them. We care not for their well-being but only for our own. If we look back at the story, it is Judah's plan that keeps Reuben from returning Joseph to his father. How often do our selfish plans thwart the will of God and the good of others?

We cannot explore this narrative without also addressing the behavior of the other brothers. More than any others, they represent human nature at its worst. They are motivated by jealousy,

271

bitterness, and anger. The brothers have no concern for Joseph or how his death might affect their father. They simply hate Joseph and want to get rid of him.

The brothers' actions in the story might present an opportunity to examine the nature of human hatred and jealousy. One might explore these dynamics in the nuclear family or in the global family. How prevalent is hate in our homes and in our world? What is at the root of it? How do we justify it?

The question remains, Where is God in this story? Of course, chapter 45 offers a response to that question, but, if we just had these verses to work with, what could we say? Perhaps we could leave that question with the congregation. When humans behave badly, when we give in to our jealousy and anger, when we let our pettiness govern our actions, where indeed is God? (Carol Cavin-Dillon)

LASTING RENEWAL

ROMANS 10:5-15

In our world today, a person does not have to look far in order to hear rhetoric about renewal. When we turn on our televisions, we hear politicians promote projects for economic, social, and urban revitalization, and we listen to talk show hosts speak of becoming our best person. When we go to a local bookstore, we find sections dedicated to self-help and self-improvement. Even when we drive by our neighborhood churches, we see signs advertising aid for those individuals struggling with relevant problems of this era. Each of these renewal efforts and projects respectively benefits those seeking help, but as a church, are we mirroring the world in our attempts to bring revitalization? Or, are we proclaiming the gospel as a message that offers lasting renewal?

This very issue of renewal captivated Paul's attention when he wrote his letter to the Romans. Always longing to be in Rome, a letter offering help to a congregation struggling with problems between Jewish and Gentile Christians would suffice for now instead of face-to-face contact. An ongoing battle among early

Christians focused on the tension between Jew and Gentile. In his letter, Paul emphasizes righteousness or a right relationship with God as a requirement for renewal. Some Jews believed that a strict adherence to the Torah could save them. History, however, reveals that this kind of legalism always fails because it ignores a person's faith in God. When we seek righteousness and salvation through our own merit and efforts, we inevitably fail. We fall into frustration for we are unable to achieve lasting renewal.

In Romans 10:5-15, Paul speaks of renewal under the assumption that God cannot be limited in whom God saves. God offers salvation to both the Jew and Gentile, and each is invited to embrace a life of righteousness through faith. Where legalism failed for the Jews, faith enables a person to embrace a life of righteousness. Paul frames faith as the beginning point of righteousness because it leads to salvation, but faith only comes from the Spirit, not from a person's own work. The righteousness one receives comes from Jesus Christ because only the Messiah can restore individuals and give life. Regardless of race or ethnicity, a faith in God through Christ offers renewal to both Jews and Gentiles, for the Lord forms all people into children of God. Individuals who enter a covenantal life of faith in God are enabled to live out the gospel each and every day. In following Christ, people discover true renewal.

Perhaps many Christians first experienced renewal in a local congregation. Christ forms our church communities and gives our congregations an identity by regenerating individuals into children of God. In response, we are invited to facilitate renewal with those in need. Offering rejuvenation to others, however, occurs when believers embody the good news of Christ with other people. Therefore as Christians, we take an active role in our own renewal rather than passively accepting a gift from God. By sharing the gifts we have received from God, we find lasting renewal in our lives and enable others to participate in the life-giving power of Jesus Christ. When we selfishly keep the gospel to ourselves, renewal is inhibited for both others and ourselves. So how well are we as a church proclaiming the gospel and, thus, fostering renewal? Perhaps we should take our cue from Paul, who encouraged his fellow Roman Christians to go and "bring good news" to others so that they too can experience the life-giving power of Christ. Go, Christian brothers and sisters, bringing good news to others so that all who call "on the name of the Lord shall be saved" (v. 13). (Mark D. White)

IT'S 3:00 IN THE MORNING

MATTHEW 14:22-33

"It's three o'clock in the morning, / We've danced the whole night thru." Some of you will recognize the lyric to "Three O'Clock in the Morning" by Dorothy Terriss. Three o'clock in the morning, late time, good time, dancin' time, romancin' time. But when most people think 3:00 A.M., they are not thinking "best of times," but "worst of times." Three o'clock is an hour associated with insomniacs, worry warts, and social deviants. If you can't sleep, 3:00 A.M. is tossing-and-turning time. If someone isn't home by 3:00 A.M., it becomes floor-pacing time. If the telephone rings at 3:00 A.M., it's palm-sweating time. If people are out in the streets at 3:00 A.M., it's up-to-no-good time. And 3:00 A.M. is no time to be awakened by that quartet of sounds, which includes rumbling stomachs, dripping faucets, crying babies, and furry things crawling in the walls.

In our text, it is 3:00 in the morning for the friends of Jesus. If you want to paint a picture of waves and wind, paint away. Throw in some rain, if you like. A little sleet. No stars. Disciples retching over the boat's side. But don't put down your brush without finding some way to paint fear. Then ask yourself, Why are these disciples in this predicament? They are out in the storm because Jesus sent them. Don't let that slip by. Jesus sent them. "Made the disciples" go, says the text. It is the obedient church that experiences the storm. It is the obedient Christians who find themselves in troubled seas.

For some, it's 3:00 in the morning emotionally. Bruised and battered, down and defeated, guilty and grieving. Such feelings are always the worst in the middle of the night. An individual on a stool hears the bartender announce, "Last call." Pushing the glass forward, we almost hear the phrase, "I came in here to

AUGUST 7, 2005

drown my sorrows only to discover they've learned how to swim."

For others, it's 3:00 in the morning ethically. People don't make the best choices when the majority of the world is sleeping. Anonymity after midnight covers a multitude of sins. Temptation is incredibly nocturnal. My favorite 3:00-in-the-morning song, "Help Me Make It Through the Night" by Kris Kristofferson, speaks to moral compromises made at that hour.

> I don't care what's right or wrong
> ....
> Let the devil take tomorrow.

Still others fear it is 3:00 in the morning ecclesiastically. They look at their denomination and wonder if it will weather the storm. Numbers are down. Influence is down. Faith is watered down. Once they were sailing. Now, they're surviving.

Flying from Melbourne to Athens, a professor of hydrology raises the issue of God with author Robert Fulghum. But, pointing to the Indian Ocean below, his words speak of water.

> Water is everywhere.... Water comes in many forms.... But no matter the form, it's still water.
>
> ... Human beings drink water from many vessels—cups, glasses, jugs, skins, their own hands, whatever. To argue about which container is proper for the water is crazy.
>
> ... Some like it hot, some like it cold, some like it iced, some fizzy, some with stuff mixed in with it—alcohol, coffee, whatever. It does not change the nature of the water.
>
> Never mind the name or the cup or the mix. These are not important.
>
> What we have in common is thirst. Thirst!
>
> Thirst for the water of Life!
>
> (Robert Fulghum, *Uh-Oh* [New York: Villard Books, 1991], p. 139)

That's what 3:00 in the morning is all about. Thirst! Whether you're tossing on a bed or tossing in a boat. Whether the storm is without or the storm is within. Whether you're rowing like hell, or toward it. The only thing that will satisfy is the one who, in our tradition, is called "Living Water," which is precisely what we get—or who we get—if our story is to be believed, for in the fourth watch of the night, when everything seems contrary, Jesus comes to them, walking on the sea. Don't ask how. That's an unanswerable question. It's also the wrong question.

275

Walking on waves misses the point, for the miracle has less to do with a Jesus who comes by impossible means than with a Jesus who comes at impossible times. When it is darkest, he comes. When we are weariest, he comes. When the sea is so wide and our boat is so small, when we are a day late and a dollar short or a month late and a rent payment short, when the storms of life are raging, when we're up a creek with no paddle and our arms are too tired to hold a paddle if we had one, when it's too dark to see or (worse yet) too dark to hope, Jesus comes 'round.

Jesus, won't you come by here?

Now is the needin' time. (William Ritter)

AUGUST 14, 2005

Thirteenth Sunday After Pentecost

Worship Theme: As God constantly displays patience with God's people, our call to faithfulness includes an admonition to show resolve in our resolute waiting for God's goodness.

Readings: Genesis 45:1-15; Romans 11:1-2*a*, 29-32; Matthew 15:(10-20) 21-28

Call to Worship (Psalm 133:1-2*b*, 3)

Leader: How very good and pleasant it is when kindred live together in unity!

People: **It is like the precious oil on the head, running down upon the beard.**

Leader: It is like the dew of Hermon, which falls on the mountains of Zion.

People: **For there the LORD ordained his blessing, life forevermore.**

Pastoral Prayer:

Dear Lord, when we reflect upon our lives as a community of faith, we acknowledge that we do not always dwell in peace with our sisters and brothers. Division and conflict creep into our relationships in ways that baffle us. Too often the root of these ruptures in our ideal loving relationships exists in our human pride. We want our opinions valued. We want our wishes known. We want our desires fulfilled. Regularly we deal with others who also want their way. Our pride, too often, is an occasion for our sin and separation from one another.

Grant us a new vision of ourselves, O Lord. Remind us that it is Jesus who, as the Anointed One, emptied himself and took the form of a servant. Help us recall that Christ freed each of us gathered here from our pride. Now we can freely serve others. Let us take the example of Jesus to heart and become more like our Messiah. Make us a people who offer fullness of life to others as we acknowledge that you, O God, have created all people in your image. Give us the will to forfeit our pride. Show us the strength to become a humble people of Christ. It is the name of Jesus Christ that we pray. Amen. (David N. Mosser)

SERMON BRIEFS

THE GOSPEL ACCORDING TO GENESIS

GENESIS 45:1-15

In the previous week's lectionary passage from Genesis, Joseph is a young man whose brothers sell him into slavery. In today's passage we find Joseph a full-grown man who holds great power in Egypt, the land to which he was sold. Much has happened in the chapters between: Joseph's service to Potiphar, his integrity in refusing Potiphar's wife, his imprisonment, his interpretation of dreams, and his faithful service to Pharaoh. Many pieces of the "in-between" story are worth exploring and preaching, but the lectionary skips over these parts and moves us quickly to the story's climax. And, indeed, there are some advantages to juxtaposing chapters 37 and 45 in the lectionary.

First of all, hearing chapter 45 the week after chapter 37 keeps the focus on Joseph and his brothers. It opens the door for the preacher to talk about family relationships in a way that most people can relate to. Joseph's relationship with his brothers was torn by their father's favoritism, by the brothers' jealousy, and, to some degree, by Joseph's own arrogance and insensitivity. Many people struggle with similar issues in their own families. In the same way that chapter 37 leaves us with a bleak outlook for the future, many people wonder if there is any hope for reconciliation in their own families.

When we pick up the story in chapter 45, we find Joseph once again in the company of his brothers. We finally get to see if the old sibling rivalry is renewed or reconciled. Will this story give us hope for our own families? What we discover in this chapter is the power of grace, the sweetness of forgiveness, and the triumph of love. In many ways this story in Genesis embodies the grace of the gospel itself.

Several elements make this moment in chapter 45 one of the most powerful and emotional scenes in the Old Testament. First, the brothers do not recognize Joseph, but he recognizes them. This recognition gives Joseph power but brings his emotions to the surface. It establishes a tension in the scene that leaves the hearer breathless until the truth is revealed. Second, the tables of power have turned. The brothers have traveled to Egypt to beg for food. It is Joseph who now holds the power of life or death over his brothers, as they had once held over him. Third, in chapters 42–44, Joseph toys with his brothers, leaving in doubt how he will treat them in the end.

We cannot wait to see what Joseph will do, for in his actions lie all our hopes for human reconciliation. The tension built up in chapters 42–44 is finally released in the beginning verses of this passage. Joseph can "no longer control himself," and he weeps "so loudly that the Egyptians heard it" (vv. 1-2). Joseph reveals himself to his brothers and asks them to "come closer." Indeed, they do draw closer, and the miracle of reconciliation happens. Joseph forgives his brothers and reaches out to them in love.

By overcoming his hurt and anger, by forgiving his brothers and saving them from starvation, Joseph gives all of us hope for reconciliation. It would have been natural for Joseph to act out of revenge and anger. Revenge would be consistent with our sinful human nature. Instead, Joseph chooses the way of God and forgives them.

This powerful moment in scripture can give us new hope for reconciliation, not just in our families but in our communities and in our world. Joseph set aside power and revenge and chose forgiveness and compassion. What would happen if individuals, political parties, or nations would act in the same way?

This text not only opens the door to the subject of reconciliation and forgiveness, but also invites an exploration of God's will. Three times in this passage (vv. 5, 7, 8) Joseph asserts that it was

God, not his brothers, who sent him to Egypt. Clearly, Joseph believes that his being in Egypt is God's will. Joseph's words make us wonder if God intended Joseph to be sold into slavery. Did God cause this terrible thing to happen to Joseph? And does God cause bad things to happen in our lives in order to bring about a greater purpose?

To deepen the discussion, we can look ahead to 50:20, when Joseph tells his brothers: "Even though you intended to do harm to me, God intended it for good." One way to deal with the question is to assume that God does not intentionally cause bad things to happen but chooses to work with and around bad human choices to bring about good. The Joseph story raises this question of how God works in the course of human history, and it leaves the question open-ended. Fortunately, open-ended questions provide fertile soil for the preacher. (Carol Cavin-Dillon)

NEVER FORSAKEN

ROMANS 11:1-2*a*, 29-32

Have you ever felt written-off by others or underappreciated? At one time, most of us could affirm sentiments of being an outcast. Childhood illustrates such a traumatic time in life when many of us felt left out. Imagine the school yard during recess where children vie for a position on a kickball team. One by one, players are chosen. Finally, you hear your name called as the last person selected. Perhaps the situation grows worse: Both teams are full, and you are relegated to the sidelines to wait for the next game. Few other experiences could be as difficult for a young person to handle. Written off as an unathletic child and one who cannot contribute leaves children with the impression that their peers have forsaken them. Whether its sports, academics, or social standing, most school children experience feelings of isolation or ostracism. Perhaps in our adult years, we have similar experiences with God. Do you ever feel like God is missing or has forsaken you?

Paul raises a similar question when he asks, "has God rejected his people?" (v. 1). This question is particularly poignant considering the growing tension between Jewish and Gentile Christians in the early church. Scripture speaks of Israel as God's beloved children, holding an irrevocable election. Why then does it seem that God is working through the Gentiles instead of the Jews? Has Israel failed as the chosen people? Drawing from an illustration in his own life, Paul reminds his Roman audience that some Jews remain true to God. Since God has chosen Israel, the Lord will never break his word or the promises of salvation offered to the children of Abraham. As Paul exemplifies, a remnant persists among the Jews, who continue to uphold their status as God's elect by faithfully following the Lord.

The appearance that the Gentile believers have replaced the Jews as God's chosen people provokes Paul's response in Romans 11. God has not rejected Israel. God has forsaken neither Jews nor Gentiles because the Lord desires the salvation of all. The extension of divine mercy to the Gentiles merely provokes jealousy from the Jews. As Paul argues, this jealousy leads Israel toward a true faith in God through Christ. By encompassing the Gentiles, God's activity illustrates that God works in unexpected ways, by embracing all people including those who feel outcast and ignored.

Divine activity among Jews and Gentiles is necessary and logical to Paul. Jew and Gentile alike fall to the same temptations by living disobedient lives. Paul reminds the early Christians in Rome that "God has imprisoned all in disobedience so that he may be merciful to all" (v. 32). Clearly, no one can merit eternal life on his or her own, but God is able to grant mercy to all. God forsakes no one, nor is anything out of control for the Almighty. Although God constantly pursues Israel, the Lord's purposes include the salvation of all and the destruction of none. In the divine working, God is impartial and no longer has a favored nation. All humans, Jew and Gentile alike, are equal before the Lord, where no one is left out because all are in need of mercy. Similar to the Jews and Gentiles of Paul's era, we too need God's mercy, but we also crave reminders that God has not forsaken us. We want the assurance that we are still God's people. In recalling Paul's own example, may we remember that God constantly works for our good and salvation. This kind of divine activity takes on unexpected forms, but it is God's way of reminding us that we are not forsaken. (Mark D. White)

THE DAY THE FOREIGN LADY GOT THE BEST OF JESUS

MATTHEW 15:(10-20) 21-28

Withdraw with Jesus to Tyre and Sidon and watch a Canaanite woman seek him out and cry: "Have mercy on me, Lord, Son of David; my daughter is tormented by a demon." To which Jesus says nothing. So his disciples say: "Send her away, for she keeps shouting after us." But the disciples are not so much moved by compassion as by expediency. This lady is a nuisance.

Finally, Jesus has no choice. She has outlasted him. She cannot be avoided. She can, however, be denied. Which is what Jesus does. Denies her, I mean.

"It is not fair to take the children's food and throw it to the dogs," Jesus says.

This is not simply a denial. This is an insult. Jesus is telling the woman: "It wouldn't be right to give the good stuff to you and your kind. And even if it were, it's not my job."

Some say Jesus is making a joke. Others say Jesus is not talking junkyard dogs here, but house dogs, puppies. Others suggest that while Jesus didn't personally equate Canaanites with dogs, he knew others thought that way, so he spoke the term aloud so people could hear how shocking it sounded. Still others say Jesus would never have said this if he hadn't been tired. In other words, cut Jesus some slack.

Still, you've got to admire the lady. She has a wonderful comeback:

"Yes, Lord, yet even the dogs eat the crumbs that fall from their masters' table."

And when the woman introduces the subject of table scraps—her willingness to settle for table scraps—and her belief that there will be healing power in table scraps, Jesus says: "Wow! What faith! Whatever you want, lady, you got it."

So what is this story about? On the surface, it's about healing. There is nothing unique here, except the mother's passionate intensity that healing must happen (and can happen). But this is not a story about healers so much as a story about outsiders. This lady is an outsider. And Jesus even calls her an outsider. Although if there are places where words attributed to Jesus may not come from the lips of Jesus, this is one of them. As George Buttrick put it: "What we must recognize is that the language of the tradition has been affected by the prejudices of those who handed it down during the long oral period before the gospels were compiled." Which is still going on—distortions of the gospel by those who preach it, I mean. I would love to believe that my prejudices never get in the way of my pronouncements. But they do.

But zero in, not on the word *dogs*, but on the word *table*. When the members of my wife's family outnumbered her mother's capacity to feed them simultaneously, such as for holiday dinners, there were always two tables. And no matter how hard she tried to give them equal status, they never had equal status. The living room table was the lesser table. But it's like that in many families. There's the big table. And there's the table where people sit who aren't at the big table. In a lot of families— including the church family—we are still trying to sort out who sits where, and why.

I suppose we could eat a little humble pie and confess that "we are not worthy so much as to gather up the crumbs under [the Lord's] table" (*The Book of Common Prayer*, 1979. Holy Eucharist I, Rite 1, p. 337). But few of us believe it. So the question is not whether we will collectively grovel but whether we will collectively share crumbs and cake, chairs and chairmanships. Countless images of the kingdom of God have tables in them. But people seem to be sitting at them rather than crawling beneath them.

Including the woman likened to a dog. Because I've seen her at the table. I'll never forget the day she got the better of Jesus. But that isn't how she remembers it. She remembers it as the day she got the best of Jesus—as in all of Jesus—with nothing held back by him. Which explains why, upon spotting her, I introduced myself. I mean, who knows when I might want her to pass me the bread? (William Ritter)

AUGUST 21, 2005

Fourteenth Sunday After Pentecost

Worship Theme: Similar to Peter, our Lord offers to all believers a hand in the formation of a gospel-like world. The keys of God's realm include faith, hope, and justice for all people.

Readings: Exodus 1:8–2:10; Romans 12:1-8; Matthew 16:13-20

Call to Worship (Psalm 124:2-4b, 6-8)

> *Leader:* Let us speak the words of faith. Let us speak God's truth.
>
> ***People:*** **"If it had not been the LORD who was on our side,**
>
> *Leader:* "when our enemies attacked us, then they would have swallowed us up alive,
>
> ***People:*** **"when their anger was kindled against us; then the flood would have swept us away, the torrent would have gone over us.**
>
> *Leader:* "Blessed be the LORD, who has not given us as prey to their teeth.
>
> ***People:*** **"We have escaped like a bird from the snare of the fowlers; the snare is broken, and we have escaped.**
>
> *All:* **"Our help is in the name of the LORD, who made heaven and earth."**

Pastoral Prayer:

Gracious God, regularly in life we feel as if we need to be snatched out of the clutches of evil just as courageous women drew Moses from the water. In their shrewd act they snatched Moses away from certain death. As we thumb through our daily newspapers and watch the news on our television sets, it is all too easy for us to allow despair to set in. Yet, as Paul once wrote the church at Rome, "For while we were still weak, at the right time Christ died for the ungodly" (Rom. 5:6). Perhaps we know ourselves as ungodly, but we do know, in fact, that our society and culture too regularly turns its back on the divine truths you impart, O God. In this circumstance our faith sometimes wavers, and we teeter on the rim of despair.

Yet, you Gracious Master, have shown us a better way. You have opened to us the portals of heaven and we have seen a vision of the world as you intended it. Let the hope found only in Jesus cling to us and bind us to your eternal will. In the name of Jesus, we pray. Amen. (David N. Mosser)

SERMON BRIEFS

CREATING BRIDGES

EXODUS 1:8–2:10

Have you ever had a dream that mimicked reality closely enough but when you tried to tell it you simply could not make sense of the story for your listeners? Such appears to be the case for the introduction to the Exodus narrative and the Moses character. The basic premise sounds clear enough, but some of the details just don't fit quite right. Brevard Childs, in his watershed commentary on Exodus, cites several elements employing foggy logic. If the Egyptians truly desired to contain the number of Israelites, better ways existed of doing so than enforcing ruthless labor. Likewise, killing off infant girls would achieve a sudden stop in population growth more effectively than slaying the boys. Childs voices other examples of foggy logic including the question of why Pharaoh was not suspicious of Moses.

Human reasoning, however, places God in a box. God's movement in creation does not have to follow our logic. For example, we tend to reason "the more, the better." Especially when working on sizable tasks, we look for strength in numbers. God, nevertheless, insists that one is enough to affect kingdom-size differences in this world. Again, our logic reasons that power and politics go hand in hand. However, God often looks to outsiders to carry out powerful acts of creation. In today's passage, God works through an individual on the edge of political power. That individual is not male like Daniel or Noah nor Hebrew like Esther or Paul. She is Pharaoh's daughter, and she stands in a critical gap.

Consider the creating power in this story. The Egyptians create supply cities while Pharaoh creates an oppressive political regime. Both of these acts work directly against God's plan for creation, particularly for creating the people of Israel. Yet, women disfranchised from political power engage in furthering God's creative vision: The midwives preserve instead of stifle life, Moses' mother elaborately plans for his survival, and Moses' sister participates in her mother's plan. Pharaoh's daughter stands in the gap between creation and power, effectively bridging the two. By having compassion on a child regardless of race, Pharaoh's daughter becomes an instrument of divine intervention, ensuring the survival of God's chosen leader.

Humanity needs more people to act as bridges for the sake of creation. Differing generations, cultures, political ideologies, and economic strata exemplify only a few places where bridges can bring about creational change. John Perkins, editor of a handbook for restoring at-risk communities, speaks of such bridge people when he calls for individuals connected with public resources to move back into struggling neighborhoods. As servants of Creator God we have a response-ability (an ability to respond) to create bridges, even if doing so doesn't always make sense. We are anchored in a gospel that declares that in giving away life, we gain it for the world. Through worship and contemplation we have the means to discern God's creative plan and the source for courage to join in.

God can and does use ordinary individuals to produce extraordinary results. Leaf through almost any family-style magazine and you will read stories of men and women working to make a difference in their corner of the world. The story of Pharaoh's daughter reminds us that our religious roots are firmly planted in an understanding of both power and creation that is kingdom-focused. God created a people, not a supply city; God emanates power that gives life, not political rule. And in case we missed the gospel of this passage, we have the stories of another individual sent by God: Jesus. (Karen Hudson)

HOLY LIVING: THE GOOD LIFE

ROMANS 12:1-8

If you were to ask ten people to describe the good life, it is likely you would hear ten different answers. Some people might want wealth, others happiness, and still others might dream of more vacation time. Answers vary from person to person and culture to culture. An interest in living better, more complete lives always exists. Both religious and secular people voice this desire. What if this question about the good life was posed to the apostle Paul? How would he answer? Perhaps Paul would begin with a discussion about holy living as the foundation of the good life, where one's mind and body join together to serve and worship God.

Paul addresses the concept of holy living in Romans 12 by offering practical advice to his Roman audience. Paul, quite often, eagerly offers practical steps to Christian communities for following God and becoming better Christians. Such is the case in Romans 12, which marks an important transition in this epistle: Many of the previous chapters served as a theological discussion or treatise, and now Paul exhorts Christians to live ethical lives grounded in Jesus Christ. Christ stands as the justification for Christian communities, who base their own lives on that of Jesus. Paul calls all Christians, both Jew and Gentile, to offer God sacrificial worship as the means of a holy life. Christian obedience rooted in Christ enables people to offer this kind of worship. Sacrificial worship defines the holy life but requires both the mind and the body.

Each and every day, Christians must choose with their minds to make sacrifices to follow and worship God. Believers must seek the transformation of their minds for an authentic witness to their faith. For Paul, the mind is sinful and rebellious, and without significantly changing its orientation, a sinful mind will cause a sinful life. Christians need renewed minds in order for their lives to better reflect the image of God within them. Transforming one's mind is a part of living authentically as a disciple of Jesus Christ. Therefore, a renewed mind is able to please, serve, and honor God in ways that an undisciplined one is unable. A disciplined mind discerns the will of God.

Discerning God's will as part of the holy life encompasses both the individual believer and the community of saints. Individuals strive after an embodiment of holiness, while the body of Christ seeks to nurture each believer in achieving this task. To little surprise, God works through the body, both literally and figuratively. God used the human body in the Incarnation to reveal the Messiah and to communicate the divine will. God also relies on the body of Christ, a diverse organism with an infinite number of human gifts and talents, to carry out divine plans. As a result, all members of this body, not just certain parts, are called to apply their gifts to living and fulfilling the Christian life. As Christians, Paul reminds us that when employing our gifts, we must use sober judgment or disciplined thinking as a means of evaluating ourselves and our own talents. We are then able to use our gifts for the good of our Christian communities, impacting the life within these communities and facilitating unity. God has given us grace to perform many tasks, so our calling as individuals and as a church is that together we might become a transformed people who embody holy living and, thus, experience the good life. (Mark D. White)

THE KEYS OF THE KINGDOM

MATTHEW 16:13-20

Every once in a while, a text contains so many lessons that I never know where to begin. So, I'll start with Peter. Jesus asks him a question. Peter then comes up with the right answer, for which he is "blessed" and rewarded. The question involves the identity of the Son of Man. After others answer falsely, Peter answers correctly—"You are the Messiah, the Son of the living God" (v. 16)—for which Peter should receive a gold star, claim a brass ring, pass go, and collect two hundred dollars. Except Peter had a little help, given the words of Jesus: "For flesh and blood has not revealed this to you, but my Father in heaven" (v. 17).

Still, it was a heady moment, although short-lived. Shortly afterward, upon hearing Jesus' first prediction of his passion, Peter says something like, "Nothing like that's going to happen on my watch, Lord." Which leads to Jesus calling Peter "satanic." Talk about having the wind stripped from your sails!

All of this makes me wonder. If Peter is identified with the church's foundation, what does it mean to have the word *satanic* applied to the church's core? I suppose it means that even the brightest and best are a day late and dollar short where constancy and fidelity are concerned. At its core, the church is always going to mute its witness and compromise its Lord. Peter, of course, is trying to save his hero's hide. The shadow of the cross looms large over everything that is happening here. But Peter can't see it and seeks only to shield Jesus from it. But everything that happens from this point forward has death written all over it.

What amazes me is the willingness of Jesus to entrust the church to such flawed vessels. Then again, what other choice does he have? None of us should read these passages and sit smug in our selection. I recall the troubling dream of an esteemed colleague. It comes to him whenever the church bestows another accolade upon him. In his dream, he is standing in line outside heaven's gate. Slowing things down is the fact that someone is conducting interviews. Sure enough, it is Peter himself. More surprising is my friend's discovery that the person two or three ahead of him is none other than Mother Teresa. When the beloved saint of Calcutta reaches the one to whom the kingdom's keys were given, my colleague leans forward to eavesdrop on the conversation. All he can hear is Peter saying, "Quite frankly, Teresa, we expected a whole lot more of you." Whereupon my colleague tries to take cuts in reverse or wakes from sleep in a cold sweat.

As to whether the "keys" were given to Peter (as a preindication of the papacy) or to those who testify correctly to the person and work of Jesus Christ, this has been a source of dispute between Roman Catholics and Protestants for decades. At least in theological circles. Quite frankly, I haven't met a Roman Catholic in forty years who claimed ecclesiastical superiority on the basis of this passage. But if you want to fight over it, I'll load you up with commentaries to stack in your corner.

Of greater interest is the word *keys*. I associate them with locks. And I associate locks with doors. Clearly, somebody in this passage is given awesome authority. To whatever degree such keys have been placed in my hands, my first thought is, "Don't lose them." And my second thought is, "Don't abuse them." It has been the nature of my ministry to lock as little as possible. I would rather have it said that I opened more doors than I closed, built more bridges than I burned, and welcomed more people than I turned away. Preaching years ago on the possible breadth of the kingdom's guest list, I offended a parishioner who wanted to see a few doors slammed in a few faces. Accosting me at the door, she screamed: "If you mean I might have to share heaven with the likes of Charles Manson, then I don't want to go." Taken aback by her vehemence, I stood in stunned silence. "So what do you think of that?" she asked. And the only words that came to mind were, "I guess beggars can't be choosers." (William Ritter)

AUGUST 28, 2005

Fifteenth Sunday After Pentecost

Worship Theme: Servant leadership, whatever else it must be, is based on genuine love. Both Jesus and Moses led people because of a great love for God that drove everything they did.

Readings: Exodus 3:1-15; Romans 12:9-21; Matthew 16:21-28

Call to Worship (Psalm 105:1-5, 45c)

Leader: O give thanks to the LORD, call on his name, make known his deeds among the peoples.

People: **Sing to him, sing praises to him; tell of all his wonderful works.**

Leader: Glory in his holy name; let the hearts of those who seek the LORD rejoice.

People: **Seek the LORD and his strength; seek his presence continually.**

Leader: Remember the wonderful works he has done, his miracles, and the judgments he uttered.

People: **Praise the LORD!**

Pastoral Prayer:

God of Grace and God of Glory, you have given us a story to tell to the world. It is the story of your redeeming love, O God. It is a story where love triumphs over hate and good conquers iniquity. Let us live into this story as we tell it and tell it as if the life of the world depended on it. Everyone loves a good story, and this story is so wonderful that the New Testament calls it the "good news."

Lord, as we begin to contemplate a new school year and a time to return to our regular rhythm of life after our summer break, make us mindful of holy worship. As we discipline our lives, may we establish occasions for meditation, reflection, and prayer. As liturgy is the "work of the people," let us pray and live together as the called-out community of faith. Give us a common vision and help us seek common ground so that we can become again the people of God. In Jesus' righteous name we pray. Amen. (David N. Mosser)

SERMON BRIEFS

SURPRISED BY GOD

EXODUS 3:1-15

By its very nature, a surprise is an unexpected event. And the very best surprises are pleasurable. This dramatic happening in the life of Moses, although unanticipated, was the watershed event in his life. Here at the burning bush he learned of God's will for his future and the future of God's people. Moses' response to God's challenge changed the remainder of his life and the history of the Israelites. So remarkable was Moses' life that it took four books in the Old Testament to tell his story! More is said about Moses in the New Testament than any other Old Testament prophet. His name would be forever linked with the Jewish people and their exodus from captivity to freedom. The surprise revelation at the burning bush was the moment of truth for Moses.

Any encounter with God involves revelation and response—God's choosing to reveal himself and the human's response to that revelation. In the case of Moses, God disclosed himself to this shepherd while he was "keeping the flock" on the back side of Mt. Horeb, possibly an alternate name for Mt. Sinai. Although some scholars might debate this, what God revealed to Moses seems to be more important than where it happened. A bush was burning but not consumed. Fire is often used in the Old Testament as a symbol of God's presence (see Gen. 15:17; Exod. 13:21-22; 19:18; 1 Kings 18:38-39).

Called by his name, Moses responded, "Here I am." The similarity of this call and that of Isaiah, Jeremiah, and Ezekiel is striking (see Isa. 6:1-13; Jer. 1:4-19; Ezek. 1:26–3:4). This was "holy ground" and Moses was asked to take off his shoes. In verse 5 we have the first occurrence of the word "holy" in the Bible. Any place where a person meets God is a holy place and should be approached with reverence!

It is revealed that this is the God of Abraham, Isaac, and Jacob, making it clear that Moses was not dealing with some strange new deity but the covenant God of the Hebrew people. God's demonstration showed that God had heard the cry, seen the affliction, and recognized the sufferings of the Hebrew people. Furthermore, God intended to deliver them from the Egyptians.

God commissioned Moses to be the agent in bringing Israel out of Egypt. While Moses might have applauded when he heard about God's knowledge of Israel's oppression, he seems less enthusiastic when God calls him to be the agent of that deliverance! Moses not only offered excuses but also questioned God's wisdom in choosing him for the job. Most of us feel inadequate for the job God asks us to do and without God's help we are. However, God offers us resources, just like Moses.

God countered Moses' objections with the promise of divine presence and a sign. The sign was that after the deliverance from bondage, Israel would serve God on this very mountain, a sign that became reality as the liberated people were led to Mt. Sinai to receive from God the Ten Commandments.

The name which God gave Moses was "I AM WHO I AM." The idea seems to be that God is saying, "I will always be there for you." It is inappropriate to think of God as the One who only "was" or even as the one who only "will be." God is the one who always "is."

God has not ceased to call people to do divine work, and, in many cases, this involves the element of surprise. Sometimes God uses nature, as God did with Moses, sometimes people, sometimes circumstance. Whatever the situation, to the unbeliever, nothing extraordinary seems to be happening. To the believer, however, this happening comes alive with the presence of God. Like Moses of old, whatever the call, we must be willing to investigate and respond. Be willing to be surprised by God! (Drew J. Gunnells, Jr.)

GUIDELINES FOR LIFE

ROMANS 12:9-21

Whoever coined the phrase, "rules are meant to be broken," probably discovered a unique following of people eager to fulfill that statement's vow. A rebellious spirit runs through many of us who are not big fans of rules. We do not like being told what to do. When we think of rules, perhaps memories of summer camp flood our minds. Strict guidelines for meals, activities, bedtime, and even chores required our careful attention; otherwise some form of punishment would be rendered. As children, we may not have fully comprehended the value of these rules or grasped that these guidelines actually improved camp life, kept kids safe, and taught discipline. As adults, we hope to see the value of rules by adhering to them.

Just as camp rules serve the common good, Paul offers a number of suggestions concerning the pattern of Christian living to help the believers in Rome. Although they are not rules in the strict sense, the practical guidelines of Romans 12:9-21 provide advice in how Christians should act toward each other and toward outsiders. Paul roots his advice in Christ; the Christian life should mirror the life of Jesus. Although some Christian communities, such as certain monasteries, establish their own rule for proper behavior, Paul's suggestions provide a measuring stick that helps communities grow and mature by comparing their behavior to the apostle's suggestions. Of course, Paul's list is not exhaustive; one could always add rules or helpful standards, but this counsel, as a starting point, provides Christians practical guidelines for life.

Paul begins this passage by outlining how Christians should relate with one another. Individuals who embody these suggestions foster growth within their own faith communities. Building up community begins by demonstrating love to each other. Christians can build up their communities by being affectionate, being industrious, serving God, rejoicing in hope, being patient in suffering, praying, and sharing with other needy Christians. Paul speaks of important virtues like love, hope, and hospitality. Although Paul does not spell out everything a Christian should do, his advice provides Christians with a workable list of behaviors that all should seek to embody in their relationships with each other.

As equally important as the internal relationships are between Christians, so too is the way Christians relate to outsiders. Romans 12 shifts its focus beginning with verse 14 by highlighting Christians' external relationships. What responsibility do Christians have to those outside of their community? As Paul outlines this responsibility, he assumes that Christians will encounter persecution, if they have not already experienced it. For this reason, Paul forbids vengeance and retaliation: "Do not repay anyone evil for evil" (v. 17). A Christian response to persecution should come as a blessing rather than as a curse. With the danger of persecution on the horizon, some Christians asserted their superiority over pagans, non-Christian Jews, or even their fellow Christians. Paul attacked this behavior. Christians should not act or live in aloof ways, but rather, believers should establish common ground with those who are different.

In many ways, Paul's suggestions for Christian living parallel the life of Jesus. Much like Jesus' admonition to love your enemies, Paul admonishes believers to allow their actions, particularly positive actions, to change their enemies. The thrust of his argument is that God will eventually bring about justice, which should not be the ultimate concern of Christians. These guidelines are not meant to be summer camp rules or serve as a definitive list of behaviors for Christians. Heeding Paul's suggestions, however, makes for an effective Christian witness to the world and enables us to strengthen the relationships within our own faith communities. (Mark D. White)

REDEFINING MESSIAHSHIP

MATTHEW 16:21-28

When I became a Christian at age twelve my pastor promised me that as a follower of Jesus, I had a friend who would always stick closer to me than a brother. I have found that to be true, but I am still learning what it means. It does not mean what I originally assumed. I reasoned that with Jesus as my traveling companion, I was surely bound for appealing and impressive places. But over the past two decades, Jesus and I have visited some depressing and confusing places, and I have often had to redefine my understanding of what it means to follow Jesus.

So, too, did Peter need this kind of redefinition. Just when Peter thought he had the Lord all figured out he received some depressing and confusing news as to where they were going. Jesus announced he was going to a cross and then called his followers into the same path. Our text comes on the heels of Peter's well-known confession, "Thou art the Christ, the Son of the living God" (Matt. 16:16 KJV). The truth that Peter had recognized was so significant that Jesus declared his church would be built on it. However, Peter still had a faulty concept of Christ's mission and methods. And so, "from that time forth" Jesus began presenting his disciples with a terrifying reality they did not want to face: God's will was for this freshly recognized Christ to suffer and die.

Thus began the painful process of redefining messiahship. We all have our false concepts and expectations about Jesus. God sometimes corrects these by exposing us to new insights and realities that do not fit our previous understanding of who Jesus is and how God operates. We are forced to rethink the issues of faith as Peter was. In Peter's mind, Jesus was about to ruin a perfectly good ministry by getting himself killed. "Lord, think of all the people you will be letting down," he seems to say. But Jesus was thinking of all the people he would be lifting up. Jesus was thinking of the multitudes that would be made right with God through this depressing and confusing step that seemed so wrong to Peter.

This seemingly wrong step helps us to better understand the Lord's harsh words to Peter in verse 23. Jesus addressed Peter as Satan because Peter's desire opposed God's will. Peter was speaking as Satan might speak. Peter may have meant well, but he was out of line. The disciple's place is that of following in the way Christ has chosen (even if that way is unappealing or unimpressive), not leading Christ in the way we would like for him to go.

Redefining messiahship can be a slow and painful process. It was for Peter. In fact, Peter was still wrestling with it the night before the Crucifixion. That may have been part of the reason

Peter denied Jesus those three times. He still did not agree with where the Lord was going. But Peter eventually worked through it. In time, he became a preacher of the cross, the very thing he had so vigorously opposed early in his development. Peter "got behind"—where he belonged—and allowed the Lord to redefine his concept of messiahship. To follow Jesus is to let Jesus do the leading, even in those depressing and confusing times when we do not appreciate where Jesus is going. (Lance Sawyer)

REFLECTIONS

SEPTEMBER

Reflection Verse: *"Be patient, therefore, beloved, until the coming of the Lord. The farmer waits for the precious crop from the earth, being patient with it until it receives the early and the late rains." (James 5:7)*

PATIENCE: CONSTANT PERSEVERANCE
James 5:7-11

My friend, the late Steve Monk, used to pray with some fervor, "Lord, give me patience, and give it to me right now!" I would guess that this is a prayer that not a few of us preachers have also contemplated, if not actually prayed, over the years. If this prayer for patience is your prayer, then you are in good company. In our Psalter, the psalmist knows that waiting for God to act can take all the willpower we can muster. For example, the psalmist asks:

> How long, O LORD? Will you forget me forever?
>   How long will you hide your face from me? (Ps. 13:1).
> How long, O LORD, will you look on? (Ps. 35:17).
> How long, O LORD? Will you be angry forever?
>   Will your jealous wrath burn like fire? (Ps. 79:5).
> How long, O LORD? Will you hide yourself forever?
>   How long will your wrath burn like fire? (Ps. 89:46).

Even the prophet Isaiah asks, "How long, O Lord?" (Isa. 6:11). Our Gospel stories also address patience with respect to Jesus' ministry. Once, after a temple incident, "the disciples came to him privately, saying, 'Tell us, when will this be, and what will be the sign of your coming and of the end of the age?' Jesus answered them, 'Beware that no one leads you astray'" (Matt. 24:3-4). Like most pastors, the disciples too are somewhat impatient. We are prompted about the issue of patience because the Bible so often speaks of patience in ways far more momentous than we often employ the word. James follows this biblical tendency, speaking as it does about patience. James tells his flock, "Be patient, therefore, beloved, until the coming of the Lord. The farmer waits for the precious crop from the earth, being patient with it until it receives the early and the late rains. You also must be patient. Strengthen your hearts, for the coming of the Lord is near" (James 5:7-8).

Of course, the kind of patience that the Bible usually praises is the patience of waiting for God to finish God's business with the world, in theological jargon, "eschatological patience." Eschatology simply describes the content of the doctrine of the last things. At its most basic level, eschatology suggests that, at some point in the world's history, all will cease. Then, God will complete God's work begun at creation. Most of what the Bible describes in terms of patience addresses this awareness. Consequently, Paul writes, "Now concerning the times and the seasons, brothers and sisters, you do not need to have anything written to you. For you yourselves know very well that the day of the Lord will come like a thief in the night" (1 Thess. 5:1-2).

However great a concern the day of the Lord will be for us— and I suggest that it is a large concern—our rather more simple and necessary interest pertaining to patience is as a virtue. Patience is a virtue that we either want to practice or wish we could practice. Most preachers I know want to be more patient people, but the question is how. The "how" hill is a tricky one to climb.

For one thing, we need to know that gaining patience is an uphill climb. The modern media rarely extol the virtue of patience. If we carefully examined the thousands of advertisements we constantly see and hear, we would notice repeated key words along the way. *Instant, immediate,* and *fast-acting* are all words used in the most positive sense to sell whatever is the product of the moment. These commercials could easily lead people to believe that only the fastest or the quickest is the best. It would be easy to chalk up this kind of thinking to our modern world, but even the Bible subtly provides this point of view as well.

In the story of David and Goliath, for one example, the biblical writer assures our perceptions of both David and Goliath by highlighting certain features. The story describes Goliath as having a "helmet of bronze on his head, and he was armed with a coat of mail; the weight of the coat was five thousand shekels of bronze. He had greaves of bronze on his legs and a javelin of bronze slung between his shoulders. The shaft of his spear was like a weaver's beam, and his spear's head weighed six hundred shekels of iron" (1 Sam. 17:5-7). Everything we read about Goliath in this description is big and strong—but also inevitably slow.

By contrast, "David ran quickly toward the battle line to meet the Philistine. David put his hand in his bag, took out a stone, slung it, and struck the Philistine on his forehead; the stone sank into his forehead, and he fell face down on the ground" (1 Sam. 17:48-49). Although slow and steady may win the race between the tortoise and the hare, in this biblical story it is the slow, ponderous giant Goliath who literally has his head handed to him. For most people in our society fast and quick is the way to go—and fast and quick rarely have time to be patient.

Second, we as spiritual leaders of our congregations need to recognize that some things can only get better with time. The wisdom that life gives us is not something we can gain "at once," "immediately," or "instantaneously." Rather, to be wise, one must experience what life dishes out and then measure how we respond. The phrase "experience is the best teacher" is true on multiple levels. Resembling a fine, aged steak, there are some things that we cannot rush. For this reason, James recommends waiting in patience like the farmer who waits "until [the crop] receives the early and the late rains." We cannot hasten some things. Whether it is our relationship with God or our relationships with those whom we love, some things simply take time. Our culture has forgotten this fact of life.

Third, from the biblical perspective, being patient is a virtue. Cleary the Bible speaks about patience most often with regard to waiting for the Lord's return. Jesus said, "Whoever is faithful in a very little is faithful also in much" (Luke 16:10). But also let's consider this question, "Could not the opposite also be true?" If we are have the ability to wait in patience for God, can we not also be patient with those we love and also with ourselves? So often we worry about what we will do next that we miss the joy and prospects that the present moment affords.

Being patient with another person is difficult, but it also honors that relationship. Patience in life is that constant perseverance over the things that cannot mature "at once," "immediately," or "instantaneously." Rather, patience is an attitude of hope in which time and forbearance eventually help us live wisely, and therefore, abundantly. For this reason, patience is one of the monuments to right living.

May we mull over two final thoughts? First, Jeremiah, who knew more than a little about waiting on God, said with the greatest conviction, "The LORD is good to those who wait for him" (Lam. 3:25). Thus, if being patient is not your "cup of tea," then consider it a spiritual discipline along the lines of prayer, meditation, and Bible study. To employ patience in life and in our ministries is to put our lives in the hand of one who will give us great things. Although he certainly was not a Christian, the wise Aristotle sagely remarked, "Patience is bitter, but its fruit is sweet."

The final word I want to share comes from one of our preachers, Jay Darnell, who said in a staff meeting better than I could ever say it, "Faith picks up the cross. Love binds it to the soul. Patience bears it to the end."

As believers who seek abundant life, we pastors will practice the virtue of patience—with God, others, and ourselves. If we need a reminder of one of the foundational characteristics of abundant life, then there is a pillar with the word *patience* inscribed on it. Amen. (David N. Mosser)

SEPTEMBER 4, 2005

Sixteenth Sunday After Pentecost

Worship Theme: The path of least resistance regularly tempts people. However, in the church of Jesus Christ, believers confront those who violate the community's sacred covenant out of loving concern.

Readings: Exodus 12:1-14; Romans 13:8-14; Matthew 18:15-20

Call to Worship (Psalm 149:1-5, 9*bc*)

> *Leader:* Praise the LORD! Sing to the LORD a new song, his praise in the assembly of the faithful.
>
> *People:* **Let Israel be glad in its Maker; let the children of Zion rejoice in their King.**
>
> *Leader:* Let them praise his name with dancing, making melody to him with tambourine and lyre.
>
> *People:* **For the LORD takes pleasure in his people; he adorns the humble with victory.**
>
> *Leader:* Let the faithful exult in glory; let them sing for joy on their couches.
>
> *People:* **This is glory for all his faithful ones. Praise the LORD!**

Pastoral Prayer:
When we worship you, O God, it is a day of joy and celebration. You have given us every good blessing that we enjoy, and our mood today is one of thanksgiving. Help us be a grateful people for the bounty placed at our disposal. Not only this, but as

stewards of these divine blessings help us share these blessing with others. We worship here in the name of Jesus, therefore we feel Jesus' presence among us. Let us rejoice and give thanks for the divine estate in which you declare us heirs.

Give us the discernment and vision to love our neighbor as ourselves. You have revealed to us, O Gracious Lord, that our loving our neighbor fulfills the divine law. Make us a people who live just lives. Make us a people who share justice and its blessing with those among whom we abide. Give us the will to love others even when the path to loving others presents difficult obstacles. For where there is love, there is a way through the wilderness. Bestow on us loving hearts and a ministry to match our gifts for the tasks necessary to proclaim your holiness to a world in need. In Christ's name we pray. Amen. (David N. Mosser)

SERMON BRIEFS

LET'S MAKE A DEAL

EXODUS 12:1-14

The children said to their parents in the days of their engagement: This month shall be the month of our wedding; it shall be the beginning of the years of our marriage. Tell all your friends and family that, on this day, they are to dress in their finest and celebrate with us.

This parody of the text could go on, at times offering humorous reminders of all the dos, don'ts, and details of modern wedding planning. This is not to suggest that wedding planning and Passover preparation correspond, but they both raise similar questions. As for weddings, one theory claims that all couples decide they should elope but make that decision only after the dress is bought, the church and reception hall are booked, and time is too late. Certainly skipping all of the hoopla and headaches of a wedding presents an enticing alternative to decision-weary brides and grooms. So why go to all of the trouble? Why make such a big deal out of the event?

The same could be asked of Passover ritual. The details

303

concerning when, how, and with whom to celebrate the Lord's passing over at first seem unnecessary. Why worry about how to cook the lamb and how to eat it when the important point is to mark the doorposts with the lamb's blood? Moreover, doesn't God already know who God's chosen people are? Don't they already have the sign of circumcision? Why go to all this trouble?

The text answers: "This day shall be a day of remembrance for you" (v. 14). Go to all the trouble to observe this day in this particular manner so that you will remember—not so that God will remember, but so that you will remember and celebrate and observe. The cadence of the preceding text beats out this emphasis: "This month shall mark for you the beginning." "You shall keep it until the fourteenth day." "You shall let none of it remain.... You shall eat it.... You shall eat it hurriedly." "The blood shall be a sign for you."

God doesn't need blood on the door to identify Hebrew households any more than God needs a wedding to recognize when two people's hearts are joined, a baptism to understand that Holy Spirit has entered a life, or ordination to know when someone has accepted the responsibility of divine servanthood. We humans, on the other hand, are different. Making big deals out of important events helps us to remember why and how we started along the path we journey.

In the case of the Passover, God as Creator of the world, now creates a people, renewing the covenant made with Abraham and, in a sense, restoring to the world a divine orderliness from the beginnings of creation. The people will need this memory and the lesson it teaches, namely that at times when all possibilities seem exhausted and hope dashed they can trust in God. Why? Because God is a Creator God who brings into being things, people, opportunities, and forms not yet imagined.

This text reminds us to go to all the trouble to observe high points in our lives in a "big deal" manner so that we, too, will remember. Remember joy from a wedding day, peace during baptism, the calling of ordination, pride at graduation, or the anticipation of a job. Why do we need the memories? So that we will know God: Creator, Provider, Savior, Sustainer, Counselor, Friend. (Karen Hudson)

ARE THERE ANY REQUIREMENTS?

ROMANS 13:8-14

Two coaches were asked to give the basic requirement of their respective sports. Both coaches pulled out their rule books and began to spout off requirements, but both were told that they had to simplify their answers to one basic requirement. The baseball coach finally answered, "Keep your eye on the ball." To that, the basketball coach said, "Just get the ball in the basket, I don't care whether you see it or not!"

Most subjects have basic requirements that help us understand those subjects better. Our faith is no different. As Jesus was asked, "Teacher, which commandment in the law is the greatest?" I imagine him thumbing through all the scrolls of his day in his head, thinking about all of the laws and requirements, but finally answering, " 'Love the Lord your God with all your heart, and with all your soul, and with all your mind.' This is the greatest and first commandment. And a second is like it: 'You shall love your neighbor as yourself' " (Matt. 22:36-39). In Luke's Gospel, Jesus then goes on to tell that masterful story of the good Samaritan who helped his neighbor. This was really a shocking story for a Samaritan to be the one who reflected the greatest commandment!

To love is a Christian's basic requirement. This idea must have stuck with Paul throughout his years of ministry. Paul had written the great love chapter to the Corinthians telling them that without love they had nothing, but now he tells the Roman church that this basic requirement extends beyond those within the Christian community. Paul tells them to love neighbors of any and every persuasion. It's not like the saying, "When in Rome do as the Romans." Rather, Paul says, "When in Rome, or Jerusalem, or Judea, or Samaria, or wherever you are, do what is required as a follower of Christ."

Love is the principle by which all else is measured. It is the key for those of us who live under the grace of Christ. Love is the fulfillment of the law. Once you know the basic requirement of a sport, you work at mastering it. So too, in faith, once we know that the basic requirement of us is to love, we must strive to master what love means, why it matters, and how it helps us to live as Christ instructed.

This is where Paul comes in. He basically says, "love is not a sentiment for someone or something. Love is not just a feeling for the opposite gender." Paul warns about getting love confused with the desires of the flesh. Paul says love is shown by our actions, by what we do. We know of God's love because of what God has done for us. This is most vividly displayed in the sending of God's only Son.

We work at loving our spouses, family, and friends, but for us to love an enemy means that we are commanded to work for that person's good. That is hard for us to do. How do you work for the good of an enemy? Nationally, how does a country work for the good of other countries that act as our enemies? How do we as missionaries work for the good of others without placing our own societal and ethical standards on them?

Paul says that we can't lose sight of the light of the past or the light of the future salvation. The impact of God's future on our present makes all the difference. Knowing the promise of the future keeps us from falling back and looking to ourselves for salvation. Our love must be tempered by the hope of God's final salvation of the world.

In the meantime, we must put on Christ. During Halloween, there are a lot of children who will put on costumes and try to look like different characters, but it's not until they begin to act like their characters that people will really know who they are. That is true for us, too. To put on Christ is to act like Christ. Then, people will really know of God's love. (Ryan Wilson)

ASKING, AGREEING, AND GETTING

MATTHEW 18:15-20

I have almost concluded that God does not honor "football" prayers. I am not referring to those controversial pregame prayers from the press box. I am talking about those perfectly legal, but seemingly ineffective, petitions offered by Christian fans from the stands. "Oh Lord God of Israel, wouldst thou please part the defense of thine enemies that thy runner may go forth?" "Dear God, safely guide thy quarterback's pass into the arms of our blessed receiver." Maybe I am exaggerating just a little, but prayers of that nature are routinely offered up by desperate believers in situations of "fourth and goal." There are actually times when hundreds of Christians are praying together in one accord, "agreeing together" for the salvation of the home team. But big games are still lost in spite of Jesus' sure and certain promise about heaven and earth moving in response to the request of united prayer efforts.

Jesus was apparently either wrong about what he said or some of us have been wrong about what he meant. What he said was, "if two of you shall agree on earth as touching any thing that they shall ask, it shall be done for them" (v. 19 KJV). What some of us think he meant was that God will do anything we want him to do if only we can find at least one other Christian to ask him for the same thing. This was the attitude that some of Jesus' disciples took. In Mark 10, James and John practically quoted these words back to him as if to say, "All right Lord you promised, so give us the seats of honor when you take the throne!" Jesus responded, "Ye know not what ye ask." Neither does anyone else who thinks his words were an unconditional, money-back guarantee that can be cut out and pasted wherever suits us best.

The promise is part of a lesson Jesus taught about how our relationships with others affect our relationship with God. In this week's passage, Jesus began by talking about how to be reconciled to a brother and wound up talking about how to have power in prayer. It may just be that those two subjects are related, like a symphony, where a host of instruments and instrumentalists are in complete obedience to the conductor and in complete harmony with each other. There is something powerful—something moving—about that. This is the kind of powerful movement we are promised "where two or three are gathered together" in his name (v. 20 KJV).

Surely Jesus can be present in the smallest of congregations. But his purpose was not to provide us with the minimal number who must be present on Sunday morning in order to have church. Church "happens" wherever Christ is present. We can count on his presence where two or more are united in obedience to Christ and in harmony with one another. When there is agreement on earth, earth is more like heaven, and the prayers we pray truly can move both heaven and earth. Jesus really gets into the "midst" of an agreement like that. That is the kind of agreement in which church "happens" and prayers get answered. That is the way to "Ask, Agree, and Get." (Lance Sawyer)

SEPTEMBER 11, 2005

Seventeenth Sunday After Pentecost

Worship Theme: God frequently calls believers to advance when our inclination is to retreat. God repeatedly calls us to welcome those who do not act or think as we do. The most difficult task that God calls us to carry out, however, is forgiving others as God first forgave us.

Readings: Exodus 14:19-31; Romans 14:1-12; Matthew 18:21-35

Call to Worship (Exodus 15:1b-3, 6-7, 11, 21)

Leader: I will sing to the LORD, for he has triumphed gloriously; horse and rider he has thrown into the sea.

People: **The LORD is my strength and my might, and he has become my salvation; this is my God, and I will praise him, my father's God, and I will exalt him.**

Leader: The LORD is a warrior; the LORD is his name.

People: **Your right hand, O LORD, glorious in power—your right hand, O LORD, shattered the enemy.**

Leader: In the greatness of your majesty you overthrew your adversaries; you sent out your fury, it consumed them like stubble.

People: **Who is like you, O LORD, among the gods? Who is like you, majestic in holiness, awesome in splendor, doing wonders?**

All: Sing to the LORD, for he has triumphed gloriously; horse and rider he has thrown into the sea.

Pastoral Prayer:

God of Creation, we pray today that we might join in your plan of creation. In ages past, you liberated Israel from her bondage in Egypt. Today we give thanks that you liberated us from the bondage to sin and death through your son and our Messiah, Jesus Christ. In this freedom, we pray that you, O Lord, liberate us from the judgmental spirit so pervasive in today's world. Every person, so it seems, judges whether or not another person's actions are upright, wholesome, and praiseworthy. A critical spirit has invaded our thinking as well. Forgive us for this trespass against others as you open us to fair dealings in our actions and thoughts with regard to others. Most of all give us a spirit of forgiveness that comes from your gracious presence in our lives. Fill our cup with your goodness, O Lord. In Jesus' sanctified name we pray. Amen. (David N. Mosser)

SERMON BRIEFS

STORYTELLING AS FAITH SUSTAINING

EXODUS 14:19-31

When you were little, what was the incident that everyone in your family talked about for years? What about the event seemed amazing and inexplicable? Does anyone in your family still talk about it? How has perception of the event changed over time? How did life change afterward? During the event, who spoke of God? How was God described? How did your perception of God change because of what happened?

Perhaps similar questions inspired the authors of Exodus to tell the tale we hear in Exodus 14. Regardless of various views on the historicity of the narrative, the crossing of the Red Sea is an event recalled by the Hebrew nation as a pivotal point in the already high drama of the creating of the Hebrew nation. It is a story told over and over again, emerging as a linchpin in the Jewish liturgical calendar.

Why, do you suppose, did ancient writers choose this story to tell? Fans of Charlton Heston will recognize the dramatic screenplay potential imbedded here, although positing that as a reason for success reflects more on modern American expectations than on ancient motivation. Far from highlighting Israel, a close reading of the text finds that it talks as much about the destruction of the Egyptians as about the safe passage of the Israelites. Furthermore, any serious consideration of the question, "Who was God to the Egyptians?" demands critical review of our own and the text's theology.

So why is this story told in this way? Perhaps one answer stems from verse 19. "The angel of God who was going before . . . moved and went behind them." Thus far in the Exodus narrative God has been in the forefront of Israelite movement (Exod. 13:22). Now, just when the Israelites face chaos from in front and behind, God's presence in the angel moves to the back. Shouldn't God be going before them, preparing the way? Is the human Moses really in tune with God enough to replace the heavenly angel at this juncture? As the story unfolds we hear of Israel making an incredible step of faith as they enter the sea. Their faith asserts that God will see them safely through this crossing, that God will be present in new ways, all the time creating fresh possibilities in the circumstances at hand. In this moment of a crisis of faith, the Israelites shine brightly. Indeed, celebrating such a milestone in faith merits retelling the story for future generations in order to comprehend what it looks like to know that I AM is Lord.

Nevertheless, this story demands further contemplation because it includes a description of the decimation of the Egyptian army. Even ages later, as the writer of Hebrews reflects on faith, the inclusion of the Egyptian defeat remains (Heb. 11:29). So why include in a story of faith a gruesome reminder of God's judgment? Terence Fretheim posits a suggestion that may shed some light. He sees the Egyptians as embodying destruction and chaos that work to subvert God's creational plan (See Terence E. Fretheim, *Exodus*, Interpretation: A Bible Commentary for Teaching and Preaching [Louisville: John Knox Press, 1991], pp. 158-61). Knowing that God not only creates new potential for life but also triumphs over forces attempting to disrupt creation moves faith from hindsight to hope's sustenance. Such faith recognizes the creative possibility for "things not seen" (Heb. 11:1) and purports assurance that God brings them into existence.

Return to the story your family told over and over. What does it teach you about faith? How would you recount the story to younger generations? May you continue to tell "so the people [will fear] the Lord and believe" (v. 31). (Karen Hudson)

TAKING A SEAT WITH MISTAKEN IDENTITY

ROMANS 14:1-12

Many times in the life of faith, we find ourselves looking at other people who bear the name of Christian and we decide to take a seat on the judge's bench. We call the courtroom to order, and we pass judgment on the unrighteous offenders!

Paul knew this all too well from his background. Paul had taken his seat at the judge's bench, and he had terrorized first-century Christians. Paul justified his actions through his faith. He was keeping the law. He was staying pure. Paul was trying to do what he thought God would have him to do. But, his encounter with Jesus showed him his mistake. He had taken a seat at the judge's bench with mistaken identity. Paul thought he was the judge, but Christ showed him that he was the one who was guilty.

Consequently, Paul writes to the Romans to welcome "those who are weak" and addresses the weak and the strong (the spiritually immature and spiritually mature). The amazing thing is how Paul brings both groups into the picture, and you can almost imagine both groups beginning to smile.

Then, Paul addresses two issues of the church of the day: dietary laws and sacred day laws. "Those who eat must not despise those who abstain, and those who abstain must not pass judgment on those who eat; for God has welcomed them" (v. 3). Paul writes that while someone's diet may show their level of maturity, it does not give them the right to pass judgment, because God has welcomed both the weak and the mature. And concerning holy days, Paul writes, "Some judge one day to be better than another, while others judge all days to be alike" (v. 5). Paul suggests that both should hold strong convictions about it, but they should do so to honor the Lord.

I find this line of thinking to be very relevant for today. I wonder what Paul would have to say about our cultural issues, and I wonder which side of these issues he would view as strong or weak. We often say that people are more conservative or liberal in their beliefs, and I wonder if Paul would allow us to substitute these words for weak and strong. The cultural norms make us wonder about our freedom in Christ and how our freedom can be expressed in our culture. Where do we draw the line?

Paul's real issue is what is known today to be a judgmental mentality. Whether being more conservative or liberal, whether being weak or strong, Paul warns both sides about having a judgmental mentality. This mentality believes that I am right and anyone else who doesn't see things exactly as I see them is wrong. This mentality goes a step further by condemning and trying to correct any thought besides one's own.

I think Paul would remind the weak and the strong that we see through a glass dimly. In fact, Paul suggests that the more important thing is not the issue of the day. While our position on certain issues of the day may indicate who is stronger or weaker in their faith, and while it is important to strive to mature in one's faith, the most important thing is to remember that we are living for God. Someday we will all be accountable to God. In the meantime, whether weak or strong, we must not judge each other. Paul implies that we as humans, whether weak or strong, have a tendency to mistake our identity. We try to play god. Worse yet, we play a condemning and uninformed god. By passing judgment, we are the ones who are full of ignorance and prejudice. We are passing judgment on ourselves. (Ryan Wilson)

ACCOUNTS UNPAYABLE

MATTHEW 18:21-35

An assumption underlying this parable seems to be that sins accumulate like a debt. When another person does us wrong we often feel as though they owe us something. Our natural desire is to make them pay. Those with especially sensitive consciences may even be, to some degree, aware of this indebtedness. This is manifest in such everyday expressions as, "Is there anything I can ever do to make it up to you?"

I have come to realize that there is nothing I can do to "make up" for most of the wrongs I have committed. The damage we do when we hurt other people cannot usually be undone no matter how sorry we are or how guilty we feel. There is a sense in which we are all beholden to each other and to God. The servant in the parable owed his king ten thousand talents. It was a crushing debt considering that the imperial taxes for all of Judea, Idumea, and Samaria combined were only six hundred talents per year.

Jesus likely used this hyperbolic figure to emphasize how helpless we are and how merciful God is. The poor man who owed his king ten thousand talents was subject to lose everything he owned and everybody he loved. He would spend the rest of his life in the futile attempt to "make it up." The forgiveness he received was nothing short of amazing, but even grace carries an obligation. Jesus warned that if we do not forgive others, then God will not forgive us.

Our dilemma is that God's grace is easy to receive, but hard to imitate. There is something in us that cannot stand the thought of forgiving a person we absolutely dislike. One of my biggest frustrations is that most of the people I need to forgive have not asked me to forgive them. They do not generally even acknowledge they have done anything wrong, nor do they show any remorse. But if I only forgive those who beg me to I will probably only be able to forgive two or three more people over the course of the next fifty years. Meanwhile, I will probably need God's forgiveness two or three thousand times. According to Jesus, I will have to do better than that.

One thing that helps me survive is the realization that apologies do not usually undo damage or "make up" debts anyway. I have a four-year-old son who still thinks they do. He sometimes hits his two-year-old brother, then quickly confesses and apologizes to both brother and father in a desperate attempt to atone for his sins before judgment overtakes him. As his father, I am glad he is learning to say "I'm sorry," but those words do not have as much power as he presumes. I do forgive him, but not because of the apology. I forgive my son because I love him; and that is the reason God forgives us. We can never imitate God with exactitude or with the same magnitude, but we can imitate the loving Spirit. Love is the force that makes forgiveness possible. Love can cover a "multitude of sins." We cannot pay all the debts we owe, nor can we expect payment on all the debts owed to us. But we can love. If we can really love, then we will find that we can really forgive. (Lance Sawyer)

SEPTEMBER 18, 2005

Eighteenth Sunday After Pentecost

Worship Theme: Our God is a God of providence. Whether it is the food we eat or the work of our hands given as a sacred stewardship, God provides for our needs. Rather than begrudge God's graciousness toward others, believers are free to rejoice in God's goodness toward us.

Readings: Exodus 16:2-15; Philippians 1:21-30; Matthew 20:1-16

Call to Worship (Psalm 105:1-6, 45c)

Leader:	O give thanks to the LORD, call on his name, make known his deeds among the peoples.
People:	**Sing to him, sing praises to him; tell of all his wonderful works.**
Leader:	Glory in his holy name; let the hearts of those who seek the LORD rejoice.
People:	**Seek the LORD and his strength; seek his presence continually.**
Leader:	Remember the wonderful works he has done, his miracles, and the judgments he uttered.
People:	**O offspring of his servant Abraham, children of Jacob, his chosen ones.**
All:	**Praise the LORD!**

Pastoral Prayer:
In our scurrying about to scratch out a living for ourselves and our loved ones, Lord of All, we too often forget the real founda-

316

tion you provide for our lives. We too regularly assume the burdens of life by ourselves when you are prepared to lift life's burdens. We forget that it was Jesus who reminded those who had ears that "my burden is light" (Matt. 11:30). Give us the assurance of faith, O Lord of Creation, that you are the source of providence and that you know how to provide for our every need. Create in our lives not only the buoyancy that faith gives but also the grace to treat our sisters and brothers with the kind of love you desire for all people. Forgive us where we fail, and buoy us upon the waters of mercy. In the name of Jesus our Christ we pray. Amen. (David N. Mosser)

SERMON BRIEFS

EXPERIMENTAL THEOLOGY

EXODUS 16:2-15

One day my husband came home and asked, "Do you have the fixings for chocolate chip cookies?" Sure enough, I did and proceeded to make some the next day. After one bite, my husband grimaced and asked what I had done to the recipe. Admittedly, I had tried to be health conscious and had substituted applesauce for cooking oil, the result of which was speckled, cake-like cookies, not the chewy, melt-in-your-mouth kind that he expected. I knew of the applesauce substitution with cakes and muffins but had to experiment to see if it worked with cookies.

Exodus 16 finds the Israelites also in a try-it-and-see period. My seminary Old Testament professor noted that Exodus 13–19 describes a progression: first God reveals God's self, then God and the Israelites enter a time of testing such revelation, next God reveals God's self again, and finally the people are called and commissioned. Our text falls in the middle of the experimental part of the cycle. God reveals God's self as the one who delivers, leading the Israelites out of bondage in Egypt (Exodus 13). The people explore to what extent God will continue to deliver, and God probes to see "whether they will follow [God's] instruction or not" (v. 4). Such experimentation allows for the demonstration and proof of who I AM is so that the people will more fully respond to what "you shall be" (Exod. 19:6) entails.

Moses and Aaron refuse to deal with the Israelite's demands for food, seemingly having had enough of their complaining merely days after crossing the Red Sea. God, however, chooses to reply not in condemnation but by offering further revelation of the divine self. Certainly, we could understand if God wanted to do a touch of smiting. These same Israelites who have just experienced exemption from plagues, liberation from Egypt, and water purification, not to mention the miraculous sea crossing, now say that they would rather have stayed in Egypt and died! But God has bigger plans for these people and elects to show that the I AM who delivers liberation also literally delivers daily bread. God chooses dialogue over judgment.

Judgment in the Old Testament, in fact, seems to come more from when people stop calling out to God than from when they call out in complaint. Isaiah speaks to the coming judgment because the people do not know God and have turned away from the Lord (Isa. 1:3-4). Amazingly, Holocaust survivors testify to the Exodus truth, claiming that arguing with God, even accusing God of abandonment, remains a statement of belief. Engaging in dialogue opens avenues for revelation and ultimately for partnering divine and human creativity.

The cycle of revelation, testing, revelation, and commissioning continues. We see it in the stories of Jesus in the Gospels and in the beginning of the church described in Acts and the Epistles. The message urges that we continue to engage God in dialogue and experiment with our experience of God's revelation. Revelation in today's text illustrates what trust and provision look like. Israel had to learn how to trust their Deliverer. God showed that provision comes in creative and unexpected ways; certainly, Israel didn't have manna in mind when they cried out—quail maybe, but not manna. Like trying applesauce in cookies, testing our understanding of God is not wrong, although we might get unexpected results. But then, what better way to remember God as Creator. (Karen Hudson)

LIVING OR DYING, WE WIN!

PHILIPPIANS 1:21-30

Whether or not you like the apostle Paul you have to admire him and his viewpoint on so many things, especially living and dying. This morning we begin a two-part study in the life of this most interesting individual. We'll call this morning's study "Living or Dying, We Win!"

His was a life worth living before Christ. Paul was young, connected, successful, well-educated, and a leader in his faith. Many young men his age during his time would have gladly traded places with him because of who he was and who he was becoming. Yet, we get a glimpse of a person searching for meaning in his life in all that he did.

In today's stressed-filled lives, many are the parallels we can draw between a person such as Paul and us. Paul wanted the best life had to offer as he knew it, and so do we. Quite honestly, he wanted to win! Paul had been present at the stoning of Stephen, the first Christian martyr. It is said, almost in passing, that he approved of this murder. And not only did he approve of it, he sought more. By arresting and killing more Christians, Paul would win! But thanks be to God that Paul found real meaning in his encounter with Jesus Christ on the Damascus Road. His experience was so meaningful that Paul tells the faithful in Philippi a bold statement that probably confounded them as it does us: "For to me, living is Christ and dying is gain." Paul's outlook on his life was that it had meaning enough now to continue living to serve Christ. His dying, Paul believed, was to be total gain. For us, those words speak of deep roots in Christ Jesus. It tells us of a living relationship with the living Lord. So real is Christ that to die is to gain entrance into an eternal relationship with Jesus.

John Wesley shares of his experience while at sea with the Moravians as they journeyed toward the colony of Georgia and how he was taken aback by almost party celebration during a fierce storm. Wesley feared he was going to die, while the Moravians were celebrating the possibility. This experience caused him to reexamine his relationship with Jesus Christ. The Moravian believers had an inner spiritual strength that Wesley did not yet possess.

319

Paul is honest as he explains that he was not sure which he preferred, living or dying. To stay alive meant more work and more victories for Jesus and his gospel. Yet, the thought of an eternal reward in Christ was also very inviting for Paul, knowing that death was not something to fear. Yet, Paul knows that at that point in his life he was to continue working toward winning new believers and strengthening the old ones.

Paul then encourages the faithful to live their lives in ways that will allow them to boast "in Christ." His command: "Live your life in a manner worthy of the gospel of Christ ... standing firm in one spirit, striving side by side with one mind for the faith of the gospel" (v. 27). Paul considered it a great privilege to believe in Christ and to suffer for him as well, for, in the end, the reward would be great: a never-ending relationship with Christ Jesus. In these times when winning is so important to so many, why not win at something that pays off eternally? Walking with Christ in such a way that allows us to die in a way that glorifies God is to win! (Eradio Valverde, Jr.)

THANKS FOR GOD'S ETERNAL UNFAIRNESS

MATTHEW 20:1-16

This parable is perplexing. To most people it appears to be a story that tells of an injustice committed against those who have worked throughout "the heat of the day" (v. 12 NIV). Those hired late in the day are paid the same wage as those who have labored all day long. In the eyes of nearly everyone, this would appear to be an injustice.

The story also seems to undermine a healthy work ethic. How is it that those who work only a little, and presumably produce only a little, are rewarded equally with the more productive workers? Our society celebrates honest work. We value those who give "an honest day's work for an honest day's pay." Those important principles are undercut by this parable.

Further, to those who are alert to political and economic issues, this story would seem to smack of socialism. Rather than paying the workers according to their contribution, the owner pays them according to their need. Surely everyone needs a day's pay, but do all earn it? Simplistic understandings of socialism appear to undergird the moral values of the parable. People get what they need rather than what they earn. Surely such a world might degenerate into a place where no one works and all expect someone else to provide for their needs!

Our perplexity grows as we consider this to be a story of Jesus. We expect Jesus to be fair in all things. We expect Jesus to uphold our values. We want Jesus to be sensitive to the political complexities of his words. Surely Jesus would not be an advocate for obvious unfairness. Surely Jesus would not support values destructive to a productive society. Everything in the story seems contrary to our view of good sense and common fairness. It is perplexing to find Jesus associated with these views!

Well, friends, to understand this parable we must first agree that it is not about economics. This may be "no way to run a railroad" or a vineyard, but Jesus is not talking about human economic enterprises in this story. Rather, he teaches about "the kingdom of heaven." In other words, this is a story about God, not human economics.

A fair day's wage can be earned, but a place in the kingdom of God cannot. God's love and acceptance cannot be earned. Love and acceptance are gifts given as God chooses, not as we would choose. Just as the owner of the vineyard chooses to give each worker a full day's wage, so God chooses to give us a full day's wage of God's love and acceptance. Don't we have to admit that this is almost as difficult to swallow as the story of the generous employer?

We who occupy the pews and pulpits of churches too often secretly want God to benefit us in proportion to the time we have spent laboring in God's vineyard. It may offend us to think God's love is not parceled out in proportion to the Sunday school classes taught, the choir practices attended, the sermons endured, or the offerings tossed into the collection plate. God's reign is characterized by God's freely given love. It is not about our earning it. It is about the very nature of God, which is to give. Given how far short of the kingdom of heaven our efforts have produced, aren't we all laborers who have arrived late in the day and contributed little? Thanks be to God that we who have contributed so little to the harvest are blessed with God's generous love. (Carl L. Schenck)

SEPTEMBER 25, 2005

Nineteenth Sunday After Pentecost

Worship Theme: The authority that Jesus as the Messiah brings to those who believe is an authority of faithfulness. Jesus embodied his teaching. The test of authentic faith matches a believer's lofty professions with his or her conduct.

Readings: Exodus 17:1-7; Philippians 2:1-13; Matthew 21:23-32

Call to Worship (Psalm 78:4*b*, 12-16)

> *Leader:* "We will tell to the coming generation the glorious deeds of the LORD, and his might, and the wonders that he has done.
>
> **People:** **"In the sight of their ancestors he worked marvels in the land of Egypt....**
>
> *Leader:* "He divided the sea and let them pass through it, and made the waters stand like a heap.
>
> **People:** **"In the daytime he led them with a cloud, and all night long with a fiery light.**
>
> *Leader:* "He split rocks open in the wilderness, and gave them drink abundantly as from the deep.
>
> **People:** **"He made streams come out of the rock, and caused waters to flow down like rivers."**
>
> *All:* **Let us praise God and God's marvelous works!**

Pastoral Prayer:
  O God of the Journey, guide us as we move through the days of our lives. Be our light as we tread through life's dark places. Be

our strength when our own strength fails. Remind us to constantly submit to Jesus who knew what it meant to be fully human as you also made him fully divine. Jesus took the form of a servant. By Jesus' example we can know the way.

Let us cling to the path of righteousness even when other paths tempt us to stray. Inspire in us, O God of Mercy, a heartfelt longing to work in your vineyard for your people and creation. Make us stewards of Jesus' authority that opens the portals of heaven so we catch a glimpse of you and your intention for life. When we fall short of our mark, then forgive us and set us anew on the path that leads to you. We pray in humbleness of spirit in Jesus' name, the pioneer and perfecter of our faith. Amen. (David N. Mosser)

SERMON BRIEFS

IMAGINE THE BEST

EXODUS 17:1-7

There is an old saying that an optimist sees a glass as half full; a pessimist sees a glass as half empty; an engineer sees the glass as twice as big as it needs to be.

The people of Israel are wandering in the desert. They have been sustained by manna, but they grow tired of the manna and complain. They regret the day when they left Egypt and wonder if God is no longer caring for them. God's response is to send quail.

The Hebrews are very thirsty and need water. "Did you take a wrong turn, or did you intend to lead us out here to die," they ask their leader. Moses responds with a question of his own: "Why do you test the Lord?" We can almost hear the anger and frustration Moses must feel in these repeated bouts of immaturity and impatience.

People today often raise the same question when they read this portion of the history of Israel. How is it that the Hebrews could continue to doubt and lack trust in God's intentions and goodness? The answer to that question points to something basic in the human condition.

Our perception of our lives is a reflection of our inner state. If we are anxious and afraid, our thoughts lead us to the dark places of doubt and even despair. We are impatient with our discomfort. We want a quick fix. We are consumed by worry. We look around for someone or something to blame. We forget that we have been called to journey to a place that awaits us.

Perception is a function of our maturity. When we are growing in maturity we can tolerate our pain because we know that it is demanded in our growth. We learn from our experiences. We discover that confidence and determination are thoughts we can choose as surely as we can choose thoughts of frustration and worry. We learn that we can follow a course of action based on our confidence that God is leading us through the wilderness. We have a vision of the future that calls us forward.

One element this story shares with another significant event in the journey of the Hebrews is the rod of Moses. The rod is the instrument Moses uses to express the power of God. As Moses carries the rod, it is a symbol of the possibilities of God's power. The people complain to Moses who holds the symbol. The Hebrews have the opportunity to look at a symbol of what God can make possible. Their anxiety masks the possibilities that are in plain sight.

Albert Einstein once said that imagination is more important than knowledge. Maturity is the capacity to manage our anxiety in ways that help us see the possibilities and "live" in their direction. As Moses demonstrates, those who trust God's leadership have in their view the symbols and signs of God's active saving power. Prayer, worship, reading the Scriptures, and living in the community of Christ helps us to manage our anxiety and fears so that we do not lose God's gift of imagination. (Bob Holloway)

YOU'RE BETTER THAN ME!

PHILIPPIANS 2:1-13

Last Sunday we began to look at the life of the apostle Paul. We found that his life was similar to many of ours today. Paul wanted to win, at first, until he realized what true winning really was. Winning was living a life worthy of the gospel, and dying was to enter into a continuation of such a life for all eternity.

Today, we examine what Paul says in chapter 2 of his letter to the believers in Philippi. As we said last Sunday, whether you like Paul or not, you have to admire him. Paul advanced the gospel in his time farther than any other evangelist. And not only as an evangelist but also as a pastor. Paul's letters are responses to crises or words of encouragement during times of stress and trials. Such is the case in this passage. Paul encourages the believers to strive to live their lives in a unique way. Instead of the popular notion of "everyone for themselves," Paul stresses, "everyone for everyone." Instead of "looking out for number one," make yourself number two and try harder. Let's examine these point by point as we get to what we will call, "You are better than me."

Paul's starting point is for all believers in that fellowship of Philippi to be of one mind. He stresses this twice, at the beginning of this passage and at the end. How many organizations and groupings can we think of where there is truly only one mind? Is that true in your family? In your workplace? With your friends? In your church? What then, could Paul possibly mean in saying we should be of the same mind. In most families the "one mind" would be "stay together, love one another, get along as much as possible, learn to forgive and overlook mistakes, be a family." In your workplace, you may have a mission statement that summarizes the goals of your organization. Perhaps it says, "Everyone pull together," "be a team," and so forth. In your church, it may also be a mission statement about what you believe God is calling your church to be in that particular place and time. We all know that, although we have the same mission statement, we won't always get along, but we should still love each other enough to work together for the good of the gospel. Look ahead to what Paul writes in verse 5, "Let the same mind be in you that was in Christ Jesus." Paul is actually the original author of WWJD! If we have the same mind that was in Christ Jesus, we certainly need to ask ourselves prior to every decision, "What would Jesus do?"

Paul stresses the need for humility to be present in our working together. Set the goals of the church above your "selfish ambition or conceit," working together with humility to the point that we can truly regard others as better than ourselves. Here it is

2005; can we believe this statement? Yes, we can if we remember that the basic reality of the gospel of Jesus is that it calls for people to do the unexpected and to live lives that surprise others. This is no exception. Jesus knows that, for us to accomplish all that God intends for us, we must work together, putting others ahead of ourselves so that we can win others to God's reign. If this is not yet true in us, today is the day to start with a new attitude toward others and toward ourselves. (Eradio Valverde, Jr.)

UNDER AUTHORITY

MATTHEW 21:23-32

A professor interpreting the results of a psychological profile taken by a first-year student said, "According to these findings you are a person who does not accept things simply on the basis of authority. If that is accurate, you may question what I am telling you." "Oh," replied the student, "I didn't know you were an authority!"

Today's Gospel lesson is all about authority. It begins with Jesus' opponents challenging his authority to teach. Jesus cleverly turns the question upon the questioners by asking them about the authority of John the Baptizer. Jesus set a trap for his opponents. Any answer they give could be used against them.

Following this exchange, Jesus tells a parable. This story, commonly called the parable of the two sons, recounts two sons who say one thing and do another. It would be easy to get distracted with the inconsistency of their words and deeds. This is not Jesus' point. Jesus responds to those who questioned his authority by telling of the authority of a father. While the sons respond in different ways both verbally and behaviorally, in each case, they are responding to the authority of the father. The parable, like the preceding confrontation with his opponents, is about authority.

This subject of authority, and specifically Jesus' authority, is not as easy or comfortable as we might think. We say Jesus is "Lord and Savior," but we are much more comfortable with the Savior part of his identity than we are with Jesus as Lord. Like the second son in the parable, we are likely to verbally affirm Jesus' authority, but not live under that authority. Examples are nearly endless, but today we will look at two.

First, we are resistant to Jesus' authority to teach us about our obligations to our neighbor. Jesus teaches an ethic of radical obligation to our neighbors. We are generally content in dealing with our neighbors from a perspective of simple fairness. Jesus pushes us farther than we want to go. Jesus teaches that we are to love our neighbor as ourself. This love has many dimensions, but it consistently seeks to do that which is best for the neighbor. This love of neighbor has us feed the hungry neighbor, clothe the naked neighbor, and visit the sick neighbor. The love of neighbor that Jesus teaches puts the needs of the neighbor at least on a par with our own. In the real world, this is a difficult teaching. Does Jesus have authority over our lives in this regard?

Second, we are resistant to Jesus' authority to teach us the identity of our neighbor. As difficult as it is to love our likable neighbors, Jesus teaches that our neighbor is the hated and mistrusted Samaritan. Our neighbor is the person at work who undercut us when we were in line for promotion. Our neighbor is the enemy. Jesus would have us extend the love we give to those near and dear to us to those we dislike and mistrust. This is a hard teaching. It is Jesus' teaching. Does Jesus have authority over our lives in this regard?

Authority. It is not an easy word. We who are accustomed to living our lives our way resist submitting our ways to the authority of another. Even Jesus Christ. Yet, our text is quite clear about Jesus' authority. It is also clear about those who say Jesus has authority but behave as if he does not. In the living of our lives does Jesus have authority over us? Of the two sons in the parable, which are we? (Carl L. Schenck)

REFLECTIONS

OCTOBER

Reflection Verse: *"Now when they saw the boldness of Peter and John and realized that they were uneducated and ordinary men, they were amazed and recognized them as companions of Jesus." (Acts 4:13)*

BOLDNESS: CONFIDENCE PRODUCED BY FAITH
Acts 4:13-22

When people act with the courage of conviction it is the bold person who understands what is at stake with regard to their action. Boldness is not arrogance. Rather, boldness describes a person who looks squarely at circumstances and proceeds with bravery and daring. Whatever consequences come—and consequences will come to be sure—the bold person knows with certainty that doing the right thing is worth the risk. In the Christian faith, the bold person acts with risk for the building up of community and not for personal gain. Jesus, no doubt, is our best biblical example of such boldness. Given the earthly end of Jesus' life and that Jesus doubtless knew full well what was in store for him as a result of his ministry, we can hold Jesus up as the epitome of boldness. Jesus possessed a poise borne of faith. Faith in God and the trust that radiated from this faith enabled Jesus to challenge the powers and principalities of his age—and ours.

When Luke tells the story of the early church, he suggests that the things that happened to Jesus are the same sorts of things that happened to the disciples. In this case Peter and John heal a person and speak out boldly in the name of God. As a "reward" for the healing of this man "lame from birth" (Acts 3:2), or an individual that today we would describe as a person with a disability, the religious authorities arrest Peter and John. The religious authorities then interrogate them with this question: "By what power or by what name did you do this?" (v. 7). By the power of the Holy Spirit Peter tells them that the power of Jesus Christ healed the man. Luke wants us to know that this inspired speech comes as a gift from the Holy Spirit because, as Luke also notes, "they were uneducated and ordinary men." This scene before the religious authorities fulfills the promise that Jesus earlier made to the disciples. Luke writes that Jesus pledges to the disciples that, "When they bring you before the synagogues, the rulers, and the authorities, do not worry about how you are to defend yourselves or what you are to say; for the Holy Spirit will teach you at that very hour what you ought to say" (Luke 12:11-12). Luke's story from Acts 4 illustrates both the boldness of the disciples and the surprise of the religious authorities.

After the religious authorities' cross-examination of Peter and John, we might expect these disciples to pray for protection from those who arrested and persecuted them. Yet, we read quite a different prayer in Acts. After release, Peter and John return to their companions and relate the interrogation's details. Subsequently, Luke tells us they offered a prayer clearly inspired by the Holy Spirit. "Sovereign Lord, who made the heaven and the earth, the sea, and everything in them . . . look at [the religious authorities'] threats, and grant to your servants to speak your word with all boldness" (Acts 4:24, 29). As prayers go, this is an absolutely magnificent one. At the same time, it is also a prayer that bewilders those of us who generally want to take the safe route or maintain a secure course of action. Not these early Christians. They were after the truth and wanted to proclaim it boldly.

Not everyone possesses boldness as a natural inclination. These "uneducated and ordinary" disciples prayed for boldness and received it as a Holy Spirit gift. The preacher in Ecclesiastes said, "I saw that under the sun the race is not to the swift, nor the battle to the strong, nor bread to the wise, nor riches to the intelligent, nor favor to the skillful; but time and chance happen to them all" (9:11). However, Luke reminds us that those who are bold in the Lord may indeed carry the day.

I offer here for evidence two examples of guiding boldness that provided benefits for a community that would have been lost without a bold act of leadership. These two examples come from American history.

The first example of boldness comes from President Andrew Johnson's secretary of state, William H. Seward. Seward was responsible for negotiating the purchase of Alaska from Russia and was so anxious to get it that he started negotiating with the Russian minister before he had cleared it with President Johnson. He began with an offer of $5 million, but the Russian minister held out until the offer was $7 million.

Congressional approval for the money was difficult because of growing tensions between Congress and the President. But, it finally approved the purchase, and on October 18, 1867, Alaska officially became a territory of the United States. However, Seward became the subject of many jokes, the most famous being Alaska's nickname of "Seward's Folly." He once was asked what was the most significant thing he'd ever done in his career; he replied, "The purchase of Alaska! But it will take a generation to find that out" ("Seward's Folly," n.p., n.d. Online: http://www.everythingalaska.com/eta.sfy.html).

A second example of necessary boldness comes from President Truman's decision to dismiss the ever-popular Douglas MacArthur during the Korean War. At the time of the pronouncement it was one of the most unpopular decisions a sitting president ever made. In retrospect, however, Truman's decision in the early 1950s may have kept the United States out of a war with China, perhaps even another world war. In speaking with labor leader William Hillman, Truman remarked, "I wonder how far Moses would have gone if he had taken a poll in Egypt? What would Jesus Christ have preached if He had taken a poll in the land of Israel?" (Alonzo L. Hamby, *Man of the People: A Life of Harry S. Truman* [New York: Oxford University Press, 1995], p. 558). What sustained Truman was first thinking that he was right and then calling forth the boldness to act accordingly.

Clearly today's church is not persecuted as was the early church. However, what often happens to the modern church may be just as pernicious: damned with faint praise, ignored or belittled, regularly pitied, usually satirized. Regardless of how our culture sees us, our task today is to speak boldly in the name of the Lord. Believers can speak boldly because our "Exhibit A" to the truth of the gospel is the people who have changed lives. Only a bold presentation of the Christian faith can enable others to

embrace the life of discipleship. Discipleship is not merely build-
ings, or budgets, or honors, or awards. Rather, bold discipleship is
sharing a faith that changes people. Bold discipleship is simply
speaking fearlessly the words of the gospel that can give addicts,
criminals, those wandering without meaning, and those consumed by a critical spirit the healing tonic that we call the love of
God in Christ Jesus our Lord. Can you speak a bold word?

If we pastors require a reminder about one of our faith's foundational characteristics of abundant life, then we might look to a
pillar with the word *boldness* inscribed on it. Amen. (David N.
Mosser)

OCTOBER 2, 2005

Twentieth Sunday After Pentecost

Worship Theme: The law was one of God's many holy gifts to Israel. Over time, however, people recognized that the law's power to save was negligible. Then, Christ came not only to fulfill the law but also to offer believers the treasure of salvation by faith.

Readings: Exodus 20:1-4, 7-9, 12-20; Philippians 3:4*b*-14; Matthew 21:33-46

Call to Worship (Psalm 19:7-10, 14)

Leader: The law of the LORD is perfect, reviving the soul; the decrees of the LORD are sure, making wise the simple;

People: **The precepts of the LORD are right, rejoicing the heart; the commandment of the LORD is clear, enlightening the eyes;**

Leader: The fear of the LORD is pure, enduring forever; the ordinances of the LORD are true and righteous altogether.

People: **More to be desired are they than gold, even much fine gold; sweeter also than honey, and drippings of the honeycomb.**

Leader: Let the words of my mouth and the meditation of my heart be acceptable to you,

People: **O LORD, my rock and my redeemer.**

Pastoral Prayer:

Lord of Law and Lord of Grace, today we come before your holy presence to worship you and to praise your sacred name. Too frequently in life we see law and grace in conflict with the other. Yet, in your divine wisdom, you offer to us each of these divine gifts—law and grace. Let us strive for the discernment to perceive the law's blessing. You gave the sacred law, O God, as a guide to your people. You gave the law so that the people of the promise might abide in covenant community together. At the same time, however, we know that the law does not hold the power to save us. Rather, the law only became our custodian until the time of Christ's coming in power and glory. May we cling to Christ's grace and let it become for us the law of faith by which we live in your eternal blessedness. Let Christ's spirit be fulfilled for us in the rule of faith. Forgive us our shortcomings as we open ourselves to newness of life. In the name of Jesus we pray. Amen. (David N. Mosser)

SERMON BRIEFS

GROW UP

EXODUS 20:1-4, 7-9, 12-20

The struggle began as they pulled out of the driveway. The energetic daughter had unfastened her car seat and was attempting to stand up. Dad, not wanting to stop the car, pushed her back into the seat. She stood up once again. This continued for a few moments until Dad in frustration stopped the car and placed her in the car seat with some authority. As he was pulling away she said, "I may be sitting down on the outside, but I am standing up on the inside."

Boundaries are important at any age. Boundaries keep us safe even though, at times, we feel restricted. At times *no* is a wiser and more compassionate word than *yes*. The Ten Commandments are boundaries that, while stated in the negative, create the climate in which our relationship with God and with each other can flourish.

The commandments are not simply God setting a standard for the people of Israel through which they can earn God's goodness toward them. Rather, the commandments are yet another expression of God's grace leading them out of slavery to their own needs and appetites and the sometimes deceiving temptations of seemingly urgent circumstances. They are as much a sign of God's saving covenant as the parting of the Red Sea. Without the commandments to guide them, they journey toward some other Pharaoh willing to enslave them.

To understand the Ten Commandments in this way has two helpful elements. First, this understanding helps Christian disciples recognize the place of the commandments in their desire to follow Christ. From this perspective, our obedience is a response of gratitude. In gratitude we accept our freedom to reject the commandments as ten easy steps to earning God's love. They do not become a litmus test for the obedience of others through which we humbly place ourselves a little higher on the righteousness scale. The commandments become a reference point in our struggles so that we can recognize temptations, our need for repentance, and the depth of God's mercy.

The commandments are also helpful in another way. In our prayerful reflection and in the life of prayer and reflection in the Body of Christ, these commandments can point us to the deepest realities. As boundaries they point to what are healthy and life-giving necessities in our relationship with God and with others. Gratitude directs us to the spirit of the law and not just the words.

Someone once said, "the better the relationship the fewer the rules." Our prayerful and grateful encounters with the Ten Commandments can lead us to know in heart and mind what is essential. The spirit of the commandments moves us from childish disobedience to mature freedom. (Bob Holloway)

FINDING THE BEST BARGAIN

PHILIPPIANS 3:4*b*-14

Bargains receive great emphasis in the marketplace. Hardly a day goes by that most of us don't get something in the mail that tells about a bargain of some sort somewhere. Finding real bargains is tricky, however.

How do you find the best bargains? First, you need to know where to look. We have learned that in sales advertisements, the prices are not really very low, and the quality of the merchandise is sometimes poor. Second, to find the best bargain, you need to be sure that the bargain is really what you want. Third, you ought to be able to afford the bargain. Fourth, a bargain ought to be worth it. I suppose that somewhere there is a bejeweled watchband on sale for $50,000, marked down from $100,000. Even so, most of us can get along just fine without it.

What does this brief primer about bargains say to us about life? Of course, finding the best bargain in life surpasses in importance by far the matter of finding the best bargain in the marketplace. Jesus asked, "What does it profit them if they gain the whole world, but lose or forfeit themselves?" (Luke 9:25). When our very lives for now and for eternity are at stake, getting the greatest bargain is far more important than whether or not we save a couple of dollars at a store.

How do you find the greatest bargain in life? In Philippians 3:8 Paul testified, "I regard everything as loss because of the surpassing value of knowing Christ Jesus my Lord. For his sake I have suffered the loss of all things, and I regard them as rubbish, in order that I may gain Christ." Consider how we can speak of life in Christ as life's greatest bargain.

In finding life's greatest bargain, one needs to know where to look, just as in the marketplace. Where do you look to find what life is all about and what is most satisfying in life? Look to scripture's testimonies of people of faith as they came to know and walk with Jesus. Look to Christian history's stories of stalwart, adventurous Christians. Look to your own acquaintances with such people of faith today. All of these sources can verify that life in Christ is life's greatest bargain.

We said that a bargain must be of use to us. When we look at Jesus clearly, we find ourselves wanting to say with Peter, "Lord, to whom can we go? You have the words of eternal life" (John 6:68). Who else but Christ can help us with the problem of sin and guilt (see Rom. 5:8; 6:23)? Who else can help us deal with our difficulties, even help us overcome them (see Rom. 8:37;

Phil. 4:13)? Who else can turn our lives around, bringing freshness and joy (see 2 Cor. 5:17)? Who else can give us purpose in life (see Mark 1:17; John 10:10)? Who else can bring us the hope of resurrection (John 11:25-26)?

But can you afford this bargain? Yes, for Jesus requires all we have and no more. Indeed, Jesus gives himself to us if we will just receive.

Is following Jesus worth it? Someone has suggested that life is like a department store that some malicious practical joker entered during the night. The person took nothing and destroyed nothing. Rather, the night visitor merely switched the price tags around, leaving the cheapest items with the most expensive price tags and vice versa. When morning came, no one noticed the changes. The result was that shoppers paid outrageous prices for shoddy, useless merchandise.

Paul seems to suggest that he had gotten the price tags of his life straightened out. It is time that we do so, too. We will find that the greatest bargain in life is life in Christ. (Ross West)

WARNING

MATTHEW 21:33-46

Today's text must be approached with great care and confession. This parable of Jesus tells of the wicked tenants who do not recognize the rightful owner. In fact, after mistreating the owners' servants, they murder the heir in hopes of coming into possession of the vineyard. These are seriously nasty and wicked people. In the context of Jesus' time and ministry this parable was directed against the religious leaders. More precisely, it was directed against the Jewish religious leaders of the time.

Here we must exercise much care and kneel in confession. Within Christianity has lurked the ugly cancer of anti-Semitism. We cannot deny it, and we dare not ignore it. This passage from Matthew's Gospel is one of those New Testament texts that has been twisted and misused into fuel for the anti-Semitic fires that burn the soul of Christianity. We must not approach this text today without acknowledging its demonic misuse in the history of Christianity.

At the same time, we must learn its positive lessons. For our time, the issue in the parable is not the failings of the Jewish leaders of the first century, but our own failings in our own time.

The parable tells of servants who had been given much and who overreached in their desire to "have it all." The owner had provided a lovely and productive vineyard and asked only his fair share of the produce. In their greed, the servants sought to make a claim on that which was not theirs. Let us hear the story with trembling.

Couldn't the same parable apply to our stewardship of the planet? God has planted a beautiful and fruitful vineyard for our care. In our greed we are reaching for lifestyles that put too heavy a strain on the fabric of the natural world. Overpopulation, pollution, global warming, and other assaults on the natural world spring in part from our desire to "have it all." The church's voice has not been clear or convincing that stewardship of the environment is a sacred duty. Be warned, we are the wicked tenants.

Or, we could look at the many ways religious leaders have silenced their voices in the interests of self-serving desires to be accepted or popular. Virtually every denominational body has taken a position against capital punishment, yet we speak softly in a society that prefers retribution. Most Protestant bodies are officially against gambling, but we have sold out the vineyard to the easy money illusions of state lotteries and casinos. Gambling is popular, and we sell our souls by being all too quiet. Be warned, we are the wicked tenants.

We are all religious leaders, and we are all guilty. Jesus is not gentle with us. God has given us much and asks only that we give back that which belongs to God. We are to be busy serving God rather than serving ourselves. We are guilty, and in this text we are warned.

The great danger is that we will read this lesson as one directed at persons long ago and far away. No! Across the centuries, Jesus is speaking to us and reminding us of our role as servants of another. Will we heed Jesus' warning? (Carl L. Schenck)

OCTOBER 9, 2005

Twenty-first Sunday After Pentecost

Worship Theme: Jesus speaks about a king who gave a wedding banquet and thereby provides believers with an image of the kingdom of heaven. God has made covenant with God's people in many and various ways. God only asks that we respond in faith.

Readings: Exodus 32:1-14; Philippians 4:1-9; Matthew 22:1-14

Call to Worship (Psalm 106:4-6, 19-22)

> *Leader:* "Remember me, O LORD, when you show favor to your people;
>
> **People:** **"Help me when you deliver them; that I may see the prosperity of your chosen ones,**
>
> *Leader:* "that I may rejoice in the gladness of your nation, that I may glory in your heritage.
>
> **People:** **"Both we and our ancestors have sinned; we have committed iniquity, have done wickedly.**
>
> *Leader:* "They made a calf at Horeb and worshiped a cast image. They exchanged the glory of God for the image of an ox that eats grass.
>
> **People:** **"They forgot God, their Savior, who had done great things in Egypt, wondrous works in the land of Ham, and awesome deeds by the Red Sea."**
>
> *All:* **We are God's forgiven people. Let us worship God in joy and faithfulness.**

Pastoral Prayer:

O God of Pillar and Fire, you are faithful to your people when your people forsake you and turn to other gods. Your patience is beyond our comprehension. Again and again you forgive us and turn us toward you. Give us the inner resolve to accept your pardon, O God, embracing it, and allowing your divine forgiveness to be a shelter for our lives. You have set a banquet before us and ask us to sit at places of honor. Sometimes your grace seems too good to be true and we have difficulty receiving your gift. However, we pray you to send the Holy Spirit upon us gathered to praise your holy name. Somehow we hope against hope that we can come to ourselves and recognize the blessedness of your kingdom. We pray for this wisdom in the name of Jesus Christ. Amen. (David N. Mosser)

SERMON BRIEFS

WHAT SHAPE IS AN IDOL?

EXODUS 32:1-14

When we think of idolatry, we generally think of some other country, some other time, or some other person. Idolatry, like the sin of covetousness, is something someone else is doing. With idolatry, simply and perhaps, innocently, we often fall into the trap of self-deception. The truth is all have idols. While the idolatry of Israel was self-evident, ours is just as prevalent and maybe all the more sinister. Why should we be content to worship idols rather than the great and universal God?

The occasion for this lapse into idolatry on the part of the Hebrew people probably comes from two things: the absence of Moses from the camp and the idolatrous background of the people themselves. Moses was on Mount Sinai for forty days and nights (Exod. 24:18), a time span Moses had not anticipated. This became a challenge to the faith of the people as well as a test of their character.

Although Israel had seen the invisible God in action, they still wanted a god they could see. As a result they requested Aaron to make gods to go before them, an action based on ignorance and a lack of respect for Moses. Aaron prepared the image of a calf and proclaimed a feast. The bull, a symbol of strength and vitality, was often used among ancient peoples to represent deity. The Egyptians worshiped the god Mnevis, a golden calf, so it was understandable that the Israelites wanted a golden calf of their own! The people gladly took off their jewelry and earrings and gave them to Aaron to use in making this image. This was in direct disobedience to the command God has just given them: "You shall not make for yourself an idol, whether in the form of anything that is in heaven above, or that is on the earth beneath, or that is in the water under the earth" (Exod. 20:4). The Israelites arose early in the morning to offer burnt offerings and to sit down to eat and drink. They may have thought they were worshiping God; however, their apparent sincerity was no substitute for obedience or excuse for disobedience.

What shape is an idol? Need it be in the shape of man or beast? Could it be anything that humans can devise as an object of worship and devotion? An idol is worshiped, not for its shape, but for its imagined power. Most modern idolaters worship gadgets and material things rather than images. Does it really matter which of our toys we make into a god? Maybe our idol is primitive like a rabbit's foot. Perhaps the idol is a flashy new automobile, a sizable bank account, a job title, a finely decorated house. Idolatry lies in the heart of the worshiper, not in the idol itself. The real tragedy is that idols give us nothing while promising everything and then take away even that which we have.

God was ready to destroy the entire nation because of their sin. Had Moses not interceded for them, this would have happened. Moses, however, pleas for mercy, and God spares them. God's wrath is real, so also is God's mercy. The idol had to be destroyed. Consequently it was melted, beaten to pieces, and strewn upon the waters.

Most of us, like the Israelites, are prone to idolatry. We can even take religious things, things meant to point us to God, and worship them instead of the living God. Some worship their particular church instead of the Lord of the church. Some worship their pastor, instead of the Great Shepherd of the sheep. Some worship the Bible, meant to reveal God to us, instead of the God revealed therein. An idolater is always spiritually disabled, deprived of forgiveness and power. To be saved from this tragedy, we must turn to the power of the real God, not to any human-made substitute. (Drew J. Gunnells, Jr.)

AT PEACE IN A RESTLESS WORLD

PHILIPPIANS 4:1-9

Restlessness seems to be a given in our world. This restlessness sometimes goes beyond dissatisfaction. Indeed, often it seems that conflict dominates the lives of many people. Such feelings of restlessness likely include us. We, too, wonder how we can find peace in the restlessness of our lives and our world.

This passage in Philippians acknowledges our concern for peace and points us to the peace that we seek. Paul was quite familiar with the restlessness of the world of his day. He was in prison. Paul's life was in danger. He had few possessions. He was familiar with anger, conflict, dissatisfaction, and restlessness in his world. Yet Paul was at peace (see Phil. 4:11). Consider what Philippians 4:1-9 can teach us about finding peace in our own restless world.

First, what is this peace that we seek? Peace in the Bible and in life is always peace in the midst of difficulty and trouble rather than the absence of difficulty and trouble (see John 16:33). Peace is the sense of well-being that exists as we deal rightly and constructively with the restlessness of our world and our lives. If we want peace in a restless world, we must seek the peace that flowers and grows in droughts and storms as well as on days of abundance and calm.

How can we get this peace? We can see at least six ideas in this passage. Surely one of them will help you. (1) We can get peace by building positive relationships with people. Seeking to see the best in others and to be reconciled with people with whom we are in conflict is important if we want peace. (2) We can have peace by learning to "rejoice in the Lord always." We don't need to deny the dark side of life, but a song in our hearts goes a long way toward bringing peace in our lives. (3) We can achieve peace by being gentle with other people. Just before we say harsh words to someone, we could help ourselves as well as them by waiting a moment and reconsidering our words. (4) We can have peace by remembering the Lord's nearness (v. 5). We need to look at our lives each day from the perspective of eternity. Taking a long look would enable us to see what is truly important in life rather than only what is worrying us at the moment. (5) We can have peace by praying instead of worrying. When we worry, we are only exalting ourselves as if it is expected and possible that we be perfect and in control of every circumstance. Relying on God rather than worrying is a better way for our hearts to have peace. (6) We can have peace if we think, especially if we think the right thoughts. When we fill our minds with degrading thoughts about others and about ourselves, we should not be surprised when we do not have peace in our lives.

What does such peace do for you? Verse 7 states that "the peace of God, which surpasses all understanding, will guard your hearts and your minds in Christ Jesus." The Greek word translated "guard" suggests that God's peace is like a guard at a fortress, keeping out those things that are harmful. God's peace, referring really to God, stays awake, watching for danger so that we may sleep in peace (see Psalms 27; 46:1-3; John 14:18).

Do you want this peace? If you do, you can have it as you surrender to the Lord and the Lord's way and practice in your life the things that make for peace. (Ross West)

GETTING BETWEEN US AND GOD

MATTHEW 22:1-14

The Bible is full of stories about weddings. Early in the book of Genesis we have the stories of the marriage of Isaac to Rebekah and of Jacob to his two wives. Later we read of the weddings of Samson, King David (in his case several weddings!), and others. In Old Testament times, like our own, weddings were accompanied with great banquets. Eating and drinking and dancing have been means of celebrating weddings for centuries.

In fact, the metaphor of the banquet is one that weaves

throughout the Bible. Isaiah envisions the reign of God as a time when there will be a great feast on Mount Zion with fine wines and great festivity. The writer of Psalm 23 looks forward to a day when God will prepare a banquet. In our time and culture, banquets and feasts are so common they lose a good deal of their charm. We are more concerned about losing weight than eating enough. But in biblical times and the subsistence cultures of those times, banquets or feasts were rare indeed. They represented life at its best. No wonder biblical writers described God's reign as a banquet.

Jesus was no exception. In today's parable Jesus compares the kingdom of heaven to a wedding banquet. This was a familiar image to his listeners. However, in Jesus' story the theme takes on a new twist. The invited guests do not come! They have other business that is more important to them than the wedding banquet.

This story calls us to give attention to our lives. What are the things we allow to get between us and the kingdom of heaven? What is more important to us than God's reign? Before we too quickly answer that nothing is more important than God, perhaps we had better examine our gods. The twentieth-century theologian Paul Tillich described God as a person's "ultimate concern." Whatever is most important to us is our god.

There are many good things that are not God. In the parable, people were distracted by family and business affairs. Family is a good thing, but it is not God. Business and commerce are good things, but they are not God.

October 19, 1987, was Black Monday for the financial markets. The Dow-Jones average fell 508 points in a single day. In Miami, a longtime investor came to his brokerage office and asked to see his broker and the office manager. They gathered in the conference room and the investor took a gun from his briefcase and killed the broker, office manager, and then himself. The bull market, the golden calf, had become a god that had failed.

For too many, faith is like a grandfather clock. It is a family heirloom that we would not consider abandoning. But we also don't expect it to keep good time, to be relevant. We certainly do not regulate our lives by it. So it is with the gospel. What is getting between you and God? (Carl L. Schenck)

OCTOBER 16, 2005

Twenty-second Sunday After Pentecost

Worship Theme: Scripture is unyielding about believers' loyalty to God. The teachers of Israel tried to trap Jesus into choosing between God and the emperor. Our culture also subtly attempts to ensnare us. May we believers be as "wise as serpents and innocent as doves" (Matt. 10:16).

Readings: Exodus 33:12-23; 1 Thessalonians 1:1-10; Matthew 22:15-22

Call to Worship (Psalm 99:2-6, 9)

Leader: The LORD is great in Zion; he is exalted over all the peoples.

People: **Let them praise your great and awesome name. Holy is he!**

Leader: Mighty King, lover of justice, you have established equity; you have executed justice and righteousness in Jacob.

People: **Extol the LORD our God; worship at his footstool. Holy is he!**

Leader: Moses and Aaron were among his priests, Samuel also was among those who called on his name. They cried to the LORD, and he answered them.

People: **Extol the LORD our God, and worship at his holy mountain; for the LORD our God is holy.**

Pastoral Prayer:

O God our God, when we attend to our worship vows it is an acknowledgment of allegiance to you and your kingdom. In our weakness we bow down to other idols that in their seductive lure blind us to your benevolence to us. In our clouded judgment our world's lesser gods pull us toward thinking that they might satisfy our wants. However, in our most faithful moments, we concede that you alone can furnish our needs. Revive in our hearts that spirit of unquestionable devotion to you, O God of Righteousness, which causes us to cleave to your ways as we sojourn in the world. Make us the faithful disciples that Jesus first called when he beckoned the eleven saying, "Follow thou me" (John 21:22 KJV). Let our devotion to you and your kingdom be a sign of our ultimate allegiance to your sovereignty over our lives. In the name of the one who came to give us abundant life, we pray. Amen. (David N. Mosser)

SERMON BRIEFS

A GLIMPSE OF GLORY

EXODUS 33:12-23

Years ago there was a story that made its way into preacher's sermons about a little boy who came home from his first day at school and was asked by his mother, "What did you learn today in school?" "Nothing," he answered, "I've got to go back tomorrow!" While we see glimpses of God's glory everywhere, we can never fully fathom this mystery at one sitting: We must always go back tomorrow!

There are three requests in our text that Moses makes to God. First, Moses asked for an experienced person to guide them in their journey across the desert. God's answer is given in Numbers 10:29-33 and was Hobab the Midianite. The second request had to do with the presence of God and is stated in verses 16 and 17. All Moses had at this point was a promise and a name he could use. Moses was seeking some visible manifestation of God. If God went with the people, they would not have to make pilgrimages back to Sinai to worship. God replied, "My presence shall go with thee, and I will give thee rest" (v. 14 KJV). In the Hebrew language the

345

word for presence is the word "face." Moses was delighted and dared to say, "If this doesn't happen, don't lead us any further."

Moses then waxed very bold and made a third request, "Show me thy glory" (v. 18 RSV). Moses and God talked in the Tent of Meeting, just as friends do; however, Moses actually wanted a revelation surpassing any previous revelation God had given. The Lord answered Moses' request in part telling him that God would place him in the cleft of the rock, probably a small cave, and would cover him with God's hand as God passed by. This would give Moses a chance to glimpse something of God's glory, but Moses would not see God's face. We cannot see God fully because we are finite and morally imperfect.

There is also the thought here that we "never see God coming, we only see him going." While we live life forward, we understand it best backward. Regularly only as we reflect on life does it strike us that God was in it all along!

What Moses wanted, God accomplished in the coming of Jesus. The glory of God was fully manifested in Jesus Christ. John speaking of this wrote, "And the Word was made flesh, and dwelt among us (and we beheld his glory, the glory as of the only begotten of the Father), full of grace and truth" (John 1:14 KJV).

Jesus spoke of this glory, praying for future believers, "Father, I will that they also, whom thou hast given me, be with me where I am; that they may behold my glory, which thou hast given me: for thou lovedst me before the foundation of the world" (John 17:24 KJV).

What the psalmist said—"The heavens declare the glory of God; and the firmament sheweth his handiwork" (19:1 KJV)—is true. We do see God in a blade of grass, in a beautiful sunrise, in the chemistry of humankind, in the stars of the heavens; however, we see God most clearly in Jesus our Savior.

I have used song lyrics at funerals that seem to strengthen people and speak of this glory:

> Just think of stepping on shore and finding it heaven
> ....
> Of waking up in glory and finding it home.
> (Don Wyrtzen, "Finally Home" [Nashville: Singspiration, 1971].)

(Drew J. Gunnells, Jr.)

A CHURCH THAT MATTERS

1 THESSALONIANS 1:1-10

The Thessalonian church, like all churches, had some problems. Some members were expecting Christ to come immediately and had quit working, waiting for that return. To live, they "sponged off" of others. Paul wrote these letters to deal with their problems. But first, Paul would commend them for being a church that mattered. How did they?

They trusted. Paul was thankful that they had responded to the gospel so well. Paul—with Silvanus (Silas) and Timothy—had witnessed to them that they had been "chosen" by God, chosen to be loved and forgiven and blessed. The Thessalonians believed that and became "imitators of [the disciples] and of the Lord" (v. 6). They were fully convicted and depended on the power of the Holy Spirit. They discovered the joy of the faith.

God has chosen us, elected us to be recipients of the gospel. A church is founded on that gospel. We are not part of the church because our parents were or because it is a good thing to do. We are part of the church because we have responded in trust to God's grace that sought us out and called us into the kingdom. When that happens, joy fills us; we are fully convicted; and we trust the power of the Holy Spirit to help us live the faith. Trust is what matters most.

They served. The proof of their trust in Christ was their service. They threw themselves into the work. Paul talked about the "work of faith," trusting God in all they did. They gave a "labor of love," the motive for all they did. They had "steadfastness of hope," a patient endurance to stay with the faith, no matter what persecution or hardships they faced. In verses 9-10, Paul wrote of their turning from heathen gods to the true and living God and how they waited for the return of Christ. This was a waiting on tiptoe, with great excitement and hope.

A church that matters serves Christ. This church witnesses, loves people, meets the needs of others, and keeps the faith alive no matter what. A serving church finds out what needs to be done for Christ and does it. You don't have to beg people to teach Sunday school, or visit, or sing in the choir, or cut the grass. Volunteers line up to do the work. If that happened in our churches, do you think they would matter?

They witnessed. This church became an example to believers in Macedonia and Achaia. Paul did not have to tell others about the Thessalonian church. They already knew about them before Paul got there. Their faith and works were well known. They were an inspiration to others.

Do our churches have a witness? A little boy was staring at a big picture of Jesus on the wall. He turned to his Sunday school teacher and said, "It seems that if Jesus lives inside of us, he's going to stick out somewhere."

Is Jesus "sticking out" of our churches? Do others know of our faith, our love, our good works for Christ? The Thessalonian church has given me a new hope that one day, when I tell someone which church I serve, they will say, "I've heard about that church. They really love the Lord, don't they?"

The Thessalonian church had some problems. Even so, they also had a vital ministry for Christ. They trusted the gospel, they served Christ, and they witnessed for Christ. Paul was proud of them. They were a good testimony to Paul's ministry and to the power of the gospel to change lives. (Hugh Litchfield)

OF WISDOM AND MONEY

MATTHEW 22:15-22

Jesus was no fool: He knew a trap when he saw one and responded accordingly. In this and next week's Gospel lessons, Jesus escapes entrapping questions intended to destroy by turning them into answers intended to puzzle. "Give therefore to the emperor the things that are the emperor's," Jesus says (v. 21). Rather than debating whether Caesar's face on the coin is idolatrous or paying taxes is unjust, Jesus reminds the listeners that money is symbolic and temporary. This lesson is one that is lost on far too many people. Money is gained and accumulated for any number of reasons but almost always with the idea that it will last as long as it is tended carefully. Anyone who has watched stock portfolios change in this decade certainly has learned that such is not always the case! Still, people hoard money and manage it as if it were a permanent fixture on this earth. Jesus reminds us that this simply is not true.

Likewise, Jesus reminds us that God is invested in the permanent fixtures of our lives. It may be less clear what those permanent fixtures are, but we could venture some educated guesses: our lives, our faith, and our souls. All of these are the very stuff of which God made us, and thus "things that are God's." Yet, even the impermanent things of this life belong to God as they pass through our lives: time, talents, skills, passions, ideas, and material gifts (including money).

Still, Jesus relegates those impermanent things to their proper place, as being a part of this earthly world, important symbols, but not the stuff of which God made us. Woven carefully, these contrasting themes (giving the permanent fixtures of our lives alongside the impermanent things of this life to God) can be woven into a challenging stewardship sermon today.

However, the wisdom of Jesus and Jesus' care in not regarding people with partiality as he converses with his adversaries might also bring a powerful message to light. Here, Jesus speaks as respectfully of the Roman emperor as he does of God, not a common courtesy that most of his religious colleagues would have given to Caesar. Likewise, even as Jesus criticizes the Pharisees and Herodians, Jesus criticizes his own disciples. To all of them, he says "Why are you putting me to the test, you hypocrites?" (v. 18). And to all of them, Jesus offers a wise but puzzling answer about coins and emperors and God. A warning to the "would-be wise"; however, Jesus stands alone after this difficult conversation. When everyone hears Jesus' amazing words, they leave him and go away. Such is the journey of many wise followers of God, and such may be our path when we too seek the wisdom of God and share it with others. But knowing that this wisdom comes from and belongs to God, we have no choice but to share it with others, for how else can we give that which belongs to God back to God but to share it with God's people—even if it means standing alone when all is said and done. (Mary J. Scifres)

OCTOBER 23, 2005

Twenty-third Sunday After Pentecost

Worship Theme: God's ways repeatedly remain mysterious to believers. Moses merely glimpses the land of promise. Israel's faithful leaders try to trip up Jesus, whom God sent. In the midst of human confusion, however, God speaks a word of promise to God's people.

Readings: Deuteronomy 34:1-12; 1 Thessalonians 2:1-8; Matthew 22:34-46

Call to Worship (Psalm 90:2-6, 14, 16-17 RSV)

Leader: Before the mountains were brought forth, or ever thou hadst formed the earth and the world, from everlasting to everlasting thou art God.

People: **Thou turnest man back to dust, and sayest, "Turn back, O children of men!"**

Leader: For a thousand years in thy sight are but as yesterday when it is past, or as a watch in the night.

People: **Thou dost sweep men away; they are like a dream, like grass which is renewed in the morning: in the morning it flourishes and is renewed; in the evening it fades and withers.**

Leader: Satisfy us in the morning with thy steadfast love, that we may rejoice and be glad all our days. Let thy work be manifest to thy servants, and thy glorious power to their children.

People: **Let the favor of the Lord our God be upon us, and establish thou the work of our hands**

**upon us, yea, the work of our hands estab-
lish thou it.**

Pastoral Prayer:

Our dreams and our desires, O Lord, most fully come from your imaginative acts in creation and in your son, our Messiah, Jesus. Let us take our impulse for life from this Messiah. Jesus was one

> who, though he was in the form of God,
>   did not regard equality with God
>   as something to be exploited.

Rather, Jesus

> emptied himself,
>   taking the form of a slave,
>   . . . humbled himself
>   and became obedient to the point of death. (Phil. 2:6-8)

Jesus' divine act on our behalf, O Monarch of the Universe, is so grand and regal that we can hardly take it in. However, in your mercy and wisdom, O God, you accord us a foretaste of your divine splendor. Help us move through our days with a gratitude that imitates the depth of this gift. Help us share the good news with our needy world. In the name of Jesus our Christ we pray. Amen. (David N. Mosser)

SERMON BRIEFS

LEADERSHIP SECRET OF MOSES

DEUTERONOMY 34:1-12

Did you hear those amazing words describing Moses in verse 10? "No prophet has risen like Moses" (NIV). A list of Moses' accomplishments would bring us to agree with this conclusion. Moses parted the Red Sea, delivered the Israelites from slavery, brought the Ten Commandments to humanity, and led thepeople to the Promised Land. The question we will consider is, Why was Moses a great leader?

The passage we read is the final chapter in Moses' story. Let's take a look at the early years of Moses' life in Exodus to gain insight into what shaped this great leader. After growing up in Pharaoh's palace, Moses must flee from Egypt because he murdered a guard who was beating a Hebrew slave. After the murder, Moses tries to cover up the crime scene by hiding the Egyptian's body in the sand. This illustrates one of the faulty leadership qualities from Moses' youth: deceit. Later God appears to Moses in a burning bush and commands him to go back to Egypt to deliver the Hebrews from slavery. Moses responds with a list of objections and excuses why he should not go back to Egypt. Moses tells God that he is not eloquent, that he is a nobody, and that the people will not listen to him. Moses begs God to send someone else. During Moses' encounter with God at the burning bush he demonstrates other qualities. They are fear, reluctance, lack of faith, and worry. Not the leadership qualities we would expect from one of the greatest prophets who ever lived.

At this point, most of us give up. We begin to lose confidence because of our failures that God would use us to carry the message of Christ to the world. We doubt, fear, lack faith, and worry. We forget that God does not choose the most educated, well-rounded, or talented men and women to change the world.

Moses, however, does not give up or give in to his shortcomings. Instead, he begins to walk in faith and demonstrate that God had chosen the right person. Despite fear, Moses confronts Pharaoh and demands that he let the Israelites go. This is the first instance when Moses begins to rely on God's power rather than his own, and this is the secret behind Moses' success. This important leadership trait, reliance on God's power, was the one that shaped Moses' life, leadership, and ministry. Moses would have to use this leadership trait often for God to provide manna, guide the Israelites to the Promised Land, and dispose of an angry army that had Israel trapped at the Red Sea. Moses knew that God's power was sufficient to do anything, even miraculously part a sea. Moses' belief in the Lord's power led the writer of Deuteronomy to say that up to that day, there had been no one to show the mighty power or perform the awesome deeds that Moses did.

That same power is available to us today. It comes from an intimate face-to-face relationship that Moses cultivated daily. Moses listened and spoke to God often, enabling him to be in tune with

God's plan for his life and the lives of the people that Moses led. God also wants us to cultivate an intimate relationship of speaking and listening. This relationship and trust in God's power will allow us to tap into God-given leadership traits to help change the world for Christ. God longs to take our burning bush experiences of fear, worry, and insecurity, and turn them into strengths for God's kingdom. (Tim Roth)

A MINISTRY OF INTEGRITY

1 THESSALONIANS 2:1-8

With all the scandals in churches now, there is a great need for a ministry with integrity. Ministers are needed whose life and words match. There is much distrust of church leaders today.

In this section of scripture, Paul defended himself against slanderous accusations. In so doing, Paul offers good insight into what a ministry of integrity involves.

A courageous commitment. It was not easy for Paul and his colleagues to come and preach to the Thessalonians. They had been persecuted already because of their witness. It was dangerous to keep on doing it. There was opposition everywhere, not only from unbelievers, but from believers who criticized Paul's motives for ministry. However, come they did. Why? They felt that God wanted them to do it, and nothing would stand in their way. They had a strong sense of God's call to the work.

People have asked me if there were times in my ministry when I was tempted to quit. I would answer, "Every Monday morning." It's tough to do ministry. We meet opposition, not only from those outside the church, but more often from those inside it. It gets discouraging, hard, and trying.

What keeps us at it? It is the belief that God has called us to the work, and it has to be done—no matter what the price. Integrity involves a courageous commitment.

A pure motive. Evidently, many charges had been directed against Paul, especially at his motives for ministry. Paul answered them all. Paul was not "deluded," coming with sneaky motives to fool others. Paul did not come to gain the applause of others, but only the

353

approval of God. He did not come to make money off of them. Paul did not preach for personal praise. He came to minister because it was what God wanted him to do. That's the end of the story.

Why do we serve Christ? In all honesty, we struggle with mixed motives. It's pleasant to have people say nice things about us, to give us power to advise them on living their lives, and to receive personal satisfaction from what we do. I would add that it is beneficial to receive money, but most of us never have to worry about that. However, the bottom line is, Why do we serve? God has placed us there, and we want to please this God who has entrusted us with ministry. We will be criticized and opposed, and our motives will be questioned. But, a ministry of integrity is based on pleasing God.

A compassionate manner. Paul did not come as a dictator, as some had charged. Instead, Paul came with gentleness, caring for them like a mother for her children. He was willing to die for them. They were dear to him. Paul came among them and gave them his heart. They knew that. That is why all the charges against Paul would not hold water. The Thessalonians had met Paul face-to-face, and had discovered that he cared for them.

Authority is a significant issue these days. How do we exercise it? In some churches, ministers rule with an iron hand. Their word is law, their command is to be obeyed, and following without question is expected. But it is not so in a ministry of integrity. Compassion for others, suffering with others, sacrificing for others—these are the marks of that ministry. Does the minister care for us? That is the big question.

A man said, "I may not agree with all my pastor does, but the pastor sat with me all night when my wife died. I trust my pastor." That is a ministry of integrity. (Hugh Litchfield)

OF LOVE AND WISDOM

MATTHEW 22:34-46

Today's lesson divides easily into two sections, verses 34-40 and verses 41-46. Taken together, they can provide a weighty sermon, juxtaposing the simple but brilliant message of love against the complex but crucial notion that Christ is both human and divine.

The two passages can also be looked at as wisdom passages since the preacher can reflect on the amazing wisdom of Christ contrasted to the limited wisdom of even the most brilliant and well-versed of humans. To combine these two passages is tricky in a short sermon, but, given enough time, the two passages may be intertwined in any number of ways. Or, taken apart, either pericope can provide a meaningful message for the day.

In our first section, we are reminded of the basic "love theme" of Christianity, the Shema and first commandment to love God alongside the Golden Rule to love others. These well-known words of scripture can too easily be dismissed in our living, perhaps because of their overly familiar place in our minds. But anyone who has tried to love others (even the "unlovable" others) selflessly and caringly knows that loving this way is not easy. Any follower of God who has struggled to prioritize God first and foremost in every aspect of one's life knows that such a priority is seldom attended to consistently. Even the person for whom self-giving comes easily is challenged when reminded that such self-giving should be rooted in a love for self that is just as deeply entrenched and God-centered as our love for others.

Loving according to the first commandment and the Golden Rule is not an action that comes easily or enduringly. John Wesley called such love "perfect love." Striving for such love was the path toward Christian perfection, the path that early Methodists were called to follow. Most branches of Christianity today agree that such perfection is seldom, if ever, attained in our earthly life. And yet, Jesus clearly proclaims this "law of love" as the greatest of all of God's commands. With that in mind, the wise preacher will carefully unfold this text with the challenge and complexity that living such love actually involves. How are we to love others when we struggle with self-hatred? How are we to love others when we are self-absorbed? How are we to love those who harm and hate us? How are we to love God when we feel abandoned or betrayed by God? How are we to love when we are stretched too thin in our obligations of love and kindness? How are we to love when loving puts our lives and our loved ones at risk? Such questions can be woven into a powerful message of love, or even stewardship if the church's season requires such a focus.

Conversely, Jesus quickly turns his seemingly simple message into another puzzle when he asks the Pharisees an equally challenging series of questions. First, Jesus asks them the question of the Messiah's lineage, an obvious lead-in to the answer that the Messiah will come from the lineage of David. But to then quote Psalm 110:1 "The LORD says to my Lord" and ask how David can call his own son Lord asks the Pharisees to go into the puzzling world of rabbinic dialogue and midrash. Many Christian scholars take this to mean that Jesus calls the Pharisees to understand Christ's dual role as both divine and human. But such an interpretation neglects the primary result of this dialogue: Jesus finally silences the scribes and Pharisees in the seemingly endless debates of these late Matthean chapters. Whatever Jesus may have meant, Jesus again proves his indisputable wisdom and ability to out-debate even the most profound of scholars. This passage can easily stand alone as a preachable text on the wisdom of Jesus. Or, you may prefer to delve into the christological claim implied here that the Messiah is both fully human (David's son) and fully divine (David's lord). (Mary J. Scifres)

OCTOBER 30, 2005

Twenty-fourth Sunday After Pentecost

Worship Theme: Believers can afford to be humble because the God of righteousness has sent Jesus to show us life's true path. No longer do we bear our own burdens but rather give these burdens to Christ who carries them for us.

Readings: Joshua 3:7-17; 1 Thessalonians 2:9-13; Matthew 23:1-12

Call to Worship (Psalm 107:1-3, 6-7)

Leader:　　O give thanks to the LORD, for he is good; for his steadfast love endures forever.

People:　　**Let the redeemed of the LORD say so, those he redeemed from trouble and gathered in from the lands, from the east and from the west, from the north and from the south.**

Leader:　　O give thanks to the LORD, for he is good; for his steadfast love endures forever.

People:　　**Then they cried to the LORD in their trouble, and he delivered them from their distress; he led them by a straight way, until they reached an inhabited town.**

Leader:　　O give thanks to the LORD, for he is good; for his steadfast love endures forever.

All:　　**O give thanks to the LORD, for he is good; for his steadfast love endures forever.**

Pastoral Prayer:

O Covenant God, we offer ourselves to you to use as you will. We today surrender all we have to your holy kingdom. In Jesus we have a guide who has condescended to become one of us for our eternal benefit. For this impenetrable gift we offer our thanksgiving and praise. But even more than praise we resolve this day to turn to you and await your divine instruction. Direct us in your ways as we sojourn through our world. Furnish us with the will not only to attend to our religious duties in worship but also to carry that worshiping spirit into our daily lives. Make us people who feed the hungry, clothe the naked, and visit the alienated—those who too often go through life separated from others and alone. O God, grant us a zeal to spread the good news to a world in deep need of the gospel. As we take notice of others' needs, repeat again to us what you have first offered on our behalf in Christ. In the name of Jesus, the Anointed One of God, we pray. Amen. (David N. Mosser)

SERMON BRIEFS

CROSSING OVER

JOSHUA 3:7-17

This passage can be a difficult premise for a sermon, in part because we would just as soon not mention the "ethnic cleansing" in verse 10, where the foreign tribes are driven out. With that said, it may be permissible to allegorize this chapter, for, indeed, it seems to be symbolic and evocative on its face. Make what you will of the Hebrew numerology in this chapter (3, 7, and 12 being the most important and holy numbers in the Bible): 3 days (v. 2), 7 foreign tribes (v. 10), 12 sacred individuals (v. 12). But the clear message here is about God's presence and protective grace through Joshua for the people. The Lord informs Joshua that a miracle will happen that will evoke in the minds of the Israelites the sign of Moses (and thus impart the mantle of Moses upon the new leader, Joshua). Using the ark of the covenant—itself a sacramental/symbolic object—Joshua and the priests cause the water to cease flowing in the Jordan so that the people may cross over freely. Anyone who has watched Charlton Heston in the movie *The Ten Commandments* remembers that Moses' most flashy miracle was the parting of the Red Sea. This symbolism is glaringly obvious. More subtle is the allegorical symbolism regarding salvation and, perhaps, an anticipation of the Messiah. The name *Joshua* means, in Hebrew, "God saves." *Jesus* is the Greek form of Joshua. In Matthew 1:23, we are told that Isaiah's words (Isa. 7:14) regarding one named "Immanuel" is a messianic prophecy of Jesus, and that the name *Immanuel* means "God with us." This brings us full circle back to Joshua 3:7, where the Lord said to Joshua, "I will be with you." Jesus echoed this promise, saying "I am with you always" (Matt. 28:20).

Further allegorical license might allow us to work the theme of "crossed over" and "crossing on dry ground" to the Promised Land. We find the phrase eight times in seven verses in Joshua. Here we might quote Jesus in John 5:24 (NIV): "I tell you the truth, whoever hears my word and believes him who sent me has eternal life and will not be condemned; he has crossed over from death to life." One might even add Luke 16:26, where Jesus tells a parable of heaven and hell, explaining that "a great chasm has been fixed, so that those who want to go from here to you cannot, nor can anyone cross over from there to us" (NIV). We finally cite Ephesians 2:14-16 (NIV):

> For he himself is our peace, who has made the two one and has destroyed the barrier, the dividing wall of hostility, by abolishing in his flesh the law with its commandments and regulations. His purpose was to create in himself one new man out of the two, thus making peace, and in this one body to reconcile both of them to God through the cross, by which he put to death their hostility.

In sum, Joshua 3 teaches us that the God of the Covenant is with us; God saves; and God helps us cross over from death to life—hopeful themes brought to fruition by the New Covenant and the cross. (Lance Moore)

A MINISTER OF INTEGRITY

1 THESSALONIANS 2:9-13

Paul seemed to get more personal in his defense against the accusations made toward him. Not only Paul's ministry but also his life was a testimony to integrity. Paul urged the Thessalonians to "remember," for if they did, they would not believe the charges against him.

What makes up a life of integrity? Hard work. He labored and toiled and worked day and night so that he wouldn't be a burden to them as he preached the gospel. Paul probably plied his tent-making skills so that he could pay his own way. While some in the church had quit working as they waited for the return of the Lord, Paul didn't. He worked, he carried his own weight, he did not depend on them to support him. He worked hard at the work of Christ.

To serve Christ is hard work. If we are lazy, we will not accomplish much. If we are ministers, the work of the church is a never-ending affair. If we are laity, serving Christ and the church comes amid full-time jobs and numerous other commitments. Sometimes, it seems that we do work day and night. Unfortunately, usually 70 percent of the church membership lets the other 30 percent do most of the work. To be a person of integrity, we need to do our part.

Live right. Paul set a good example among them with conduct "pure, upright, and blameless" (v. 10). Paul lived what he preached. He did not manipulate them or abuse them or trick them. Paul's life was an open book, and when they read it, it was the story of a character with great integrity.

Servants of Christ need to live pure, upright, and blameless lives. We live what we preach and we believe. Our lives are a living testimony to the truth of the gospel.

Some students at West Point were debating the merits of Christianity. One asked, "After all, what is a Christian anyway?" After a pause, one said, "Oscar Westover." The discussion ended. One student, living his faith every day, silenced all the arguments against Christianity. It still will.

Love well. Paul changed the image from a mother/nurse to a father, tenderly caring for his children. Paul did the three tasks ministers do. He "urged" or "exhorted" them, teaching them the truth about Christ. He "encouraged" them, comforting them in their difficulties. He "pleaded" with them to live a life worthy of God. Paul desired that they learn the faith, trust the faith, live the faith. His love for them was strong. He did not give up on them.

Paul said, "As you know," indicating that they had experienced that love and seen it in action in Paul's life.

When we care for people, we want them to know and love Christ. I remember a woman who loved her husband into the faith, but it took twenty years. She said, "I never gave up hope. For you see, I love him." Servants of integrity love that way—and that long.

Humility. Praise and honor go to God. This was the goal of Paul's work. Paul's coworkers accepted the word not as a "human word" but as "God's Word." Paul pointed beyond himself to God. Paul did not want to make followers for himself but followers of God.

Our ultimate hope of ministry is not that people will see us but that they will see God. There is a danger that preachers can create their own disciples, loyal only to them. No one should be loyal to a preacher, only to God. We do not preach ourselves. We preach Christ.

A minister of integrity—Paul was that. Christ still needs such persons. The world will take notice of servants of integrity. (Hugh Litchfield)

HUMBLE LIVING IN A PROUD WORLD

MATTHEW 23:1-12

Today's scripture continues Jesus' conversation from Matthew 22. Much of Jesus' cryptic preaching can be unfolded more easily when the two chapters are read together. For example, the call to look toward only one teacher and instructor reflects back to the great commandment (22:37-38). Without that reference, the message may sound harsh or even unreasonable. With that reference, however, one begins to see that the Jesus of Matthew's Gospel is once again calling followers to the worship of God and God alone. Allegiances to other teachings or teachers and even reverence for our own parents (whom we are called to honor) are not to replace or prevail over our allegiances to and reverence for God. Although a seemingly obvious message for any follower of God, the message is lost at many points in human history. In Jesus' day, the scribes and Pharisees elevated their own rules and regulations to the level of God's law. In our day, we likewise elevate other things to the level of God's law. Even worthy values, such as patriotism, religious fervor, family commitments, fiscal responsibility, or social ethics, we exalt to a level that surpasses our commitment to Christ. Of course, less worthy values also sneak into our list of priorities and behaviors: selfishness guised as self-protection, pursuit of financial gain masked as careful money management, judgmentalism masked as savvy thinking, along with many other temptations. In any case, priorities that replace God's place in our lives become idolatrous. This is the temptation against which Matthew's Jesus calls us to guard. This is the temptation to practice differently than we preach, a temptation that people of God have always faced.

When we remember that such temptations of wrong practice are uniquely ours when we teach and preach and profess and believe in the call to love and serve, then we can understand how easily we can be humbled. After all, those who do not profess or accept God's grace will never have to "fall from grace." Only those who strive to follow God, who claim to worship Christ, who yearn to live by the Spirit are in danger of becoming like the Pharisees who taught well, but practiced poorly. After all, if we are not teaching selflessness and we live selfishly, we may be guilty of selfishness, but we will not be guilty of hypocrisy. Likewise, when we are professing godly living but practicing lives of sin, we are guilty of both the sin in our lives and the hypocrisy of our unpracticed teachings.

How then are we to dare teaching or preaching, professing or believing in our call to love and serve? Surely, we know that we will never live up to our teaching or our preaching. Confessing that reality may be the key to godly living, and to this passage. We may instruct, but we have only one instructor. We may be children of God, but there is only one perfect Son of God. We may be serving, but the greatest person of all time served us all the way to his death upon a cross. With this truth in mind, we will find the humility and the grace to follow Christ and live in the Spirit of love.

When we exalt servanthood rather than success, we will find

ourselves living as Christ calls and following where God leads. Such lives are lives that will bring us close to Christ. Such lives are lives that allow God's Spirit to flow through us and touch others. Such lives are lives that will bring us into the kingdom or realm of God. (Mary J. Scifres)

REFLECTIONS

❧

NOVEMBER

Reflection Verse: *"In humility regard others as better than yourselves." (Philippians 2:3)*
"The reward for humility and fear of the LORD / is riches and honor and life." (Proverbs 22:4)

HUMILITY: GENTLENESS OF SPIRIT
Proverbs 22:4 and Philippians 2:1-13

As pastors who care for their flocks, we all know that this is a humbling responsibility. At the same time, we also know that the kind of influence we exert over individuals and the communities of faith we lead can be something of a heady experience. Sometimes it is easy to forget our humility and fall into our pride. I suggest that, for pastors, possessing the gentleness of spirit—that which we might call humility—is one of the foundational pillars of the Christian life. Surely humility is one trait that is essential to those who lead others toward the kingdom of God.

Perhaps we will never know, but tradition has it that Solomon composed his proverbs while residing in the King's palace. There is not much evidence to support this claim, but likewise little evidence suggests that the viewpoint is incorrect. Chiefly, a proverb is a pithy piece of wisdom that suggests right living. Proverbs 22:4 alerts readers that, "The reward for humility and fear of the LORD / is riches and honor and life." Humility, thus, is one synonym among others for "the fear of the Lord."

A previous "pillar of abundant Christian living" recalls that the fear of the Lord is one way to confess loyalty to God. When we possess the fear of the Lord, we subject ourselves to God's realm. Humility is like the fear of the Lord in that it is an attitude of the faithful toward God. This humble attitude essentially reminds people that we are not God. It also suggests that we rely totally on God for all life. Humility is a counterweight to the human tendency to pride or self-assertion. Humble people recognize that life unfolds within the larger perspective of a great and glorious God. Our God is so magnificent and so potent that we live absolutely at the behest of the divine. As pastors we know that our congregations much prize humility, but occasionally pastors so hone the art of humility that it serves neither God nor us very well.

In common life we all see examples of what we might call "false humility." What are we talking about when we speak of "false humility"? When one of my parishioners remarked, "Humility is overrated," I think what she really meant was a reference to "false humility." False humility feigns a modesty that is really absent. False humility is the deceptive practice of pretending to be more humble than we actually are or should be. However, false humility is also irritating because it drips with insincerity and habitually becomes a tool of manipulation. Not only is false humility hypocritical, it is also deceitful. To possess false humility is to be pretentious.

A few years ago I attended a pastors' continuing education seminar. A presenter from a relatively large and distant church offered a session on pastoral care. He began by telling us "my associate ministers are more gifted than I am, but I am there to encourage them and push them to be the best they can be." We knew of his reputation for competence, therefore, his humility seemed exaggerated. He persisted with generous seasonings of phrases like "Clearly, many of you are more able than I" and "I wish I knew half as much about pastoral care as most of you do." Yet, most of us knew that he knew more than we would ever know about counseling troubled people. This highly capable pastor, for all his good intention, tainted his insights by downplaying his considerable proficiency. Sometimes, without realizing it, our false humility becomes almost as grating as arrogance. Some people could even equate false humility with pride.

Authentic humility is the character trait we pastors possess that plainly reminds us that we might occasionally be wrong. True humility reminds us that no one is always right. Humility helps us speak a provisional word upon which others might amend or expand. Other people who have gifts and talents just as we do might add to or modify our best thinking so as to improve our common judgment. Proper humility reminds all of us that no one—not even the best among us—has the market of truth cornered.

Paul, who writes his epistle to the Philippians from a jail cell, deals with the joy he has in Christ. Paul lifts up for the congregation at Philippi his joyfulness, even in prison. Paul offers them hope in their circumstances as he embraces hope in his. Paul offers this admonition: "Do nothing from selfish ambition or conceit, but in humility regard others as better than yourselves. Let each of you look not to your own interests, but to the interests of others" (Phil. 2:3-4).

In Paul's first-century culture, people did not recognize humility as a virtue. Rather, people saw humbleness as a symptom of weakness. The "do it to others before they do it to you" philosophy held great influence then as it does now. Consequently, when Paul speaks of humility he writes as one who offers the alternative Jesus community an approach by which we relate to one another. A Christian community is one that regards "others as better than yourselves." This community identifies itself by the trait of humility. We are not doormats. More exactly, we try to empathize with other people as Christ empathizes with us. Paul follows up his urging toward authentic humility with a beautiful portrait of this theology with the "Christ Hymn" (Phil. 2:5-11).

We are called to be humble people because Jesus was humble. Did Jesus not say, "For all who exalt themselves will be humbled, and those who humble themselves will be exalted" (Luke 14:11)?

Mark's Gospel sets a scene in which Jesus calls the first disciples (Mark 1:16-20). These four first-called just happened to be fishermen. The image of discipleship as fishing is an intriguing metaphor. To catch fish one must be patient. Fishing, for amateurs, calls forth not only patience but also humility. How many times can we tangle our lines? How many times do we sink the hook in a stump, a tree branch, or an old submerged tire? How many times can our reel jam or lock up? Unless we are one of those few people who are genuine fishing experts, then one thing fishing teaches us is a deep sense of humility. Fishing for fish does this to people. How much more difficult can fishing for people be? I suggest it is even a more daunting task than fishing for mere fish. Therefore, when we share the good news we must always share it with humility.

Being fishers of people is what discipleship means. No one is outside the loving care of God. Whether one is male or female, slave or free, Jew or Gentile, God loves us all. Not only this, but God calls us to love those whom God also loves. As we pastors handle the gospel's "lures," may we do so with a humility that seems fitting for human beings who want to share the Word of God with others. *Humility* regarding our task is a pillar worthy of anyone's house of faith. Amen. (David N. Mosser)

NOVEMBER 6, 2005

Twenty-fifth Sunday After Pentecost

Worship Theme: Like the wise bridesmaids, we too prepare for God's call. Like the bridesmaids, we too know "neither the day nor the hour" (Matt. 25:13). Faithful disciples are always ready to respond to the Lord's coming!

Readings: Joshua 24:1-3*a*, 14-25; 1 Thessalonians 4:13-18; Matthew 25:1-13

Call to Worship (Psalm 78:1-7 RSV)

Leader: "Give ear, O my people, to my teaching; incline your ears to the words of my mouth!

People: **"I will open my mouth in a parable; I will utter dark sayings from of old, things that we have heard and known, that our fathers have told us.**

Leader: "We will not hide them from their children, but tell to the coming generation the glorious deeds of the LORD, and his might, and the wonders which he has wrought.

People: **"He established a testimony in Jacob, and appointed a law in Israel, which he commanded our fathers to teach to their children; that the next generation might know them, the children yet unborn, and arise and tell them to their children, so that they should set their hope in God, and not forget the works of God, but keep his commandments."**

Leader: "Give ear, O my people, to my teaching; incline your ears to the words of my mouth!"

People: **We are prepared to hear the Lord's teachings. Amen.**

Pastoral Prayer:

O God and Master of all, you who are routinely veiled, yet on occasion revealed, we pour out our prayers to you this day. We, as a people striving for faith, are prepared to respond to the disclosure of your divine nature. Help us attune our eyes and ears to the messages you send us. Let us embrace the small and seemingly insignificant ways your revelations come to us. At times your revelation comes to us in a new understanding of an old biblical story. Regularly, however, your disclosures come to us, O God, in the voice of another person, sometimes young and at other times more mature. Whoever is "Christ-bearer" for us, let us hear your word afresh. We pray this in the power and grace of Christ. Amen. (David N. Mosser)

SERMON BRIEFS

WITNESSES AGAINST OURSELVES

JOSHUA 24:1-3*a*, 14-25

Here are the preaching points from this scripture: (1) the choice, (2) the problem of false gods, (3) looking to the mighty acts of God, (4) learning from one another.

1. Choice. When I was a campus minister, one of our students walked in one day wearing a badge saying, "I'm a fool for Christ. Who are you a fool for?" It wasn't totally good grammar, but it was an excellent point. The question isn't whether you'll be a fool. That's a given. Theologically, we call that original sin. The real question is for whom you will be a fool, whom will you serve? It's not just that you must make that basic choice. You do make it, whether you realize it or not. Either you choose God, or you choose a false god—often yourself, but one way or another, you choose.

2. False gods. Joshua understood so well how hard it is to leave the false gods behind that he scoffed when the people said they would serve the Lord, even though he had just called them to do so. "You can't serve the Lord," he says. "You're not up to it. You'll fail, and God will get you." Now, that's powerful preaching.

The choice isn't between God and nothing. If it were, that would be a "no-brainer." The choice is between God and money, God and sex, God and self-will, God and ease, God and booze, God and a hundred other false little gods who want to make fools of us.

3. Looking to the mighty acts of God. Our choice is not just an individual life choice, nor do we choose only which god we shall serve. We choose also the people of whom we shall be a part. We choose a particular history and a particular tradition. When we choose God, we choose the one who brings us out of slavery, the same God who brought our people out of slavery so long ago. We may not be of Hebrew descent physically, but we are spiritual Hebrews when we choose the God of the Bible.

4. Learning from one another. Once we have made that basic decision to serve God, we have to follow it up with a hundred smaller decisions every day. Do I serve God best by doing this or by doing that? In some ways, the big decision is easier. It's the little decisions that give us trouble. Falling in love and getting married is a delight. Living together is a lot of work.

I made my wife a necklace of wooden alphabet beads. It reads, WWAGD? "What would Aunt Gertrude do?" My wife says she can't always tell what Jesus would do, because she must make decisions about matters of which the Gospels tell us little, but she sees what Aunt Gertrude does, and she knows Jesus would approve of anything Aunt Gertrude does. It's great to have someone like Aunt Gertrude in your life, someone you can count on to do it right, whatever "it" is.

We find out how to serve our God, the one whom we call Master, by looking to the saints around us and learning from them. If you don't have an Aunt Gertrude, start looking for one. (John Robert McFarland)

THE GATHERING

1 THESSALONIANS 4:13-18

Some Thessalonians had a problem. They wanted to know what would happen to the Christians who had already died when Christ returned. They knew that Christ would take them to heaven, but what about the fate of their deceased brothers and sisters?

Paul wrote these words to answer their concern. Paul wanted them to have hope. The pagans had no hope. When you died, you died, and that was that. However, because of their faith in Jesus, that was not the end of the story.

To be honest, some have used this passage to promote the idea of "soul sleep," that when a person dies, they stay in the grave until Christ's Second Coming. In my judgment, this is not what these verses mean. The big picture is that when Jesus comes—when the kingdom comes in its fullness—all who are his will be gathered together in that kingdom. No one will be left out. Those who died and those who have not will both be there. The relationship with Christ cannot be broken, even by death.

"Therefore," Paul said, "encourage one another with these words" (v. 18). That was the purpose of Paul's discussion: to give them hope. They were facing persecution and death. They needed to know that no matter what happened to them, their relationship with Christ was eternal. One day, they would all be reunited with each other. It would be a great gathering by Christ. It would be a happy day.

As I have gotten older, I seem to be attending more funerals. As I write this, I have recently returned from participating in the funeral for one of my dearest friends, Harvey. He was a minister in the prime of his life. Then, a brain tumor and nine months later, he was dead at age 54. It was a sad moment. However, his funeral was a celebration of life, not death. There was more joy than sadness. How could that be? The words of this scripture tell us. As Paul said, "we will be with the Lord forever." We come to the moment of death with hope. We grieve, just like everyone does, but not without hope. We know that death is not the final word about us. Christ has said that, and it is the word of eternal life.

371

Early in my life, I heard the moment of death described as a person leaving on a ship. Loved ones are gathered on the shore. They watch as the ship heads toward the horizon, waving good-bye through their tears. Finally, the ship disappears and someone says, "There he goes. He's gone." But on the other side of the horizon—on the heavenly shore—someone shouts, "Here he comes!" On that shore is a welcoming party, ready to welcome him home. I have imagined my homegoing and who would be on the shore to meet me. Jesus would be there. So would my father and grandparents. My mentor in the faith, Dr. Horne, would be there. Our housekeeper, who helped rear me would be waving at me. One of my former students would be there; she packed so much of life into her thirty short years. Many more would be there—and now one more. Harvey will be there. Somehow, I feel that will be a "great day in the morning."

The Thessalonians were worried about what would happen in the future. Paul said, in essence, trust Christ. Christ will not let you down. Here is the truth. If we trust Christ to take care of us today, can we not trust him to take care of us forever? (Hugh Litchfield)

CARRYING THE LIGHT

MATTHEW 25:1-13

Preparation is a proud virtue in our world today. We prepare for rainy days, holidays, parties, sermons, meetings, births, even deaths, and certainly for weddings! Even two thousand years ago, brides and grooms prepared for their weddings. So, what happened to half of the bridesmaids in today's parable from Jesus? Surely, delays on wedding days were as common then as now. Yet, five of these ten women came without sufficient oil to fill their lamps into the late hours of a delayed wedding celebration. The virtue of preparation had apparently not been taught to these women.

This may seem like a silly, superficial parable. It can be a difficult parable to preach in a time when becoming one of many wives would not be cause for great celebration. But in its context as a kingdom parable, the story brings important messages to light. After all, the coming of God's reign should be high on the priority list for Christians. Even symbolic festivals of that arrival such as the upcoming Christ the King Sunday or Christmas celebrations should be times of great rejoicing and spiritual renewal. But very few people focus sufficient preparation time through these busy months of late fall. Many will arrive on Christmas Day with nothing but empty stockings, bloated stomachs, and tired souls. Today's parable reminds us that such inadequate preparations are dangerous paths for God's followers. Ultimately, we will miss not only the celebration but also the kingdom itself.

Preaching about the coming of Christ and the realm of God can be vague and ambiguous. Many godly people simply do not feel any urgency about such arrivals. And so, this parable can also be presented as a reminder that we are carriers of God's light into a dark world, here and now, not just in some distant, unknown future. To be bearers of light, we would need to be even more prepared than the five wise bridesmaids, and certainly more generous. But, we are often as ill-prepared to carry that light and to wait for the coming of God's realm as those five foolish bridesmaids were. We neglect worship during busy seasons, we forget heartfelt resolutions from the last year, and we create harried schedules and grumpy moods during the Advent and Christmas seasons of peace and love. We forget to fill our lamps.

As we move into the busiest season of the year for many people, today's parable can challenge us to find ways for filling our lamps and shining Christ's light into a world of darkness and despair. When we take the time to listen, when we have the humility to let God's Spirit guide us, when we surround ourselves with the strong light of a community of Christ's followers, our lamps are filled and ready. Then, we can take that light out into the world. We can share that light and our love with a world of dim hope and dark corners. We can carry light that will fill the lamps of others. In doing so, we are more than just wise bridesmaids; we are generous givers of love and light.

As givers of love and light, we can create that beauty seen in churches on Christmas Eve. The lights go out with only one candle lit on the altar. The sudden darkness is a bit unnerving. Then, one by one, we share the light with those around us. Soon, the room is brighter and more Spirit-filled than any other night of the year. That's what it's like to keep our lamps filled, to carry the light, to be the light of God. (Mary J. Scifres)

NOVEMBER 13, 2005

Twenty-sixth Sunday After Pentecost

Worship Theme: God promises the return of Christ, although no one but God alone knows the day or the hour of the coming. Our task is to remain faithful as we wait for our Lord.

Readings: Judges 4:1-7; 1 Thessalonians 5:1-11; Matthew 25:14-30

Call to Worship (Psalm 123:1-2*b*, 3-4 RSV)

> *Leader:* To thee I lift up my eyes,
>
> **People: O thou who art enthroned in the heavens!**
>
> *Leader:* Behold, as the eyes of servants look to the hand of their master . . .
>
> **People: Have mercy upon us, O LORD, have mercy upon us, for we have had more than enough of contempt.**
>
> *Leader:* Too long our soul has been sated with the scorn of those who are at ease, the contempt of the proud.
>
> **People: Have mercy upon us, O LORD, have mercy upon us.**

Pastoral Prayer:
Gracious God and Loving Creator, as the days shorten we give praise to you for the light of Jesus Christ. Jesus' light illumines our path as we sojourn in your world. On this faith journey we wait for Jesus who comes, as Paul tells us, as "a thief in the night." Give us patient endurance as we wait for that blessed hope of Christ's return. We pray that you find us about the ministry tasks that you

have called us to, O God. Help us use the gifts, graces, and talents you have provided for us and make us better stewards of those gifts. Remind us that those who are faithful over a little will also be those you entrust with much more. May we be in the number of those believers whom you call "good and trustworthy" stewards. Furnish for us the strength of character and the endurance to run the race set before us. Guide us in the paths of righteousness for your name's sake. Amen. (David N. Mosser)

SERMON BRIEFS

SOMETHING TO BE SAID FOR PRAGMATISM

JUDGES 4:1-7

Judges reminds us that high-minded religion does not always generate good behavior. Pragmatism seems to be the stronger human motivator, for good and for bad. For the Israelites, again and again they would obey God when in need but then, in complacent prosperity, drift back into evil pagan practices. We are not much different from our religious forebears!

On the positive side, we find in Jewish history, occasions where the right thing was done for practical purposes even when the ideology may not have been so enlightened. The Jews were a patriarchal society. Priests were male only. Restrictions on women, both civil and religious, were far more stringent than those upon men. But when Israel faced trouble, it found a skilled female leader and the pragmatic Jews set aside custom and made Deborah their leader.

Deborah provides good opportunity to speak about the value of women in leadership. Even denominations that do not ordain women should acknowledge that God chose Deborah—a female—to lead the nation Israel and even to convey "the word of the Lord." The chauvinistic Jews had the good sense to listen to Deborah and demonstrated enough trust in her leadership to follow her direction even at the risk of death. The moral drawn from this text is that if both God and the Israelites trusted a woman's leadership, surely we can, too.

If this passage is used for a primary text, obviously the many characters and place names should be researched in a commentary or Bible dictionary, and the greater context of this point in Jewish history should be shared. For one example, the character of Sisera, the enemy commander, is an interesting one. See Judges 5:20 (NIV): "From the heavens the stars fought, / from their courses they fought against Sisera." More likely, this will be a Sunday in which the New Testament lectionary may provide the better (easier!) preaching text. But may I suggest that we do not too quickly dismiss this passage and, instead, emulate verse 4:3 and "cry out to the Lord for help" in our sermon-writing on this one. Another option may be to take inspiration from Deborah's life story, abandon the lectionary, and develop instead a sermon series entitled, "Great Women of the Old Testament." (Lance Moore)

WHAT WE'RE SAVED FOR

1 THESSALONIANS 5:1-11

In recent years, there has been a renewed interest in those things surrounding the "last days." A stroll through any bookstore reveals a multitude of books on the how, when, and where of biblical prophecies concerning the return of the Lord. The church community at Thessalonica was no different than we are in this respect. Since their earliest days, this group of Christians had anticipated the return of the Lord. Most of this community, in fact, believed that the Lord would return to earth within their lifetime. However, when some members of their community began to die before the promised return of Christ, the inevitable question arose: When will the day of the Lord come? This period of struggle had led to feelings of doubt and uncertainty with regard to the future. The church found itself in need of comfort and reassurance. They needed to be reminded that, despite appearances to the contrary, God was still in control, and their hopes for the future were still secure.

In his letter to the church at Thessalonica, Paul sought to encourage his brothers and sisters and to refocus their attention on the things that are most important for those of us living "between the times." Paul reminded them of their identity in Christ and the security that comes from this new relationship. Paul writes that, for those who live in darkness, the day of the Lord would come with surprising and inescapable force. "But you, beloved, are not in darkness, for that day to surprise you like a thief; for you are all children of light and children of the day" (vv. 4-5). As followers of Christ, these individuals had received insight into God's activity in the world. They possessed a new understanding of the will of God for creation, a new understanding of where true "peace and security" lie. Their security could be found in the one who works for our good in all things, "For God has destined us not for wrath but for obtaining salvation through our Lord Jesus Christ" (v. 9).

Yet, the challenge for this community, as well as for us, is to remember that there is a commission issued for the "children of light" as well. Abraham Smith writes that "Paul's distinction between children of the day and those of the night is not just about contrasting spheres of awareness or existence but also of contrasting spheres of action" (*New Interpreter's Bible*, vol. 11 [Nashville: Abingdon Press, 2000], p. 727). This time of waiting for Christ to return is not to be spent in idleness, but in active preparation for his return. The church has been given the gifts of faith, hope, and love in order that we might live as God's people in the world. Our task for these days is that we might become lights in a world of darkness and that we might "encourage one another and build up each other." One of my professors in seminary often talked about salvation in this way. He said that sometimes we focus so much on the end of salvation, that we forget the means and purpose of salvation. He would state, "We don't always need to ask what we are saved from, sometimes we need to ask what we are saved for." Paul's words for the church of yesterday, today, and tomorrow advise us to keep this in mind as well. There is work to be done before Christ returns, "let us keep awake and be sober." (Wendy Joyner)

GREAT POWER, GREAT RESPONSIBILITY

MATTHEW 25:14-30

"With great power comes great responsibility." Uncle Ben's words follow Peter as he leaves the car, but he quickly forgets

377

them in the excitement of participating in this wrestling match. He knows that with his special gifts, the $3,000 prize will be his! As he anticipates, he triumphs in the ring, but the box-office manager refuses to pay the full amount. Peter is furious but unable to do anything to alleviate his frustration. Until, that is, a thief enters the box office after Peter and steals all of the money. Peter allows the thief to escape, asserting that the loss of the money is not his problem. He quickly heads to the car, knowing Uncle Ben is waiting for him. As he approaches, he notices a crowd gathered near their meeting spot. To his horror, they are surrounding his uncle, who is dying from wounds inflicted by a carjacker. Peter follows the murderer, chasing him into an abandoned building. With dismay, he realizes that this is the same thief he allowed to escape earlier in the evening. As tears fill his eyes, Uncle Ben's words run through his head again, "With great power comes great responsibility" (*Spider-Man,* Columbia TriStar Home Entertainment, 2002).

Comic book fans will have already recognized this story. Peter Parker, otherwise known as Spider-Man, learned at a young age the truth of his uncle's words. Because he neglected to do what he could easily have done, the man he loved like a father was dead. "With great power comes great responsibility." While we may not have the gifts of web-slinging and "spider sense" that Peter Parker had, the same is true for each of us.

Jesus, too, had much to say about power and responsibility. In our scripture today, Jesus tells a story of three servants who were given similar jobs by their master. The amount of money each servant received differed, but their duty did not. They were to look after their master's property. The first two servants understood that their master wished them to invest the money, just as he would have done. They did so, doubling the funds, and were rewarded for their efforts. The third servant, however, was concerned only for his own well-being. Unwilling to risk losing the money and facing the master's anger, he hid the money away. After all, the master only wanted him to safeguard what he had been given. How shocked this third servant must have been when the master threw him out! How could he have misread the situation so badly?

"Throw him into the outer darkness!" Does this punishment

seem harsh to you? After all, the sin seems rather minor: The servant did not waste or steal his master's wealth. He did not refuse to acknowledge whose it was. He returned exactly what was given to him. Throughout the Gospels, however, Jesus proclaims that it is not enough to simply look out for ourselves. Rather than saving judgment only for those who do evil, Jesus consistently condemns people who do no good, such as the priest and the Levite in the parable of the good Samaritan, or the rich man "Dives," who ignores the poor man Lazarus.

"With great power comes great responsibility." Like Peter Parker, we must learn that our refusal to use our gifts has consequences. This fact is true no matter the size of our gifts, no matter how powerless we may think we are. There is no exemption from God's demand for diligence. As Christians, we have been promised the greatest power of all—that of the Holy Spirit dwelling within us. With that great power comes great responsibility. (Melissa Scott)

NOVEMBER 20, 2005

Christ the King/Reign of Christ

Worship Theme: The Reign of Christ signals that in the life, death, and resurrection of Jesus, God again claims sovereignty over God's creation. Our part as human creatures is to become subjects in the greatest realm ever conceived in the mind of God.

Readings: Ezekiel 34:11-16, 20-24; Ephesians 1:15-23; Matthew 25:31-46

Call to Worship (Psalm 100 NASB)

Leader:	Shout joyfully to the LORD, all the earth.
People:	**Serve the LORD with gladness; come before Him with joyful singing.**
Leader:	Know that the LORD Himself is God; it is He who has made us, and not we ourselves; we are His people and the sheep of His pasture.
People:	**Enter His gates with thanksgiving, and His courts with praise. Give thanks to Him; bless His name.**
Leader:	For the LORD is good; His lovingkindness is everlasting,
People:	**And His faithfulness to all generations.**

Pastoral Prayer:

On this Christ the King Sunday, O God, we are not accustomed to speaking in words of sovereignty. Yet, you are sovereign over us. You demonstrate your divine rule in our world by its creation, redemption, and ultimately, its final consummation. As our sovereign we confess that we have failed as individuals and as a church to follow your holy rule. In our insecurity and pride we have sought our own way, even when it brings disaster upon our heads and into the lives of others. Despite our hard-heartedness, O God, you continue to express your love and care for the world. You have emptied grace upon grace into our lives. All you ask is that we reverence your holy name by our worship and by our lives. Give us the will to once again understand that true freedom lies in our subjugation to your holy bidding. You call us to fullness of life. All we must do is accept your gracious invitation to be your people. Create the miracle of faith in our hearts, we pray, in the name of Jesus. Amen. (David N. Mosser)

SERMON BRIEFS

THE PASTOR AND THE PEOPLE

EZEKIEL 34:11-16, 20-24

"Shepherd" is a most significant term in the Bible. The word occurs in both the Old and the New Testament. Among the Hebrew people sheep-raising was a leading industry and the occupation of a shepherd a recognized occupation. We can hardly think of the term without thinking of the twenty-third Psalm, written doubtless by Israel's shepherd king, David, and of its affirmation, "The Lord is my shepherd."

Jesus declared himself to be the "good shepherd" (John 10:14). When the Lord gave Peter his last personal command, Jesus charged Peter to be a good shepherd, to "tend my sheep" (John 21:16). No wonder that one of the illustrative titles given to the leader of a church is that of "pastor," for the word means "shepherd." Jesus is still the "shepherd of the sheep"; however, each pastor is an undershepherd.

As Ezekiel pens the words of our text the Hebrew people are in the period of their history known as the Babylonian captivity. Ezekiel's preaching is to be an encouragement to the scattered Israelites who are experiencing trouble with unfaithful shepherds. Ezekiel was not thinking of pastors of churches but of the rulers of Israel who also had spiritual responsibilities. What Ezekiel said about unfaithful civil leaders applies with perhaps even greater force to the spiritual leaders today.

In these first ten verses we see that the unfaithful leaders showed little love or care for the people, looking out only for themselves. They did not strengthen the flock, nor care for the wounded, nor look for lost sheep. Consequently, Ezekiel promised that God would judge and discipline these false shepherds.

The glorious truth of the passage is that God himself would become the shepherd of his people Israel and would exercise his redemptive purpose through the Messiah, who is referred to as "my servant David." God would bring his people back to the homeland of promise and provide food for them "upon the mountains of Israel," and prosperity and security would characterize their life. God would bring back the strays and care for the injured and weak. In contrast God would "destroy the fat and the strong" (vv. 14, 16 KJV).

God did not want his people to suffer from self-centered leadership. Ezekiel delivered the good news that a new day of spiritual leadership was coming. We can comprehend what God was doing because we have seen this in Jesus Christ. We can understand the love, commitment, and sacrificial service God expects because God sent Jesus as our example. We can be thankful that we have been invited to be the "sheep of his pasture," and that we have undershepherds that flesh out this kind of love for God's people.

In a day when leadership is often seen as domination, we need a new look at the pastor as "shepherd." Unlike cattle, sheep are not driven. Anyone familiar with sheep knows they follow the shepherd because of his care for them. Good shepherds never have to lecture the sheep about authority. The sheep understand the authority because they trust the shepherd. Just as Jesus said, the true shepherd understands and cares for the sheep, even to the point of dying for them (John 10:1-18). When a pastor reflects this kind of lifestyle, the pastor has no worry about the "followship" of the sheep.

During this Thanksgiving season, thank God for being the

"great shepherd of the sheep" and for those undershepherds God has called to emulate the divine example. The church pastored by such a leader will minister to a community and never lack for significant kingdom service. In so doing, "the pastor and the pastor's people" will make a difference. (Drew J. Gunnells, Jr.)

PRAYING WITH POWER

EPHESIANS 1:15-23

The most basic form of prayer happens when we ask God for help. Call it Prayer 101. Think back to some of your first prayers. One of my first prayers came after some teenage mischief that I knew was not pleasing to God. I asked God to forgive me for the sin in my life, and God touched my heart after this prayer. I felt forgiven and clean for the first time. What I did not know until many years later was there was unseen power behind my prayer. It came through my seventy-year-old grandmother who faithfully prayed by name for each of her ten grandchildren. One of her many prayers was that all of her precious grandchildren would come to know Christ.

The apostle Paul also takes us on a journey of prayer in today's passage. The same power behind my grandmother's prayers is here in this passage. Grandma was a prayer warrior who spent time every day in intercessory prayer. She stressed the importance of prayer because God works through our prayers on behalf of others. A question Paul answers in this passage is, How should we pray for others?

Can you remember a time when you did something for another person and did not hear a thank you? Maybe you did the dishes, cleaned your room, gave someone a gift, or gave someone your valuable time. Perhaps their "no response" made you frustrated and angry. Jesus himself was once in a similar situation described in Luke 17. Jesus healed ten lepers from the most socially degrading disease of their time. However, only one leper came back to thank Jesus. Jesus was pleased with the leper who came back to give thanks, but disappointed in the other nine. Paul emphasizes the importance of giving continual thanks in prayer for what God has done. Paul celebrates the fact that his friends are blessed in heaven, chosen before the creation of the world, redeemed through Christ's blood, and lavished with wisdom and understanding. Paul reminds us that we should not forget that it stirs God's heart when we remember and give thanks for what God has done through our prayers in the lives of others. It pleases God in the same way Jesus was pleased with the one leper that remembered to give thanks to him.

Paul also makes it a priority to ask God to grant wisdom and revelation to his friends so they may know Christ better. We can understand why Paul prays that his friends would know Christ better when considering the life the disciples are called to live. In Mark 3, Jesus comes down from the mountainside to choose his disciples. "He appointed twelve—designating them apostles— that they might be with him" (Mark 3:14 NIV). The requirement of these disciples was simply to spend time in Jesus' presence getting to know him better. Paul prays fervently that his friends in Ephesus would spend time praying, reading, and experiencing the risen Christ so they would know Christ better. Paul knew that the twelve who spent intimate time in Jesus' presence changed the world.

Paul goes on to pray his most powerful, earthshaking prayer for his friends: that they may know the hope to which they are called and understand their glorious inheritance and the power available to them. This power is described with words that will almost take our breath away. This power in Christ is the working of his mighty strength—far above every power and dominion, above every title ever given for all times—and places Christ as the head over everything and everyone. Paul prays that his friends will know that there is nothing to fear in this lifetime, that God has won the final victory, and that they can live with confidence and freedom.

Paul gives us a model to pray with power and passion for others. It is said that one of the most prominent early churches was in Ephesus. That is not a surprise considering the fervent prayer that surrounded this church. What would happen to our churches and friends if we prayed with this same passion? (Tim Roth)

WHAT KIND OF KING IS THIS?

MATTHEW 25:31-46

Today we celebrate Christ the King Sunday. It is a time when we often focus on the majestic images of Christ. Indeed, our scripture today begins that way. "When the Son of Man comes in his glory, and all the angels with him, then he will sit on the throne of his glory. All the nations will be gathered before him, and he will separate people one from another as a shepherd separates the sheep from the goats" (vv. 31-32). This scene depicts our magnificent Lord, returning to declare that God's kingdom has come. God is the creator and sustainer of all things. God embodies every characteristic of a king: powerful, majestic, and just. God's appearance fills us with hope and fear, humbled by Christ's power and glory.

There is no doubt that this king is Jesus, because, just as Jesus did in life, he quickly turns things upside down. On earth, Jesus consistently allied himself with the downtrodden and oppressed. Jesus ate with people who were disparaged by the rest of society. Even in Jesus' parables, it is the lowly and needy who ultimately triumph. "Whoever wishes to be first among you must be your slave," Jesus reminded his disciples (Matt. 20:27).

It should come as no surprise that, on returning, Jesus continues to teach the same lessons. What kind of king is Jesus? A great judge, the ruler of all the nations. Certainly, this is true. But there is something more to this story. This is not a king concerned with the richness of the tributes his people bring. Jesus does not desire to increase his own renown.

What kind of king is this? Jesus answers that question himself. "Just as you did it to one of the least of these who are members of my family, you did it to me" (v. 40). Jesus is a hungry, ragged beggar on the side of the road. Jesus is the old woman in the nursing home, waiting for someone, anyone, to smile at her. Jesus is the stranger hovering at the back of the sanctuary, uncertain about a welcome. Jesus is the prisoner, disgusted with himself, sure that salvation is not possible.

What kind of king is this? Why would a mighty sovereign place himself on the same level as his lowliest subjects? What kind of king would lay aside his crown, step down from his throne, and humble himself so completely? Jesus, the king above all kings, did just that. It is appropriate that Christ the King Sunday comes just before Advent. It helps us remember that the God we worship is a different kind of king. Jesus left his heavenly home so that we could eventually join him there. As the hymn in the second chapter of Philippians reminds us, Jesus

> though he was in the form of God,
>> did not regard equality with God
>> as something to be exploited,
> but emptied himself,
>> taking the form of a slave,
>> being born in human likeness.
> And being found in human form,
>> he humbled himself
>> and became obedient to the point of death—
>> even death on a cross. (vv. 6-8)

What kind of king is this? Jesus is the Christ, the king of kings, who demonstrates that true power, God's power, is known in relationships, in healed lives, and most of all, in love. God has exalted Jesus, and given to Jesus the name above all names. Let us bend our knees and confess that Jesus Christ is Lord, to the glory of God. (Melissa Scott)

NOVEMBER 27, 2005

First Sunday of Advent

Worship Theme: The call from God to God's people is to "stay awake." Believers are to be attentive to the coming of the one whom God sends. This one who comes will strengthen us to the end. This is the promise from the "Faithful One."

Readings: Isaiah 64:1-9; 1 Corinthians 1:3-9; Mark 13:24-37

Call to Worship (Psalm 80:1-3, 17-19 NASB)

> *Leader:* Oh, give ear, Shepherd of Israel, Thou who dost lead Joseph like a flock; Thou who art enthroned above the cherubim, shine forth!

> ***People:*** **Before Ephraim and Benjamin and Manasseh, stir up Thy power, and come to save us!**

> *Leader:* O God, restore us, and cause Thy face to shine upon us, and we will be saved.

> ***People:*** **Let Thy hand be upon the man of Thy right hand, Upon the son of man whom Thou didst make strong for Thyself.**

> *Leader:* Then we shall not turn back from Thee; Revive us, and we will call upon Thy name.

> ***People:*** **O LORD God of hosts, restore us; Cause Thy face to shine upon us, and we will be saved.**

Pastoral Prayer:

O God, we pray to you because we need your strength and a vision. We want to envision the world as you intended it at

387

creation. Although your ways remain mysterious to us, you have promised to show us the way. Clear our minds of every impediment that clouds our judgment, and therefore, our vision. At times you hide your face from us, but you have also delivered us into the hands of our iniquity. We cry out to you in repentance and in trust. Send us a word of comfort and a word of hope. Strengthen our faith with the advent of your son, Jesus Christ, so that we can anticipate better days for our world, our nation, our congregation, and ourselves. We stand before you in anticipation. As our new church year dawns, give us that expectant hope that marks your people. In the name of Jesus, our Christ, we pray. Amen. (David N. Mosser)

SERMON BRIEFS

DEAR GOD, WHERE ARE YOU?

ISAIAH 64:1-9

This passage comes in the context of a wider and more detailed plea for God's mercy and help for a people who are in deep trouble. They have been devastated by adversaries who have trodden down the sanctuary, and "we have become like those over whom thou hast never ruled, / like those who are not called by thy name" (Isa. 63:19 RSV). In God's absence, their enemies have defeated and humiliated them. To further complicate their condition, the people have long since turned from God and sinned grievously. "In our sins we have been a long time" (64:5 RSV). The situation is so bad that there is no one to call on God. "There is no one that calls upon thy name, / that bestirs himself to take hold of thee" (v. 7 RSV).

The servant proceeds to try to justify the sinful condition of the nation. Blaming someone else for our actions is an old habit. It goes all the way back to Adam and Eve. With some degree of caution and tentativeness Isaiah blames God. "But you were angry, and we sinned; / because you hid yourself we transgressed" (v. 5). Isaiah also writes "for you have hidden your face from us, / and have delivered us into the hand of our iniquity" (v. 7). The overall force of other statements in the passage makes it clear that the Jews really know that they are responsible for their situation. It always makes us feel somewhat less guilty if we can find someone else to share the blame. As a closing argument, the servant reminds God that there is a parental obligation here. "Thou art our father; / ... we are all the work of thy hand" (v. 8 RSV). God cannot leave his children to be orphans in this hostile environment.

Against this backdrop of defeat, sin, and moral degradation, the servant pleads with God to get involved on their behalf. He does not want a timid or marginal involvement. The servant, rather, wants God to show up with such force that the enemies of the people will tremble at his presence. "O that thou wouldst rend the heavens and come down, / that the mountains might quake at thy presence" (v. 1 RSV). The servant is probably remembering how God manifested himself on Mt. Sinai where God revealed the divine name. The servant wants God to do this again. It is only by an undeniable show of God's power that the situation can be redressed.

It is important to remember and recite the mighty acts of God in the past. This is why our Jewish friends celebrate Passover each year with a Seder meal in which the specifics of their deliverance from Egypt are recited and acted out. Recollection of how God has acted in our behalf in the past is a source of faith that God will continue to act in our behalf in the future.

As we enter into the season of Advent, we sing, preach, and pray about how, in the "fullness of time," God intervened in human affairs in the coming of Jesus, the Christ. In our remembrance of the birth of Jesus, we are asking God to "do it again."

The plea of the servant in Isaiah, like the Jewish celebration of Passover and the Christian celebration of Advent is not a nostalgic rumination about wanting to go back to the "good old days." It is a cry for God to show up at this time and place to help us deal with the mess in which we find ourselves. We do not want to go back to the old days; we want God to show up in this day and time.

There is a personal dimension to this matter which we must not miss. There are times and situations in our individual lives in which we feel an overwhelming need for the power of God in our lives. We remember that God has showed up with power in the crisis experiences of our lives in the past, but we cannot live on past blessings. History is cold comfort when we are hurting right now. So we sing:

> Come, Thou long expected Jesus,
> Born to set Thy people free,
> From our fears and sins release us,
> Let us find our rest in Thee.
> Israel's strength and consolation,
> Hope of all the earth, Thou art,
> Dear Desire of every nation,
> Joy of every longing heart.
> (Charles Wesley, "Come, Thou
> Long Expected Jesus," in vol. 4 of
> *The Poetical Works of John and
> Charles Wesley* [London: Wes-
> leyan-Methodist Conference,
> 1869], p. 116)

We pray that Christ who came will keep on coming. (Thomas Lane Butts)

HURRY UP AND WAIT

1 CORINTHIANS 1:3-9

The season of Advent is upon us again. It may seem as though it has been here for months, with the reds and greens decorating the stores and shopping malls since September. However, the season in which we anticipate the birth of Christ in Bethlehem officially begins today. This is a familiar time for many of us. As we bring our own decorations down from the attic, we make lists of gifts to buy, people to visit, and goodies to bake. There are pageants to attend, parties in which we must make appearances, and family gatherings we have to plan. It almost seems routine. We do the same things every year. We get exhausted every year. Each year we swear we are going to do things differently the next year. Yet we say these things to no avail. It is as if by the time the first Sunday of Advent arrives, we are already so overloaded with commitments, we cannot wait for the last Sunday to come so we can get some rest.

Is this really what we have done to Advent? Has the lighting of the Advent wreath become a chore or a checklist to make it through the holiday season? Are we focusing on hope just to get us through Advent rather than hoping for the babe in a manger?

Paul's message in 1 Corinthians 1:3-9 gives us the encouragement to make it through the waiting and the anxious hoping we experience in Advent. Paul proclaims, "God is faithful." This is the reason we gather together at Advent, because we serve a faithful God. We know the end of the Christmas story. The census will be called. Mary and Joseph will make the journey to Bethlehem. There will be no room for them. God's son will be born in a manger.

Indeed there is much to be done to prepare our hearts, our minds, and our homes for the coming of the babe, but we are assured that, because we serve a faithful God, these things will come to pass. In the same verses, we are reminded of the strength and knowledge we have been given to be the faithful Body of Christ we have been called to be.

It is as if Paul is commiserating with us in all the duties and obligations that lie before us. Paul understands the amount of faith it takes to wait through what seems like an eternity for Christ to come. The key is that we must enact the waiting as seriously as we go about our other Advent duties. It is in the waiting that we find the peace in knowing what will come. It is in the waiting that we find the rest to help us through to the end. And it is in the waiting that we find we are in community with those who wait with us. What better gift can we give this Advent season, than to give ourselves the time and space to wait? (Victoria Atkinson White)

GOD'S TIME

MARK 13:24-37

For first-time visitors to the Navajo reservation, one of the most frustrating cultural differences is time. For the dominant society, the day is divided into neatly organized units, clearly designated by hours and minutes. If a meeting is to begin at a certain hour, it is hoped that everyone will be present at the appointed time, even a few minutes early. On the reservation, many people are on "Indian time."

Hours or minutes do not label "Indian time." Instead, events, meetings, or even church begin when the time is right. Most of the world thinks in *chronos*, humans' way of thinking about time. Many Native people think in *kairos*, God's time.

When we were expecting our first child, the doctor did his examination, interviewed us, and proclaimed January 1 as the due date. Thirty years ago, being more than a little naive, I believed and decided I wanted her to be the first child born in the new year. Not only would we get our names in the paper, but our hometown often gave prizes to Baby New Year. We could use free diaper service for a year, free formula, and a new car seat.

One week before her due date, on Christmas Eve, I started having some funny pains. My doctor assured me that the baby wasn't due for another week and to take something for gas, and he would see me in the office later that week.

I was at the hospital a few hours later—in labor. At four o'clock on Christmas morning, the doctor explained that he was going home to open presents with his family and take a nap and that he would be back in plenty of time, about 7 A.M. Not to worry, this was my first child, and I would be here for hours.

Tamara came in God's time—the right time—at 4:44 A.M. chronologically. No matter how many deliveries that doctor has made or how many sonograms or ultrasounds are done, under normal circumstances, babies arrive in God's time.

Matthew's Gospel warns of the end times with oppression, tribulation, a darkened sun and falling stars. Yet, even with all the experts proclaiming the due date, the day when the Son of Man comes in the clouds with great power and glory will be in God's time, at the right time.

Each new birth is a new beginning, for the child and the parents. The doctors can estimate when the child will be born, but no one knows for sure the child's personality or even what kind of parents the couple will be.

Just as one cannot become consumed with the signs, the

parents-to-be are buying clothes, stocking up with diapers, and painting the nursery. Matthew tells us what we should be doing in the interim. Watch! Give strict attention to your own actions and words. Be active and alert.

In this season of Advent, it is easy to get caught up in the commercialism of Christmas. The holiday becomes more important than the event that it celebrates, especially since we live in a longer and longer period of expectation. The decorations and mistletoe were dragged out to be ready the day after Thanksgiving, this weekend, but now the holiday wrappings could be seen as early as Halloween. The period of expectation is up to eight and a half weeks.

The Advent wreath reminds us of God's time: a time of joy, of peace, of hope, and most especially, a time of looking forward to new beginnings. We are living in moments no one has ever lived in before. It is our choice to live it fully, confidently, and purposefully, knowing that God's time will be fulfilled, and, if we watch, we will not be caught sleeping but prepared and ready to partake in the new life offered by the Son of Man when Jesus comes in power and might. (Raquel Mull)

REFLECTIONS

DECEMBER

Reflection Verse: *"But be doers of the word, and not merely hearers who deceive themselves. For if any are hearers of the word and not doers, they are like those who look at themselves in a mirror; for they look at themselves and, on going away, immediately forget what they were like." (James 1:22-24)*

PRAXIS: DOERS OF THE WORD
James 1:19-25

Deep into December we now complete our twelve-month journey of meditations on the theme "Twelve Pillars of Abundant Christian Living." We have labeled these twelve pillars as monuments to right living and tied them to Moses' erecting of commemorative pillars (Exod. 24:4). Represented among these monuments are the self-evident qualities of love, patience, forgiveness, assurance, and humility. Most preachers quickly recognize these pillars as being vital to a true, purposeful, and meaningful Christian life. As an old American Express advertisement might put it, "Don't leave home without them."

Other Christian qualities represented by these pillars are a bit trickier to grasp. Some of our parishioners might be hard-pressed to determine how the fear of the Lord, righteousness, discernment, or discipline might be pillars worthy enough to hold up our house of faith. Still, we have ventured a case for each. Our focal point for this final meditation offers us a most difficult word: Praxis. What in the world is praxis?

We derive *praxis* from a Greek word for "action" or "practice." By and large, philosophers are the thinkers who typically employ the word. However, theologians, too, can use praxis to sensibly emphasize useful concerns for Christian believers. Praxis signifies spiritual truth as a type of wisdom that can only be fully learned through experience. Consequently praxis engages our whole being: body, soul, and spirit. We might even advocate that, because we know what God has done for us, praxis becomes what we can do for God—with God's help, of course.

Praxis takes truth from a purely theoretical concept and moves truth to a practical and intuitive level of understanding. From this perspective we might come to know truth with the whole of our being. Praxis, to say it another way, is where theory and practice meet. A person might say that praxis is "where the rubber meets the road." From a Christian viewpoint, praxis occurs where our profession of faith meets our serving in God's realm. We, of course, have another and more familiar word for this occasion. Christians call it discipleship.

"Practice what you preach!" Whether others voice this sentiment out loud or simply use this phrase as an introspective way to measure Christian sincerity, the world watches those who profess Jesus Christ as Lord. For an opponent to call a believer a "hypocrite" is an essentially scornful description of a Christian. The dreaded word *hypocrisy* implies to "play a part" or profess to be something that one is not.

There are many charges others may level at Christians, but the most stinging to Jesus' disciples is to be dubbed a hypocrite. Hypocrites are those persons who say one thing and then do another. They are people who playact for gain. Hypocrites assume one role while, in reality, they live another role. So insistent was Jesus about following God's way that in the Sermon on the Mount Jesus bluntly addressed hypocrisy.

> So whenever you give alms, do not sound a trumpet before you, as the hypocrites do in the synagogues and in the streets, so that they may be praised by others. . . .
> And whenever you pray, do not be like the hypocrites; for they love to stand and pray in the synagogues and at the street corners, so that they may be seen by others. . . .
> And whenever you fast, do not look dismal, like the hypocrites, for they disfigure their faces so as to show others that they are fasting. Truly I tell you, they have received their reward. (Matt. 6:2, 5, 16)

Perhaps Jesus is saying that when we practice good things, for example, giving to the needy, praying, or fasting, we engage these practices because it is part of who we are as believers. The reward of such observances is in the practice itself, not for the effect it has on others who happen to watch us give or pray or fast. We give because Jesus first gave to us. We pray because Jesus prayed. Prayer was the foundation not only of Jesus' ministry among us but also of Jesus' relationship with God. We fast because it is a spiritual discipline that reminds us of Jesus' potent question, "Is not life more [important] than food?" (Matt. 6:25).

Discipleship describes the Christian practice of putting our lives where our profession is. We try as best we can, with God's help, to make our life congruent with our words. Again, we try to practice what we preach. As a parishioner once put it to me in my first parish: "Preacher, I would rather see a sermon any day than hear one." I couldn't agree more. The word *praxis* is another way to say our discipleship is active and based on solid biblical principles. Praxis means we do not divide our faith into a spiritual part and a service part; we blend them into a life pleasing to God.

In his book *How Good Do We Have to Be?* Rabbi Harold Kushner writes about his conversations with World War II veterans in 1994–95, the fiftieth anniversary of that war's major battles. What struck me about Kushner's observations was that these soldiers, fifty years after suffering and seeing their friends die, remembered not so much the hard times of soldierly life as "the experience of caring enough about something to put their lives on the line for what they cherished" (New York: Little, Brown and Company, 1996, p. 159). Can we Christians similarly say without hypocrisy that we understand our faith in Jesus Christ in this way?

A poem, *The Guy in the Glass,* offered by an alert reader, reminds us of what James tells his early readers, "For if any are hearers of the word and not doers, they are like those who look at themselves in a mirror; for they look at themselves and, on going away, immediately forget what they were like." As strange as the word *praxis* may be to our ears, it is a word that can keep our hearing and doing together for the glory of God. I sense that this poem addresses the same issue that James addressed long ago.

> When you get what you want in your struggle for pelf,
> And the world makes you King for a day,
> Then go to the mirror and look at yourself,
> And see what that guy has to say.

For it isn't your Father, or Mother, or Wife,
Who judgement upon you must pass.
The feller whose verdict counts most in your life
Is the guy staring back from the glass.

He's the feller to please, never mind all the rest,
For he's with you clear up to the end,
And you've passed your most dangerous difficult test
If the guy in the glass is your friend.

You may be like Jack Horner and "chisel" a plum,
And think you're a wonderful guy,
But the man in the glass says you're only a bum
If you can't look him straight in the eye.

You can fool the whole world down the pathway of years,
And get pats on the back as you pass,
But your final reward will be heartaches and tears
If you've cheated the guy in the glass.

This poem, by Peter "Dale" Wimbrow, Sr., was first published in *The American Magazine* in May 1934. The magazine asked readers to offer an answer to a young reader's question: "One good reason, please, why an ambitious young man should be honest."

If preachers need a token of one of the foundational traits of abundant life then perhaps there is a pillar with the word *praxis* inscribed on it, but I doubt it. Rather the pillar we seek will no doubt read "discipleship." Amen. (David N. Mosser)

DECEMBER 4, 2005

Second Sunday of Advent

Worship Theme: The Lord promises a day that will be a day of comfort and release. On the day of the Lord's promise, all people will see the Lord's glory then revealed. John prepares the way.

Readings: Isaiah 40:1-11; 2 Peter 3:8-15*a*; Mark 1:1-8

Call to Worship (Psalm 85:8-13 NASB)

Leader:	I will hear what God the LORD will say;
People:	**For He will speak peace to His people, to His godly ones; but let them not turn back to folly.**
Leader:	Surely His salvation is near to those who fear Him, that glory may dwell in our land.
People:	**Lovingkindness and truth have met together; righteousness and peace have kissed each other.**
Leader:	Truth springs from the earth; and righteousness looks down from heaven.
People:	**Indeed, the LORD will give what is good; and our land will yield its produce.**
All:	**Righteousness will go before Him, and will make His footsteps into a way.**

Pastoral Prayer:

O Lord our God of Consolation, the prophet Isaiah reminds us that, "Comfort, O comfort my people, says your God." For the divine comfort of the holy gospel we give you thanks, O God of our Ancestors. We gather to worship you and to remember your promise to our forebears, a promise that propelled them through both the wilderness and the Exile. Too often we modern people feel as if we, too, live in the wilderness, exiled in our own land. Troubles crop up in front of us and difficulties seem to surround us. These troubles and difficulties are of many and various kinds. Yet, if we can cleave to your promise, then we will see your glory. And if we see your glory, then we will have courage. Give us the stoutness of heart to face our difficulties. Arm us with the gospel of peace. Make us people committed to justice and equity in our dealings with others. Help us learn to love those for whom love is a difficult task. We can love in this way only through the grace and mercy of Jesus Christ in whose name we pray. Amen. (David N. Mosser)

SERMON BRIEFS

OVERHEARING THE HEAVENLY HOST

ISAIAH 40:1-11

Recently I called a good friend on a cell phone in Northern Florida. As the phone faded in and out I found myself overhearing someone else's conversation. We like to overhear, to listen in. Have you ever said, "I would like to be a fly on the wall during that conversation"?

If you were walking down the street and overheard a conversation on the other side of a fence, you might be tempted to try to listen in. However, if one spoke your name, you would definitely pause to lend an ear. Is that not why we come to worship, to hear our name? Is that not why we overhear the ancient conversations of scripture, to hear our name? Overhear these rapid interjections of voices in our text. You just might hear your name.

David Buttrick is instrumental in helping preachers distinguish and discern the various voices clamoring for our attention. In verses 1-2 we overhear the heavenly host, the voice of God, proclaim the end of the Exile as certainly as if it already had happened. God asks the exiles to hear an alternative perspective on reality. Many Christians today need to hear the encouraging voice of God as we labor in a land not our own.

In verses 3-5 we overhear another unidentified voice issuing orders to construct a highway upon which God comes in triumph and liberation. In verse 6*a*, we overhear yet another voice that speaks to or calls the prophet to preach to the exiles. They and we need to be reminded that God is still God and that he has not forgotten his people. In verses 6*b*-8 we are dismayed to overhear the despairing preacher respond that there is no purpose in preaching. Hope is as fleeting as the mortal life we live.

To the preacher's pessimism, the heavenly council commands that the prophet should simply present God in all his power and glory. So unique are these "good tidings" *(gospel)*, that Isaiah uses a word never used before *(basar)* to stress the gospel's unique power to deliver.

Finally in verses 9-11 we overhear two powerful but contrasting images of the God who fills on one hand the role of a powerful conquering hero and, on the other, the role of the tender shepherd. How ironic it was that Jesus' acceptance of the latter and rejection of the former initiated the conflict that contributed to his rejection on the part of many—even those he came to deliver.

Did you hear your name? As we overheard this ancient conversation, did you hear a word concerning you? You may have heard that this is a new day. However, to proceed on the right path, we may have to confess that we have been walking on the wrong path. This confession is called repentance.

Did you hear that there is someone coming not only to find you, free you, but to accompany you as well? Did you hear that this one has gone to much effort to prepare and pave the way for his coming? John Claypool said that the significance of any event is in direct proportion to the preparation we give to it. Christ's coming must be significant indeed! During this Advent season we anticipate with delight! Aren't you glad you "lended" an ear? (Gary L. Carver)

HOLD EVERYTHING!

2 PETER 3:8-15a

I remember my mother's voice. It came out of nowhere. I am absolutely positive that she had eyes in the back of her head. She could see around corners, and she reminded me of that reality each time I tried to go outside without a coat. "Hold everything," she would say. "Just where do you think you are going without your coat and your hat?" I still hear that voice. It really is true; no one loves you and looks after you like your mother. Theologically, I think God actually holds the blue ribbon when it comes to love. But, mothers would come in a close second. Can you imagine how Mary felt as she stood in the temple court and heard that a sword would pierce her own heart? She took the infant Jesus back into her arms and started her personal journey to the foot of the cross. Only the love of a mother divinely mixed with the call of the father could make that journey fruitful!

At the heart of this passage Peter provides a clear message. Peter speaks to the ages as he is thinking about the personal journey of faith. Peter says it is time to be prepared. It is time to be ready. It may not be raining right now but the sky will open sooner or later. Our job is to be prepared when the promise arrives. We will not be ready with coat, gloves, or even the warmest hat. We will be ready with the warm heart that comes by faith. Hold everything, the promise is coming!

The heart of God holds a deep longing for human creation. God desires that no one would perish. The heart of God looks forward to that day when we will be found "spotless, blameless, and at peace with him" (v. 14 NIV). The patience of God will outlast our reluctance to adopt a spirit of holiness for our own lives.

The promise has been slow in coming, but it will arrive. It is the promise of the Lord Jesus. It is the day when all things will change once again. Everything changed when the first Advent took place in Bethlehem. Now Peter says, "Hold everything! Be sure you are prepared because the arrival of the promise will change the world once again."

People in Peter's day asked the same question as modern thinkers, When will it happen? What will it look like? Why is it

401

taking so long? Peter is the apostle with all the answers. Over-anxious, impetuous Peter has become a philosopher and theolo-gian: "With the Lord a day is like a thousand years, and a thousand years are like a day" (v. 8 NIV).

The promise has been slow in coming because God's time is not our time. The Lord's *kairos* will never meet the intricate stress-producing standard of human *chronos*! Stop tapping your foot, quit looking at your watch, hold everything, and begin to live in eager expectation of God arriving in your life. Expect God to show up so your life and your world can be transformed.

In the end, we discover that the reward is contained within the promise itself. The promise of repentance, the promise of salva-tion, brings the hope of a new heaven and a new earth. The baby at Bethlehem changed everything. Now it is time for all things to be refreshed, renewed, and revived. It will be time to hear the voice of God say, "Hold everything, where do you think you are going? I have a home for you right here. It is a home of righ-teousness. Get ready. Put on the cloak of holiness and fit your feet with the gospel of peace. Be ready! My promise is true." (Randy Jessen)

YOUR VOICE IN THE WILDERNESS

MARK 1:1-8

Change is difficult, whether it is in a person, a relationship, a job, or even the furniture. I personally do not like change. Once in a while—too often for me—my daughter would say, "I wonder what the couch would look like over there." I would start a pot of coffee and make some chocolate chip cookies and her brother would drag out the vacuum cleaner because it was his job to clean around the baseboards when the couch was out from the wall. And usually, the next morning, I would forget the changes and stub my toe or run into the coffee table on my way to a fresh cup of coffee.

Within the church, a common saying when faced with change is, "We've never done it that way before."

John the Baptist is a great story of changes. Change in the

man, change in the environment, change in the message, and change in his listeners.

John the Baptist was clothed in camel's hair with a leather belt around his waist and a diet of locusts and wild honey. Scripture makes a point of sharing this with us precisely because it was different from the main society. John has always been presented as a loner, living in the wilderness. Now, he is surrounded by masses of humanity for hours each day. He has left his old lifestyle and home behind.

Don't resurrect something that God has already finished. John, in obeying God's call on his life, moved on to proclaim the message of baptism for the repentance and the forgiveness of sins. He didn't preach and baptize for a couple of hours and then run back to his place of solitude in the wilderness. He was open to change.

John's background is a little vague. We know about his birth and who his parents were. Because his father was a priest, we assume John was raised knowing and practicing the Mosaic law. But here is a new message: Repent and be baptized with water and prepare to be baptized by one who baptizes with the Holy Spirit. A new way of relating to God is on the horizon, and John gives the message with confidence and strength.

Until one comes in authority, one is not fit to *be* an authority. John appeared in the wilderness proclaiming a new message with confidence and strength. He could have whispered the message to a couple of people, to try it out, and then if they did not accept it or believe it, he could return and say, "Well, I tried." He spoke loud enough, and so many times, that the whole Judean countryside and people of Jerusalem were coming to the river Jordan.

John the Baptist gave his message with strength and confidence and people responded. He could not have spoken thusly if he had let fear rule his actions. If he had worried about how he looked and what people would say about him, he would have been trying to please people and not God. John would have failed. He instead pointed the people to God through Jesus the Christ and he spoke to those who were in the wilderness.

Another factor for us to consider is his audience. John was in the wilderness, a word often associated with those who are spiritually lost and hopeless, those who are hurting, those who are opposite of him: the fearful, the resentful, the unforgiven, the weak. It was to these that he gave his message of hope and power.

It is the season of Advent, the time to prepare for a new beginning, a new beginning not only for the church but also for us. A time of new beginnings is also in store for those who are still in their wilderness of unforgiveness, the wilderness of pain and hopelessness, the wilderness of loneliness and resentment. Who needs to hear the message of hope and power and love? Who needs to hear your voice in their wilderness? (Raquel Mull)

DECEMBER 11, 2005

Third Sunday of Advent

Worship Theme: John tells those who asked whether he was the Messiah that "I am the voice of one crying out in the wilderness" (John 1:23). John announces the one who is mightier than he, the one coming after him.

Readings: Isaiah 61:1-4, 8-11; 1 Thessalonians 5:16-24; John 1:6-8, 19-28

Call to Worship (Psalm 126:1-3, 5 NASB)

Leader: When the LORD brought back the captive ones of Zion, we were like those who dream.

People: The LORD has done great things for us; we are glad.

Leader: Then our mouth was filled with laughter, and our tongue with joyful shouting; then they said among the nations, "The LORD has done great things for them."

People: The LORD has done great things for us; we are glad.

Leader: Those who sow in tears shall reap with joyful shouting.

People: The LORD has done great things for us; we are glad.

Pastoral Prayer:

As we move closer and closer to that blessed day we call Christmas, O God, help us anticipate the good news that is so good we can scarcely believe it. Prepare our hearts and lives for this life-giving word that comes from you through your prophets. Make us ready for the word that has come to dwell among us, that word that can transform war into peace and hatred into love. Give us hearts receptive to the message of hope. This message of hope is so mysterious and so wonderful that it alters all human arrangements and makes your precious gift of life worth living. Furnish us with a light that will flood our hearts with anticipation and warm our hearts with expectation. O God, recreate in our lives the peace and goodness of the garden of creation. Make us people who wait for a world full of garlands rather than ashes. Let us give thanksgiving in joy today! In the name of Jesus we pray. Amen. (David N. Mosser)

SERMON BRIEFS

WHO DESERVES GOD'S BLESSINGS AND OUR HELP?

ISAIAH 61:1-4, 8-11

The significance of this passage is multiplied because it is the passage Jesus read to the congregation when he began his ministry in the synagogue in his hometown of Nazareth. Luke's account of this event (4:16-30) has Jesus reading only the first two and a half verses. He stops just before the phrase, "The day of vengeance of our God." Jesus begins his sermon from this text with this statement: "Today this scripture has been fulfilled in your hearing" (4:21).

Jesus' audience is glad to hear this message, but they obviously had an interpretation of the passage that was contrary to the interpretation that Jesus gave. Jesus included the Gentiles as also being rightful beneficiaries of God's blessings. The Jews were so confident that they were God's unique and chosen people that they tended to despise other people. According to William Barclay, they thought that "the Gentiles were created by God to be fuel for the fires of Hell" (*The Letters to the Galatians and Eph-*

esians, The Daily Study Bible Series [Philadelphia: Westminster, 1958], p. 125). When they heard this young man who grew up among them speak of Gentiles in a complimentary way, they were angry. They hustled Jesus out of town, to the brow of a hill. They would have thrown him down, but Jesus escaped.

Jesus begins his ministry by identifying with the poor, the sick, and the oppressed. Jesus has come to minister to them and set them free. He puts no national, cultural, or racial boundaries on his ministry. Jesus includes everyone. As Luke's account indicates, this is quite unacceptable to "the good church folks" of that day.

Jesus' choice of this passage as the platform for his ministry is reminiscent of the Magnificat (Luke 1:46-56), which E. Stanley Jones called "the most revolutionary document in the world" (William Barclay, *The Gospel of Luke,* The Daily Study Bible Series [Philadelphia: Westminster, 1956], p. 9). It also puts one in mind of the last judgment parable in Matthew 25:31-46. All nations will be judged by the same standard. Judgment is not to be made on theological correctness, but on response to the needs of the poor, the sick, and the oppressed.

Isaiah 61, the Magnificat, Jesus' first recorded sermon, and the final judgment passage in Matthew 25 bring sobering news to religious legalism and exclusiveness. What does the Lord require of us? Micah said it well: "to do justice, and to love kindness, / and to walk humbly with your God" (Mic. 6:8). It was the prophets' role to proclaim this simple but revolutionary program. It is our role to do it. It is all too easy to recite a beautiful philosophical description of religious devotion and forget we are called to respond, not just to recite. A businessman notorious for his ruthlessness announced to Mark Twain, "Before I die I mean to make a pilgrimage to the Holy Land. I will climb Mount Sinai and read the Ten Commandments aloud at the top." Twain said, "I have a better idea, you could stay home in Boston and keep them." It is not enough to "go" to church; we are called to "be church" to the poor, sick, and oppressed in the world at large. No boundaries, no one is excluded.

Anyone who gets seriously involved in a program of ministry to the kind of people and problems implicit and explicit in Isaiah 61, the Magnificat, and the teachings of Jesus will find themselves at odds with powerful forces both in and out of the church. Many benevolent funds are set up to "help deserving people." I do not think Jesus ever suggested that help should be reserved for the deserving. Who is deserving, and who is qualified to make the determination? The truth is that we would like to help nice, deserving, and grateful people who are in need of help through no fault of their own. This just about excludes everybody I have helped in fifty years in the ministry!

Those who look for avenues of service through stained-glass eyes are quickly disillusioned. Experience teaches us that the poor are not perfect, the needy are not always nice, and many who receive help are not grateful in the manner in which we would like them to be. Many who are poor and oppressed are also bitter and resentful, and any who help them may be the object of their hostility. Churches and individuals who reserve their benevolence for the deserving and grateful miss the meaning of ministry in the spirit of Isaiah and Jesus. (Thomas Lane Butts)

WHAT WE DON'T HAVE TO DO

1 THESSALONIANS 5:16-24

The renewed emphasis on the observance of the liturgical church year in many denominational traditions has been a real gift during this season of the year in particular. In reclaiming the weeks leading up to Christmas as the season of Advent, many people have found new resources for a time of spiritual preparation and renewal. The days of Advent can focus our energies toward the true meaning of these days, as they are a time for remembering the birth of Christ and awaiting the return of Christ in judgment. These days remind us that spiritual preparations are to take place in our lives, as well as the practical holiday preparations of cleaning, cooking, shopping, baking, and decorating.

It is in this season of preparation that we find this series of exhortations for Christian conduct, given by Paul to a church that was waiting anxiously for the return of Christ. At first glance, these instructions seem so straightforward and simple, that there does not appear much for the preacher to do on this Sunday. We might find ourselves simply wanting to exhort our congregation to follow these admonitions so that they might be found holy and blameless when the Lord returns. Yet, in this season of list-making, it would be easy to be lulled into complacency by reading this series of short phrases as a checklist, things we know we should do and things that we need to be working on in our lives. We could find ourselves falling into the trap of viewing this season as one of "self-improvement," with attention to our spiritual lives simply becoming one more task among the list of things that we must do: pray more, sin less, love one another.

However, what strikes me during this season of list-making is that most of the imperatives Paul catalogs are relational. The words of exhortation that Paul offers are not simply tasks to be performed, but challenges for us to reflect on how we are engaging our spiritual lives. We are encouraged to spend time on those things that will strengthen our relationship with the living Christ. We are called to examine the attitudes of our heart and the outlook of our lives. Are we rejoicing? Are we giving thanks in all circumstances? We are called to be faithful in prayer, to give attention to the words of scripture, and to avoid things that might "quench the Spirit" (v. 19) and serve to diminish the effectiveness of God's movement in our lives. Paul tells us that all of this "is the will of God in Christ Jesus for [us]" (v. 18).

Yet, perhaps the most important reminder in this passage about our relationship with God is that it is God's actions on our behalf that truly make us holy and blameless. When Paul writes, "May the God of peace himself sanctify you entirely" (v. 23), it is an important caution to those of us who think that our relationship with God is carried out in our own strength. It is only through the power and presence of God—given through Jesus and found in prayer, scripture, and the Holy Spirit—that we are enabled to be in relationship with God in the first place. This is the truly good news of the gospel proclaimed during this Advent season. In the midst of all our striving and doing, may we celebrate the presence of God given to us, for "The one who calls you is faithful, and he will do this" (v. 24). (Wendy Joyner)

ARE WE A SIGN OR A DESTINATION?

JOHN 1:6-8, 19-28

The news is always embarrassing: Someone who was not what he claimed to be has been discovered to be a fraud. The University of Notre Dame experienced that embarrassment a few years ago when the coach it had hired was found to not hold the degree he reported on his résumé. We live in a world where many times people pretend to be something other than what they are. Here is one who claims to be a doctor but has no medical degree, one who says she is a lawyer but has never been to law school, one who claims to be single but is found to be married. The age of pretension, the time of the great pretenders, is what we might name our moment of history.

This is what makes our text so refreshing. When the Jews question John the Baptist about his identity, thinking that perhaps he could be the Messiah, John quite openly and adamantly says, "I am not the Messiah." John was clear about his role in the grand scheme of God's working. He was a "voice of one crying out in the wilderness, / 'Make straight the way of the Lord,'" as John echoed the ancient Isaiah. He would not claim to be what he was not. John was a sign that was to point the way to the truth, but John refused to pretend that he was the truth.

John the Baptist models a behavior from which the church can draw rich lessons. The church is never the end of faith. It points the way to the object of our faith, which is Jesus. We exist to serve Jesus. Everything about us and all that we do should point to the one who is the "true light." This word is necessary in an age when the church can sometimes pretend to be the be-all and end-all of faith. The church is always a sign that points the way, which means that sometimes it must examine itself to make sure it is not in the way!

Jesus, the gospel teaches, is "the true light, which enlightens everyone." In this time of national exclusivism and religious suspicion of traditions different from our own, it is tempting to claim that we have a special revelation from God. I heard a young pastor say the invocation at a community gathering shortly after the World Trade Center had been attacked. He prayed, "God, you are the God of America." Well, God may be the God of America, but he is also God of the cosmos. Part of the revelation that Jesus, the true light, brings is the reminder that God is larger than all our creeds and wider than our national boundaries.

On this third Sunday of Advent we remember our brother John the Baptist, who pointed beyond himself to the one he called the "Lamb of God," and remind ourselves that this one gave himself for the sins of the whole world, not just our world. Perhaps the message we need to bring to the world this Advent is that the light that shines through Christ is a revelation that all of us are children of God. This means that people we do not understand and may not even like are children of God. The light that enlightens everyone is a reminding light that teaches us that we cannot say, "My Father who is in heaven" until we learn to say "Our father who is in heaven."

To a religious system that had come to believe it had a corner on the truth, John brought a word that a true light was coming into the world, and it would enlighten everyone. Later, in the glow of that light, Peter and Paul and others came to the awareness that God loved the Gentiles too. That same light glows in our world and is teaching us that God loves the very people we love to hate, whomever they are. And we, by God's grace, are a sign that points the way to the enlightening light. Praise God for such a ministry in a dark and hurting world! (Chris Andrews)

DECEMBER 18, 2005

Fourth Sunday of Advent

Worship Theme: God promises David through the prophet Nathan that God will build a house of David and his lineage. In the promised birth of Jesus, God completes the house of faith.

Readings: 2 Samuel 7:1-11, 16; Romans 16:25-27; Luke 1:26-38

Call to Worship (Luke 1:47-55 NASB)

> *Leader:*   "My spirit has rejoiced in God my Savior.
>
> *People:*   **"For He has had regard for the humble state of His bondslave;...count me blessed.**
>
> *Leader:*   "For the Mighty One has done great things for me;...and His mercy is upon generation after generation....
>
> *People:*   **"He has done mighty deeds with His arm; He has scattered those who were proud in the thoughts of their heart.**
>
> *Leader:*   "He has brought down rulers from their thrones, ...He has filled the hungry with good things;...
>
> *People:*   **"He has given help to Israel His servant, ... as He spoke to our fathers."**

Pastoral Prayer:

O God of Magnificent Promise, we live in the hollow of your almighty hand. You have revealed yourself in the child born of Mary. In this birth we glimpse more of you than in any other way. Through the agency of the Holy Spirit you overshadow your servant Mary, and she brings to life the light-bearer of the world. In his life we have a perfect template, which shows us the outlines of peace, justice, compassion, and mercy. Help conform us, your people, O God, to the image of Christ whom you send to save your people. Give us a song in our hearts so that we, too, might sing with joy the songs of Zion. Create within our circles of influence a care and compassion for those who are less fortunate than we. Provide in our church's life a sense of the sacred worth for all your creatures and give us the will to seek out the last, the lost, and the least. May we give to them the hope that you provide for us in Jesus, our Lord and Master. It is in his holy and sacred name that we pray. Amen. (David N. Mosser)

SERMON BRIEFS

POUND THOSE NAILS!

2 SAMUEL 7:1-11, 16

Have you ever stumbled into something great but didn't know it at the time? In 1985, I was serving in a town in northeast Colorado. I received a call from the leader of our local pastor's group inviting area pastors to a special lunch. He wanted to introduce a man who had a vision for creating housing for the poor.

We all faithfully arrived and sat around long tables in the basement of the Episcopal church. We listened attentively to a tall, soft-spoken man named Millard Fuller. He shared the vision of his fledgling organization called Habitat for Humanity. No one in the room had ever heard of Millard Fuller or the ministry he founded, but we listened and then went to lunch at the café a block away. Everyone thought it was a great idea, but no one thought it would really catch on. By 1994, Habitat for Humanity was building homes across the United States and creating low-cost, quality housing in more than forty countries around the world. It all goes back to a vision that God gave to Millard Fuller.

King David had a different kind of vision to build a distinctive type of structure. It dawned on him that the king lived in a rich palace of cedar while the ark of God remained in the traveling

413

tabernacle. He thought it would be wonderful to build a beautiful home for the Lord. David felt called to honor God by building something more stable that a traveling tent.

The prophet Nathan originally gave David the green light but a nighttime vision began to change everything for David. Ultimately, David was prevented from building the temple of God. In return, God promised to build a different kind of house for David. His house would become a dynasty of spiritual leadership that would point the people to the Messiah. In fact, the house of David and his kingdom was to endure, while the house of worship that Solomon ultimately provided for God would fall.

I think of Joshua 24:15 and the powerful commitment that brought renewal to the people and to the covenant of God. "As for me and my household, we will serve the LORD." Those words continue to provide a spirit of unity for families that become a house. How many families have you seen that do not qualify as a house or a home?

Solomon would build the temple, but God would build the house of David. Only God can bring a gathering of generations together to create a house. Today we recognize the significant differences that exist between generations. We think differently. We learn differently. We hold different values. We even worship differently. Only God can take all of those differences and create one house that is built to honor God.

The tabernacle was created at God's instruction to provide a place for the postexodus people of Israel to worship. Now the house of David will provide the ultimate reason to worship. David's house and line will lead us to a stable in the little city of Bethlehem. The house of David will bring us the Lord Jesus. God's promise comes to completion. The house of David will endure. It will be established forever. It will become the hope of the world.

Two features stand out. First, we must become a part of the family. We must make ourselves available for adoption into the family of God. Second, we must create earthly families based on things that will endure. Are you building a house, or are you just pounding nails? (Randy Jessen)

WHAT IS PAUL TRYING TO TELL US?

ROMANS 16:25-27

Textual critics debate about the placement of these verses, but these three verses make for a wonderful benediction. Just as Paul began his writing to the Romans, here he closes with a celebration of God's salvation. God, who had taken care of God's people down through the centuries, has now fulfilled the message of the prophets in Christ. Through this announcement in Christ, God's message of salvation has been made clearly known as a message for all nations.

While some Christians don't really know much about the Old Testament and while there are on occasion a few like Marcion who reject Hebrew Scripture altogether, Paul proclaims that Christ was the fulfillment of the promise of God. So on the fourth Sunday of Advent, we celebrate God's ultimate gift. We celebrate the royal announcement of God's purpose unfolding before our eyes. We join in the celebration of the revelation of God's mysteries being made known to us in the flesh. We celebrate that in Jesus the veil has been removed revealing God's eternal plan.

Love is an action, and God showed us love by God's action in Jesus Christ. We are allowed a balcony seat to see God's perspective on how Jesus came to be Lord over a redeemed creation. Paul is being a witness for all to hear. In three short verses, Paul tells of his faith in a God who has been active throughout the centuries but who has made known the eternal plan in Jesus Christ. Paul expects a response. Paul expects everyone to hear, believe, and obey.

The writing reminds us that a doxology of praise is central to all we do and say in our faith. Above all, we are to proclaim that Jesus Christ is King. In Jesus, the final victory of God's grace has been made known, and we are called to be a part of the restoration and redemption of the cosmos! We trust and await fulfilled promises as God has shown us God's redemptive care for creation through Jesus.

What is Paul trying to tell us? Paul invites us into the story of faith. Paul bids us to come and know the only wise God, who, although mysterious, comes to be fully known in Jesus Christ. For that action, we give glory and honor forever and ever. Amen. (Ryan Wilson)

MISSION: IMPOSSIBLE

LUKE 1:26-38

If you are not old enough to remember the hit television show *Mission: Impossible,* then perhaps you have seen the movie versions starring Tom Cruise. A spy is given an assignment so difficult it is considered nearly impossible, but, of course, he succeeds. We viewers never harbor a doubt that the "impossible mission" will succeed on the screen. In real life, however, we have great difficulty believing the impossible.

Mary, the mother of Jesus, may be the "favored one" of God, but she is not much different from any of us. She cannot envision the impossible, the supernatural. "How can I have this baby and still be a virgin?" The angel answers, "Nothing is impossible with God." To emphasize the point, the angel adds that Elizabeth, Mary's aged and barren cousin, will have a baby as well!

Across the years, skeptics have continued to express doubts about the virgin birth. Where Isaiah gave what some deem to be a Messianic prophecy of a "virgin . . . with child" (7:14 NIV), scholars rightly point out that the Hebrew word translated there as "virgin" could also simply mean "a young maiden." However, Luke's use of the word is clear: Mary was a virgin and yet conceived a child. As C. S. Lewis has said, the people of Bible times may not have known much about reproductive science, but they certainly knew how babies are made! Those who dismiss the possibility of a virgin birth do so against the biblical text. They have the same sort of empirical approach to miracles that Mary initially voiced: Miracles are not rational, not possible.

The death and resurrection of Jesus is a mirrored miracle of his birth. Indeed, it was another Mary who met Jesus on Easter Sunday with disbelief. She could not believe her eyes; in fact, she told herself it could *not* be Jesus (he's dead!), it must be the gardener! Both Marys eventually conceded that God had indeed wrought a miracle in Jesus. God has brought the impossible into reality, which is the very definition of *miracles* and is at the core of religion. True religion is not solely about words and laws and liturgies, it is about the supernatural, the miraculous infusion of Divine Spirit into human life. The teachings of Jesus are a fine moral guide even for the secular empiricist, but the miracles confirm a more amazing message, implicit in our opening verse regarding Gabriel: The angel (and thus also the Christ Child) is "sent by God." The omnipotent Creator God has sent the very "Son of the Most High" into a particular time and place to a specific woman, Mary. The bold claim of Christianity, what Karl Barth calls "the Scandal of Particularity," what others call "Christocentric theology," may at first seem far-fetched: God became incarnate in a little baby, the son of a peasant woman named Mary. Like Mary, we may be allowed to first meet this miraculous claim with an incredulous pause. But at some point, God's expression of love toward us through the Spirit's interjection into our everyday world calls for a response from us. May we say, with Mary, "Here am I, the servant of the Lord; let it be with me according to your word" (v. 38). (Lance Moore)

DECEMBER 25, 2005

Christmas Day

Worship Theme: The salvation of our God, Isaiah suggests, the ends of the earth shall see. This salvation has come in the creative word of creation and, now, in the word made flesh. This word enfleshed is full of grace and truth.

Readings: Isaiah 52:7-10; Hebrews 1:1-4 (5-12); John 1:1-14

Call to Worship (Psalm 98:1-6 NASB)

Leader: O Sing to the LORD a new song, for He has done wonderful things, His right hand and His holy arm have gained the victory for Him.

People: **The LORD has made known His salvation; He has revealed His righteousness in the sight of the nations.**

Leader: He has remembered His lovingkindness and His faithfulness to the house of Israel; all the ends of the earth have seen the salvation of our God.

People: **Shout joyfully to the LORD, all the earth; break forth and sing for joy and sing praises.**

Leader: Sing praises to the LORD with the lyre; with the lyre and the sound of melody.

People: **With trumpets and the sound of the horn shout joyfully before the King, the LORD.**

Pastoral Prayer:

Joy to the world, we sing and pray, O God, for you have come to dwell with your people. You come in Jesus, your holy Word made flesh. At the birth of the Messiah we rejoice that we have met you, O God, face-to-face. You, Lord of all, are the one who knows our frame and the thoughts of our hearts. When we cry out in our anguish as human creatures, "Who sees us? Who knows us?" it is you, Gracious Lord, who answers us to the depths of our souls. Today we heap praise upon your holy name for the birth of Jesus, our Messiah. Let us sing with zest and verve as we offer thanksgiving for that inexpressible gift of salvation offered to us in Bethlehem's manger.

As we approach a new year, may we have the confidence that assurance in faith provides for the living of these days. Grant us your pardon as we enter into joyful and abundant life through Jesus Christ, in whose name we pray. Amen. (David N. Mosser)

SERMON BRIEFS

GOOD NEWS FOR EVERYBODY

ISAIAH 52:7-10

Isaiah speaks for God as he recites the oppressions and indignities of Israel. God says, "I am coming to take charge of the situation." Verses 7-10 constitute a hymn of ecstatic joy for the very feet of the messenger who is coming from the mountain with the good news: "Your God reigns." It is an enthronement announcement of the reign of a new king. The past has been bleak, but the future is filled with hope. It is good news.

This announcement brings joy to the hearts of the Jews, but it is a circumscribed salvation. It is for the Jews only. The other nations will see it, but they are not included in it.

> The Lord has bared his holy arm
> before the eyes of all the nations;
> and all the ends of the earth shall see
> the salvation of our God. (v. 10)

The hymn of joy at the announcement of salvation and peace anticipates another announcement, in another time, which is not circumscribed. It is for all people. It is for all times. Let us turn to that royal announcement by the herald angels.

In Luke's account of the birth of Jesus a herald angel appears to simple shepherds in the field. The shepherds were initially afraid. The angel said: "Be not afraid; for behold, I bring you good news of a great joy which will come to all the people; for to you is born this day in the city of David a Savior, who is Christ the Lord" (Luke 2:10-11 RSV).

In the Christmas pageant a five-year-old was given the part of the angel who announced the birth of Jesus to the shepherds. He rehearsed his opening lines over and over; "Fear not: for, behold, I bring you good tidings of great joy, which shall be to all people" (KJV). He was ready. The rehearsals went fine, but no one had anticipated the impact of a packed house on the memory of a five-year-old. On the night of the pageant the announcing angel rushed out on the stage, looked at the crowd and forgot his lines, but he remembered the spirit of the occasion, and he said, "Don't be scared! I've got good news for everybody!"

The child muffed his lines, but he did not miss the meaning of the coming of Christ. When we strip away the theological words with which we characteristically describe the Incarnation, the unadorned meaning is simple: Do not be afraid; it is good news. It is for everybody. It is for all time.

The good news that comes with the Babe of Bethlehem is that we are all included in the saving love of God. About three years ago our associate pastor was giving the children's sermon to an unusually large group of children. Children were packed into every corner of the chancel area. She ended the brief homily by saying, "And God loves you and you and you," pointing as she spoke in three different directions. She paused to let this profound message sink in. During the silence, a child down at the far end of the chancel behind the baptismal font toward which she had not pointed, said in a wee, small voice, "What about me?" This child represents a category of people that is larger than most of us know: those who live below the radar screen of normal attention or who wonder if they are too small or too bad or too insignificant to be included.

The good news is that God's inclusive, unconditional love is not only greater than we know but also greater than we *can* know. No matter how articulate we may be, we never have enough words.

There is a hymn that makes the point clear:

> Could we with ink the ocean fill,
> And were the skies of parchment made;
> Were ev'ry stalk on earth a quill,
> And ev'ry man a scribe by trade;
> To write the love of God above
> Would drain the ocean dry;
> Nor could the scroll contain the whole,
> Tho' stretch'd from sky to sky.
> (Frederick M. Lehman, "The Love of God,"
> *Sing to the Lord* [Kansas City, Mo.: Lillenas,
> 1993], no. 86)

All eyes and ears are turned to the mountains and the sky as we wait to hear again the good news of peace, liberation, and redemption. Today is the day! Can you hear it? Listen! (Thomas Lane Butts)

FRAGMENTS AND FASHIONS!

HEBREWS 1:1-4 (5-12)

When one is about to preach on a text, it is expedient to reveal one's vast knowledge about the who, what, when, and where of the word upon which one is about to expound. I would tell you who wrote the book of Hebrews, but I do not know. It was a preacher of the first rank, a master of classical rhetoric and the Greek language and one familiar with the congregation, although separated from it. I would tell you when he wrote the book of Hebrews, but I do not know. The best guess is that it was written between 60 A.D and 100 A.D. with a leaning toward the latter because of the more highly developed Christology.

I would tell you what the book of Hebrews is, but I do not know. Some say it is a sermon, some say it is a letter, similar to those of Paul.

I would tell you to whom the book of Hebrews was written,

but I do not know. We do know that they were tired. They were tired of worship, ministry, ridicule, prayer, and some had even begun to lag in faithful attendance. I do know, however, how the unknown author sought to bring relief to his beleaguered congregation. He preached to them about Jesus. Hardly a novel idea, but one that was most effective. Perhaps he knew that our attitudes about just about everything begin with our view of God. If we get Jesus right and sincerely seek to follow him, much will fall into place. So, this peerless preacher engages the congregation in dialogue about the most fundamental element of our faith. Who is Jesus, and how has God sought to communicate to us through him?

God has spoken, as Thomas G. Long translates it, through "many fragments and many fashions" (Thomas G. Long, *Hebrews*, Interpretation: A Bible Commentary for Teaching and Preaching [Louisville: John Knox Press, 1997], p. 4). God has spoken (1:1). God, from the get-go, has sought to make God's self known in episodes of speech punctuating seasons of silence. To Abraham, Samuel, the Canaanite woman, or through John the Baptist, God's voice was heard only after periods of time when it was not heard. Perhaps God uses the silence to make us more attentive.

God also speaks "in many fashions." God seeks to be known through visions, dreams, divine urgings, gut reactions, the beauty of night, the stories of villains and heroes, the law, and the spirit of it. God speaks through a mother's love, the flight of a bumblebee, political leaders, and the language of prayer. In infinite ways and through the best and the worst, God is here, screaming for attention.

But God has spoken most definitely, ultimately, and most fully through his Son (1:2). If you want to know what God looks like, look at Jesus. If you want to know what the worthwhile life is like, look at Jesus. If you want to know how to interpret scripture, history, the universe, look at Jesus. It is Jesus! Jesus is the superior revelation of God, the focal point of history, the key to understanding life, and the purpose of the existence of the universe.

The expert in oral communication uses an early church hymn to describe, although limited, the ultimate first and last Word of God. "Whom he appointed heir of all things, and through whom he made the universe. The Son is the radiance of God's glory and the exact representation of his being, sustaining all things by his powerful word" (Heb. 1:2b-3a NIV).

Will Campbell had been the unofficial pastor to Waylon Jennings, traveling with him on tours. Will thought that he would talk to him about his spiritual condition. "What do you believe about Jesus?" Waylon said, "Uh-huh." A man of few words. A few weeks later he decided he would ask again. "What do you believe about Jesus?" Waylon said, "Well, let me ask you, all of the books that have been written about Jesus have they ever improved on Jesus?" Will said, "No." Jennings said, "Well, then that's what I believe. I believe in Jesus."

Can't beat that! Uh-huh! (Gary L. Carver)

LOVE WITH SKIN ON IT

JOHN 1:1-14

On this Christmas Day we are blessed to have a reading from the Gospel of John, which is not unlike the soaring hymns of this season. Just as Christmas carols are played in malls and on secular radio stations and received with joy by people who do not practice or even acknowledge faith in Christ, so these words about "The Word" would have been intriguing, if not downright inspirational, to people of John's world.

For centuries philosophers in Greece had speculated about the divine Word *(Logos)* and its relationship to the universe. No doubt the collection of verses we read today would have awakened their interest. But John is addressing a different audience. He is speaking to those raised in the Jewish tradition rather than in the Greek. They, too, would certainly respond to his hymn of the Word. Did not their ancient scriptures declare that by the Word of the Lord an unformed chaos had been transformed into an ordered universe (Genesis 1)? Had not the psalmist said that by the Word of the Lord the heavens were made and all the host of them by the breath of his mouth (Ps. 33:6)? Prophet and psalmist and the wise men and women of Israel's tradition had declared this Word to be the powerful instrument of divine activity.

Yet this praise of the divine Word was open to one form of serious misunderstanding. As soon as a group of writings were set apart as sacred, as had happened with the Torah, the danger arose that they would be regarded as in themselves the Word of God and, therefore, worthy to receive honor and praise. So the Torah came to be exalted in Israel's life.

No doubt John had seen this elevation of the written word in Israel's worship ritual. In a dramatic way, he changes the whole reference to "The Word." "The Word" is identified! No longer are the written words of the Torah held up for the people to reverence. Now "The Word" is the living Word, who took on human form and appeared among men and women: "And the Word became flesh and lived among us" (v. 14).

Incarnation is the theological term used to describe this "Word become flesh." Incarnation is the essence of Christmas Day; it is what the angels and shepherds and star and Mary and Joseph are about. It is love with skin on.

There is a cute story about a little girl who was put to bed one night by her parents. But it was one of those nights when the shadows in her bedroom assumed strange shapes, and the little one felt scared. She sought out her parents for comfort. They told her to go back to bed and to remember that God was with her in the bedroom and would take care of her. She dutifully returned to her darkened room, only to find the shadows even more frightening. So she sought out her parents again and said, "I know God is in my room, but could you come too, because I need someone with skin on."

That is Christmas: love with skin on. That is what John was witnessing to with his hymn about The Word. That is what we celebrate this glorious Christmas Day!

Let us remember that there is nothing theoretical about the Christian faith. It is always made real by its physical presence through acts of kindness and deeds of mercy and loving presence. It is love with skin on. It is "the Word become flesh" that "lives among us . . . full of grace and truth."

Merry Christmas! (Chris Andrews)

BENEDICTIONS

Season of Advent
Go forth under the protection of the Almighty, Creator, Redeemer, and Sustainer. Go forth and be the people of God. Amen.

"The peace of God, which surpasses all understanding, will guard your hearts and your minds in Christ Jesus" (Phil. 4:7).

"Those who wait for the LORD shall renew their strength,
they shall mount up with wings like eagles,
they shall run and not be weary,
they shall walk and not faint" (Isa. 40:31).
In this blessed season of Advent wait with patience for the salvation of our God! Amen.

In the bleak midwinter and in any scorching heat, the Lord is our light and our salvation. God's Spirit of strength and patient endurance be yours as you go out into the world proclaiming God's goodness and God's greatness to humankind trapped in despair. Remember the Lord is your guide and your shield. Amen.

Christmas Season
May the Lord, made in a likeness of our flesh, remind each of us of God's tender mercies given as a gift of grace to a people whom the Lord created. Take the Christmas joy of Christ and give it to the world, in the name of the Father, the Son, and the Holy Ghost. Amen.

As candles burn bright and the carols ring out harmoniously, share the wonder of Christ's incarnation with all you meet. Let the truth of the gospel shine forth in your life, knowing that you

THE ABINGDON PREACHING ANNUAL 2005

are under the protection of the Almighty from now and hence-forth. Amen.

Season After Epiphany

As your depart this sacred place, take with you the grace of the Lord Jesus Christ, the love of God, and the communion of the Holy Spirit. Be of good cheer, for the light of Christ has over-come the darkness of the world. Amen.

"There are many who say, 'O that we might see some good!' / Let the light of your face shine on us, O LORD" (Ps. 4:6)! Do not hide your light under a basket, O people of God. Rather, let the light of love shine in your life forever. Amen.

God asks us to be missionaries to the world. Go from this sanctu-ary to sing and shout the good news to the whole earth that Jesus Christ is Lord. Let the convictions of our heart persuade those without hope that there is a God indeed! Amen.

As God brought Jesus to the waters of baptism, may God bring us to these cleansing, healing waters as well. May God's Spirit remind us that we are daughters and sons of the Most High. Go and proclaim the victory over sin and death by our God—Father, Son, and Holy Spirit. Amen.

Season of Lent

As we are a people forgiven of sin, so let us now become a forgiv-ing people. May God's grace burn within us as we go as a recon-ciled and reconciling people. Wherever we go, we go in the name of God, the Son, and the Holy Spirit. Amen.

"Let the redeemed of the LORD say so, / those he redeemed from trouble" (Ps. 107:2). Amen.

As we sing, "O Sacred Head, Now Wounded," know with assur-ance that our God has provided the Lamb for our salvation. Go forth with the confidence of the people of God. Be the people of God. Amen.

Remember the words of the psalmist,
>"The LORD is my light and my salvation;
> whom shall I fear?
>The LORD is the stronghold of my life;
> of whom shall I be afraid?" (Ps. 27:1). .

As you reenter the world, go with the confidence that God lights your path and provides a way when there seems to be no way. Go in God's strength. Amen.

Season of Easter

Gracious God, as we leave this sacred time, we know that like those of old we, too, have many questions. We ask with other disciples, "Where is the Lord?" Help us find comfort in another question: "Why do you look for the living among the dead?" Remind us of the heavenly promise, "He is not here, but has risen" (Luke 24:5). Christ has risen indeed!

In our moments of doubt and in our moments of despair, O God, grant us a glimpse of your purpose for creation. In Christ all things dwell. Glory be to the Father, to the Son, and to the Holy Spirit. Amen.

As the Almighty God has raised Jesus from the grave, may our God raise us to new life in the power of the Holy Spirit. Amen.

Paul asked with passion, "Where, O death, is your victory? / Where, O death, is your sting?" (1 Cor. 15:55). Today the creation resounds with the affirmation that God has conquered sin and death. May we celebrate the resurrection of Christ with lives dedicated to the gospel and its hope for humankind. Amen.

Season After Pentecost

"The LORD watch between you and me, when we are absent one from the other" (Gen. 31:49).

Bless now your church, O God, as we scatter to serve our risen Savior. Give us the courage and will to do your bidding today, tomorrow, and forever. In the name of the Father, Son, and Holy Spirit. Amen.

May God's grace enfold you;
May Christ's peace be upon you;
May the Holy Spirit's encouragement guide you, all your days.
Amen.

May the holy bread of heaven feed you as you walk with the Lord. As we depart our time of worship and praise, may the light of Christ guide our steps and bring us once more to the temples of the Lord. We pray this and all things in the name of the Creator, the Savior, and the Mighty Counselor. Amen.

Other Liturgical Occasions

"It is done! I am the Alpha and the Omega, the beginning and the end. To the thirsty I will give water as a gift from the spring of the water of life" (Rev. 21:6). Gracious God give to us, the thirsty, from the spring of the water of life so that we, too, may drink. Amen.

Our prayer today, O God, is that of the faithful Ruth, who left her people and her gods to worship you and you alone. "May the LORD reward you for your deeds, and may you have a full reward from the LORD, the God of Israel, under whose wings you have come for refuge" (Ruth 2:12).

In our hour of need, you, O Lord Almighty, have answered our prayer with a story and a promise. The story is one of Jesus and his redeeming love. The promise is that you will always be with us. For this we dedicate our thankful lives in humble gratitude. Amen.

"May the LORD give you increase, / both you and your children" (Ps. 115:14). Amen.

(David N. Mosser)

TEXT GUIDE*

THE REVISED COMMON LECTIONARY (2005—YEAR A)

Sunday	First Lesson	Psalm	Second Lesson	Gospel Lesson
1/2/05	Eccl. 3:1-13	Ps. 8	Rev. 21:1-6a	Matt. 25:31-46
1/9/05	Isa. 42:1-9	Ps. 29	Acts 10:34-43	Matt. 3:13-17
1/16/05	Isa. 49:1-7	Ps. 40:1-11	1 Cor. 1:1-9	John 1:29-42
1/23/05	Isa. 9:1-4	Ps. 27:1, 4-9	1 Cor. 1:10-18	Matt. 4:12-23
1/30/05	Mic. 6:1-8	Ps. 15	1 Cor. 1:18-31	Matt. 5:1-12
2/6/05	Exod. 24:12-18	Ps. 99	2 Pet. 1:16-21	Matt. 17:1-9
2/13/05	Gen. 2:15-17; 3:1-7	Ps. 32	Rom. 5:12-19	Matt. 4:1-11
2/20/05	Gen. 12:1-4a	Ps. 121	Rom. 4:1-5, 13-17	John 3:1-17
2/27/05	Exod. 17:1-7	Ps. 95	Rom. 5:1-11	John 4:5-42
3/6/05	1 Sam. 16:1-13	Ps. 23	Eph. 5:8-14	John 9:1-41
3/13/05	Ezek. 37:1-14	Ps. 130	Rom. 8:6-11	John 11:1-45
3/20/05	Isa. 50:4-9a	Ps. 31:9-16	Phil. 2:5-11	Matt. 26:14–27:66
3/27/05	Acts 10:34-43	Ps. 118:1-2, 14-24	Col. 3:1-4	John 20:1-18
4/3/05	Acts 2:14a, 22-32	Ps. 16	1 Pet. 1:3-9	John 20:19-31
4/10/05	Acts 2:14a, 36-41	Ps. 116:1-4, 12-19	1 Pet. 1:17-23	Luke 24:13-35
4/17/05	Acts 2:42-47	Ps. 23	1 Pet. 2:19-25	John 10:1-10
4/24/05	Acts 7:55-60	Ps. 31:1-5, 15-16	1 Pet. 2:2-10	John 14:1-14
5/1/05	Acts 17:22-31	Ps. 66:8-20	1 Pet. 3:13-22	John 14:15-21
5/8/05	Acts 1:6-14	Ps. 68:1-10, 32-35	1 Pet. 4:12-14; 5:6-11	John 17:1-11
5/15/05	Acts 2:1-21	Ps. 104:24-34, 35b	1 Cor. 12:3b-13	John 7:37-39

*This guide represents one possible selection of lessons and psalms from the lectionary. For a complete listing see *The Revised Common Lectionary*.

429

Sunday	First Lesson	Psalm	Second Lesson	Gospel Lesson
5/22/05	Gen. 1:1–2;4a	Ps. 8	2 Cor. 13:11-13	Matt. 28:16-20
5/29/05	Gen. 6:9-22; 7:24; 8:14-19	Ps. 46	Rom. 1:16-17, 3:22b-28 (29-31)	Matt. 7:21-29
6/5/05	Gen. 12:1-9	Ps. 33:1-12	Rom. 4:13-25	Matt. 9:9-13, 18-26
6/12/05	Gen. 18:1-15	Ps. 116:1-2, 12-19	Rom. 5:1-8	Matt. 9:35–10:8 (9-23)
6/19/05	Gen. 21:8-21	Ps. 86:1-10, 16-17	Rom. 6:1b-11	Matt. 10:24-39
6/26/05	Gen. 22:1-14	Ps. 13	Rom. 6:12-23	Matt. 10:40-42
7/03/05	Gen. 24:34-38, 42-49, 58-67	Ps. 45:10-17	Rom. 7:15-25a	Matt. 11:16-19, 25-30
7/10/05	Gen. 25:19-34	Ps. 119:105-112	Rom. 8:1-11	Matt. 13:1-9, 18-23
7/17/05	Gen. 28:10-19a	Ps. 139:1-12, 23-24	Rom. 8:12-25	Matt. 13:24-30, 36-43
7/24/05	Gen. 29:15-28	Ps. 105:1-11, 45b	Rom. 8:26-39	Matt. 13:31-33, 44-52
7/31/05	Gen. 32:22-31	Ps. 17:1-7, 15	Rom. 9:1-5	Matt. 14:13-21
8/7/05	Gen. 37:1-4, 12-28	Ps. 105:1-6, 16-22, 45b	Rom. 10:5-15	Matt. 14:22-33
8/14/05	Gen. 45:1-15	Ps. 133	Rom. 11:1-2a, 29-32	Matt. 15:(10-20), 21-28
8/21/05	Exod. 1:8–2:10	Ps. 124	Rom. 12:1-8	Matt. 16:13-20
8/28/05	Exod. 3:1-15	Ps. 105:1-6, 23-26, 45c	Rom. 12:9-21	Matt. 16:21-29
9/4/05	Exod. 12:1-14	Ps. 149	Rom. 13:8-14	Matt. 18:15-20
9/11/05	Exod. 14:19-31	Exod. 15:1b-11, 20-21	Rom. 14:1-12	Matt. 18:21-35

*This guide represents one possible selection of lessons and psalms from the lectionary. For a complete listing see *The Revised Common Lectionary*.

Sunday	First Lesson	Psalm	Second Lesson	Gospel Lesson
9/18/05	Exod. 16:2-15	Ps. 105:1-6, 37-45	Phil. 1:21-30	Matt. 20:1-16
9/25/05	Exod. 17:1-7	Ps. 78:1-4, 12-16	Phil. 2:1-13	Matt. 21:23-32
10/2/05	Exod. 20:1-4, 7-9, 12-20	Ps. 19	Phil. 3:4b-14	Matt. 21:33-46
10/9/05	Exod. 32:1-14	Ps. 106:1-6, 19-23	Phil. 4:1-9	Matt. 22:1-14
10/16/05	Exod. 33:12-23	Ps. 99	1 Thess. 1:1-10	Matt. 22:15-22
10/23/05	Deut. 34:1-12	Ps. 90:1-6, 13-17	1 Thess. 2:1-8	Matt. 22:34-46
10/30/05	Josh. 3:7-17	Ps. 107:1-7, 33-37	1 Thess. 2:9-13	Matt. 23:1-12
11/6/05	Josh. 24:1-3a, 14-25	Ps. 78:1-7	1 Thess. 4:13-18	Matt. 25:1-13
11/13/05	Judg. 4:1-7	Ps. 123	1 Thess. 5:1-11	Matt. 25:14-30
11/20/05	Ezek. 34:11-16, 20-24	Ps. 100	Eph. 1:15-23	Matt. 25:31-46
11/27/05	Isa. 64:1-9	Ps. 80:1-7, 17-19	1 Cor. 1:3-9	Mark 13:24-37
12/4/05	Isa. 40:1-11	Ps. 85:1-2, 8-13	2 Pet. 3:8-15a	Mark 1:1-8
12/11/05	Isa. 61:1-4, 8-11	Ps. 126	1 Thess. 5:16-24	John 1:6-8, 19-28
12/18/05	2 Sam. 7:1-11, 16	Luke 1:47-55	Rom. 16:25-27	Luke 1:26-38
12/25/05	Isa. 52:7-10	Ps. 98	Heb. 1:1-4 (5-12)	John 1:1-14

*This guide represents one possible selection of lessons and psalms from the lectionary. For a complete listing see *The Revised Common Lectionary.*

CONTRIBUTORS

Tracey Allred
Durham Memorial Baptist
  Church
521 Crossview Lane
Durham, NC 27703

Chris Andrews
First United Methodist Church
930 North Boulevard
Baton Rouge, LA 70802-5728

Stephen Bauman
Christ Church, United Methodist
520 Park Avenue at Sixtieth Street
New York, NY 10021

Scott Bullard
5328 Garrett Road
Durham, NC 27707

Thomas Lane Butts
First United Methodist Church
324 Pineville Road
Monroeville, AL 36460

Gary Carver
First Baptist Church
401 Gateway Avenue
Chattanooga, TN 37402-1504

Carol Cavin-Dillon
Brentwood UMC
309 Franklin Road
Brentwood, TN 37027

Mike Childress
St. Andrews UCC
2608 Browns Lane
Louisville, KY 40220

Jerry Gunnells
1205 Dominion Drive, E.
Mobile, AL 36695

Tracy Hartman
Baptist Theological Seminary
3400 Brook Road
Richmond, VA 23227

Bob Holloway
First United Methodist Church
313 N. Center
Arlington, TX 76011

Karen Hudson
5709 Drayton Drive
Glen Allen, VA 23060-6381

Randy Jessen
1830 Starstone Court
Colorado Springs, CO 80919

Wendy Joyner
Fellowship Baptist Church
P.O. Box 1122
Americus, GA 31709

Gary Kindley
First United Methodist Church
5601 Pleasant Run Road
Colleyville, TX 76034

Hugh Litchfield
6012 Currituck Road
Kitty Hawk, NC 27948

Robert Long
St. Luke's United Methodist
    Church
222 N.W. 15th Street
Oklahoma City, OK 73103-3598

Mike Lowry
University United Methodist
    Church
5084 DeZavala Road
San Antonio, TX 78249

**Timothy S. Mallard, Chaplain,
    U.S. Army**
United States Army Command
    and General Staff College
7045 Ashleigh Manor Court
Alexandria, VA 22315

John Mathis
High Hills Baptist Church
211 S. Halifax Road
Jarratt, VA 23867

John Robert McFarland
1007 Riverview Road
Sterling, IL 61081-4323

Lance Moore
First United Methodist Church
324 Pineville Road
Monroeville, AL 36460

David Mosser
First United Methodist Church
P.O. Box 88
Graham, TX 76450

Raquel Mull
2220 Utah, N.E.
Albuquerque, NM 87110

Timothy Owings
First Baptist Church
P.O. Box 14489
Augusta, GA 30919

Dennis Phelps
Severns Valley Baptist Church
P.O. Box 130
Elizabethtown, KY 42702

William Ritter
First United Methodist Church
1589 W. Maple Road
Birmingham, MI 48008

Tim Roth
Chapelwood United Methodist
    Church
11140 Greebay Drive
Houston, TX 77024

Lance Sawyer
P.O. Box 1052
Monroeville, AL 36461

Carl Schenck
Manchester United Methodist
    Church
129 Woods Mill Road
Manchester, MO 63011-4339

Mary Scifres
3810 67th Avenue Court N.W.
Gig Harbor, WA 98335

Melissa Scott
Colonial Avenue Baptist Church
4165 Colonial Avenue S.W.
Roanoke, VA 24018

Jeffrey Smith
Woodway FUMC
9191 Woodway Drive
Waco, TX 76712

Thomas Steagald
Marshville United Methodist
  Church
P.O. Box 427
Marshville, NC 28103

Eradio Valverde, Jr.
Trinity UMC
6800 Wurzbach Road
San Antonio, TX 78240

Ross West
Positive Difference
  Communications
100 Martha Drive
Rome, GA 30165-4138

Mark White
302 North Estes Drive
Chapel Hill, NC 27514

Victoria Atkinson White
302 North Estes Drive
Chapel Hill, NC 27514

Ryan Wilson
First Baptist Church
P.O. Box 828
Columbus, GA 31902-0828

Philip Wise
Second Baptist Church
6109 Chicago Avenue
Lubbock, TX 79424

Sandy Wylie
P.O. Box 986
McAlester, OK 74502

INDEX

OLD TESTAMENT

NEW TESTAMENT

Romans

1:16-17; 3:22b-28 (29-31) 193-95
3:23 194
3:24 89
4:1-5, 13-17 89-90
4:11 83
4:13-25 204-5
4:16-25 224
4:19 . . . . .88, 203
4:25 95
5:1-8 .211-12
5:1-11 .95-96
5:6 285
5:8; 6:23 .335
5:12-19 83-84
6:1b-11 218-19
6:4 126
6:5 219
6:12-23 224-26
7:15-25a 236-37
8:1-11 242-44
8:6-11 . . . . .111-12, 249
8:12-25 249-50
8:18 42
8:26-39 254-56
8:37 335
8:39 .219, 248
9:1-5 .261-62
9:6-8 218
10:5-15 272-74
11:1-2a, 29-32 280-81
12:1-8 287-88
12:9-21 294-95
12:19-21 .26
13:8-14 305-6
14:1-12 312-13
16:25-27 415-16

1 Corinthians

1:1-9 .54-55
1:3-9 .390-91
1:10-18 61-62
1:18-31 67-68
2:16 .28, 149
12:3b-13 179-81
12:4-5, 10-11 197
12:31; 14:1-2 73
13:1-13 71-73
13:7 71
15:14 73
15:55 . . . . .127, 427

2 Corinthians

5:7 267
5:17 336
5:17, 20-21 218-19
11:14-15 36
13:11-13 186-87

Galatians

2:20; 4:21-31 218

Ephesians

1:15-23 383-84
2:14-16 359
4:24 23
5:8-14 104-6
6:10-17 23-26

Philippians

1:21-30 319-20
2:1-13 . . . . .324-26, 364-67
2:3 364
2:5-11 . . . . .53-54, 118-19, 366
2:6-8 . . . . .351, 386
2:12 20
3:4b-14 334-36
4:1-9 .341-42
4:7 425
4:11 341
4:13 336

Colossians

3:1-4 .125-26
4:6 106

1 Thessalonians

1:1-10 347-48
2:1-8 .353-54
2:9-12 36
2:1-13 35-38
2:9-13 359-61
2:10 35
4:13-18 371-72
5:1-2 299
5:1-11 376-77
5:16-24 408-9

1 Timothy

1:15 194

Hebrews

1:1-4 (5-12) 421-23
1:3 172